CONQUERED CONQUERORS

ANCIENT ISRAEL AND ITS LITERATURE

Thomas C. Römer, General Editor

Number 41

SBL PRESS

CONQUERED CONQUERORS

Love and War in the Song of Songs

Danilo Verde

SBL PRESS

SBL PRESS

Atlanta

Copyright © 2020 by Danilo Verde

Library of Congress Control Number: 2020950495

To John

Contents

Acknowledgments

This book leaves me with a profound sense of gratitude and the strong feeling that my research has not been a solitary endeavor but rather a community journey.

I am very grateful to the Faculty of Theology and Religious Studies, KU Leuven for giving me the opportunity to be part of such an inspiring group of scholars. I am particularly indebted to Thieu Lamberigts (KU Leuven) and Johan Leemans (KU Leuven) for their words and gestures of encouragement and esteem. For their unflagging commitment, friendly and generous support, I would like to thank Pierre Van Hecke (KU Leuven) and Jean-Pierre Sonnet (Gregorian University, Rome), whose extraordinary competence has been an invaluable resource. Without their expertise and thorough knowledge of Biblical Hebrew language and poetry, this book would never have reached its completion. For their constructive feedback, I would also like to express my profound gratitude to Marc Brettler (Duke University), Brian Doyle (KU Leuven), and Susanne Gillmayr-Bucher (KU Linz). It would be impossible to thank all the scholars who gifted me with their precious time and challenging comments. My special gratitude goes to friends and colleagues of the European Association of Biblical Studies research unit Metaphor in the Bible and the Society of Biblical Literature research group Metaphor Theory and the Hebrew Bible for their stimulating questions and criticisms.

I also owe deep gratitude to Thomas Römer, general editor of Ancient Israel and Its Literature, and the other members of the editorial board for accepting my monograph. Many thanks are due to the editors and publishers who allowed me to use in this book the following articles and book chapters previously published in their journals and volumes: "Metaphor as Knowledge: A Hermeneutical Framework for Biblical Exegesis with a Sample Reading from the Song of Songs (Song 8:10)" (*BibAn* 6 [2016]: 45–72); "War-Games in the Song of Songs: A Reading of Song 2,4 in Light of Cognitive Linguistics" (*SJOT* 30 [2016]: 185–97); "Playing Hard to

Get: The Elusive Woman in Song 4:4" (*ETL* 94 [2018]: 1–25); "When the Warrior Falls in Love: The Shaping and Reshaping of Masculinity in the Song of Songs" (in *The Song of Songs Afresh: Perspectives on a Biblical Love Poem*, edited by Stefan Fischer and Gavin Fernandes, HBM [Sheffield: Sheffield Phoenix, 2019], 188–212); and "The Belligerent Woman in Song 1,9" (coauthored with Pierre Van Hecke, *Bib* 98 [2017]: 208–26).

I am grateful to my family, especially to my mother, for teaching me to work hard, to never give up, and to keep smiling no matter what. Much of this book is rooted in her joyful resilience. In the words of the psalm, כל־מעייני בך. Words could never express my gratitude to John. It suffices to say: אני לדודי ודודי לי.

Abbreviations

AB	Anchor Bible
ABD	Freedman, David Noel, ed. *Anchor Bible Dictionary*. 6 vols. New York: Doubleday, 1992.
ABRL	Anchor Bible Reference Library
ABS	Archaeology and Biblical Studies
ADPV	Abhandlungen des deutschen Palästina-Vereins
AfO	*Archiv für Orientforschung*
AIL	Ancient Israel and Its Literature
AJSL	*American Journal of Semitic Languages and Literatures*
Alleg. Hom.	Heraclitus, *Homeric Allegories*
Am.	Ovid, *Amores*
AnBib	Analecta Biblica
ANESSup	Ancient Near Eastern Studies Supplement Series
ANETS	Ancient Near Eastern Texts and Studies
AOAT	Alter Orient und Altes Testament
AOS	American Oriental Series
ATANT	Abhandlungen zur Theologie des Alten und Neuen Testaments
BA	*La Bible d'Alexandrie*
Bacch.	Euripides, *Bacchae*
BASOR	*Bulletin of the American Schools of Oriental Research*
BBR	*Bulletin for Biblical Research*
BC	Bloomsbury Companions
BDB	Brown, Francis, Samuel R. Driver, Charles A. Briggs, and Wilhelm Gesenius. *The New Brown-Driver-Briggs-Gesenius Hebrew and English Lexicon of the Old Testament: With an Appendix Containing the Biblical Aramaic*. Peabody, MA: Hendrickson, 1979.
BEIFAO	Bibliothèque d'étude de l'Institut français d'archéologie orientale

BETL	Bibliotheca Ephemeridum Theologicarum Lovaniensium
BHQ	*Biblia Hebraica Quinta*
BHRG	Christo van der Merwe. *A Biblical Hebrew Reference Grammar*. Bloomsbury, NJ: T&T Clark, 2017.
BHS	*Biblia Hebraica Stuttgartensia*
Bib	*Biblica*
BibAn	*The Biblical Annals*
BibInt	Biblical Interpretation Series
BibOr	Biblica et Orientalia
BibSem	The Biblical Seminar
BKAT	Biblischer Kommentar, Altes Testament
BLS	Bible and Literature Series
BMW	The Bible in the Modern World
BRev	*Bible Review*
BRP	Brill Research Perspective
BSLCC	Brill's Studies in Language, Cognition and Culture
BZAW	Beihefte zur Zeitschrift für die alttestamentliche Wissenschaft
CBET	Contributions to Biblical Exegesis and Theology
CBQ	*Catholic Biblical Quarterly*
CC	Continental Commentaries
CCL	Cambridge Companions to Literature
CCME	Culture and Civilization in the Middle East
CCTC	Cambridge Classical Texts and Commentaries
CdE	*Chronique d'Egypte*
CI	La couleur des idées
CILT	Current Issues in Linguistic Theory
CL	*Cognitive Linguistics*
CLP	Cognitive Linguistcs in Practice
ClQ	*Classical Quarterly*
CLR	Cognitive Linguistics Research
CTL	Cambridge Textbooks in Linguistics
CUFSG	Collection des universités de France, Série grecque
CurBR	*Currents in Biblical Research*
DCH	Clines, David J. A., ed. *Dictionary of Classical Hebrew*. 9 vols. Sheffield: Sheffield Phoenix, 1993–2014.
DJD	Discoveries in the Judaean Desert
DM	Deir el-Medineh

DNWSI	Hoftijzer, Jacob, and Karen Jongeling. *Dictionary of the North-West Semitic Inscriptions*. 2 vols. Leiden: Brill, 1995.
EA	Egitto Antico
EBib	Études bibliques
EBR	Klauck, Hans-Josef, et al., eds. *Encyclopedia of the Bible and Its Reception*. Berlin: de Gruyter, 2009–.
EH	Essential Histories
EHLL	Khan, Geoffrey, ed. *Encyclopedia of Hebrew Language and Linguistics*. 4 vols. Leiden: Brill, 2013.
EJEL	*European Journal of English Studies*
Eleg.	Theognis, *Elegiac Poems*
ELL	Asher, R. E., and J. M. Y. Simpson, eds. *Encyclopedia of Language and Linguistics*. 10 vols. Oxford: Pergamon, 1994.
ELS	English Language Series
EncJud	Skolnik, Fred, and Michael Berenbaum, eds. *Encyclopedia Judaica*. 2nd ed. 22 vols. Detroit: Macmillan Reference USA, 2007.
ETC	*English Text Construction*
ETL	*Ephemerides Theologicae Lovanienses*
EUS	European University Studies
FAT	Forschungen zum Alten Testament
FCB	Feminist Companion to the Bible
FGS	Functional Grammar Series
Frag.	*Fragments*
FT	*Feminist Theory*
GDBS	Gorgias Dissertations, Biblical Studies
GKC	Kautzsch, Emil, ed., and Arthur E. Cowley, trans. *Gesenius' Hebrew Grammar*. 2nd ed. Oxford: Clarendon, 1910.
GS	*Gender & Society*
HACL	History, Archaeology, and Culture of the Levant
HALOT	Koehler, Ludwig, Walter Baumgartner, and Johann J. Stamm. *The Hebrew and Aramaic Lexicon of the Old Testament*. Translated and edited under the supervision of Mervyn E. J. Richardson. 4 vols. Leiden: Brill, 1994–1999.
HBM	Hebrew Bible Monographs
HCP	Human Cognitive Processing
Hipp.	Euripides, *Hippolytus*
HSM	Harvard Semitic Monographs
HThKAT	Herders Theologischer Kommentar zum Alten Testament

Id.	Theocritus, *Idyllis*
Il.	Homer, *Iliad*
Int	*Interpretation*
ISBE	Bromiley, Geoffrey W., ed. *International Standard Bible Encyclopedia*. 4 vols. Grand Rapids: Eerdmans, 1979–1988.
ISBL	Indiana Studies in Biblical Literature
JANES	*Journal of the Ancient Near Eastern Society*
JAOS	*Journal of the American Oriental Society*
JBL	*Journal of Biblical Literature*
JEA	*Journal of Egyptian Archaeology*
JEP	*Journal of Experimental Psychology*
JHS	*Journal of Hellenic Studies*
JJS	*Journal of Jewish Studies*
JLCR	Jordan Lectures in Comparative Religion Series
JNES	*Journal of Near Eastern Studies*
JNSL	*Journal of Northwest Semitic Languages*
Joüon	Joüon, Paul. *A Grammar of Biblical Hebrew*. Translated and revised by Takamitsu Muraoka. 2nd ed. 2 vols. SubBib 27. Rome: Pontifical Biblical Institute, 2006.
JP	*Journal of Pragmatics*
JPSP	*Journal of Personality and Social Psychology*
JQR	*Jewish Quarterly Review*
JSem	*Journal of Semitics*
JSOT	*Journal for the Study of the Old Testament*
JSOTSup	Journal for the Study of the Old Testament Supplement Series
JSS	*Journal of Semitic Studies*
KHC	Kurzer Hand-Commentar zum Alten Testament
KRI	Kitchen, K. A. *Ramesside Inscriptions, Historical and Biographical*. 8 vols. Oxford: Blackwell, 1969–1990.
KTU	Dietrich, Manfried, Oswald Loretz, and Joaquín Sanmartín, eds. *Die keilalphabetischen Texte aus Ugarit*. Münster: Ugarit-Verlag, 2013. 3rd enl. ed. of *KTU: The Cuneiform Alphabetic Texts from Ugarit, Ras Ibn Hani, and Other Places*. Edited by Manfried Dietrich, Oswald Loretz, and Joaquín Sanmartín. Münster: Ugarit-Verlag, 1995.
LAEP	Longman Annotated English Poets
LAI	Library of Ancient Israel
LCC	Language, Culture, and Cognition

LCL	Loeb Classical Library
LD	Lectio Divina
LGE	Lyricorum Graecorum quae exstant
LHBOTS	The Library of Hebrew Bible/Old Testament Studies
LL	*Language and Literature*
LLPB	Le livre de poche Biblio
LP	*Lingua Posnaniensis*
LR	Le livre et le rouleau
LS	*Language Sciences*
LSAWS	Linguistic Studies in Ancient West Semitic
LSJ	Liddell, Henry George, Robert Scott, Henry Stuart Jones. *A Greek-English Lexicon.* 9th ed. with revised supplement. Oxford: Clarendon, 1996.
LT	*Literature and Theology*
LXX	Septuagint
MdB	Le Monde de la Bible
Mor.	Plutarch, *Moralia*
MQ	*Midwest Quarterly*
MS	*Metaphor and Symbol*
MT	Masoretic Text
NBE	Nueva Biblia española: Comentario teológico y literario
NEA	*Near Eastern Archeology*
NICOT	New International Commentary on the Old Testament
NIDB	Sakenfeld, Katharine Doob, ed. *New Interpreter's Dictionary of the Bible.* 5 vols. Nashville: Abingdon, 2006–2009.
NIDOTTE	VanGemeren, Willem A., ed. *New International Dictionary of Old Testament Theology and Exegesis.* 5 vols. Grand Rapids: Zondervan, 1996.
NIVAC	NIV Application Commentary
NJB	New Jerusalem Bible
NRSV	New Revised Standard Version
NRTh	*Nouvelle revue theologique*
OBO	Orbis Biblicus et Orientalis
OBT	Overtures to Biblical Theology
OJLS	Opera Journeys Lecture Series
OLA	Orientalia Lovaniensia Analecta
OP	L'ordre philosophique
Or	*Orientalia*
OTE	*Old Testament Essays*

OTL	Old Testament Library
OTS	Old Testament Studies
OtSt	*Oudtestamentische Studiën*
P.Beatty	Kenyon, Frederic G., ed. *Chester Beatty Biblical Papyri*. London, 1933–1941.
P.Harr.	*The Rendel Harris Papyri of Woodbrooke College, Birmingham*. Vol. 1, edited by J. Enoch Powell. Cambridge, 1936. Vol. 2, edited by Revel A. Coles et al. Zutphen, 1985.
P.Oxy.	Grenfell, Bernard P., et al., eds. *The Oxyrhynchus Papyri*. London: Egypt Exploration Fund, 1898–.
Par.	Beazley, John D., ed. *Paralipomena: Additions to Attic Black-Figure Vase-Painters and to Attic Red-Figure Vase-Painters*. Oxford: Clarendon, 1971.
PBM	Paternoster Biblical Monographs
PD	Parole de Dieu
PHSC	Perspectives on Hebrew Scriptures and Its Contexts
PMG	Alcman, *The Partheneion Maidens' Song*
POS	Pretoria Oriental Series
PT	*Poetics Today*
PTS	Patristische Texte und Studien
QG	Philo, *Questions on Genesis*
QUCC	*Quaderni Urbinati di Cultura Classica*
RB	*Revue biblique*
RCL	*Review of Cognitive Linguistics*
RetBib	Retorica biblica
RIDA	*Revue Internationale des droits de Tantiquite*
RPT	Rhetorical Philosophy & Theory
SAOC	Studies in Ancient Oriental Civilizations
SBFLA	*Studii Biblici Franciscani Liber Annus*
SBLDS	Society of Biblical Literature Dissertation Series
SBS	Stuttgarter Bibelstudien
SemCl	*Semitica et Classica*
SGLG	Sammlung griechischer und lateinischer Grammatiker
SHCANE	Studies in the History and Culture of the Ancient Near East
SJOT	*Scandinavian Journal of the Old Testament*
SocPsy	*Social Psychology*
SOTBT	Studies in Old Testament Biblical Theology
SPQ	*Social Psychology Quarterly*
SR	*The Sewanee Review*

SSN	Studia Semitica Neerlandica
StBib	Studi biblici
StBibLit	Studies in Biblical Literature
StJ	Studies in Judaism
StPho	Studia Phoenicia
STR	Studies in Theology and Religion
SUB	Scandinavian University Books
SubBi	Subsidia Biblica
SymS	Symposium Series
TAD	Porten, Bezalel, and Ada Yardeni, eds. *Textbook of Aramaic Documents from Ancient Egypt*. 4 vols. Jerusalem: Hebrew University Press, 1986–1999.
TB	Theologische Bücherei: Neudrucke und Berichte aus dem 20. Jahrhundert
TDNT	Kittel, Gerhard, and Gerhard Friedrich, eds. *Theological Dictionary of the New Testament*. 10 vols. Grand Rapids: Eerdmans, 1964–1976.
TDOT	Botterweck, G. Johannes, and Helmer Ringgren, eds. *Theological Dictionary of the Old Testament*. 15 vols. Grand Rapids: Eerdmans, 1977–2006.
Test. and Frag.	Plato (comic poet), *Testimonia and Fragments*
TG	Thinking Gender
ThJ	*Theatre Journal*
ThWAT	Botterweck, G. Johannes, and Helmer Ringgren, eds. *Theologisches Worterbuch zum Alten Testament*. 9 vols. Stuttgart: Kohlhammer, 1970–.
TLOT	Jenni, Ernst, and Claus Westermann. *Theological Lexicon of the Old Testament*. 3 vols. Peabody, MA: Hendrickson, 1997.
TSBA	*Transactions of the Society of Biblical Archeology*
UF	*Ugarit-Forschungen*
VT	*Vetus Testamentum*
VTSup	Supplements to Vetus Testamentum
WBC	Word Biblical Commentary
WO	*Die Welt des Orients*
ZAW	*Zeitschrift für die alttestamentliche Wissenschaft*
ZDMG	*Zeitschrift der deutschen morgenländischen Gesellschaft*

And while I did not know whether to flee from her or move even closer, while my head was throbbing as if the trumpets of Joshua were about to bring down the walls of Jericho, as I yearned and at once feared to touch her, she smiled with great joy, emitted the stifled moan of a pleased she-goat, and undid the strings that closed her dress over her bosom, slipped the dress from her body like a tunic, and she stood before me as Eve must have appeared to Adam in the garden of Eden.

—Umberto Eco, The Name of the Rose (trans. Weaver)

1

Introduction

War is the father of all (beings) and king of all.
—Heraclitus, *Frag. 53* (trans. Marcovich)

Over the past decades, much research has been devoted to one of the most common human experiences: the experience of falling in love, an all-consuming attraction of one person toward another person, involving the body, the mind, and the entire range of human emotions. The experience of two people falling in love simultaneously is universal to humans, transcending cultural boundaries, and embedded in the space-time coordinates of the experience. As a human universal, this experience can be found in all cultures and throughout human history. As social and cultural constructions, however, the conceptualization, the linguistic form, and the literary representation of falling in love vary from culture to culture, from language to language, and from literature to literature. Hence the ongoing inquiry into the various understandings of falling in love in different historical periods, cultural contexts, and literary traditions.[1] This book investigates ancient Israel's understanding and aesthetics of falling in love in one of the masterpieces of world literature: the Song of Songs. More precisely, it inquires into the Song's use of military language.

Speaking of love in military terms is very common in literature and everyday speech. Suffice it to mention Ovid's poetic line "Every [male] lover serves as a soldier, also Cupid has his own camp" (*Am.* 1.9 [Showerman]); Sappho's famous description of Helen (*Frag.* 16); the military

---

1. Victor Karandashev, *Romantic Love in Cultural Contexts* (Cham, Switzerland: Springer, 2017); William R. Jankowiak, *Intimacies: Love and Sex across Cultures* (New York: Columbia University Press, 2008); Elaine Hatfield and Richard L. Rapson, *Love and Sex: Cross-cultural Perspectives* (Lanham, MD: University Press of America, 2005).

characterization of love/rs in Andalusian and Islamic literature; the trou-
badours' representation of *l'amour courtois*; Shakespeare's famous line "My
eye and heart are at a mortal war/How to divide the conquest of thy sight"
(*Sonnet* 46.1); and the poem *Love's War* attributed to John Donne.[2] As for
everyday language, common expressions such as "Better put on my war
paint," "He is known for his conquests," "She surrendered to him," "She
fled from his advances," and so on are only a few examples of how profoundly the concept of war plays a part in structuring human thinking/
talking about love.[3]

The Song is no exception: LOVE IS (also) WAR is one of the poem's main
Leitmotivs (§1.1). Although several stimulating and noteworthy studies
have investigated the Song's metaphors, surprisingly the poem's warlike
imagery has never been thoroughly and extensively researched, and much
scholarly research on the Song's figurative language has completely overlooked the developments of metaphor studies outside biblical exegesis
(§1.2). The theoretical framework on which this book draws is cognitive
linguistics, which currently represents the reference point for academic
research on metaphorical phenomena and which, in recent years, has shed
new light on the figurative language of biblical literature (§1.3).[4] Grounded
in cognitive metaphor theories, the Song's warlike imagery will be investigated on three levels, that is, the clause level, the semantic/conceptual
level, and the communicative level (§1.4). A few preliminary questions,
concerning both the Song and the hermeneutical premises of this work,
will be addressed at the end of this first chapter (§1.5).

---

2. For Andalusian and Islamic literature, see Shari Lowin, *Arabic and Hebrew
Love Poems of al-Andalus*, CCME 39 (London: Routledge, 2013).

3. George Lakoff, *Women, Fire, and Dangerous Things: What Categories Reveal
about the Mind* (Chicago: University of Chicago Press, 1987), 411.

4. See, for instance, Danilo Verde and Antje Labahn, eds., *Networks of Metaphors in the Hebrew Bible*, BETL 309 (Leuven: Peeters, 2020); Labahn, ed., *Conceptual
Metaphors in Poetic Texts: Proceedings of the Metaphor Research Group of the European Association of Biblical Studies in Lincoln 2009*, PHSC 18 (Piscataway, NJ: Gorgias, 2013); Pierre Van Hecke and Antje Labahn, eds., *Metaphors in the Psalms*, BETL
231 (Leuven: Peeters, 2010); Van Hecke, ed., *Metaphor in the Hebrew Bible*, BETL 187
(Leuven: Peeters, 2005).

1.1. Overview of the Song's Military Imagery

One of the most astonishing features of the Song's figurative language is the involvement of the entire human world in the poem's celebration of love. The lovers' dialogues and monologues constantly evoke all the main elements of both the natural and cultural environment. Not only does the natural and cultural world construct the scene in which the passion of the Song's lovers takes place; it also provides the lovers with thoughts and words to describe and talk to each other. The Song's encompassing embrace of surrounding reality even includes one of the most unsettling aspects of human experience: war. Indeed, on several occasions the poem describes the lovers in military terms, and their courtship as a war-game, which is surrealistically played out against the background of exotic flowers, lush trees, vivacious animals, and pleasing scents.

The very first image of war occurs in 1:9:

SONG 1:9
To a mare that is among Pharaoh's chariots
I liken you, my friend.[5]

לססתי ברכבי פרעה
דמיתיך רעיתי

Some lines after, the woman describes her beloved as a conquering warrior:

SONG 2:4
He has brought me to the house of wine,
and his army on me is love.

הביאני אל־בית היין
ודגלו עלי אהבה

Song 3:6–8 describes a royal wedding procession escorted by Israel's warriors:

SONG 3:6–8
Who is this going up from the desert
like columns of smoke,
perfumed with myrrh and frankincense,
from all kinds of the merchant's powders?
Look! Solomon's litter!
Sixty warriors are around it,

מי זאת עלה מן־המדבר
כתימרות עשן
מקטרת מור ולבונה
מכל אבקת רוכל
הנה מטתו שלשלמה
ששים גברים סביב לה

---

5. Unless otherwise indicated, all biblical translations are my own. The translations of the Song's warlike metaphors will be justified in the following chapters.

from the warriors of Israel.   מגברי ישראל
All of them are equipped with a sword,   כלם אחזי חרב
experts in war.   מלמדי מלחמה
Each with his sword on his thigh   איש חרבו על-ירכו
because of terrifying nocturnal dangers.   מפחד בלילות

While 2:4 portrays the man as conqueror, 4:4 represents the woman as a fortified, well-defended city:

SONG 4:4
Like the tower of David is your neck,   כמגדל דויד צוארך
built in courses;   בנוי לתלפיות
thousands of shields are hung on it,   אלף המגן תלוי עליו
all quivers of warriors.   כל שלטי הגבורים

The image of the man as conqueror, already found in 2:4, again occurs in 5:10:

SONG 5:10
My beloved is dazzling and ruddy,   דודי צח ואדום
deployed among myriads [of soldiers].   דגול מרבבה

Chapter 6 contains two controversial military images:

SONG 6:4
You are beautiful, my love, like Tirzah,   יפה את רעיתי כתרצה
longed for like Jerusalem,   נאוה כירושלם
frightening as an army with deployed banners.   אימה כנדגלות

SONG 6:12
I am shocked; she turned me   לא ידעתי נפשי שמתני
into the chariots of Amminadib.   מרכבות עמי-נדיב

Immediately after, the poem mentions a military dance:

SONG 7:1
—Come back, come back, O Shulammite;   שובי שובי השולמית
Come back, come back, that we may admire you!   שובי שובי ונחזה-בך
—Why do you want to admire the Shulammite   מה-תחזו בשולמית
like the dance of the two camps!   כמחלת המחנים

Finally, the poem's last chapter contains two images of war:

SONG 8:6–7
Set me as a seal on your heart,
as a seal on your arm,
for strong as death is love,
vehement as Sheol is passion.
Its flashes are flashes of fire,
a raging flame of Yah.
Many waters cannot quench love
nor rivers drown it away.
Should one offer all the wealth of
      his house for love,
he would be utterly scorned.

שימני כחותם על־לבך
כחותם על־זרועך
כי־עזה כמות אהבה
קשה כשאול קנאה
רשפיה רשפי אש
שלהבתיה
מים רבים לא יוכלו לכבות את־האהבה
ונהרות לא ישטפוה
אם־יתן איש את־כל־הון
ביתו באהבה
בוז יבוזו לו

SONG 8:10
I am a city wall,
and my breasts are like towers.
Thus, I have seemed to him
like one who finds and provides peace.

אני חומה
ושדי כמגדלות
אז הייתי בעיניו
כמוצאת שלום

Even though military images are not numerous, they are spread through-out the Song's eight chapters. Such imagery includes military metaphors, similes, and scenes. Martial metaphors are sometimes expressed by the formula "A *is* B" (5:10; 8:10). On some occasions, however, they are expressed through more complex linguistic expressions (2:4; 6:12). Similes are usually expressed through the formula "A is *like* B" (4:4; 6:4; 8:10), and only once through the verb "to compare/to liken" (1:9). Finally, I distinguish scenes from metaphors and similes; scenes are not descriptive statements ("you are..., I am...," etc.) but dynamic representations of events or actions: that is, the wedding processions (3:6–8) and the military dance (7:1).

1.2. Scholarly Research on the Song's (Military) Metaphors

When we read the main monographs and the plethora of studies and commentaries on the Song's metaphors, we cannot fail to notice that current scholarship has several lacunae. The theoretical frameworks from which exegetes draw often seem to be outdated. The Song's troublesome language of war is not foregrounded; often it is not even recognized, and sometimes it is considered too odd for a love poem and therefore neglected or misinterpreted. A systematic and exhaustive analysis of all the Song's military images in light of the last achievements of metaphor studies is wanting.

1.2.1. Monographs on the Song's Figurative Language

Whoever works on the Song's metaphors cannot prescind from careful study of some milestones on the poem's figurative language, such as works by Othmar Keel, Hans-Peter Müller, Jill Munro, and Fiona Black.[6]

Keel investigated the Song's similes and metaphors in his erudite monograph *Deine Blicke sind Tauben* (1984) and summarized his research results in his later commentary *Das Hohelied* (1986).[7] Keel consistently warns exegetes not to underestimate the remarkable cultural chasm separating the Song from its modern readers. According to him, since the Song is from a different milieu, what its metaphors evoke to its modern, Western audience might not reflect the poem's original intent. The inquiry into the Song's metaphors, therefore, cannot bypass a careful investigation of its *Umwelt* in order to recover those ancient cultural conventions from which the poem drew. To this purpose, Keel suggests a concentric hermeneutical model. First, he argues, the Song's metaphors should be read in light of their immediate context in the poem. Second, readers should contextualize the metaphors in the whole Hebrew Bible, giving priority to those texts that are closer to the Song in both form and content. Finally, the Song's metaphors should be understood within the poem's broader context, namely, the Song's land. By "land," Keel concretely means the land of Palestine as *Natur* but especially as *Kulturwelt*.[8] Keel contends that, by studying Syria-Palestinian archaeological findings, we have access not only to the Song's general cultural milieu but also to a specific symbolic system,

---

6. Brian P. Gault has recently authored a monograph on the Song's body metaphors in light of conceptual metaphor theory. See Brian P. Gault, *Body as Landscape, Love as Intoxication: Conceptual Metaphors in the Song of Songs*, AIL 36 (Atlanta: SBL Press, 2019). The present book had been submitted and accepted before the publication of Gault's work, which therefore will not be treated here.

7. Othmar Keel, *Deine Blicke sind Tauben: Zur Metaphorik des Hohen Liedes*, SBS 114–115 (Stuttgart: Katholisches Bibelwerk, 1984); Keel, *Das Hohelied*, BKAT 18 (Zürich: Theologischer Verlag, 1986); Keel, *The Song of Songs: A Continental Commentary*, trans. Frederick J. Gaiser, CC (Minneapolis: Fortress, 1994).

8. Keel, *Deine Blicke*, 22–24.

a traditional repertoire of erotic images, that were unique to Palestine and shaped the poem's figurative language.

Following traditional interpretations of metaphorical phenomena, Keel considers the identification of the so-called *tertium comparationis* crucial to understanding the meaning of the Song's metaphors and similes. Whereas many exegetes (e.g., W. Rudolph and Gillis Gerleman) had argued that *metaphorized* and *metaphorizing* share physical, visible similarities, Keel asserts that the external form does not play any role in the Song's metaphors and that the *tertium comparationis* concerns the functional, dynamic dimension of the realities in question.[9] In his opinion, for instance, the metaphor of the woman's eyes as doves in Song 1:15 does not describe how eyes and doves *physically are and appear* to the man. They rather describe what they *do*. Since the function of eyes is "to look at," and in the ancient Near East the function of doves was to be messengers of love, the correct interpretation of what the man says in Song 1:15 is "Your glances are messengers of love."[10]

Keel devotes an entire chapter to the comparison of the woman's neck, nose, and breasts to towers (4:4; 7:5; 8:10).[11] While several authors had understood the similes in 4:4 and 7:5 as referring to the cylindrical shape of necks and towers, Keel coherently follows his approach and argues that, since towers defend citadels, the metaphor in question conveys the image of an unconquerable, self-confident woman. Furthermore, he reads the simile of the nose in 7:5 (אפך כמגדל) as portraying a threatening woman—the threat of an insurmountable resistance—due to the well-known connection between "nose" and "snorting/anger," expressed by the Hebrew lexeme אף. Finally, he understands Song 8:10 as referring to the woman's attempt to haughtily parry the man's courtship, an attempt that, in Keel's opinion, is vain because she can only capitulate, like a citadel in front of a vanquishing army.

Some of Keel's statements are in line with current understandings of metaphor, and this becomes even more surprising when we consider that his bibliography does not include any of the pioneering studies that were already opening new perspectives on metaphorical phenomena between the late 1970s and the early 1980s. The author's emphasis on the hermeneutical relevance of the Song's milieu is particularly up to date, finding

---

9. Keel, *Deine Blicke*, 27–30.

10. Keel, *Song of Songs*, 71.

11. Keel, *Deine Blicke*, 32–38.

support in modern research on the tangled bond between metaphor and culture.[12] As Zoltán Kövecses recently summarized:

> There is a fair amount of consensus in the study of how metaphors are interpreted that the comprehension of particular metaphorical expressions requires familiarity with the context in which the metaphor is used.... In other words, much of the experimental work on metaphor comprehension indicates that metaphor interpretation can take place only in context; that is, metaphor interpretation varies with context and, thus, metaphor and context are closely linked.[13]

Keel's belief that the Song's metaphor primarily creates conceptual images recalls current emphasis on the cognitive dimension of metaphorical phenomena.[14] He also has the merit to focus on one of the most neglected clusters of metaphors: those images that portray the woman as a fortified citadel under siege.

Keel's inquiry, however, also includes some problematic aspects. First, he presents a one-way relationship between the Song's metaphors and their cultural context. In other words, he investigates how a deeper knowledge of Palestinian imagery can help to understand the Song's figurative language (from *Umwelt* to the Song), but he does not consider how the Song's metaphors enrich and improve our knowledge of that culture (from the Song to *Umwelt*). While he emphasizes metaphors as *products of culture*, he neglects to consider that they are also, so to speak, both *open windows into culture* and *producers of culture*. As argued by George Lakoff and Mark Turner in *More than Cool Reason* (1989), while poetic metaphors reflect cultural conventions, they also rework those conventions and either create innovative conceptualizations or modify, at least in part, the conceptual universe to which they belong. The relationship between metaphor and context is circular: while culture undeniably governs metaphor production, metaphors themselves may also affect their cultural context.[15] In this regard, the next chapters will show that the Song's metaphorical

---

12. On the importance of context for the production and comprehension of metaphors, see Zoltán Kövecses, *Where Metaphors Come From: Reconsidering Context in Metaphor* (Oxford: Oxford University Press, 2015); Kövecses, *Metaphor in Culture: Universality and Variation* (Cambridge: Cambridge University Press, 2007).

13. Kövecses, *Where Metaphors Come From*, xi.

14. Keel, *Deine Blicke*, 86.

15. Kövecses, *Where Metaphors Come From*, 99.

discourse on human love in terms of war is one of the most original conceptualizations of eros in the ancient Near East—even though the ancient Near Eastern conceptual universe provided the soil in which this unique metaphor grew. The second drawback of Keel's method is his focus on the *tertium comparationis*, which he always identifies with the *function* of both metaphorized and metaphorizing elements. According to cognitive linguistics, the *tertium comparationis* is by no means the core of metaphor (see *infra*). Moreover, Keel's claim that the salience of the Song's metaphors resides in their *functional* dimension seems to be quite reductive, since metaphor usually entails a cross-mapping of several conceptual elements. Overlooking the visual dimension is particularly problematic, especially in a poem in which the characters glance at each other and constantly describe what they see.

A second well-known monograph on the Song's figurative language is *Vergleich und Metapher im Hohenlied* (1984) by Müller, who investigates the poem's metaphors and similes by combining rhetorical analysis, a sociological approach to language, and the history of religions. Starting with the distinction between receiver (*Vergleichsempfänger*), donor (*Vergleichsspender*), and *tertium comparationis* (*Dritte des Vergleichs*), Müller illustrates three ways in which similes are built, namely, by (1) predicative construction, (2) appositional construction, and (3) metaphor. According to him, metaphor is nothing more than a simile in which the donor replaces the receiver.[16] He argues that the Song's figurative language is embedded in ancient ritual incantations, which aimed to create real associations between receiver and donor, so that the former could assume the properties of the latter. Since all elements of nature were thought to possess a kind of soul, ritual ceremonies had the purpose of giving humankind access to that vital force by the magical power of the word. According to Müller, through expressions such as "I liken you," the recipient acquired the numinous force possessed by the animal/plant invoked. In other words, in Müller's view, the Song reflects a stage in which metaphor creation was considered a performative linguistic act, creating magical connections between donor and receiver. He argues that metaphor, in which the donor entirely replaces the receiver, marks the peak of such a magical process. Additionally, he contends that the Song's metaphors fulfilled the religious

---

16. Hans-Peter Müller, *Vergleich und Metapher im Hohenlied*, OBO 56 (Freiburg: Universitätsverlag, 1984), 11.

yearnings of archaic fertility cults. Despite the fact that the Song demy-thologized its cultural background and, thereby, became a secular poem, its metaphors held the power to overcome the barrier separating human-ity from cosmos. Within the context of the Yahwistic religion—testified by the metaphorization of love as "a flame of Yah" (Song 8:6)—the poem's lovers assumed a "theomorphic value" thanks to metaphors, making the experience of YHWH possible to each other. Oddly, Müller does not pay any particular attention to the Song's warlike imagery, even though he employs some military metaphors and similes as examples of the poem's performative language and numinous character.[17]

Müller's monograph is particularly challenging, for both its merits and drawbacks. Its attention to the syntactic construction of the poem's similes and metaphors is especially noteworthy, since it reminds us that we can access the underlying conceptual systems of literary texts only by analyz-ing words and the way words are connected to each other. *Vergleich und Metapher*, however, also has some shortcomings. First, Müller's syntacti-cal analysis is a traditional taxonomic collection of data without semantic consequences. Despite their titles, respectively *Syntaktische Beobachtun-gen* and *Semantische Beobachtungen*, chapters 1 and 2 are just juxtaposed, without explaining how the syntactic analysis of metaphors and similes sheds new light on their semantic content. Second, the title *Vergleich und Metapher* suggests the priority of simile and the comprehension of metaphor as a kind of simile, as Müller clearly asserts.[18] On the contrary, modern studies of metaphor convincingly claim that the relationship between metaphor and simile is exactly the opposite.[19] Simile is a form of metaphor, rather than the other way around. Finally, Müller's thesis of a phase in the development of language in which the use of metaphor was connected to a magic view of reality is highly conjectural, not supported by any kind of evidence, and weakened by cognitive linguistics, which highlights how metaphor is, on the contrary, an ordinary way through which humans speak and think.

Certainly much clearer and easier to understand is the monograph *Spikenard and Saffron: The Imagery of the Song of Songs* (1995) by Munro, who aims "to explore the way in which the images operate throughout the

---

17. Müller, *Vergleich und Metapher*, 16–17, 32–33.

18. Müller, *Vergleich und Metapher*, 11.

19. Barbara Dancygier and Eve Sweetser, *Figurative Language*, CTL (Cambridge: Cambridge University Press, 2014), 137–50.

poem as metaphors for love."[20] According to Munro, the Song's images belong to three imaginative fields, namely, court, family, and nature, within which it is possible to distinguish smaller groups of images. While in the first three chapters she identifies and describes three broad imaginative fields, with their own subgroups of images, Munro devotes a fourth, conclusive chapter to uncovering "how the images work together."[21] It is important to note that she does recognize some military metaphors but only as images radiating from the main image of kingship.[22] In the final chapter, titled "Images in Spaces and Times," she argues that the Song organizes its imaginative fields through a kind of "emotional drama" that presents the experience of love from the perspective of the woman.[23] In conclusion, she suggests that the Song's metaphors of love have a pedagogic intent of wisely warning young women against flippancy.[24]

As Tod Linafelt comments, Munro "demonstrates a keen interpretative eye and a creative mind" throughout her novel investigation of the Song's figurative language.[25] Her choice of situating individual metaphors within their broader metaphorical system, as opposed to the traditional treatment of isolated metaphors, is a noteworthy aspect of novelty. However, we would be remiss to overlook certain weaknesses. Munro only gathers the small units of images into clusters, and she only explores the Song's imaginative fields on a lexical level, without any reference to the poem's concept(s) of both love and lovers. Disappointingly, this results in tedious catalogues of images that do not enhance the comprehension of the poem's concept of love. But the main problematic aspect for the present research is the inadequate attention devoted to the warlike metaphors, which the author considers just as a subgroup of the royal imagery.[26] The Song's warlike images should be considered in their own conceptual domain, that is, WAR. While it is true that the domain WAR sometimes intersects with other domains, such as COURT, overlapping does not mean conflation.

---

20. Jill M. Munro, *Spikenard and Saffron: The Imagery of the Song of Songs*, JSOTSup 203 (Sheffield: Sheffield Academic, 1995), 16.

21. Munro, *Spikenard and Saffron*, 117.

22. Munro, *Spikenard and Saffron*, 19.

23. Munro, *Spikenard and Saffron*, 142.

24. Munro, *Spikenard and Saffron*, 147.

25. Tod Linafelt, review of *Spikenard and Saffron: The Imagery of the Song of Songs*, by Jill M. Munro, *JBL* 118 (1999): 350–51.

26. As also noted in Tremper Longman, *Song of Songs*, NICOT (Grand Rapids: Eerdmans, 2001), 13–14.

More recently, Black authored *The Artifice of Love: Grotesque Bodies in the Song of Songs*, in which she shows how the Song's body imagery aims to baffle and tease its readers.[27] Black argues that the juxtaposition of unexpected elements in the Song's descriptions of the lovers portrays the lovers' bodies as "playful, disconcerting, unsettling, dangerous"—in a word, "grotesque"—affecting both the book's gender politics and the readers' responses.[28] She presents the common way through which scholars usually read the Song's body images, namely, as complimentary descriptions, and she proposes that the grotesque might be an alternative perspective. After illustrating some examples of the grotesque both in literature and in art during the period of the Renaissance and how the grotesque has been considered by literary criticism, Black analyzes the Song's four descriptions of the lover's body (4:1–5; 5:10–16; 6:4–7; 7:1–10), "in light of a heuristic that privileges the unexpected, variability and difference."[29] Finally, she investigates how the Song's grotesque bodies present desire and the relationship between the two lovers and the implications for the reader. While according to several scholars the Song is a rare example of equality between man and woman in the Hebrew Bible, Black argues that the woman is much more grotesque than the man. By going beyond the contraposition between androcentric and gynocentric characters in the poem, Black eventually argues that the hermeneutics of the grotesque allows us to consider the paradoxes of the Song as a mirror of "the conflicted nature of love."[30] The Song simultaneously attracts and repels the reader so that the reader, like the Song's lovers, will never be satisfied by the text. As far as the Song's warlike imagery is concerned, Black only focuses on the metaphorization of the woman as a city.[31] In this regard, by rejecting the Song's description as "complimentary," Black comments: "When the violence and chaos of war is added to this picture, the results are compounded: to be sure, valor and victory are here, but these can never be achieved without estrangement and loss."[32]

---

27. Fiona C. Black, *The Artifice of Love: Grotesque Bodies in the Song of Songs*, LHBOTS 392 (London: T&T Clark, 2009), 2.
28. Black, *Artifice of Love*, 3–4.
29. Black, *Artifice of Love*, 124.
30. Black, *Artifice of Love*, 227.
31. Black, *Artifice of Love*, 153–59.
32. Black, *Artifice of Love*, 159.

Black succeeds in showing that the presence of grotesque elements in the Song provides an ulterior mode of reading the Song and speaking of human desire. The main merit of *The Artifice of Love* is certainly its serious consideration of the troublesome dimension of the Song's imagery, which aims to perplex the reader. As the author writes: "All is not verdant, robust and alive in the natural body as the lovers configure it.... Nature implies not only fecundity, enjoyment and excess, but their opposites as well."[33] Unfortunately, she does not deal with all the Song's warlike images, which, as I have shown, remain almost unexplored by all major monographs on the Song's metaphors.

1.2.2. Other Studies

It would impossible to reconstruct and summarize all scholarly comments and observations on the Song's metaphors, even if we only focused on the past few decades. There are some studies, however, that are worth mentioning, because either they are essential reference points to whoever engages the Song's figurative language, or they make clear that the Song's military language has received only scant attention (if any) and that an up-to-date approach to the poems' metaphors is needed.

Francis Landy undoubtedly is one of the authors who has contributed the most to the interpretation of the Song's metaphors, pointing out that "the Song largely consists of metaphors, and there can be no analysis of it without an attempt to interpret them: through the images one comes to the meaning."[34] He convincingly argues that the Song's metaphors are simultaneously "extremely lucid and extraordinarily refractory." They are lucid in that they communicate emotionally what being in love is. They become refractory, however, when one "struggles to rationalize them."[35] In his monograph *Paradoxes of Paradise* (1987), Landy emphasizes the ambiguity and enigmatic nature of the Song's metaphors, arguing that the ambivalence pervading its metaphors tells of the ambivalent relationship between the lovers and the world.[36] The Song simultaneously portrays

---

33. Black, *Artifice of Love*, 153.
34. Francis Landy, "The Song of Songs and the Garden of Eden," *JBL* 98 (1979): 514.
35. Landy, "Song of Songs," 514.
36. Francis Landy, *Paradoxes of Paradise: Identity and Difference in the Song of Songs*, BLS 7 (Sheffield: Almond, 1987), 265.

the lovers as both part of and separate from their world. They are *like* the world and, at the same time, different. Ultimately, the Song's many paradoxical images well express the paradoxical and subversive nature of beauty. As Landy suggestively says: "Beauty is a stranger, a gift, taking us by surprise, wonderful and terrible."[37] As for the Song's martial imagery, Landy recognizes only a few military metaphors, on which he makes psychoanalytical remarks. For instance, in his view, the military image of the mare representing the woman in 1:9 induces "a transfer of phallic energy that is doubly threatening. A woman who is as powerful as a man endangers his supremacy."[38] At the same time, however, Song 1:9 ironically "hints at her proper subservience, as a member of the king's entourage [i.e., the beloved man], as an adornment to his court, on whom he hangs his tropes and jewelry, the gold and silver pendants, and chains of 1:10–11."[39] Landy's comments on nonmilitary interpretations of the contested root דגל are also noteworthy. Although he does not provide a solution for such a debated case, the author points out that many commentators seem to consider beauty and wonder as incompatible, and, therefore, they often provide bathetic readings of the Song.[40]

In the same period, Robert Alter wrote his seminal monograph on biblical poetry, titled *The Art of Biblical Poetry*, in which he devotes an entire chapter to the Song's metaphors, titled "The Garden of Metaphor."[41] According to Alter, figurative language plays a more prominent role in the Song than in the rest of the Hebrew Bible.[42] Although biblical Hebrew poetry regularly uses metaphors and similes, the Song's use of figurative language is unique for several reasons. First, in the Song the process of figuration is frequently foregrounded. The Song often puts the operation of comparison in front of the reader, for instance, by employing the root דמה ("to be like") or the transitive verb "to liken," as in 1:9. Alter argues that, in doing so, the Song calls for the reader's attention to "the artifice of metaphorical representation."[43] Second, metaphors and similes are much more

---

37. Landy, *Paradoxes of Paradise*, 170.

38. Landy, *Paradoxes of Paradise*, 168.

39. Landy, *Paradoxes of Paradise*, 168.

40. Landy, *Paradoxes of Paradise*, 131 n. 1.

41. Robert Alter, *The Art of Biblical Poetry*, rev. ed. (New York: Basic Books, 2011), 231–54.

42. Alter, *Art of Biblical Poetry*, 236.

43. Alter, *Art of Biblical Poetry*, 241.

flamboyant in the Song than elsewhere in the Hebrew Bible. As a result, on several occasions, especially when the lovers describe each other's body, the correspondence between image and referent becomes very unclear, and the poet "gives free rein to the exuberance of figurative elaboration."[44] Such a fluid distinction between figure and referent is the third peculiarity of the Song's use of figurative language, thanks to which the Song becomes a teasing game transforming the pleasure of love into the pleasure of playing with language.[45]

A few years after Landy's and Alter's contributions, Harold Fisch wrote an essay titled "Song of Solomon: The Allegorical Imperative," which forms part of his monograph on biblical Hebrew poetry.[46] Like Landy, Fisch argues that the Song's figurative language recalls the language of dreams, with a free flow of symbolic and ambiguous images. As the author explains:

> You may see a horse in a dream, and it may mean many things, but of one thing you may be sure: it does not simply mean a horse! If we think of the language and imagery of the Song of Solomon as a whole in terms of dream symbolism as the text, I think, requires us to, then the search for the so-called literal meaning, a search that has so much exercised the commentators, becomes very questionable.[47]

Even though neither Fisch nor Alter comments extensively on the Song's warlike metaphors, they both quote the military metaphors to make their point on the peculiarities of the Song's poetics. Fisch, for instance, refers to 6:4 as a good example of the Song's symbolic language; Alter uses 1:9 to explain how the Song involves the reader in the metaphorical process and 4:4 to show the Song's extravagant language.[48]

Some of Landy's, Alter's, and Fisch's ideas can be found in articles by Jean-Pierre Sonnet, although Sonnet reworks those previous contributions in a very original way.[49] Besides adding new considerations on the

44. Alter, *Art of Biblical Poetry*, 247.

45. Alter, *Art of Biblical Poetry*, 248.

46. Harold Fisch, "Song of Solomon: The Allegorical Imperative," in *Poetry with a Purpose: Biblical Poetics and Interpretation*, ISBL (Bloomington: Indiana University Press, 1990), 80–103.

47. Fisch, "Song of Solomon," 89.

48. Fisch, "Song of Solomon," 93; Alter, *Art of Biblical Poetry*, 241, 249–52.

49. Jean-Pierre Sonnet, "Du chant érotique au chant mystique: Le ressort poé-

relationship between dreamlike language, metaphor, and metonymy using Sigmund Freud, Roman Jakobson, and Jacques Lacan, Sonnet has a short paragraph that profoundly inspired the present study. He notices that the Song's lovers seem to play a war-game.[50] This idea had already been proposed by Luis Alonso Schökel.[51] Inspired by Alonso Schökel, Sonnet refers to warlike metaphors (1:9; 2:4; 4:4; 6:4; 8:10) and uses those warlike metaphors to explain what he considers one of the main distinctive features of the Song's use of figurative language, that is, that once a metaphor is installed in the Song, it needs to develop throughout the poem.[52] For Sonnet, as for Landy, Fisch, and Alter, the Song's warlike metaphors seem to have a kind of paradigmatic value for understanding the Song's peculiar use of figurative language.

More recently, Elaine James addressed the Song's metaphors that intertwine war and cityscape.[53] After examining how the city appears in the Song (3:1–5; 5:2–8), she considers how the city metaphorically represents the woman (4:4; 6:4; 7:5; 8:9–10). James points out that in the Song the city is an ambivalent place that both fosters and endangers the lovers' relationship. This ambivalence also emerges when the urban and the military overlap in the descriptions of the beloved woman. As she puts it, "The Song playfully casts the lovers in a battle of the sexes, in which the young woman is a threatened city, and her lover is the encroaching enemy."[54] The urban imagery intertwining the military imagery "emphasizes her beauty and intimidating grandeur, while it also plays on the obverse dimensions of the protective functions of urban architecture, underscoring the young

---

tique du Cantique des cantiques," in *Regards croisés sur le Cantique des cantiques*, ed. Jean-Marie Auwers, LR 22 (Bruxelles: Lessius, 2005), 79–105; Sonnet, "Le Cantique: La fabrique poétique," in *Les nouvelles voies de l'exégèse: En lisant le Cantique des cantiques*, ed. Jacques Nieuviarts and Pierre Debergé, LD 190 (Paris: Cerf, 2002), 159–84; Sonnet, "Le Cantique, entre érotique et mystique: sanctuaire de la parole échangée," *NRTh* 119 (1997): 481–502; Sonnet, "Figures (anciennes et nouvelles) du lecteur: Du Cantique des cantiques au Livre entier," *NRTh* 113 (1991): 75–86.

50. Sonnet, "Du chant érotique," 94.

51. Luis Alonso Schökel, *Il Cantico dei Cantici: La dignità dell'amore* (Casale Monferrato: Piemme, 1990), 75.

52. Sonnet, "Du chant érotique," 95.

53. Elaine T. James, *Landscapes of the Song of Songs: Poetry and Place* (New York: Oxford University Press, 2017), 88–117.

54. James, *Landscapes of the Song of Songs*, 88.

woman's vulnerability in the lovers' encounter."[55] James rightly argues that the Song's representation of the woman as city clearly draws on a vast repertoire of images personifying cities as women, images quite widespread both in the Hebrew Bible and in ancient Near Eastern literature in contexts of war and destruction, emphasizing vulnerability. The Song, in her view, employs the motif city-as-woman in a surprising way: to portray the battle of the sexes, in which the woman, on the one hand, is depicted as vulnerable and, on the other hand, resolves her vulnerability through her surrender—by welcoming her lover (8:10). James's overall reading of the Song's cityscape is very much in line with what is proposed here, although her use of the ancient Near Eastern motif city-as-woman, and, therefore, her insistence on the vulnerability of the Song's woman is debatable. In my view, she overlooks that the ancient Near Eastern metaphor (DEFEATED) CITY IS WOMAN and the Song's metaphor WOMAN IS (FORTIFIED) CITY are completely different. As chapter 2 will show, the Song does draw on the ancient Near Eastern motif city-as-woman, but, by switching source and target domain and by picturing the woman as fortified, it turns that motif upside down. I contend that the entire point of the Song's metaphor WOMAN IS CITY is to emphasize the woman's grandeur, rather than her vulnerability.

As for commentaries, over the last few decades a remarkable number of them have been published that, in different ways, have certainly elucidated many aspects of the Song's discourse. Nevertheless, commentaries on the Song published in the last thirty years seem to have completely overlooked the developments of metaphor studies in contemporary linguistics, of which there is no sign in the commentaries' introductory chapters to the Song's imagery, or throughout the comments, or even in the bibliography. This is even more surprising when we consider that the Song is mainly made up of metaphors, and therefore we would expect up-to-date theoretical frameworks on and clear methodologies for working with metaphors. Furthermore, the Song's warlike imagery seems to be one of the most problematic aspects in the poem's figurative language. While I will detail current readings of the Song's military images in the next chapters, I will only give a few examples here.

First, several scholars do not even recognize the Song's military scenery. As Tremper Longman has sharply noted, nonmilitary interpretations

---

55. James, *Landscapes of the Song of Songs*, 108.

of the Song mainly depend on the fact that "*it seems odd* to have military metaphors in a love poem."[56] Second, although a few scholars recognize some military images in the Song, many explanations are dubious. For instance, Gianni Barbiero argues that Song 2:4 contains a military metaphor in which the man is described as conqueror and affirms that the woman is conquered by love *rather than* by force.[57] In so doing, Barbiero creates an opposition between "force" and "love" that sounds very unconvincing if love is conceptualized in terms of a war of conquest. Several authors explain 2:4 by referring to different issues, such as belonging and commitment, man as a refuge for the woman, and man's royal dignity, without explaining from where and how we can derive these concepts.[58] The same exegetes also explain 2:4 through other metaphors (MAN IS REFUGE and MAN IS KING), imposing on the text different conceptual domains and, therefore, different conceptualizations of the experience of love. With respect to the image of the fortified and armed city (4:4; 6:4; 8:10), not only does the role of specific elements remain dubious, but also their general meaning is still unsettled. In 4:4 it is still unclear whether the warriors' hanging of their weapons on the tower signifies surrender or defense of the citadel and whether the line suggests her "impregnability," his "confidence," or the "power of love."[59] Likewise, does the image of towers and wall in 8:10 refer to her "chastity," her "sexual maturity," or her "chastity and independence"?[60]

---

56. Longman, *Song of Songs*, 180.

57. Gianni Barbiero, *Song of Songs: A Close Reading*, trans. Michael Tait, VTSup 144 (Leiden: Brill, 2011), 90.

58. Belonging and commitment: Longman, *Song of Songs*, 113. Man as a refuge for the woman: Cheryl J. Exum, *Song of Songs*, OTL (Louisville: Westminster John Knox, 2005), 115. Man's royal dignity: Roland E. Murphy, *The Song of Songs: A Commentary on the Book of Canticles or the Song of Songs*, Hermeneia (Minneapolis: Fortress, 1990), 136.

59. Her impregnability: Duane A. Garrett, "Song of Songs," in *Song of Songs, Lamentations*, Duane A. Garrett and Paul R. House, WBC 23b (Nashville: Nelson, 2004), 190–91; his confidence: Elie Assis, *Flashes of Fire: A Literary Analysis of the Song of Songs*, LHBOTS 503 (New York: T&T Clark, 2009), 124–25; the power of love: Exum, *Song of Songs*, 164–65. For the warriors' hanging of their weapons as signifying surrender or defense of the citadel, see Keith R. Crim, "Your Neck Is Like the Tower of David (The Meaning of a Simile in Song of Solomon)," *VT* 22 (1971): 70–74.

60. Her chastity: Yair Zakovitch, *Das Hohelied*, HThKAT (Freiburg: Herder, 2004), 187–89. Her sexual maturity: Longman, *Song of Songs*, 146. Her chastity and independence: Murphy, *Song of Songs*, 159.

Carol Meyers's inspiring study "Gender Imagery in the Song of Songs" is also worth mentioning. Within the hermeneutical horizon of feminist exegesis, she presents the architectural imagery of the poem and points out that military, architectural metaphors in 4:4; 7:5; and 8:10 suggest a stunning, subversive idea of female power.[61] While Meyers rightly emphasizes the resulting powerful portrayal of the woman, not only does her exclusive focus on the female character cloud the role of the man; it also prevents a more relational comprehension of the lovers' games of seduction. With respect to 3:7–8, comments on the presence of warriors do not go beyond the simple observation that the royal litter is escorted by armed men who evoke David's bodyguard (2 Sam 23:8–39), without questioning the meaning and role of such a military scene within the poem.[62] Scholars have faced specific philological questions in 8:6–7 and investigated the dialectic between *love and death* in light of ancient Near Eastern literature, but very little has been said about the military atmosphere of these verses.

In sum, when we look at current scholarly research on the Song's metaphors it seems evident how scant is the attention that exegetes have paid to the interpretation of the poem's military language, as well as to the relatively recent developments in metaphor studies. This book will try to fill these lacunae.

1.3. Theoretical Framework

Over the past decades, several fields of research, such as linguistics, psychology, neurosciences, philosophy, theology, and so on, have produced an impressive number of studies on metaphorical phenomena. Undoubtedly, cognitive linguistics currently is the main research field and the main reference point for scholarly inquiry on what is usually considered the queen of tropes. Without detailing the intricacies of cognitive metaphor theories, I will here outline the basics of conceptual metaphor theory, blending theory, and other more recent developments that will be used to explain the Song's metaphor LOVE IS WAR.

---

61. Carol L. Meyers, "Gender Imagery in the Song of Songs," in *A Feminist Companion to the Song of Songs*, ed. Athalya Brenner, FCB 1 (Sheffield: Sheffield Academic, 1993), 204.

62. See the discussion in Marvin H. Pope, *Song of Songs: A New Translation with Introduction and Commentary*, AB 7C (Garden City, NY: Doubleday, 1977), 436–40.

In 1980, George Lakoff and Mark Johnson authored what is now considered the manifesto of conceptual metaphor theory, a study significantly titled *Metaphors We Live By*, which introduces the notion of "conceptual metaphor."[63] Whereas metaphor has often—but not always—been treated as a decorative artifice of language, as an extraordinary instrument of rhetoric and imagination, Lakoff and Johnson argue that metaphor is a pervasive linguistic phenomenon, implemented daily in a variety of communicative situations. The use of metaphor is universal and cross-cultural, suggesting that metaphor does not only concern the human way of talking. Rather, it must have something to do with the mechanisms of the human mind. According to Lakoff and Johnson, "Metaphors as linguistic expressions are possible precisely because there are metaphors in a person's conceptual system."[64] In other words, we talk metaphorically because much of our concepts are structured metaphorically. Our ordinary conceptual system, by which we think, is metaphoric in itself, so metaphor is not only a figure of speech but first and foremost a figure of thought. For instance, the common use of a series of expressions on the occasion of a debate, such as "Your claims are indefensible," "He attacked all the weak points of my argument," and "I have destroyed her reasoning," seem to imply the concept ARGUMENT IS WAR, a concept that is metaphorical in itself. According to Lakoff and Johnson, not only do the metaphorical concepts of our mind shape our language, but they also inform our actions. For instance, many of the things that take place during an argument are partially structured by the concept of war: those who are engaged in a discussion really act like they are in war, using strategies, considering each other enemies, and acting like there are winners or losers. Metaphor, therefore, is something we live by, whether we are aware or not.

According to conceptual metaphor theory, the cognitive process that generates the metaphorical concepts of our mind consists of conceptualizing a segment of experience (e.g., ARGUMENT), called the target, in terms of the accumulated knowledge of another segment of experience (e.g., WAR), called the source. Hence the notion of conceptual metaphor (e.g.,

---

63. George Lakoff and Mark Johnson, *Metaphors We Live By* (Chicago: University of Chicago Press, 1980). Lakoff presented a more sophisticated version of his conceptual metaphor theory some years later. See George Lakoff, "The Contemporary Theory of Metaphor," in *Metaphor and Thought*, ed. Andrew Ortony (Cambridge: Cambridge University Press, 1993), 202–51.

64. Lakoff and Johnson, *Metaphors We Live By*, 6.

ARGUMENT IS WAR): the mind creates a set of conceptual correspondences, called mapping, between conceptual elements of the source and conceptual elements of the target. One of the best-explored examples in English is a cluster of metaphorical expressions such as "I am simmering," "I am boiling," and "I am steaming," which imply the conceptual metaphor ANGER IS HEAT AND PRESSURE OF A CONTAINED LIQUID.[65] In this case, the mapping can be represented as in figure 1.1 below. Conventionally, the conceptual metaphor is written in small caps (ANGER IS HEAT AND PRESSURE OF A CONTAINED LIQUID), as are the conceptual domains (CONTAINER and SELF). The two conceptual structures can be graphically represented by two squares (or circles) with or without dotted borders. The arrow indicates the unidirectional, asymmetric projection of some conceptual elements of the source (a, b, c, etc.) on the target (a', b', c', etc.), so that A IS B, and not B IS A. Furthermore, figure 1.1 only shows some selected mappings (a/a', b/b', c/c', d/d', e/e'). Whereas other conceptual projections are possible (f/f'), the source domain contains some conceptual elements that do not play any role in the process of mapping (g). Likewise, the entire conceptual structure of the target is not the object of the metaphorical process (h). The partial nature of metaphorical mappings is technically called metaphorical highlighting.[66]

Several years after the first developments of conceptual metaphor theory, Gill Fauconnier and Mark Turner developed Lakoff's model by cre-

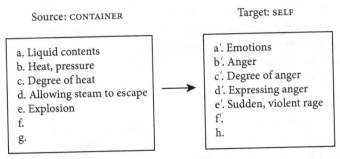

Fig. 1.1. Mapping of ANGER IS HEAT AND PRESSURE OF A CONTAINED LIQUID. Based on Barbara Dancygier and Eve Sweetser, *Figurative Language*, CTL (Cambridge: Cambridge University Press, 2014), 29, table 2.3.

---

65. Dancygier and Sweetser, *Figurative Language*, 75.

66. For more details, see Zoltán Kövecses, *Metaphor: A Practical Introduction* (Oxford: Oxford University Press, 2010), 103.

ating a new paradigm called blending theory, which was first adopted in biblical scholarship by Pierre Van Hecke.[67] According to blending theory, the metaphorical process involves four spaces: (1) input 1, which corresponds to the source domain of conceptual metaphor theory; (2) input 2, which corresponds to the target domain of conceptual metaphor theory, (3) the generic space, which is the well-known *tertium comparationis*, namely, what the two domains have in common and what makes the mapping possible; and (4) the blended space, namely, a new structure in which the elements of the first two domains are blended, producing a whole that cannot be gathered from single domains. For instance, the conceptual structure of the sentence "This surgeon is a butcher"[68] can be represented as in figure 1.2 below. Both a surgeon and a butcher employ sharp tools on a body for a purpose (generic space). The mind connects the source domain BUTCHERY and the target domain SURGERY through a series of correspondences, which blend and shape the conceptualization of the surgeon as an incompetent person. The blended space certainly represents the main novelty of blending theory with respect to conceptual metaphor theory. In this view, metaphor is not the mere result of cross-mapping different conceptual domains. Rather, it is an entirely new concept produced by blending source and target. For instance, in the previous example, the metaphor SURGEON IS BUTCHER creates the new concept of INCOMPETENCY, which as such does not belong either to the domain BUTCHERY or to the domain SURGEON (neither a butcher nor a surgeon is incompetent by definition) and which is entirely created through the metaphorical process.

Neither conceptual metaphor theory nor blending theory aimed to provide a model for the interpretation of literary metaphor. They rather intended to explain the cognitive mechanisms underlying the production of metaphor, pointing out the metaphorical dimension of human mind. Nev-

---

67. Gill Fauconnier and Mark Turner, "Rethinking Metaphors," in *The Cambridge Handbook of Metaphor and Thought*, ed. Raymond W. Gibbs (Cambridge: Cambridge University Press, 2008), 53–66; Fauconnier and Turner, *The Way We Think: Conceptual Blending and the Mind's Hidden Complexities* (New York: Basic Books, 2002). See also Seana Coulson and Todd Oakley, "Blending Basics," *CL* 11 (2000): 175–96; Joseph E. Grady, Todd Oakley, and Seana Coulson, "Blending and Metaphor," in *Metaphor in Cognitive Linguistics*, ed. Raymond W. Gibbs and Gerard J. Steen (Amsterdam: John Benjamins, 1999), 101–24; Pierre Van Hecke, "Conceptual Blending: A Recent Approach to Metaphor: Illustrated with the Pastoral Metaphor In Hos 4,16," in Van Hecke, *Metaphor in the Hebrew Bible*, 215–31.

68. Kövecses, *Metaphor*, 315–16.

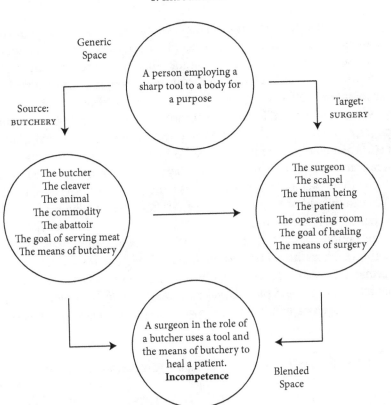

Fig. 1.2. Blend of SURGEON IS BUTCHER. Based on Zoltán Kövecses, *Where Metaphors Come from: Reconsidering Context in Metaphor* (Oxford: Oxford University Press, 2015), 316, fig. 19.3.

ertheless, very soon scholars started investigating the relationship between literary and nonliterary metaphor in light of cognitive metaphor theory, using both conceptual metaphor theory and blending theory to unravel the meaning of specific literary metaphors and to investigate the conceptual systems behind specific literary works.[69] Following the insights of conceptual metaphor theory, according to which the same conceptual metaphor is

---

69. Lakoff himself faced the question of literary metaphor in George Lakoff and Mark Turner, *More than Cool Reason: A Field Guide to Poetic Metaphor* (Chicago: University of Chicago Press, 1989). For an overview of scholarly debate on literary metaphor after the "cognitive veer," see Elena Semino and Gerard Steen, "Metaphor in Literature," in Gibbs, *Cambridge Handbook of Metaphor and Thought*, 232–46.

entailed by different metaphorical expressions,[70] some scholars pointed out that poems, plays, and novels often contain extensive metaphors underlying the sentence level. Paul Werth argues that in literature we can find "an entire metaphorical 'undercurrent' running through a whole text, which may manifest itself in a large number and variety of 'single' metaphors."[71] In this view, a literary text is made up of root metaphors (also called megametaphors, extended metaphors, and sustained metaphors) underlying clusters of surface metaphors (or micrometaphors or nonextended metaphors).[72] A literary text, therefore, presents many layers: through the surface layers, to which single metaphorical expressions belong, we have access to the conceptual subworld of the text. Here we can find megametaphors expressing the text's gist and its "fundamental cultural frames."[73] In line with Werth, several studies focus on the relationship between megametaphors and micrometaphors in poetic texts and narratives. For instance, Donald C. Freeman analyzed the megametaphors that give coherence to the language, characters, events, and plot of Shakespeare's *Macbeth*.[74] Antonio Barcelona showed that LOVE IS A UNITY OF TWO COMPLEMENTARY PARTS is one of

---

70. For instance, the conceptual metaphor LIFE IS PATH is entailed by a cluster of common metaphorical expressions, such as "Look how far we've come," "We're at a crossroads," "We'll just have to go our separate ways," "We can't turn hack now," "I don't think this relationship is going anywhere" (see Lakoff and Johnson, *Metaphor We Live By*, 44–45).

71. Paul Werth, "Extended Metaphor: A Text-World Account," *LL* 3 (1994): 80.

72. The notion of extended metaphors is by no means new. In 1975, in a well-known contribution to biblical hermeneutics, Paul Ricœur underscored that metaphors are not "isolated events of discourse." According to Ricœur , "There are often clusters or networks of metaphors underlying either a whole poem, or the entire work of a poet." See Ricœur, "Biblical Hermeneutics," *Semeia* 4 (1975): 94. A few years later, Benjamin Harshav (Hrushovski) analyzed the presence of extended metaphors in both modern poetry and nonpoetic texts. According to Hrushovski, metaphor analysis cannot be limited to either one word or the boundaries of sentence: "We must observe metaphors in literature not as static, discrete units, but as dynamic patterns, changing in the text continuum." See Benjamin Hrushovski, "Poetic Metaphor and Frames of Reference: With Examples from Eliot, Rilke, Mayakovsky, Mandelshtam, Pound, Creeley, Amichai, and the New York Times," *PT* 5 (1984): 5–43. This article has been recently republished: Benjamin Hrushovski, *Explorations in Poetics* (Stanford, CA: Stanford University Press, 2007), 32–74.

73. Werth, "Extended Metaphor," 101.

74. Donald C. Freeman, "Catch[ing] the Nearest Way: *Macbeth* and Cognitive Metaphor," *JP* 24 (1995): 689–708.

the most dominant conceptual metaphors in *Romeo and Juliet*, making the play's view of romantic love systematic and coherent.[75]

This perspective will be very helpful in better understanding the creation of conceptual coherence in the Song through the undercurrent conceptual metaphor LOVE IS WAR. A clarification of the term *coherence*, however, is necessary. As Marc Brettler points out, "Unfortunately, despite the large number of studies claiming coherence of one kind or another, most studies do not offer a clear understanding of the term, assuming, instead, that it is transparent or understood. Most ignore the well-documented use of the term 'coherence' in non-biblical disciplines, especially literary study and linguistics."[76] Outside biblical scholarship, the notion of coherence has played a crucial role in the fields of new criticism and linguistics from the 1970s onward.[77] Whereas new criticism mainly regarded coherence as a property of the text, several linguists have rather argued that coherence is a mental phenomenon, that is, something that the reader creates.[78] Moreover, coherence can be distinguished as local and global. Local coherence concerns single and/or adjacent sentences, whereas global coherence is something that goes beyond the sentence/paragraph boundary, including the entire literary work.[79] Empirical experiments have shown that the human mind has a strong inclination to make texts cohere,

---

75. Antonio Barcelona Sánchez, "Metaphorical Models of Romantic Love in *Romeo and Juliet*," *JP* 24 (1995): 667–88.

76. Marc Z. Brettler, "The 'Coherence' of Ancient Texts," in *Gazing on the Deep: Ancient Near Eastern and Other Studies in Honor of Tzvi Abusch*, ed. Jeffrey Stackert, Barbara Nevling Porter, and David P. Wright (Bethesda, MD: CDL, 2010), 412.

77. Myers argues that literary criticism can be considered "the special activity of seeking the coherence which it postulates as a property of literary texts." See David G. Myers, "Robert Penn Warren and the History of Criticism," *MQ* 34 (1993): 375–76. Among linguistic studies on the notions of coherence and cohesion, see Ted J. M. Sanders and Henk L. W. Pander Maat, "Cohesion and Coherence: Linguistic Approaches," *ELL* 2:591–95; Michael A. K. Halliday and Ruqaiya Hasan, *Cohesion in English*, ELS 9 (London: Longman, 1976).

78. John D. Murray, "Logical Connectives and Local Coherence," in *Sources of Coherence in Reading*, ed. Robert F. Lorch and Edward J. O'Brien (Hillsdale, NJ: Lawrence Erlbaum, 1995), 107–25; Paul van den Broek, Kirsten Risden, and Elizabeth Husebye-Hartmann, "The Role of Readers' Standards for Coherence in the Generation of Inferences During Reading," in Lorch and O'Brien, *Sources of Coherence*, 356–67.

79. Jason E. Albrecht and Edward J. O'Brien, "Updating a Mental Model: Maintaining Both Local and Global Coherence," *JEP* 19 (1993): 1061–70.

even when these texts clearly do not hold together.[80] The appearance of a coherent representation of a certain text, however, is not exclusively due to the reader's mind. As Ellen van Wolde explains, coherence "is a dynamic interaction process between the text and the reader."[81] Through its linguistic elements of cohesion, the text itself contributes to look coherent in front of the reader's eyes. As Zoya Rezanova and Konstantin Shilyaev put it: "*Coherence* refers to the cognitive interconnections that make up the conceptual and content structure of the text. *Cohesion* is mostly concerned with linguistic relations between the units of the text and its lexical content in particular."[82] However interrelated, the notions of coherence and cohesion are by no means synonymous.

A further distinction needs to be made. The term *coherence* does not equal the term *unity*, which is "a compositional and authorial category," referring to whether a literary work is written by one or more authors, with or without editorial interventions, and to whether a text is a unitary whole or is composed of different fragments and layers.[83] In other words, whereas coherence is a mental representation emerging from the interplay between the text's elements of cohesion and the reader, unity is an exclusive property of the text.

The presence of extended metaphors in a literary work, therefore, is something that the reader's mind recovers and reconstructs in light of the text's micrometaphors; that is, the presence of extended metaphors says very little about whether a literary work (e.g., the Song) is unitary on the authorial and/or compositional level. Extended metaphors are broad conceptualizations of realities (e.g., LOVE IS WAR), conceptualizations that, in principle, might also be found in composite works and that might be used by different authors/redactors who share the same conceptual universe. It is my contention that, whereas LOVE IS WAR as such neither proves nor excludes the authorial or compositional unity of the Song, it certainly

---

80. For a clear presentation of some of these experiments, bibliography, and relevance for biblical studies, see Jeffrey Stackert, "Pentateuchal Coherence and the Science of Reading," in *The Formation of the Pentateuch: Bridging the Academic Cultures of Europe, Israel, and North America*, ed. Jan C. Gertz et al., FAT 111 (Tübingen: Mohr Siebeck, 2016), 253–68.

81. Ellen van Wolde, "The Creation of Coherence," *Semeia* 18 (1998): 168.

82. Zoya Rezanova and Konstantin Shilyaev, "Megametaphor as a Coherence and Cohesion Device in a Cycle of Literary Texts," *LP* 57 (2015): 32.

83. Brettler, "'Coherence' of Ancient Texts," 410.

fosters the reader's perception of the poem as coherent and therefore as conceptually unitary.[84]

Before describing how the analysis of the Song's metaphor LOVE IS WAR will be conducted, Gerard Steen's remarks on the necessity of a multilevel approach to literary metaphor need to be mentioned, since much of the following analysis is grounded in his proposal. While cognitive linguistics emphasized the cognitive dimension of metaphor, Steen has repeatedly suggested that the complexity of literary metaphor also requires that other registers are observed. As Steen puts it, "Every metaphor has linguistic, conceptual and communicative properties and the combination of these properties constrains or even determines the structure and function of a metaphor in the processes of discourse."[85] As a result, Steen proposes a three-dimensional model, extending the analysis of poetic metaphors to (1) their literary expressions, (2) underlying and resulting conceptualizations, and (3) communicative purposes.

According to Steen, conceptual metaphor theory has drastically separated the propositional and conceptual dimensions of metaphor. Lakoff had argued: "If mappings are confused with names for mappings, one might mistakenly think that, in this theory, metaphors are propositional. They are anything but that: metaphors are mappings, that is, sets of conceptual correspondences."[86] Steen, on the contrary, points out that propositional and conceptual aspects are by no means mutually exclusive, since "propositions can be regarded as the bridge between language and thought."[87] In other words, we have access to the conceptual level only by means of words and the way words are connected to each other. An encompassing study of metaphors, therefore, requires primarily a focus on its vocabulary, grammatical, and syntactical structures (especially in poetry, I would add, in which the use of language dictates meaning).

---

84. More on the Song's coherence, cohesion, and extended metaphors can be found in Danilo Verde, "Love Is Thirst and Hunger: Extended Metaphors and the Coherence of the Song's Words for Love," in *The Song of Songs in Its Context: Words for Love, Love for Words*, ed. Pierre Van Hecke, BETL 310 (Leuven: Peeters, 2020), 359–75.

85. Joanna Gavins, "Metaphor Studies in Retrospect and Prospect: An Interview with Gerard Steen," *RCL* 12 (2014): 504.

86. Lakoff, "Contemporary Theory of Metaphor," 207.

87. Gerard J. Steen, "Analyzing Metaphor in Literature: With Examples from William Wordsworth's 'I Wandered Lonely as a Cloud,'" *PT* 20 (1999): 502.

Steen certainly recognizes that cognitive linguistics has operated a revolution by claiming that metaphor "is not the deviant language of poets, politicians, and patients, as was the dominant view for more than two millennia, but one basic building block of a lot of language, thought, and communication."[88] The emphasis on metaphor as a ubiquitous phenomenon in language and thought, as well as on our conceptual system as metaphoric, undoubtedly broke new ground in linguistic studies, affecting the entire research on metaphorical phenomena of the last three decades. Nevertheless, not only does Steen critically review some aspects of conceptual metaphor theory; he also suggests that in literary studies an exclusive focus on the conceptual level runs the risk of neglecting other registers, such as style and communicative goals.[89]

By combining cognitive linguistics with psycholinguistics and discourse analysis, Steen underscores that literary metaphor "does not only manifest a linguistic form and a conceptual structure, but also a communicative function."[90] In this regard, the author makes a crucial distinction between deliberate and nondeliberate metaphor. While the former aims to change the addressee's perspective on the metaphor's target, the latter does not possess such a goal. Nondeliberate metaphor may still be considered intentional to some extents, insofar as language as such is intrinsically intentional. However, not all metaphors have the specific goal of changing the addressee's point of view. Steen argues, "When metaphor is used deliberately … it functions as a special device in communication, making people think outside the box of the target domain and review that from another box inside some Source domain.… To me, this form of actual thinking outside the box is the true power of metaphor, and it is special."[91]

---

88. Gerard J. Steen, "The Cognitive-Linguistic Revolution in Metaphor Studies," in *The Bloomsbury Companion to Cognitive Linguistics*, ed. Jeannette Littlemore and John R. Taylor, BC (London: Bloomsbury, 2014), 118.

89. See Gerard J. Steen, "Metaphor in Language and Thought: How Do We Map the Field," in *Cognitive Linguistics: Convergence and Expansion*, ed. Mario Brdar, Stefan Thomas Gries, and Milena Žic Fuchs, HCP 32 (Amsterdam: Benjamins, 2011), 117–56; Steen, "Metaphor and Style," in *The Cambridge Handbook of Stylistics*, ed. Peter Stockwell and Sara Whiteley (Cambridge: Cambridge University Press, 2014), 315–28; Steen and Raymond W. Gibbs, "Questions about Metaphor in Literature," *EJES* 8 (2004): 337–54.

90. Gerard J. Steen, "The Paradox of Metaphor: Why We Need a Three-Dimensional Model of Metaphor," *MS* 23 (2008): 221.

91. Gavins, "Metaphor Studies," 497.

Authors draw readers' attention to an alien source domain and make the readers think outside the box of the target domain in various ways, for example, through unconventional metaphors, extended metaphors, or linguistic signals such as unfamiliar syntactic constructions, soundplay, parallel structures, or by combining metaphor with other tropes such as hyperbole, irony, and so on. As I will attempt to show, this is usually the case for the Song's warlike metaphors.[92]

1.4. Metaphor Analysis in Three Steps

In light of the understanding of metaphor described above, the Song's use of military metaphors can be represented as in figure 1.3: LOVE IS WAR is an undercurrent conceptual metaphor, which runs throughout the entire Song and emerges in four clusters of surface metaphors, that is, WOMAN IS FORTIFIED CITY, MAN IS CONQUEROR, WOMAN IS CONQUEROR, and LOVE IS STRIFE. These clusters are expressed through several figurative expressions, namely, military metaphors, similes, and scenes. The following chapters will analyze clause constructions, semantics and conceptualizations, and the communicative goals of each figurative expression within the four respective surface metaphors. From a methodological point of view, metaphor analysis will be conducted in three steps.

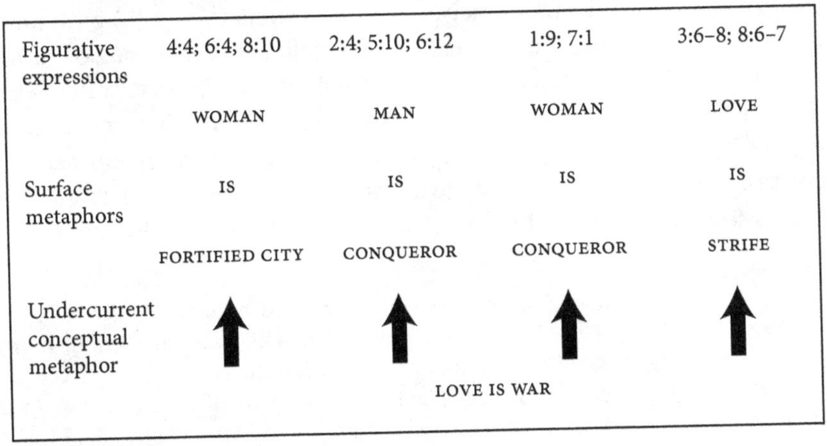

Figurative expressions	4:4; 6:4; 8:10	2:4; 5:10; 6:12	1:9; 7:1	3:6–8; 8:6–7
	WOMAN	MAN	WOMAN	LOVE
Surface metaphors	IS	IS	IS	IS
	FORTIFIED CITY	CONQUEROR	CONQUEROR	STRIFE
Undercurrent conceptual metaphor	⬆	⬆	⬆	⬆
		LOVE IS WAR		

Fig. 1.3. LOVE IS WAR in the Song.

---

92. Gerard J. Steen, "The Contemporary Theory of Metaphor—Now New and Improved!," *RCL* 9 (2011): 41–42.

The first step concerns the clause and its word order.[93] While in Biblical Hebrew the default word order of verbless clauses is subject-predicate, the most frequently recurring order of constituents in verbal clauses is verb-subject-object. Nevertheless, the word order may be inverted in both verbless and verbal clauses. Furthermore, other constituents may occupy the first position. In verbal clauses, when the verb is preceded by constituents (e.g., subject, object, prepositional phrases, etc.), the word order is regarded as marked, and modern grammarians use the linguistic category of fronting in order to indicate "the placement of a complement or adjunct of a [Biblical Hebrew] verbal clause in front of the verbal constituent of that clause."[94] Verbless clauses may also be marked, either by inverting the word order from subject-predicate to predicate-subject or by fronting phenomena. Traditional grammars have not paid great attention to fronting phenomena, and Takamitsu Muraoka mainly explains it through the category of emphasis.[95] More recently, other scholars have proposed several explanations.[96] In this regard, the pragmatic categories of topic and focus used by functional grammar have been particularly productive. The former is "who/what is talked about," and the latter is the asserted, more salient information, namely, "what is said."[97] As *A Biblical Hebrew Reference Grammar* (§47.2.1) explains, fronting phenomena may have different semantic-pragmatic functions, including (1) activating or reactivating an identifiable entity or entities; (2) marking the focus of an utterance; (3) marking a sentence focus, namely, a report on some events; (4) grounding an utterance temporally or spatially; (5) signaling simultaneous or nearly simultaneous actions; and (6) creating formal patterns, especially in poetry. The purpose of the clause analyses is to investigate whether and to what extent the Song's military metaphors, similes, and scenes present peculiar constructions that (1) contribute to a better understanding of the figurative expressions and (2) draw the reader's attention to the source domain WAR.[98]

---

93. For an overview of scholarly research on word order in Biblical Hebrew, see Pierre Van Hecke, *From Linguistics to Hermeneutics: A Functional and Cognitive Approach to Job 12–14*, SSN 55 (Leiden: Brill, 2011), 62–110.

94. Christo van der Merwe, "Explaining Fronting in Biblical Hebrew," *JNSL* (1999): 173.

95. Joüon §§155–56.

96. Van der Merwe, "Explaining Fronting," 173–86.

97. Simon C. Dik, *The Structure of the Clause*, part 1 of *The Theory of Functional Grammar*, FGS 20 (Berlin: de Gruyter, 1997).

98. Bourguet points out that syntax plays the crucial role of making a certain

The second step concerns the lexicon employed by the Song's meta-phors, similes, and scenes at stake, which will be analyzed in light of some of cognitive semantics' achievements.[99] Since the 1960s, semantics has argued that the meaning of words cannot be separated from the semantic fields or domains to which they belong. A semantic field or domain can be defined as "a segment of reality symbolized by a set of related words."[100] Cognitive semantics has further developed this basic assumption by clarifying that (1) domains are not only linguistic structures but first and foremost conceptual representations, and (2) words express concepts that are tied together within a conceptual domain because the realities to which they refer are experienced together.[101] In this view, the meaning of a word depends on the conceptual domain it evokes. For instance, the word *knife* can be used either within the domain EATING or within the domain FIGHT-ING. Whereas in the former case it indicates a kitchen tool, in the latter the same word assumes the connotation of a weapon.[102]

Furthermore, cognitive semantics has pointed out that the meaning of lexical items is not to be considered a property of words, but rather as a construction depending on different uses within different linguistic contexts. Using an example from William Croft and Alan Cruse, in expres-sions such as "John moored the boat to the *bank*" and "I know a *bank* whereon the wild thyme blows" (Shakespeare), the word *bank* assumes its meaning from the context, namely, from the utterance in which it is used.[103]

---

metaphor "stand up and be counted," as Doyle aptly puts it. See Daniel Bourguet, *Des métaphores de Jérémie*, EBib 9 (Paris: Gabalda, 1987); Brian Doyle, *The Apocalypse of Isaiah Metaphorically Speaking: A Study of the Use, Function and Significance of Meta-phors in Isaiah 24–27*, BETL 151 (Leuven: Peeters, 2000), 78.

99. For an extensive presentation of cognitive semantics, see Leonard Talmy, *Toward a Cognitive Semantics*, 2 vols. (Cambridge: MIT Press, 2000); Ronald W. Lan-gacker, "The Contextual Basis of Cognitive Semantics," in *Language and Conceptual-ization*, ed. Jan Nuyts and Eric Pederson. LCC 1 (Cambridge: Cambridge University Press, 1997), 229–52.

100. Laurel J. Brinton, *The Structure of Modern English: A Linguistic Introduc-tion* (Amsterdam: Benjamins, 2000), 112.

101. Charles J. Fillmore, "Frame Semantics," in *Linguistics in the Morning Calm*, ed. the Linguistic Society of Korea (Seoul: Hanshim, 1982), 11–37; Fillmore, "Frames and the Semantics of Understanding," *Quaderni di semantica* 6 (1985): 222–54.

102. Günter Radden and René Dirven, *Cognitive English Grammar*, CLP 2 (Amsterdam: Benjamins, 2007), 11.

103. William Croft and Alan D. Cruse, *Cognitive Linguistics*, CTL (Cambridge: Cambridge University Press, 2004), 109–10.

Words, therefore, are inherently polysemous, in the broad sense that the meaning of a word varies with its uses. In this regard, cognitive semantics employs the category of "meaning potential" in order to indicate all possible meanings that a word may convey, while considering the specific use of a word in a specific context as a process through which a portion of its meaning potential is isolated, creating a "bounded sense unit."[104] In other words, once a word is employed in a specific linguistic context only some conceptual aspects are, so to speak, triggered. As Jens Allwood argues, the activation of a specific meaning of a lexeme does not depend on the lexeme as such, but mainly on (1) the linguistic expression as a whole, and (2) the memory of past activations of that lexeme.[105] The notion of meaning potential is crucial to the present research. The Song's military imagery is sometimes expressed through lexical items that may also have nonmilitary meaning if they are considered either individually or in other contexts. For instance, the lexeme סוס ("horse") has a broad meaning potential and does not necessarily indicate a warhorse; likewise, מגדל ("tower") does not necessarily refer to fortifications, nor does it always recall military scenarios; גברים may also have the meaning of "mighty men," and so on. Nevertheless, in light of cognitive semantics and of the notion of meaning potential, I show that these (and other) lexemes do activate the conceptual domain WAR in the Song. Once the military meaning of the images at stake is established, I attempt to explain the resulting conceptualization of both love and lovers in light of cognitive metaphor theory.

As a third step, I will investigate the function of the warlike imagery within the Song to determine whether and to what extent the Song's military language is unconventional and challenging with respect to the rest of the poem, the Hebrew Bible, and cognate literature. While it would be a worthwhile and revealing project to assess the issue of the representation of love in military terms in the entire ancient Near East, for the sake of feasibility I focus on Egyptian love poems, which are usually recognized as the closest parallel to the Song from a literary point of view.[106] The

---

104. Croft and Cruse, *Cognitive Linguistics*, 109–10.

105. Jens Allwood, "Meaning Potential and Context: Some Consequences for the Analysis of Variation in Meaning," in *Cognitive Approaches to Lexical Semantics*, ed. Hubert Cuyckens, René Dirven, and John R. Taylor, CLR 23 (Berlin: de Gruyter, 2003), 43–45.

106. For quotations and translations of Egyptian texts, I rely on Michael V. Fox, *The Song of Songs and the Ancient Egyptian Love Song* (Madison: University of Wiscon-

research on the relationship between the Song and the love poems from New Kingdom Egypt started in the nineteenth century and is still the object of much scholarly interest.[107] However, the conceptual metaphor LOVE IS WAR in Egyptian love poems has not been researched hitherto. I will also consider Ugaritic literature, since its mythological texts use expressions, literary patterns, and images that bear resemblance to some of the Song's warlike imagery.[108] I will show that the Song's warlike imagery has undeniable connections with a reservoir of motifs and images and with the conceptual universe of the ancient Near East. At the same time, the Song's warlike imagery presents remarkable aspects of unconventionality, challenging ancient (and modern) understandings of romantic love and gender roles.[109]

---

sin Press, 1985). Moreover, I also consulted the following studies: Bernard Mathieu, *La poésie amoureuse de l'Égypte Ancienne: Recherche sur un genre littéraire au Nouvel Empire*, BEIFAO 115 (Cairo: Institut français d'archéologie orientale du Caire, 1996); Edda Bresciani, *Letteratura e poesia dell'Antico Egitto*, I Millenni (Torino: Einaudi, 1990).

107. See issue 46 of the journal *Die Welt des Orients* (2016), which is entirely devoted to the relationship between the Song and the Egyptian love poems of the Ramesside period (1300–1100 BCE). See also Renata Landgráfová and Hana Navrátilová, *Sex and the Golden Goddess I: Ancient Egyptian Love Songs in Context* (Prague: Czech Institute of Egyptology, 2009); Antonio Loprieno, "Searching for a Common Background: Egyptian Love Poetry and the Biblical Song of Songs," in *Perspectives on the Song of Songs/Perspektiven der Hoheliedauslegung*, ed. Anselm C. Hagedorn, BZAW 346 (Berlin: de Gruyter, 2005), 105–35; Pascal Vernus, "Le Cantique des Cantiques et l'Égypte pharaonique," in Hagedorn, *Perspectives on the Song of Songs*, 150–62; Alviero Niccacci, "Cantico dei cantici e canti d'amore egiziani," *SBFLA* 31 (1991): 61–85; John B. White, *A Study of the Language of Love in the Song of Songs and Ancient Egyptian Poetry*, SBLDS 38 (Missoula, MT: Scholars Press, 1978); Friedrich M. Müller, *Die Liebespoesie der alten Ägypter*, 2nd ed. (Leipzig: Hinrichs, 1932); Hermann Gunkel, "Ägyptische Parallelen zum Alten Testament," *ZDMG* 63 (1909): 531–39; Charles W. Goodwin, "On Four Songs Contained in an Egyptian Papyrus in the British Museum," *TSBA* 3 (1874): 380–88.

108. For quotations and translations of Ugaritic texts, I rely on Nicolas Wyatt, *Religious Texts from Ugarit: The Words of Ilimilku and His Colleagues*, BibSem 53 (Sheffield: Sheffield Academic, 2002). I also consulted Gregorio del Olmo Lete, *Mitos, leyendas y rituales de los semitas occidentales* (Barcelona: Trotta, Edicions de la Universität de Barcelona, 1998).

109. I here use the adjective *romantic* in the broad sense of mutual passion and desire experienced by two lovers within their relationship.

1.5. Preambles

1.5.1. On the Song's Literary Structure

The question of the role of the conceptual metaphor LOVE IS WAR in the Song implies a previous clarification of whether the book is here understood as a unified composition or a compilation of diverse songs.

It is well known that scholars largely disagree on how to understand the literary organization of the Song.[110] On the one hand, some of the Song's characteristics (e.g., same topic, atmosphere, figurative language, catchwords) lead exegetes to speak in terms of poetic unity, or even of narrative unity.[111] On the other hand, signs of disunity (e.g., unexpected interruptions between portions of texts, abrupt changes of speakers, inconsistencies) support the widespread idea that the Song is a collection of different poems, written by one or more authors, with or without the work of a redactor.[112] Both positions undoubtedly have some ground in the text. As far as the present research is concerned, the Song is considered something in between: it is not unitary, if by *unitary* one means a narrative plan in which a love story develops in a consistent way from beginning to end, with a prologue, a plot, and an epilogue. However, it is not just a collection either, if by *collection* one means a group of disparate, unrelated poems,

---

110. Marc Z. Brettler, "Unresolved and Unresolvable Problems in Interpreting the Song," in *Scrolls of Love: Ruth and the Song of Songs*, ed. Peter S. Hawkins and Lesleigh Cushing Stahlberg (New York: Fordham University Press, 2006), 185–98.

111. Poetic unity: see, for instance, Barbiero, *Song of Songs*, 17–24; D. Philip Roberts, *Let Me See Your Form: Seeking Poetic Structure in the Song of Songs*, StJ (Lanham, MD: University Press of America, 2007); Mary Timothea Elliott, *The Literary Unity of the Canticle*, EUS 23: Theology 371 (Frankfurt am Main: Lang, 1989). Narrative unity: see, for instance, Iain Provan, *Ecclesiastes, Song of Songs*, NIVAC 16 (Grand Rapids: Zondervan, 2001); Yair Mazor, "The Song of Songs or the Story of Stories," *SJOT* 4 (1990): 1–29. The so-called dramatic approach might be considered a type of narrative reading of the Song. See, for instance, Matthias Hopf, *Liebesszenen: Eine literaturwissenschaftliche Studie zum Hohenlied als einem dramatisch-performativen Text*, ATANT 108 (Zurich: Theologischer Verlag, 2016); Franz Delitzsch, *Hoheslied und Kohelet*, BKAT 4 (Leipzig: Dörffling & Franke, 1875). For the study of the Song as a mixture of poetry and narrative, see Stefan Fischer, *Das Hohelied Salomos zwischen Poesie und Erzählung*, FAT 72 (Tübingen: Mohr Siebeck, 2010).

112. See, e.g., Keel, *Song of Songs*, 15–22; Murphy, *Song of Songs*, 57–67; Longman, *Song of Songs*, 54–56; Jesús Luzarraga, *Cantar de los Cantares: Sendas del amor*, NBE (Estella: Verbo Divino, 2005), 121.

randomly put together. The Song rather seems to be a compilation of several cleverly organized love poems sharing refrains, motifs, metaphors, vocabulary, and subtle cross-references. Sonnet thinks of the Song as a kind of kaleidoscope, presenting a series of variations on the same theme, a series of "fragments" of the lovers' discourse, as Roland Barthes would say.[113] Sonnet's metaphor of a kaleidoscope is particularly appropriate to describe the Song and to explain its double characteristic of being simultaneously unitary and fragmented. Like a kaleidoscope, the Song projects a main motif, that is, "the lovers' mutual desire" or, as Elie Assis puts it, "the longing for union with the beloved."[114] Like a kaleidoscope, the Song gives shape to this motif through several patterns, each of which also displays its own motifs. These patterns are the poems' literary units (see the table at the end of this chapter), which are simultaneously interrelated and separated. They are interrelated due to the repetition of figurative expressions, lexemes, refrains, and so on. They are separated by the presence of end formulas. The end formulas are either formulas of invitation (3:5, 10; 5:1b; 8:14), formulas of intimate union (6:3; 7:11), or both (2:6–7, 16–17; 8:3–4). Not only do these end formulas mark and distinguish the different patterns of the main theme; they also have the function of reiterating the main theme (i.e., the lovers' mutual desire) by creating a continuous *da capo*.[115] The result is the overall image of the lovers' mutual desire as a never-ending dynamic and as an unfinished business. Even the very last words of the Song leave the reader with the strong feeling that both the lovers' mutual desire and the poem might continue forever.

1.5.2. On the Song's Date of Composition

Since the issue of the Song's date of composition is relevant to some of my claims about the poem's warlike metaphors, I will briefly clarify my understanding of the poem's position in the history of biblical literature.

The Song's date of composition is, at first sight, very difficult to establish.[116] The absence of historical allusions makes the dating of the Song extremely problematic and attempts to collocate the Song in the period

---

113. Sonnet, "Du chant érotique," 82.
114. Assis, *Flashes of Fire*, 23.
115. See my reading of the development of the Song's discourse at the end of this chapter.
116. See, e.g., Exum, *Song of Songs*, 47; Longman, *Song of Songs*, 19; Robert

of Solomon are not very persuasive. As Michael Fox argues, even if we take the Song's references to Solomon literally (1:1, 5; 3:7; 8:11)—and I do not think we should—it is not enough to date the poem to the tenth century BCE, since poets could and did write about King Solomon for centuries afterwards.[117] An inquiry into the *Sitz im Leben*, in the traditional form-critical sense, would not be very helpful, as Keel points out.[118] Love poems may be written under many possible circumstances and conditions. Comparative studies have also been inconclusive. It is interesting to note that scholars have used the very same argument, that is, the similarities between the Song and the Egyptian love poems, to place the Song in the tenth century (Gerleman) and between the eighth and the sixth centuries (Keel), while affinities between the Song and the poetry of Theocritus have been used to date the poem to the late Hellenistic period (Garbini).[119]

In my view, the language of the Song is all we have for trying to determine the Song's period of composition. A recent attempt to date the Song in light of linguistic criteria has been made by Scott Noegel and Gary Rendsburg.[120] According to the authors, the Song presents several grammatical and lexical features that are typical of Northern Israelian Hebrew, in light of which the Song should be dated to the tenth century.[121] Noegel and Rendsburg, however, do not really present positive arguments that lead conclusively to such an early date. They rather argue against a late date, trying to explain that the apparent late linguistic features of the Song can be interpreted in a different way. It is very striking that the authors do not engage with and do not even quote F. W. Dobbs-Allsopp's study titled "Late Linguistic Features in the Song of Songs," which has provided the most comprehensive and compelling research on this subject, showing that the Song's language is much closer to the phase of Hebrew language

---

Gordis, *The Song of Songs and Lamentations: A Study, Modern Translation, and Commentary* (New York: KTAV, 1974), 23.

117. Fox, *Song of Songs*, 187.

118. Keel, *Song of Songs*, 11–14.

119. Gillis Gerleman, *Ruth; Das Hohelied*, BKAT 18 (Neukirchen-Vluyn: Neukirchener Verlag, 1981), 75–77; Keel, *Song of Songs*, 4–5; Giovanni Garbini, *Cantico dei Cantici*, Biblica: Testi e Studi 2 (Brescia: Paideia, 1992), 293–96.

120. Scott B. Noegel and Gary Rendsburg, *Solomon's Vineyard: Literary and Linguistic Studies in the Song of Songs*, AIL 1 (Atlanta: Society of Biblical Literature, 2009).

121. Fox, *Song of Songs*, 189 n. 12.

known as Late Biblical Hebrew with respect to orthography, grammar, syntax, and lexicon.[122]

The scholarly attempt to be more precise only leads to unconvincing speculations. For instance, relying on Heinrich Graetz and Hans-Josef Heinevetter, Barbiero has recently tried to locate the Song during the reign of Ptolemy Euergetes (246–221 BCE), dismissing a later date simply because a period of wars started in Palestine after the accession to the throne of Antiochus III. In the author's view, a period of war would not be propitious to the composition of a love poem.[123] I wonder, however, when war has ever stopped poets and novelists from writing about love. All we can say is that the *terminus ad quem* is the first century BCE, due to the presence of manuscripts of the Song at Qumran that are dated from the early Herodian period to circa 50 CE, as well as due to the fact that the Greek version seems to have been redacted between the first century BCE and the first century CE.[124] The likely period of the final composition of the Song, therefore, seems to be between the fourth (maybe fifth) and the second century BCE.

In sum, although the Song's date of composition is difficult to pinpoint, the poem's language seems to suggest that the Song is a late biblical book. This does not exclude, in principle, that some of its parts might be more ancient and later reworked during the editorial phase. This question belongs to the prehistory of the book. As Cheryl Exum puts it, on this matter anything that can be said "is only an educated guess."[125]

---

122. F. W. Dobbs-Allsopp, "Late Linguistic Features in the Song of Songs," in Hagedorn, *Perspectives on the Song of Songs*, 27–77. Fox had already argued that the Song's language resembles Mishnaic Hebrew (Fox, *Song of Songs*, 187–91).

123. Barbiero, *Song of Songs*, 36. Heinrich Graetz, *Schir Ha-Scirim oder das salomonische Hohelied* (Wien: Braumüller, 1871), 79–91; Hans-Josef Heinevetter, *"Komm nun, mein Liebster, Dein Garten ruft Dich!": Das Hohelied als programmatische Komposition*, BBB 69 (Frankfurt am Main: Athenäum, 1988), 221–23.

124. Emanuel Tov, "Canticles," in *Qumran Cave 4.XI: Psalms to Chronicles*, ed. Eugene Ulrich et al., DJD 16 (Oxford: Clarendon, 2000), 195; Tov, "Three Manuscripts (Abbreviated Texts?) of Canticles from Qumran Cave 4," *JJS* 46 (1995): 88; Jean-Marie Auwers, "Les Septante, lecteurs du Cantique des Cantiques," *Graphe* 8 (1999): 37; "Introduction," in *Le Cantique des Cantiques*, ed. Jean-Marie Auwers, BA 19 (Paris: Cerf, 2019), 77–79.

125. Exum, *Song of Songs*, 47.

1.5.3. On the Meaning of the Song's Warlike Metaphors

Since the purpose of this book is not only to establish the presence of the conceptual metaphor LOVE IS WAR in the Song but also to explain its meaning within the poem, a previous clarification of what *meaning* stands for in this research is required.

Over the last few centuries and until recently, biblical hermeneutics has been strongly characterized by the identification of the meaning of biblical texts with so-called *intentio auctoris*. In this view, the art of biblical interpretation has often consisted in the attempt to understand the thoughts and intentions of biblical writers, regardless of the exegetes' awareness and their explicit statements. Such a focus on the *intentio auctoris* was grounded in a relatively recent, Western understanding of literature. As Terry Eagleton writes, "On this theory, a literary work is the sincere expression of some experience that the author has had, and which he [*sic*] wishes to share with others. This is a fairly recent idea, dating mostly from romanticism. It would no doubt have come as a surprise to Homer, Dante and Chaucer."[126] The idea that to understand a text mainly equals to understand *what the author meant* was already widespread in the eighteenth century. It further developed throughout the nineteenth century thanks to the influential works of Friedrich A. Wolf, Georg A. F. Ast, and Friedrich D. E. Schleiermacher, and it persisted during the twentieth century, as the work of Eric Hirsch makes clear.[127] In 1967 and 1976, Hirsch tried to strenuously defend the relevance of the *intentio auctoris* by distinguishing between the "intended meaning" of a work and its "significance" for the readers.[128] According to the author, a literary work only has one meaning (i.e., the *intentio auctoris*), whereas it can acquire different significance for different readers.

---

126. Terry Eagleton, *How to Read Literature* (New Haven: Yale University Press, 2014), 135.

127. Friedrich A. Wolf, *Museum der Altertumswissenschaft* (Berlin: Realschulbuchhandlung, 1807–1810); Wolf, *Vorlesungen über die Enzyklopädie der Altertumswissenschaft* (Leipzig: Lehnhold, 1831); Georg A. F. Ast, *Grundlinien der Grammatik, Hermeneutik und Kritik* (Landshut: Thomann, 1807); Friedrich D. E. Schleiermacher, Hermeneutik und Kritik (Berlin: Reimer, 1838). See Maurizio Ferraris, *Storia dell'ermeneutica* (Milano: Bompiani, 2008).

128. Eric Donald Hirsch, *The Aims of Interpretation* (Chicago: University of Chicago Press, 1976); Hirsch, *Validity in Interpretation* (New Haven: Yale University Press, 1967).

Hirsch's work represented a vigorous attempt to counter the new understandings of meaning that arose during the twentieth century thanks to new criticism, reader-response theory, and deconstructionism, as well as the philosophical hermeneutics of authors such as Hans-George Gadamer and Paul Ricœur.[129] Even though not all these literary movements share the same understanding of what meaning is, they all agree on one point: the meaning of a text cannot be reduced to the authorial intention, but it emerges from the text itself (new criticism), the reader (reader-response theory), and the *Horizontverschmelzung* (Gadamer)—or it is something that nobody can quite grasp, since a text can only generate multiple and contradictory interpretations (deconstructionism). To put it simply, whereas for a few centuries the meaning of a text was mainly identified with the *intentio auctoris*, the notion of meaning has recently become everything *but* the *intentio auctoris*. The title of Barthes's classic essay "La mort de l'auteur" summarizes such an epochal overturn.[130]

This book does not concern itself with authorial intention. The meaning of the Song's warlike metaphors is here considered neither a mere creation of the reader nor a mere property of the text but rather a creative construction produced by the encounter between the world of the text and the world of the reader. This implies, on the one hand, that the meaning of the Song's warlike metaphors is not considered to be something that the poem contains, but rather something that the reader creates and, on the other hand, that the way the Song's warlike metaphors are constructed "imposes some constraints ... prompting the reader to respond to it in certain ways," as Greig Henderson says.[131] I will attempt to show how the Song tries to reawaken and drive the reader's attention to the metaphor LOVE IS WAR. The category of estrangement—which belongs more to the perspective of new criticism in general and Russian formalism in particu-

---

129. Hans G. Gadamer, *Wahrheit und Methode* (Tübingen: Mohr Siebeck, 1960); Paul Ricœur, *De l'interprétation: Essai sur Sigmund Freud* (Paris: Le Seuil, 1965); Ricœur, *Le conflit des interprétations: Essais d'herméneutique I* (Paris: Le Seuil, 1969); Ricœur, *Du texte à l'action: Essais d'herméneutique II* (Paris: Le Seuil, 1986); Ricœur, *L'herméneutique biblique* (Paris: Le Cerf, 2000).

130. Roland Barthes, "La mort de l'auteur," in *Le bruissement de la langue: Essais critiques IV* (Paris: Seuil, 1984), 63–69.

131. Greig Henderson, "A Rhetoric of Form: The Early Burke and Reader-Response Criticism," in *Unending Conversations: New Writings by and about Kenneth Burke*, ed. Greig Henderson and David Cratis Williams, RPT (Carbondale: Southern Illinois University Press, 2001), 130.

lar[132]—will often be used to explain that the Song's military images are constructed in such a way that the reader is forced to stop and think of love in military terms. The presence of unfamiliar syntactic constructions, the use of enjambing lines, the sudden and unexpected appearance of the domain WAR, and the Song's reworked versions of ancient Israel's cognitive scenarios will be explained as the Song's "response-inviting structures," as Wolfgang Iser would say.[133] Thanks to these response-inviting structures, readers are prevented from losing themselves within the literary text and are challenged to become conscious of both the text and themselves, to renew their perception of both love and the Song, and to progressively realize that LOVE IS (also) WAR.

My references to *the reader*, therefore, can be considered references to the so-called implied reader:[134] an ideal reader who shares with the text knowledge, culture, and attitudes without which the text would never achieve its communicative goals. At the same time, however, I am aware that the provided interpretation of the meaning of the Song's military metaphors is grounded in the Song's text as much as in the literary and cultural background, the experience of love, and the inner world of this actual reader—that is, me. As Landy says, "Understanding a text is always a work of comparison, both with our own experience, of love for instance, and with other texts, within the same literary tradition or beyond it."[135] In this view, what we as readers bring to the encounter with the Song's metaphors is as crucial to the interpretation as what the Song's metaphors bring to us. Whether this is a resource or an obstacle to my exegesis is not for me to judge.

---

132. The phenomenon of estrangement, which is often associated with the concept of "alienation-effect" of Bertolt Brecht (*Verfremdungseffekt*), is grounded in the concept of "defamiliarization" coined by Russian formalism and, more precisely by Shklovskij, according to whom such a technique is the very core of poetry. See Viktor Shklovskij, "Art as Technique," in *Literary Theory: An Anthology*, ed. Julie Rivkin and Michael Ryan (Oxford: Blackwell, 2004), 17–23; Lawrence Crawford, "Viktor Shklovskij: Différance in Defamiliarization," *CL* 36 (1984): 209–19. For a critical presentation of the concept of estrangement/defamiliarization, see Terry Eagleton, *How to Read a Poem* (Malden, MA: Blackwell, 2007), 48–64.

133. Wolfgang Iser, *The Act of Reading: A Theory of Aesthetic Response* (London: Routledge, 1978), 34.

134. Iser, *Act of Reading*, 34.

135. Landy, "Song of Songs," 513.

The Song's Development

			End formulas
I	1:2–2:7	*In medias res*	2:6–7

I   1:2–2:7   *In medias res*   2:6–7
1:2–4: The woman's desire
1:5–6: The woman and the daughters of
Jerusalem
1:7–8: The woman's search for the man
1:9–2:3: The lovers' dialogue
2:4–5: The satisfaction of the woman's desire

II   2:8–17   *Da capo*   2:16–17
2:8–9: The arrival of the man
2:10–15: The man's song

III   3:1–5   *Da capo*   3:5
3:1–4: The woman's search for the man

IV   3:6–11   *Da capo*   3:11
3:6–10: The journey of Solomon's litter

V   4:1–5:1   *Da capo*   5:1b
4:1–15: The man's song
4:16–5:1a: The lovers' dialogue

VI   5:2–6:3   *Da capo*   6:3
5:2–7: The woman's search for the man
5:8–6:2: The woman's dialogue with the daughters of Jerusalem

VII   6:4–7:11   *Da capo*   7:11
6:4–12: The man's song
7:1: The Shulammite
7:2–10a: The man's song
7:10b: The woman' response

VIII   7:12–8:4   *Da capo*   8:3–4
7:12–8:2: The woman's song

IX   8:5–14   *Da capo*   8:13–14
8:5–7: The woman's song
8:8–10: The woman's dialogue with the brothers
8:11–12: The woman's song

Woman Is Fortified City

She gently raised two white supports, firm as rocks, which had well sustained many assaults, seeing they had been furiously attacked and had not softened.

—Honoré de Balzac, *Les Cent Contes drolatiques* (trans. May)

This first chapter presents the first cluster of the Song's military metaphors and similes featuring the beloved woman as a fortified city (4:4; 6:4; 8:10).[1] All these verses contain marked syntactic constructions that underline the importance of the employed military imagery. While 4:4, 6:4, and 8:10 are conceptually connected by the same representation of the woman as a fortified city, they focus on different features and provide diverse conceptualizations of the poem's female lover; that is, she is presented as ELUSIVE in 4:4, SUBLIME in 6:4, and MATURE in 8:10. Both the linguistic expressions and the conveyed conceptualizations of femininity in these passages are highly unconventional with respect to both the Hebrew Bible and cognate literature.

2.1. The Elusive Woman (Song 4:4)[2]

SONG 4:4
Like the tower of David[3] is your neck,   כמגדל דויד צוארך

---

1. In line with cognitive metaphor theory, throughout this book similes will be considered types of metaphors (see Dancygier and Sweetser, *Figurative Language*, 137–50).

2. The following is a reworked and extended version of Danilo Verde, "Playing Hard to Get: The Elusive Woman in Song 4:4," *ETL* 94 (2018): 1–25.

3. For the spelling דויד instead of דוד as one of the many signs of the Song's late language, see Dobbs-Allsopp, "Late Linguistic Features," 27–77. It is well-known that there is no evidence for the existence of a tower of David in biblical times, neither

built in courses,[4]
thousands of shields are hung on it,
all quivers[5] of warriors.

בְּנוּי לְתַלְפִּיּוֹת
אֶלֶף הַמָּגֵן תָּלוּי עָלָיו
כֹּל שִׁלְטֵי הַגִּבּוֹרִים

Current translations and commentators seem to overlook the peculiarity of the syntactic construction of 4:4, as well as what such construction entails on the semantic, conceptual, and communicative level.

The NRSV, for instance, translates this verse "*Your neck is like* the tower of David" (so also, among others, NJB, Patrick Hunt, and Edmeé Kingsmill).[6] Song 4:4, however, presents a case of inverted word order (*Like the tower of David* is your neck), which should be kept in the trans-

---

in archaeological findings nor in literary sources. Hence, some scholars suggested reading דּוֹד ("beloved") instead of דָּוִיד ("David"). See, for instance, Petronella W. T. Stoop-Van Paridon, *The Song of Songs: A Philological Analysis of the Hebrew Book Shir Ha-Shirim* (Leuven: Peeters, 2005), 193. This emendation is unnecessary, however, not only because מגדל דויד may be a reference to an imagined tower of David, a belief shared between author and audience, but also because the Song contains other innuendos to David, as Frolov has recently shown. See Serge Frolov, "The Comeback of Comebacks," in *On Prophets, Warriors, and Kings: Former Prophets through the Eyes of Their Interpreters*, ed. George J. Brooke and Ariel Feldman, BZAW 470 (Berlin: de Gruyter, 2016), 41–64.

4. The expression בנוי לתלפיות is a famous *crux interpretum*. I follow Garrett, according to whom it might indicate that the tower is built with cut stones tightly fitted together. Such building would have the double advantage of being both aesthetically beautiful and difficult for the enemies to scale (see Garrett, *Song of Songs*, 140).

5. The meaning of שלט is debated. In the Hebrew Bible it occurs seven times (2 Sam 8:7; 2 Kgs 11:10; Jer 51:11; Ezek 27:11; Song 4:4; 1 Chr 18:7; 2 Chr 23:9), and it is often considered a synonym of מגן, "shield" (see NRSV). Nevertheless, Borger convincingly suggested the meaning of "quivers," which (1) fits the seven occurrences of the term in the Hebrew Bible; (2) relies on Jer 51:11, in which שלט follows the verb מלא, "to be full, to fill"; (3) is supported by an inscription found in the palace of Darius I, in which the Akkadian *šaltu* bespeaks the image of a quiver; and (4) is confirmed by its occurrence in Targumic Aramaic. See Rykle Borger, "Die Waffenträger des Königs Darius," VT 22 (1972): 385–98; see also *HALOT* 1409–10. As Barbiero argues, "The two terms *māgēn* and *šeleṭ*, therefore, are not synonymous but complementary, the first indicating the weapons of defence, the second those of attack of the 'mighty men' who are defending the tower" (*Song of Songs*, 187).

6. Patrick Hunt, *Poetry in the Song of Songs: A Literary Analysis*, StBibLit 96 (New York: Lang, 2008), 45; Edmée Kingsmill, *The Song of Songs and the Eros of God: A Study in Biblical Intertextuality*, Oxford Theological Monographs (Oxford: Oxford University Press, 2009), 77.

lation since it underscores the military image and asks for the reader's attention to its meaning and its role within its immediate context. Many interpretations of the simile of the tower have been suggested. The woman is said to be portrayed as proud and self-aware (e.g., Keel), beautiful (e.g., Yair Zakovitch), adorned (e.g., Roland Murphy), redoubtable (e.g., Munro), discouraging to her lovers (e.g., Hunt), powerful (e.g., Meyers), awe-inspiring (e.g., Exum), and defensive (e.g., Duane Garrett).[7] Dobbs-Allsopp even argues that the image of the armed tower suggests that the woman "will provide safety and shelter for her lover," while in James's view Song 4:4 focuses on "the young woman's vulnerability in the lovers' encounter."[8] Many of these readings are by no means mutually exclusive, whereas some others seem to be contradictory: for instance, does 4:4 emphasize that the Song's woman is awe-inspiring (e.g., Exum), protective (e.g., Dobbs-Allsopp), or vulnerable (e.g., James)?[9] Conceptual contradictions, though they may be present due to the polysemy of metaphor, need to be explained. The presence of so many different interpretations, moreover, raises serious methodological questions: how do we decide which conceptual elements play a role in a given linguistic context? Just because a metaphor can be conceptually very dense does not imply that that metaphor means everything and anything, namely, that all possible conceptual elements (e.g., power, vulnerability, defense, refuge, etc.) connected to the source domain in question (e.g., TOWER) are simultaneously active.

It is also unclear whether and to what extent 4:4 presents an unconventional metaphor with respect to the rest of the Hebrew Bible and cognate literature.[10] Keel points out that in the ancient Near East "a woman might symbolize an unconquered city (or nation)."[11] These kinds of observations, however helpful, only emphasize the common aspects between the Song's figurative language and its milieu's imagery, overlooking possible elements of novelty in the Song on both the poetic and the conceptual level.

---

7. Zakovitch, *Das Hohelied*, 187–89; Murphy, *Song of Songs*, 159; Munro, *Spikenard and Saffron*, 42; Hunt, *Poetry in the Song of Songs*, 255; Meyers, "Gender Imagery in the Song of Songs," 202; Exum, *Song of Songs*, 164; Garrett, *Song of Songs*, 190–91.

8. F. W. Dobbs-Allsopp, "The Delight of Beauty and Song of Songs 4:1–7," *Int* 59 (2005): 267; James, *Landscapes of the Song of Songs*, 108.

9. Exum, *Song of Songs*, 165; Dobbs-Allsopp, "Delight of Beauty," 267; James, *Landscapes of the Song of Songs*, 102.

10. Technically speaking, Song 4:4 starts with a simile.

11. Keel, *Song of Songs*, 147.

2.1.1. The Marked Word Order

Song 4:4 presents a peculiar syntactic construction that underscores the simile of the armed tower, an image that develops through two verbless clauses:

Clause		Position 2	Position 1
1	Apposition of predicate	*Subject*	*Predicate*
	בנוי לתלפיות	צוארך	כמגדל דויד
2	Apposition of subject	*Predicate*	*Subject*
	כל שלטי הגבורים	תלוי עליו	אלף המגן

The Hebrew text presents a case of inverted word order (predicate-subject): "*Like the tower of David* is your neck." The predicate (כמגדל דויד), which is the focus of the utterance—the foregrounded, more salient information about the subject—occupies the fronting position. Not only does the first clause invert the default word order of verbless clauses in Biblical Hebrew, that is, subject-predicate, but it is also unusual in comparison with the poem's other similes. With the exception of 4:3–4 and 6:7, indeed, the Song's forty-three similes constructed through the preposition כ present the default word order subject (target)-predicate (source).[12] The same default word order subject (target)-predicate (source) is also present in texts belonging to the literary genre *waṣf*, with only four exceptions.[13]

Song 4:3

like a crimson thread are your lips
like a slice of pomegranate is your cheek[14]

כחוט השני שפתתיך
כפלח הרמון רקתך

---

12. Only on two occasions we can find the typical construction כ + protasis + כן + apodosis (Song 2:2, 3). In addition, on five occasions the poem introduces similes through the verb דמה (1:9; 2:9, 17; 7:8; 8:14).

13. Texts belonging to the literary genre *waṣf* include Song 4:1–7; 5:10–16; 6:4–7; 7:2–8. The *waṣf* is a widespread literary genre in Palestinian, Arab, and Egyptian literature, in which lovers describe one another's body. See Mathieu, *La poésie amoureuse*, 187–88; White, *Study of the Language*, 114–16, 148–49; Friedrich Horst, "Die Formen des althebräischen Liebesliedes," in *Gottes Recht: Studien zum Recht im Alten Testament*, ed. Friedrich Horst and Hans W. Wolff, TB 12 (München: Kaiser, 1961), 176–87.

14. The lexeme רקה seems to refer to the temple in Judg 4:21; 5:26. In Song 4:3, I

Song 4:4
like the tower of David is your neck

כמגדל דויד צוארך

Song 6:7
like a slice of pomegranate is your cheek

כפלח הרמון רקתך

The inverted word order in 4:3–4 and 6:7 marks the predicates and, thereby, the sources of the similes. Different explanations of the pragmatic function of the fronting phenomenon in 4:3–4 and 6:7 are certainly possible. The change in the word order might be a case of *variatio*, namely, a stylistic device that breaks the repetition of phonetic, morphological, and syntactic structures to provide a more vivacious text. It might also aim at capturing the reader's attention. The reader, indeed, expects the scheme "your X is like Y" started in 4:1. The inverted scheme "*like Y is your X*" in 4:3–4 and 6:7 surprises readers and, thereby, reawakens their attention. By marking the focus of the similes through the fronting position, the images of the crimson thread, the pomegranate, and the tower of David acquire prominence in front of the reader's eyes. The fronting position points out that of all things it is *to a crimson thread, to a pomegranate*, and *to the tower of David* that the beloved man compares her lips, cheek, and neck. To give an example in English, this is the difference between the sentence "*That* I don't know" and the more neutral "I don't know that."[15]

While the similes in 4:3–4 and 6:7 stand out due to their inverted word order, the simile of the tower in 4:4 stands out in the group 4:3–4 even more, because it is further developed through two more clauses, that is, כל שלטי הגבורים and אלף המגן תלוי עליו.[16] In doing so, the syntax of 4:4 expands the reading time, focusing the reader's attention on the image of the tower, which therefore requires special investigation.

---

understand רקה as a synonym of לחי, "jawbone-cheek," mainly because the *waṣf* develops the description of the lovers' body from top to bottom, or vice versa. After the mention of hair, teeth, and lips, a reference to either the woman's temple or her brows would contradict the verticality of the description.

15. Danilo Verde and Pierre Van Hecke, "The Belligerent Woman in Song 1,9," *Bib* 98 (2017): 211.

16. Such a long construction is not unusual in the Song, which alternates short (e.g., 4:11; 5:11; 8:10) and long similes (e.g., 3:6; 4:1–2; 5:12).

2.1.2. Woman/City at War

In 4:4 two different conceptual domains overlap, that is, CITY and WAR, which are used as source domains for the target domain WOMAN. As shown in figure 2.1, the domain CITY is activated by the lexeme מגדל and by the metonymic process *tower-fortifications-city*. The domain WAR is activated by the lexemes גבורים, שלט, מגן, and by the metonymic process *warriors and military equipment-army-war*. Finally, the domain WOMAN is activated by the lexeme צואר and by the metonymic process *neck-body-woman*.

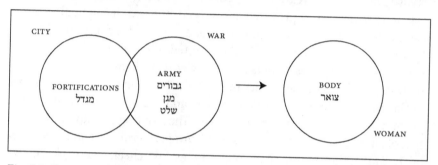

Fig. 2.1. Conceptual domains in Song 4:4

In the Hebrew Bible the lexeme מגדל ("tower") does not always refer to military fortifications or urban structures. In a few places, the Hebrew Bible mentions agricultural constructions, built in the middle of fields, vineyards, and orchards, to store the harvest or watch over properties and cattle (e.g., Isa 5:2).[17] In addition, in Gen 11:4–5, מגדל might refer to another kind of tower, namely, the *ziqqurat* of Babel, which belonged to a temple complex.[18] Nevertheless, most of the time מגדל indicates an architectural structure for

---

17. Keith N. Schoville, "מִגְדָּל," *NIDOTTE* 2:841–42; Schoville, "Fortifications," *ISBE* 2:346–54; Edward B. Banning, "Towers," *ABD* 6:622–24; Diether Kellerman, "מִגְדָּל," *ThWAT* 4:642–46.

18. Whether the tower of Babel mentioned in Gen 11:4–5 refers to a tower of a religious building or formed part of the city fortifications is debated. On the one hand, the biblical tower of Babel has often been understood as a cultic structure. See, for instance, Gordon J. Wenham, *Genesis 1–15*, WBC 1 (Waco, TX: Word, 1987), 234–46. Other scholars, however, point out that the text of Genesis is actually unclear. See Theodore Hiebert, "The Tower of Babel and the Origin of the World's Cultures," *JBL* 126 (2007): 29–58.

defending a city. In a series of texts, מגדל seems to refer to a fortified citadel inside the city itself (see Judg 8:9, 17; 9:50–57; 2 Kgs 9:17), and, especially in exilic and postexilic texts, it indicates towers built in the wilderness as forts (see 2 Chr 26:10; 27:4) or forming part of the city walls (see Jer 31:38; 2 Chr 14:6; 26:9; Neh 3:1). In the latter case, towers were built as part of the city wall at regular intervals, in a square or semicircular shape, and were equipped with balconies from which the defenders could throw burning weapons and stones. They were also built on either side of the gates in order to control and protect the entrances, which were the weakest points in a citadel. Moreover, towers represented the place from which the besieged citadels declared their surroundings to enemies.[19] The widespread urban/military use of מגדל, that is, the past activations of the lexeme, suggests that also in 4:4 the term might have such a military/urban meaning, which is definitively activated by the image of warriors hanging their shields, a reference to Ezekiel's description of the fortified city of Tyre:

EZEKIEL 27:10–11

Paras and Lud and Put were in your army,	פרס ולוד ופוט היו בחילך
your mighty warriors,	אנשי מלחמתך
they hung shield and helmet in you,	מגן וכובע תלו־בך
they gave you splendor.	המה נתנו הדרך
Men of Arvad and Helech	בני ארוד וחילך
were on your walls all around,	על־חומותיך סביב
men of Gamad were at your towers.	וגמדים במגדלותיך היו
They hung their quivers all around your walls	שלטיהם תלו על־חומותיך סביב
they made perfect your beauty.	המה כללו יפיך

Although we might consider Ezek 27:10–11 a continuation of the previous ship image (Ezek 27:1–9), Walther Eichrodt and Walther Zimmerli rightly notice that it also describes Tyre as a fortified city.[20] Several

---

19. See the drawings of Assyrian sieges reported in Philip J. King and Lawrence E. Stager, *Life in Biblical Israel*, LAI (Louisville: Westminster John Knox, 2001), 238; Yigael Yadin, *The Art of Warfare in Biblical Lands in the Light of Archaeological Discovery* (London: Weidenfeld & Nicolson, 1963), 420–25.

20. Walther Zimmerli, *A Commentary on the Book of the Prophet Ezekiel*, Hermeneia (Philadelphia: Fortress, 1983), 2:59–61; Walther Eichrodt, *Ezekiel: A Commentary*, OTL (Philadelphia: Westminster, 1970), 386. On the ship image, see Ian D. Wilson, "Tyre a Ship: The Metaphorical World of Ezekiel 27 in Ancient Judah," *ZAW* 125 (2013): 249–62; Carol A. Newsom, "A Maker of Metaphors: Ezekiel's Oracles against Tyre," *Int* 38 (1984): 151–64.

archaeological and literary sources provide evidence of the ancient custom of hanging shields not only on ships' upper rails but also on cities' fortifications.[21] While Ezek 27:10 still refers to Tyre as a splendidly armed ship, Ezek 27:11 lets the target city of Tyre emerge in the foreground, due to the explicit mention of walls and towers. The result is a kind of ambiguous, figure-ground image, in which the target ARMED CITY and the source ARMED SHIP occur simultaneously, conveying ideas such as paraded military power, steadiness, invincibility, and architectural beauty. By alluding to the city of Tyre in Ezek 27:10–11, therefore, Song 4:4 makes it clear that the tower of David is part of the city walls, entailing the metaphor WOMAN IS FORTIFIED CITY.[22] In order to understand which concepts are associated with the image of tower and how such concepts are projected into the domain WOMAN, an investigation of the metaphorical use of מגדל in the Hebrew Bible and in the rest of the Song is required.

Outside the Song, מגדל is mainly associated with two concepts, namely, DEFENSE and ARROGANCE. The conceptual association TOWER ↔ DEFENSE occurs both in the Psalter and in Proverbs. In Ps 48:13, not only does מגדל refer to Jerusalem's towers; it also conveys the idea of the holy city as a place protected by YHWH in order to discourage enemies' assaults. In Ps 61:4, YHWH himself is portrayed as a strong, protective tower. Likewise, Prov 18:10 employs the image of a tower to describe YHWH as a safe refuge.[23] On other occasions, מגדל metaphorically represents the negative concepts of PRIDE, PRETENTIOUSNESS, ARROGANCE, and excessive SELF-CONFIDENCE. This seems to be the case with the tower of Babel, which evokes unrestrained human ambition.[24] The conceptual association

---

21. Zimmerli, *Ezekiel*, 2:60.

22. The reference to Tyre within the Song is in line with some biblical texts that connect the Phoenician city to the king of Jerusalem (1 Kgs 5; 7; 9).

23. Rotasperti points out that despite the fact that the book of Proverbs often draws on the domain CITY, the only occurrence of מגדל can be found in 18:10. See Sergio Rotasperti, *"Sorgente di vita è la bocca del giusto": L'arte della metafora nel libro dei Proverbi*, StBib 75 (Bologna: Dehoniane, 2016), 11. In Prov 18:10, STRONG PROTECTION and SECURITY clearly emerge from the syntagma מגדל־עז, "tower of strength/ strong tower," as well as from the verb שגב, "to be high."

24. A long-standing tradition has read the story of Babel as referring to human pride. Several scholars have more recently focused on the theme of dispersion. See Peter J. Harland, "Vertical or Horizontal: The Sin of Babel," *VT* 68 (1998): 515–33; Ellen van Wolde, *Stories of the Beginning: Genesis 1–11 and Other Creation Stories*

TOWER ↔ ARROGANCE also occurs in some prophetic texts, as in Isa 2:15, 17,[25] and in Isa 33:18, "counting the towers" bespeaks a negative, excessive attitude of self-confidence. Furthermore, in the already mentioned texts of Ezek 26–27, the demolition of towers is a sign of the humiliation of Tyre's hauteur, and Ezek 30:6 explicitly associates arrogance with a place called Migdol. As far as the Song is concerned, the metaphorical use of מגדל always has a positive connotation and is much more developed, with respect to both the linguistic expression and the conceptual level. The lexeme מגדל here occurs four times with reference to the woman's neck (4:4; 7:5), nose (7:5), and breasts (8:10).[26] In 4:4, the image of the tower develops through three characterizations: (1) מגדל דויד, (2) בנוי לתלפיות, and (3) אלף המגן תלוי עליו כל שלטי הגבורים. The mention of David, that is, the king par excellence, seems to be fictional and used to make the description of the woman more lofty and royal. The second characterization (בנוי לתלפיות) seems to intertwine two conceptual elements, that is, BEAUTY and INACCESSIBILITY. Finally, the third characterization (אלף המגן תלוי עליו כל שלטי הגבורים) gives the idea of the city's ostentatious military power, as well as its beauty.

The sequence of the three characterizations of the tower contributes toward presenting the image in a very dynamic way: the concepts of DEFENSE and INACCESSIBILITY—inherent to the image of tower—are emphasized by the characterization "built in courses," which also adds the

---

(London: SCM, 1996), 167–68. Without denying the complexity of the story of the sin of Babel, the conceptual association TOWER ↔ ARROGANCE in the rest of the Hebrew Bible supports the reading of Gen 11:1–9 as *also* a story about human pride.

25. "Against every high tower, and against every impregnable wall …, the *haughtiness* of people will be humbled, and the *pride* of men will be brought low, and YHWH alone shall be exalted on that day."

26. According to the MT, the lexeme מגדל also occurs in Song 5:13: לחיו כערוגת הבשם מגדלות מרקחים. In light of Egyptian iconography, Keel suggests that מגדל here refers to cones of ointments that both men and women used to wear on their heads. Due to the heat of the body, these cones probably liquefied and impregnated the body. See Othmar Keel, *The Symbolism of the Biblical World: Ancient Near Eastern Iconography and the Book of Psalms* (Winona Lake, IN: Eisenbrauns, 1997), 187. Nevertheless, this interpretation does not perfectly fit Song 5:13, which mentions the man's cheeks, rather than his head. I therefore follow Murphy, according to whom מגדלות should be read מְגַדְּלוֹת (*piel*, participle, feminine, plural of גדל, "to put forth/to grow"), in line with ancient versions. The resulting translation, according to Murphy, might be: "his cheeks, like beds of spice that put forth aromatic blossoms" (*Song of Songs*, 164–66).

concept of BEAUTY. The concept of DEFENSIVE, INACCESSIBLE BEAUTY is further developed by the mention of warriors at the end of the line. Finally, the image of warriors hanging their weapons on the tower represents, so to speak, the *climax* of the simile, emphasizing the tower as not only well-defended and beautifully adorned, but also awe-inspiring. As far as the target צואר is concerned, Keel argues that in the Hebrew Bible the image of the neck is usually associated with concepts of PRIDE and HAUGHTINESS.[27] Nevertheless, it should be noticed that when the term צואר ("neck") and its cognate ערף are used metaphorically, they are primarily associated with ideas of power/submission (see Jer 31:38; 2 Chr 14:6; 26:9; Neh 3:1). For instance, the expressions "your hand shall be on your enemies' *neck*" in Gen 49:8 and "he has grasped me by the *neck* and shook me to pieces" in Job 16:12 clearly refer to an exercise of power. According to Job 41:14, the Leviathan's strength lies in its neck ("In its *neck* abides strength"). On several occasions, צואר is even coupled with words such as על and מוטה, usually translated "yoke" (see Gen 27:40; Deut 28:48; Isa 10:27; Jer 27:2). The concepts of PRIDE and HAUGHTINESS, to which Keel refers, are actually only derivative from the prototypical conceptual association NECK ↔ POWER/SUBMISSION: a well-erected neck becomes an image of pride and haughtiness when it indicates the refusal to submit to the yoke of a higher power (e.g., God, enemies, etc.; see Hos 10:11; Ps 75:6; Job 15:26). The widespread conceptual association NECK ↔ POWER/SUBMISSION in the Hebrew Bible, the biblical conceptual association TOWER ↔ DEFENSE, and the description of מגדל in 4:4 seem to suggest that the simile of the tower refers to the woman's defensive attitude and to her strength. In 7:5 the image of tower is used twice: the woman's neck is said to be "like a tower of ivory" and her nose "like a tower of Lebanon." Although the Hebrew Bible never mentions an ivory tower elsewhere, it refers to "ivory palaces" (Ps 45:9), "ivory house" (1 Kgs 22:39), and "ivory houses" (Amos 3:15) as expressions of sumptuous beauty. The simile of the woman's neck as an ivory tower suggest ideas of BEAUTY, ELEGANCE, and SPLENDOR, not only due to the preciousness of ivory but also to its color and smoothness.[28] As far as כמגדל הלבנון is concerned, while some commentators argue that the expression indicates a rocky spur of the mountain chain of Lebanon,[29] the

---

27. Keel, *Deine Blicke*, 32–39.

28. Annette Schellenberg, "Ivory," *EBR* 13:544.

29. See, e.g., Paul Joüon, *Le cantique des cantiques: Commentaire philologique et exégétique* (Paris: Beauchesne, 1909), 287–88.

other occurrences in the Song make the interpretation of מגדל as part of the city wall more likely. The characterizations "of Lebanon" and "overlooking Damascus," evoke the charm of far-off, exotic lands, while at the same time activating the concepts of CONTROL and SURVEILLANCE. Indeed, the verb צפה typically refers to sentries' activity of monitoring the city or the land (see 1 Sam 14:16; 2 Sam 18:24–27; 2 Kgs 9:18, 20; Isa 21:6; 52:8). Song 7:5 seems to suggest that while she has, so to speak, "her nose in the air" and seems to be distant (כמגדל הלבנון) and oriented toward faraway places (פני דמשק), she is actually monitoring (צופה) from top to bottom the movements, approaches, advances, and interests of those who surround her. The double image of tower in 7:5 seems to portray the woman as beautiful and splendid (כמגדל השן) and as playing the seductive game of seeming distant, uninterested, and even haughty (כמגדל הלבנון), while she is actually very alert and attentive to the courtship she is receiving.

Finally, Song 8:10 presents the common conceptual association TOWER ↔ POWER, while at the same time it adds the concept of GRANDEUR ("I am a city wall and my breasts are like towers"). Some scholars contend that the woman is here asserting her chastity;[30] the context, however, supports a different interpretation. Immediately beforehand, the woman's brothers have expressed their negative, frustrated attitude toward her sexual life and devalued the woman's femininity and sexual maturity by considering her childlike (8:8). By developing the architectural imagery of 8:8–9, the simile of towers in 8:10, on the one hand, metaphorically represents the woman as a fortified city and thereby conveys the idea of a strong woman, able to protect herself. On the other hand, it creates a strong contrast with 8:8. While the brothers consider her a *little girl* and *sexually immature* ("we have a little sister, and she has no breasts"), she asserts that she is an *adult woman* and *sexually mature* through the hyperbolic simile of the tower ("my breasts are towers!").

To sum up, the metaphorical use of מגדל in the Hebrew Bible presents two basic conceptual associations, namely, TOWER ↔ DEFENSE and TOWER ↔ PRIDE. The Song elaborates on both, blending the concepts of SELF-DEFENSE, INACCESSIBILITY, POWER, GRANDEUR, and BEAUTY, in order to describe the woman's game of seduction through which she seduces and, at the same time, parries the man (4:4; 7:5), as well as her ability to defend and look after her sexual maturity (8:10).

---

30. See, e.g., Pope, *Song of Songs*, 683.

In light of cognitive metaphor theory and of the analysis hitherto conducted, Song 4:4 can be represented as in figure 2.2 (see below). The domains in question are TOWER and NECK/WOMAN. The target is NECK/WOMAN and not simply NECK because the man is describing an element of the woman's body, so that what he says of the neck metonymically refers to the woman. We can only speculate on the generic space of this metaphor, namely, what in the poet's eyes TOWER and NECK have in common and what might have activated the simile. It might be their shared cylindrical, erect shape and/or the fact that the jewelry adorning the woman's neck resembles little shields hanging on towers and city walls, as several scholars have suggested.[31] In any case, the identification of the generic space (traditionally called *tertium comparationis*) is not very important from the perspective of cognitive metaphor theory. What does matter is the identification of the elements of the source domain that are activated in the metaphorical process. These elements are not merely the physical characteristics of TOWER (e.g., height, material) but rather the conceptual associations that are culturally embedded. We certainly do not have immediate access to the poet's mind. We do have, however, other biblical texts that provide evidence that in ancient Israel towers were associated with concepts of DEFENSE, POWER, INACCESSIBILITY, GRANDEUR, and so on. Since the Song shares with the rest of the Hebrew Bible the same cultural context and conceptual universe, we can legitimately assume that these conceptual associations are also present in the poem's use of the image of the tower.

As for the target domain NECK/WOMAN, whereas in cognitive linguistics' graphic representations of metaphors the target domain usually presents specific elements that are cross-mapped with elements of the source domain, I suggest only highlighting the elements of beauty and sensuality. This is not very orthodox, since the precise identification of the conceptual elements of both source and target is a crucial step in cognitive metaphor analysis, especially in the model proposed by Lakoff. However, the more orthodox way of analyzing metaphor from the cognitive perspective is unconvincing and unsatisfying for two main reasons. First, the precise identification of the conceptual elements of the target domain is not always possible, especially when we are dealing with very complex literary metaphors in very ancient texts. While we can identify

---

31. See, e.g., Longman, *Song of Songs*, 146.

the conceptual cross-mapping of conventional metaphors still in use—
for example, by becoming aware of what crosses our mind when we use
these metaphors—the minds of ancient authors are not available to us, and
the attempt to precisely recover the mental operation of cross-mapping
becomes very speculative. Second, even if we were able to precisely identify the cross-mapped conceptual elements, this would not be very helpful
for the sake of the interpretation, since the cross-mapping is the "what"
of metaphorical processes, not the "so what?" In other words, the cross-
mapping can explain the cognitive mechanism underlying the creation of
a certain metaphor but not the meaning of that metaphor in a specific
poetic context. I do not suggest either that there is no cross-mapping or
that the entire structure of the target is involved. Rather, I suggest that the
interpreter's focus needs to be on what the metaphor creates. As blending
theory points out, what is crucial is not the cross-mapping, but rather the

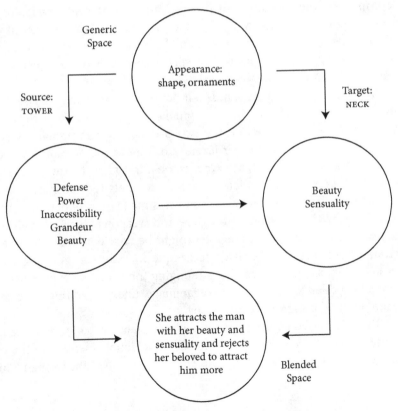

Fig. 2.2. Conceptual structure of Song 4:4

fact that the source domain restructures the target domain and creates a new conceptual representation of the target. The new conceptual representation in Song 4:4 consists in the fact that, by playing the elusive woman, the woman rejects the man to spur on his attraction—indeed, she attracts him more *through* her rejection. A tower can certainly be beautiful and inspire desires of conquest. Its function, however, is not to let conquerors in, but rather to defend the city. The purpose of having an armed tower is to threaten, discourage, and fend off attackers. Ironically, in Song 4:4 the image of the tower is used to describe the woman's seductive strategy, through which she rejects the man in order to arouse him even more and in order to encourage him to step forward.

2.1.3. Playing Hard to Get

Within the fifth literary unit of the poem (4:1–5:1), 4:4 forms part of the description of the woman's body in 4:1–7, an enchanted admiration of the woman's body enveloped by the double exclamation "How beautiful you are, my friend, how beautiful!" (4:1) and "You are altogether beautiful, my love; there is no flaw in you" (4:7), which respectively open and close the man's bewitching and longing words.

Within 4:1–7, Song 4:4 stands out not only for its syntactic construction (see *supra*) but also for its conceptual content. The simile of the tower is the only one that draws on the two overlapping conceptual domains CITY and WAR, while the other lexemes belong to the domain NATURAL ENVIRONMENT. As a result, the architectonic image of the tower emerges as an odd, heterogeneous element among animals (goats, sheep, fawns, gazelles) and fruits (pomegranate), and it is made even odder and rather disturbing by the mention of warriors and weapons. Through a drastic change of source domains, Song 4:4 might be considered an example of estrangement, namely, a stylistic technique that aims at grasping readers' attention, slowing down and prolonging their reading experience, by means of sudden shifts in figurative language, unexpected linguistic constructions, and unfamiliar expressions.

The role played by such a strange image seems to be to reinforce the theme of the elusive woman introduced by the double mention of the veil (4:1, 3).[32] The man is describing what he can glimpse of the woman while

---

32. Some exegetes argue against the meaning of "veil" for the rare Hebrew lexeme

she is hiding herself behind her veil, only allowing a partial view of her body. On the one hand, behind her veil she looks flirty and coquettish (the simile of doves), attractive and desirable (the simile of the lips), chaotic and overwhelming (the simile of leaping goats), fertile and full of life (the similes of sheep and gazelles bearing twins and the simile of the pomegranate). On the other hand, because of her veil she also presents an aspect of elusiveness and unreachability, which the simile of a beautiful, well-adorned, well-built, and well-defended tower develops and emphasizes. In other words, she appears to the man as, at one and the same time, alluring *and* inaccessible. Furthermore, the image of the tower, like the image of the veil, suggests that the woman is alluring *because* she is (apparently) inaccessible. By flirting behind her veil and, at the same time, showing her neck like an armed tower, she plays the game of the elusive woman who seduces by rejecting. At the very moment in which she hides herself behind her veil (pretending to be unavailable) and lets the man see her neck (pretending to be unconquerable), she is actually feeding the fire of the man's passion, who plays her game of seduction. By comparing the woman's neck to the fortified city of Tyre, on the one hand, he recognizes that his beloved is not easy to conquer, but, on the other hand, he might ironically imply that, eventually, he will overcome her resistance. Just as the unconquerable Tyre collapsed in spite of her fortifications, the woman is going to capitulate, sooner or later.[33] After all, such a magnificent tower of David is still the tower of the beloved (דּוֹד/דָּוִיד). Consequently, instead of retreating, he goes ahead with his conquest by glancing at her breasts (4:5), until he finally decides to step forward: "I will get me to the moun-

---

צמה, which occurs in Song 4:1, 3; 6:7 and in Isa 47:2. See, for instance, Stoop-Van Paridon, *Song of Songs*, 177–81. The meaning of "veil," suggested by several Hebrew lexicons (e.g., *HALOT*, BDB) is supported by the use of צמה in Isa 47:2 (גלי צמתך), a text that portrays the uncovering of a garment, and makes sense in the Song's description of the woman. As Van der Toorn has shown, the use of the bridal veil was very widespread in the ancient Near East, as a symbol of chastity and appurtenance. See Karel van der Toorn, "The Significance of the Veil in the Ancient Near East," in *Pomegranates and Golden Bells: Studies in Biblical, Jewish, and Near Eastern Ritual, Law, and Literature in Honor of Jacob Milgrom*, ed. David Wright (Winona Lake, IN: Eisenbrauns, 1995), 327–33.

33. According to LaCocque, "What was said of Tyre with derision by the prophet is now applied to the Shullamite with admiration!" See André LaCocque, *Romance, She Wrote: A Hermeneutical Essay on Song of Songs* (Harrisburg, PA: Trinity Press International, 1998), 105.

tain of myrrh and to the hill of frankincense!" (4:6).[34] The image of the neck/tower does not ward the man off but, on the contrary, turns him on even more. As an aphorism attributed to Italian novelist Antonio Fogazzaro says, "In war and in love, it is retreats that trigger advances." The man's conclusion clarifies that her elusiveness is nothing other than part of her irresistible, flawless beauty: "You are altogether beautiful; there is no flaw in you" (4:7). In other words, the image of the armed tower features a precise moment within the dynamic of courtship, in which, on the one hand, the elusive woman attracts by parrying and, on the other hand, the man hangs in the thrilling balance between stepping backward and forward.

The theme of *the elusive woman* is found elsewhere in the poem, albeit through different domains and images. It already occurs in 2:14, in which she is compared to "a dove in the clefts of the rock, in the covert of the cliff," while the beloved man begs her: "Let me see your face! Let me hear your voice!" The scene ends with some ambiguous words spoken by the woman. After the enigmatic invitation to catch the foxes (2:15), which probably alludes to the theme of *obstructed love*,[35] she describes the happy ending of the man's courtship (2:16). Eventually, however, she sends him back to the place from whence he came (2:17). According to 2:9, he had come from the mountains, "like a gazelle or a young stag." In other words, her game of seduction consists in being elusive (2:14), giving herself to the man (2:15–16), and rejecting him (2:17). In this way, she stokes the fire of their passion and makes eros an unfinished business. The description of the woman as "locked garden," "locked well," and "sealed spring" in 4:12 might also refer to the man's experience of the woman's elusiveness and inaccessibility. Paradoxically, this very garden becomes accessible to the beloved man in 4:16, in which the woman explicitly invites her lover to eat its luscious fruit. In this back-and-forth movement, the woman keeps him in a constant state of suspense that increases the poem's erotic tension. Sometimes, however, the woman's game of seduction does not work

---

34. I understand the expression אֵלֶךְ לִי אֶל־הַר הַמּוֹר וְאֶל־גִּבְעַת הַלְּבוֹנָה as a case of double entendre, with an innuendo to the woman's breasts.

35. According to Alter, "Since vineyards tend to be metaphorical in the Song (cf. 1:6) and are figuratively associated with the body of the beloved, one may propose the following reading: there are in the world pesky agents of interference that seem to obstruct love's fulfilment, as foxes despoil a vineyard, but our own special vineyard remains flourishing and intact, our love unimpeded" (Robert Alter, *The Writings*, vol. 3 of *The Hebrew Bible* [New York: Norton, 2019], 594).

out. For instance, in the famous scene of the man knocking at the woman's door (5:1–6), she starts playing the elusive woman by using some very ambiguous words:

SONG 5:3
I took my garment off,
how could I put it on?
I bathed my feet,
how could I soil them?

פשטתי את־כתנתי
איככה אלבשנה
רחצתי את־רגלי
איככה אטנפם

She seems not to be willing to let him in, but at the same time, she alludes to her nudity, giving the impression that she actually aims at her lover's arousal.[36] Her game of seduction, however, lasts too long, with the unfortunate, unexpected result that the man leaves. Finally, the theme of *the elusive woman* occurs also in 7:5, which is particularly interesting not only because it belongs to a *waṣf* (7:1–6), like 4:4, but first and foremost because 7:5 compares the woman's neck to a tower and describes her through the source domain CITY, as the references to Heshbon, Bath-rabbim, and Damascus suggest. The vertical image of towers, as well as their characterization as "ivory tower" and "tower of Lebanon," makes the woman appear magnificent, imposing, and aristocratic. The mention of the distant, northern cities of Heshbon and Damascus also gives her an exotic aspect, and the final expression "your nose is like a tower of Lebanon overlooking Damascus" portrays her as dominant and unattainable to anyone who wishes to approach her. Different from 4:4, however, Song 7:5 does not foreground the domain WAR, using only the domain CITY.[37]

Only 4:4, therefore, picks up the theme of *the elusive woman* introduced by the image of the veil and evoked in other parts of the poem and reelaborates it in military terms. The representation of the woman as a fortified city that repulses a military attack, that is, the man's advances, is unique to 4:4. The overlap of the domains WAR and CITY also occurs in 6:4, in which the woman is first compared to the beautiful cities of Tirzah and Jerusalem and then is defined as "terrible as an army with deployed banners." Song 6:4 does not seem to describe the woman rejecting her lover,

---

36. A number of alternative readings of these verses have been suggested. For an overview of other possible interpretations, see Exum, *Song of Songs*, 194–95.

37. The verb צפה ("to keep guard, watch attentively") might allude to the image of sentinels or watchmen, but this lexeme alone does not make a military scenario emerge.

however; rather, it seems to describe the woman as overwhelming (see §2.2). In 2:4, the same root דגל is used to describe the sexual experience of love as a military siege, in which the man conquers the woman like an army takes a citadel and plants its standard as a sign of victory (see ch. 3 below). Song 4:4, on the contrary, features a different moment in the erotic dynamic, namely, the moment in which the union is delayed. By playing the elusive woman, the woman makes it clear that such a conquest of love is not to be taken for granted, and that, far from being just a male affair, the experience of eros also depends on the extent to which she makes herself available. In doing so, the woman acts as the one who calls the shots of erotic seduction, keeping her lover's desire at bay and, at the same time, feeding the fire of their eros.

When we consider the rest of the Hebrew Bible and ancient Near Eastern literature, the description of the Song's representation of the woman's neck as a tower emerges as unique. The only text of the Hebrew Bible in which the image of an armed tower and the underlying metaphor WOMAN IS FORTIFIED CITY is used to describe a woman is in Song 4:4. Neither the lexemes מגדל, מגן, שלט, and גבור nor cognate expressions belonging to the conceptual domains FORTIFIED CITY and WAR ever occur in the Hebrew Bible to depict a woman. Egyptian love poems do not contain any similar images either. Regarding Ugaritic poems, despite the fact that they often present the relationship between deities in belligerent terms, they do not describe goddesses as cities, but rather as warriors. Likewise in Sumerian literature, shields and quivers are connected with the warrior goddess Inanna, for example, in Inanna and Ebiḫ (c.1.3.2), while the metaphor of the tower is applied to male gods, as in the following from A šir-namšub to Ninurta (c.4.27.07): "Hero Ninurta, you are the towering wall of your city. Hero Pabilsaĝ, you are the towering wall of your city. Hero Niĝirsu, you are the towering wall of your city; may your august name be invoked!" What we find abundantly both in the Hebrew Bible and in cognate literature is the reverse metaphor, namely, CITY IS WOMAN rather than WOMAN IS CITY.[38] The prophets often describe cities in female terms, as daughters,

---

38. The scholarly literature on the feminization of cities in the Hebrew Bible is very abundant. The following studies are particularly worth mentioning: Carol J. Dempsey, "The 'Whore' of Ezekiel 16: The Impact and Ramifications of Gender-Specific Metaphors in Light of Biblical Law and Divine Judgment," in Gender and Law in the Bible and the Ancient Near East, ed. Victor H. Matthews, JSOTSup 261 (Sheffield: Sheffield Academic, 1998), 57–78; Robert P. Carroll, "Whorusalamin: A Tale of Three

virgins, fiancées, brides, and mothers (e.g., Isa 1:8; 50:1; 60:4; 62:1–2; Jer 2:2; 50:42; Ezek 23:4; Amos 5:2). Cities are metaphorized as raped women, bondwomen, women in labor, sterile widows, and prostitutes (e.g., Isa 1:21; 23:12; 40:12; 47:3, 9; 52:1; Jer 2:20–23; 13:27; Nah 3:4; Mic 4:10). Several authors provide evidence that the prophets' feminization of cities rests on a widespread tradition in both ancient Near Eastern and Greek milieus.[39] John Schmitt, for instance, mentions the interesting case of the Amarna Letters, in which the Akkadian word for "city," which is grammatically masculine, is made feminine. He argues that such an unexpected change is due to the scribes' intention of following the ancient metaphorical tradition of portraying cities as women.[40]

Although some disagreement exists on whether the metaphor CITY IS WOMAN has any mythological background, there is no doubt about the fact that the representation of cities in female terms constitutes a conventional metaphor that was "deeply entrenched and hence well-known and widely used" in the Song's *Umwelt*.[41] Furthermore, several studies on the metaphor (DEFEATED) CITY IS WOMAN have shown that both the Hebrew Bible and cognate literatures adopted such an image mainly in order to describe scenes of military conquests in terms of the submission of a woman to a man.[42] While according the feminization of cities in the

---

Cities as Three Sisters," in *On Reading Prophetic Texts: Gender-Specific and Related Studies in Memory of Fokkelien van Dijk-Hemmes*, ed. Bob Becking and Meindert Dijkstra, BibInt 18 (Leiden: Brill, 1996), 67–82; Renita J. Weems, *Battered Love: Marriage, Sex, and Violence in the Hebrew Prophets* (Minneapolis: Fortress, 1995); Julie Galambush, *Jerusalem in the Book of Ezekiel: The City as Yahweh's Wife*, SBLDS 130 (Atlanta: Scholars Press, 1992).

39. Mark E. Biddle, "The Figure of Lady Jerusalem: Identification, Deification, and Personification of Cities in the Ancient Near East," in *The Biblical Canon in Comparative Perspectives*, ed. K. Lawson Younger, William W. Hallo, and Bernard Frank, ANETS 11 (Lewiston, NY: Mellen, 1991), 173–94.

40. John J. Schmidt, "Yahweh's Divorce in Hosea 2: Who Is That Woman?," *SJOT* 9 (1995): 129.

41. Kövecses, *Metaphor*, 324. On whether the metaphor CITY IS WOMAN has any mythological background, see Peggy L. Day, "The Personification of Cities as Females in the Hebrew Bible: The Thesis of Aloysius Fitzgerald," in *Social Location and Biblical Interpretation in Global Perspective*, vol. 2 of *Reading from This Place*, ed. Fernando F. Segovia and Mary Ann Tolbert (Minneapolis: Fortress, 1995), 283–302.

42. Pamela Gordon and Harold C. Washington, "Rape as Military Metaphor in the Hebrew Bible," in *A Feminist Companion to the Latter Prophets*, ed. Athalya Brenner, FCB 8 (Sheffield: Sheffield Academic, 1995), 308–25.

Hebrew Bible might be regarded as just "a semantic accident" that is due to the feminine gender of the Hebrew word עִיר ("city"), it actually conveys underlying gender stereotypes, such as the understanding of women as subdued by men.[43] The metaphor (DEFEATED) CITY IS WOMAN belongs to a widespread "rhetoric of feminization," the purpose of which was to shame and ridicule the addressees of prophetic discourse.[44] Applied to enemies' male leadership, the domain WOMAN was largely associated with concepts of WEAKNESS, VULNERABILITY, UNSTEADINESS, PASSIVITY, and BEING UNDER CONTROL,[45] and the metaphor CITY IS WOMAN often transmitted a sarcastic, scornful message. The Song's metaphor WOMAN IS (FORTIFIED) CITY overturns the conventional metaphor (DEFEATED) CITY IS WOMAN: by switching source and target domains, the Song twists not only conventional figurative language, but also the concept of woman. While the prophet's sarcastic metaphor entails a conceptualization of woman as WEAK, VULNERABLE, UNSTEADY, PASSIVE, and SUBDUED, the Song produces a novel portrayal of woman as POWERFUL, IMPREGNABLE, STEADY, RESISTANT, and IN CONTROL.

The conceptualization of the Song's woman as resisting the man's power appears even more striking when we consider that in ancient Israel's patriarchal environment women were considered the property of their men (fathers, brothers, husbands, etc.).[46] The idea that a woman might reject or even just temporarily resist male sexual desire is not easy to find else-

---

43. John J. Schmidt, "The Motherhood of God and Zion as Mother," *RB* 92 (1985): 568; Biddle, *Figure of Lady Jerusalem*, 175. The expression *semantic accident* is used by Gordon and Washington, "Rape as a Military Metaphor," 317.

44. Brad E. Kelle, "Wartime Rhetoric: Prophetic Metaphorization of Cities as Female," in *Writing and Reading War: Rhetoric, Gender, and Ethics in Biblical and Modern Contexts*, ed. Brad E. Kelle and Frank R. Ames, SymS 42 (Atlanta: Society of Biblical Literature, 2008), 95–111; Claudia B. Bergmann, "We Have Seen the Enemy, and He Is Only a 'She': The Portrayal of Warriors as Women," in Kelle and Ames, *Writing and Reading War*, 129–42; Cynthia R. Chapman, *The Gendered Language of Warfare in the Israelite-Assyrian Encounter*, HSM 62 (Winona Lake, IN: Eisenbrauns, 2004).

45. Ehud Ben Zvi, "Observations on the Marital Metaphor of YHWH and Israel in Its Ancient Israelite Context: General Considerations and Particular Images in Hosea 1.2," *JSOT* 28 (2004): 363–84; Fokkelien van Dijk-Hemmes, "The Metaphorization of Woman in Prophetic Speech: An Analysis of Ezekiel XXIII," *VT* 43 (1993): 162–70.

46. Susan Ackerman, "Women in Ancient Israel and in the Bible," in *Oxford Research Encyclopedia of Religion* (April 2016), https://tinyurl.com/SBL2645a.

where in the Hebrew Bible;[47] here, the dynamic of desire between male and female is characterized by the submission of the latter to the former. One might certainly wonder whether such a conceptual twist was intentional, and whether the author of the Song intended to overturn the conventional metaphor (DEFEATED) CITY IS WOMAN and thereby the concept of woman. The so-called *intentio auctoris*, however, is very elusive, especially since we have no idea who authored the Song. Furthermore, as Eagleton writes, the authors and their intentions are by no means "the key to a work's meaning."[48] Literary texts produce a whole range of possible meanings and conceptual effects that go far beyond the intentions of the writers. In this regard, no matter whether the overturn of the metaphor (DEFEATED) CITY IS WOMAN in WOMAN IS (FORTIFIED) CITY was intentional, Song 4:4 installs a new concept of woman in the Song's androcentric *Umwelt*. At the same time, however, it must be said that the Song's elusive woman is only relatively revolutionary. Even though the woman is here represented as having power over the man and agency over her sexual desire, the Song's elusive woman is still profoundly embedded in the poem's *Umwelt*, in which playing hard to get was probably the only way women could overtly express their sexual desire without incurring social stigma.

2.2. The Sublime Woman (Song 6:4)

SONG 6:4
You are beautiful,[49] my love, like Tirzah,[50]　　　　 יפה את רעיתי כתרצה

---

47. One might recall Tamar's reaction in 2 Sam 13:12.

48. Eagleton, *How to Read Literature*, 135. See also William K. Wimsatt and Monroe C. Beardsley, "The Intentional Fallacy," *SR* 54 (1946): 468–88.

49. In the Hebrew Bible, the lexeme יפה is usually combined with terms such as תאר, "form," and מראה, "appearance" (e.g., Gen 29:17; 39:6; 41:18; Deut 21:11; 1 Sam 17:42; 2 Sam 14:27; Jer 11:16), and often occurs with reference to the body and its attractiveness (e.g., Gen 39:6; 2 Sam 13:1; Ezek 31:3; 33:32; Prov 11:22). In the Song, the lexeme יפה is mainly used to describe the woman (Song 1:8, 15; 2:10, 13; 4:1, 7, 10; 5:9; 6:1, 4, 10; 7:2, 7), and it only once refers to the man (1:16). When applied to the woman, יפה is often connected to the description of her body: specifically her eyes (1:15; 4:1), her feet (7:2), and her entire physical presence (4:7; 7:7). Consequently, יפה is to be regarded as indicating a specific element of the domain BEAUTY, namely, the outward aspect of the woman's body.

50. While the beauty of Jerusalem and the strong desire for it are often celebrated by the Hebrew Bible, Tirzah is never acclaimed for its splendor. Its mention in 6:4 is probably due to the pun between the Hebrew name תרצה, "Tirzah," and the root רצה,

longed for[51] like Jerusalem,   נאוה כירושלם
frightening[52] like an army with deployed banners   אימה כנדגלות

Song 6:4 might be considered one of the most intriguing poetic lines in the
entire poem, due to the unexpected description of the woman as "frightening as an army with deployed banners." Since the martial language of the
last colon is often considered inappropriate to a love poem, several scholars have suggested nonmilitary translations and interpretations of the
phrase אימה כנדגלות. These are the most common ones: "daunting as what
loops on high" (Alter), "awesome in splendour as they are [i.e., Tirzah and
Jerusalem]" (Exum), "overwhelming like these sights [i.e., of Tirzah and
Jerusalem]" (Gary A. Long), "daunting as the stars in their courses" (Ariel
A. Bloch and Chana Bloch), "awe-inspiring as visions!" (Murphy), and
"awesome with trophies" (Pope).[53] Other scholars, however, have recog-

---

"pleasure, beauty." That both cities were capitals could also play a role: the man does
not compare his beloved to any city, but rather to the most important ones. Furthermore, the mention of a city belonging to Israel's ancient times lends the woman a
distinguished, glorious aspect.

51. Despite the fact that in the Hebrew Bible נאוה may occasionally indicate the
quality of "being appropriate" (e.g., Pss 33:1; 147:1; Prov 17:7), the likely connection
with אוה ("longing") suggests that it also holds the meaning of "desirable." See Gerald
H. Wilson, "נוה," NIDOTTE 3:54–56; Helmer Ringgren, "נָוֶה," ThWAT 5:294–98. This
meaning particularly fits in the Song, in which נאוה indicates the woman's charm
(Song 1:5; 2:14; 4:3; 6:4). In other words, while יפה underscores the beauty of the
woman's body, נאוה specifies that her beautiful aspect elicits the man's longing. Hence,
the proposed translation "longed for like Jerusalem."

52. Outside the Song, the adjective אים is only found in the military context
described by Habakkuk, who features the Chaldeans as ferocious and terrifying (Hab
1:6–7). In the Hebrew Bible, the noun אימה ("terror") is much more frequent and indicates a state of terror produced by a threat, often in contexts of war (e.g., Exod 15:16;
Deut 32:25; Josh 2:9; Ezra 3:3; Isa 33:18; Jer 50:38; Job 20:25; 39:19–25). See Bruna
Costacurta, La vita minacciata: Il tema della paura nella Bibbia ebraica, AnBib 119
(Rome: Pontifical Biblical Institute, 1988), 63–64. As Andersen writes, the noun אימה
describes "a state of terror and a paralyzing effect in front of an enemy." See Francis
I. Andersen, Habakkuk, AB 25 (New York: Doubleday, 2001), 152. In Song 6:4, the
translation "frightening" conveys the adjective's idea of fear. The expression כנדגלות
will be extensively discussed in the text.

53. Alter, Writings, 606; Exum, Song of Songs, 210; Gary A. Long, "A Lover, Cities,
and Heavenly Bodies: Co-Text and the Translation of Two Similes in Canticles (6:4c;
6:10d)," JBL 115 (1996): 703–9; Ariel A. Bloch and Chana Bloch, The Song of Songs

nized and accepted the military imagery of 6:4,[54] and the NRSV translates the phrase אימה כנדגלות as "terrible as an army with banners."

The translation and interpretation of 6:4 proposed here is in line with the latter group of exegetes, though with new syntactic, conceptual, and communicative observations. As will be shown, Song 6:4 presents a case of syntactic parallelism, which is broken on the conceptual level in the last colon by the introduction of the military imagery. This image creates the portrayal of the woman as not merely beautiful and attractive but as sublime, due to the blending of the concepts of BEAUTY, DESIRE, and FEAR. In doing so, Song 6:4 produces the already mentioned *estrangement effect*, forcing the reader to reflect on the meaning of such a powerful (and odd) image. The reader is thereby forced to go back to 4:4, in which the domains CITY and WAR overlap, as well as to 5:10 and 2:4, in which the woman describes her lover by using the same root, דגל. Thanks to the estrangement effect, Song 6:4 develops a complex concept not only of the female character but of the entire dynamic of love. The construal of the woman as sublime entails the conceptual metaphor BEAUTY IS A FORCE that, however embedded in the aesthetics of the Hebrew Bible and its milieu, acquires a unique character in 6:4, insofar as this is the only biblical text that presents woman as one of the loci of the sublime.

2.2.1. The Symmetry of Syntax

Song 6:4 contains three parallel verbless clauses, in which three adjectives (אימה/נאוה/יפה) function as predicates and occupy the fronting position.

Comparative Phrase	Vocative	Subject	Predicate	Clause
כתרצה	רעיתי	את	יפה	1
כירושלם		[את]	נאוה	2
כנדגלות		[את]	אימה	3

(London: University of California Press, 1998), 93; Murphy, *Song of Songs*, 174; Pope, *Song of Songs*, 551.

54. E.g., Ludger Schwienhorst-Schönberger, *Das Hohelied der Liebe* (Freiburg: Herder, 2015), 134–36; Longman, *Song of Songs*, 178–80; Barbiero, *Song of Songs*, 327–32; Keel, *Song of Songs*, 212–15.

While in the first clause the subject (את) is explicitly expressed and extended through a vocative (רעיתי), it is implicit in both the second and the third clause. The three clauses end with three parallel adjuncts, which establish three comparisons (אימה כנדגלות/נאוה כירושלם/יפה כתרצה). As for the word order, the predicates occupy the fronting position. Whereas in Biblical Hebrew the most typical order of verbless clauses is subject-predicate, clauses involving a pronominal constituent often present a predicate-subject order.[55] This phenomenon also occurs in the Song (1:5, 6; 2:1, 5, 16; 5:2, 5, 6, 8; 6:3, 9; 7:11; 8:9, 10).

According to Randall Buth, the word order predicate-subject is often employed in Biblical Hebrew clauses with a pronominal subject, and its function is to point out the characteristics attributed to the subject.[56] In this view, and in light of the concept of focus, the focal predicates are par-ticularly salient (see §1.4). For instance, Song 1:5 underscores that, despite her skin tone, she is *beautiful*. 2:5 points out that she is *lovesick*; hence she needs nutritious food (see also 5:8). 6:9 underlines that she is *unique* and *flawless*. As for 6:4, due to their fronted position, *beautiful, longed for,* and *threatening* stand out as the most salient information about the topic (i.e., the woman). In other words, among all qualities possessed by the woman, the man emphasizes that *beautiful, longed for,* and *threatening* are her most prominent characteristics. At the same time, the final position of the three similes specifies and intensifies the focused predicates: her beauty is *like* the beauty of Tirzah, she is longed for *like* Jerusalem is longed for, and she is fearsome just *like* a deployed army.

While 6:4 as a whole presents a symmetrical construction on the syn-tactic level (three parallel predicates + three parallel similes), the last colon breaks the parallelism on the semantic/conceptual level.

2.2.2. Breaking the Parallelism: The *Vexata Quaestio* of דגל

The first two colons of 6:4 contain a semantic/conceptual parallelism, since BEAUTIFUL and LONGED FOR belong to the same conceptual domain BEAUTY, and TIRZAH and JERUSALEM form part of the domain CITY. The last colon breaks this semantic/conceptual parallelism through the intro-

---

55. See *BHRG* §46.2.3.1; Van Hecke, *From Linguistics to Hermeneutics*, 93, 101.
56. Randall Buth, "Word Order in Verbless Clause: A Generative-Functional Approach," in *The Verbless Clause in Biblical Hebrew: Linguistic Approaches*, ed. Cyn-thia L. Miller, LSAWS (Winona Lake, IN: Eisenbrauns, 1999), 102–3.

duction of the domains FEAR and WAR, which are respectively evoked by the adjective "frightening" and the phrase "like an army with deployed banners." Since the military interpretation of 6:4, as well as of other metaphors (2:4; 5:10), rests on the military reading of the root דגל, such a debated root requires special investigation.

The root דגל occurs four times in the Song:

Song 2:4: ודגלו עלי אהבה / הביאני אל־בית היין
Song 5:10: דגול מרבבה / דודי צח ואדום
Song 6:4: אימה כנדגלות / נאוה כירושלם / יפה את רעיתי כתרצה
Song 6:10: אימה כנדגלות / יפה כלבנה ברה כחמה / מי־זאת הנשקפה כמו־שחר

When exegetes acknowledge that דגל has a military meaning in 2:4 and 6:4, 10, they usually translate it as "banner," quoting the book of Numbers (chs. 1; 2; 10) and Ps 20:6, in which the root apparently designates the standards of Israel's troops. While a few exegetes opt for "army" in 6:4, 10 (e.g., Jesús Luzarraga, "las escuadras," Paul Joüon, "bataillons"), some other translations suggest renderings such as "army with banners" or "bannered hosts," joining the meanings of military standard and army (e.g., Michael Fishbane).[57] Garrett's translations "panoplied city" (6:4) and "panoply of heaven" (6:10) are worth mentioning.[58] According to the author, the occurrences of נדגלות in 6:4 and 6:10 have different meanings: while the former occurrence evokes the image of a fortified citadel due to the mention of the cities of Jerusalem and Tirzah (6:4), the latter evokes the semantic field of *astronomy*, because of the previous reference to the moon and the sun (6:10). In Garrett's view, therefore, the context suggests the presence of a military metaphor in 6:4. Nevertheless, Exum's comment on 6:4, 10 makes clear that the context itself might undermine a military interpretation:

> Since the disputed phrase appears here and in v. 10, where the woman is likened to the dawn, the moon, and the sun, a meaning is required that fits both contexts.... The reading I have adopted here, following Gordis, takes the participle *nidgālôt*, used as a noun here and in v. 10, as "distinguished sights" (from *dgl* II, "to look") and understand it as

---

57. Luzarraga, *Cantar de los Cantares*, 465 and 482; Paul Joüon, *Le cantique des cantiques: Commentaire philologique et exégétique* (Paris: Beauchesne, 1909), 263 and 269; Michael A. Fishbane, *Song of Songs: The Traditional Hebrew Text with the New JPS Translation* (Lincoln: University of Nebraska Press, 2015), 161 and 167.

58. Garrett, *Song of Songs*, 226.

a reference to the cities of Tirzah and Jerusalem (See Long 1996). In
5:10 the woman described the man as distinguished among the thousand; now he describes her as awe-inspiring like the sight of these two
great cities.... This interpretation fits v. 10 as well, where the woman
is described as awe-inspiring like the sight of the dawn breaking, the
moon, and the sun.[59]

Even though Exum does not have any problem relating דגל to the military
meaning of banner in 2:4 and 5:10, when it comes to 6:4, 10 she prefers to
draw on *dgl* II, "to look." Exum, like many others, follows Robert Gordis,
according to whom דגל is to be read in light of the Akkadian *dagālu*, "to
look, to stare, to contemplate."[60] Other scholars have suggested the meaning of "to wish/to intend" for the Akkadian *dagālu*.[61] In this view, the term
דגל refers to the man's glance/intention (2:4), the sight of Tirzah and Jerusalem (6:4), and heavenly visions (6:10). The Arabic *ġāya* ("emblem/sign")
has also been suggested as a parallel cognate.[62] In this last case, דגל would
indicate the sign of the house of wine (2:4) and heavenly signs (6:4, 10).

Song 5:10 is apparently less difficult, at least as far as its general sense is
concerned. Exegetes agree that דגול here indicates the concept of someone
who is so special as to be easily recognizable among myriads. This meaning is established by connecting דגול either to a standing military banner
(e.g., Daniel Lys) or to the Akkadian root "to look" (e.g., Longman).[63] Leo
Krinetzki is among those few scholars who recognize a warlike metaphor
in 5:10.[64] However, his translation, "Mein Geliebter ist licht und rot, hehrer
als zehntausend sonst,"[65] does not convey the military imagery. Similarly,
although in 2:4 and 6:4, 10 Joüon and Luzarraga translate דגל as "army,"
when it comes to 5:10 their renderings, "On le distinguerait" and "Se dis-

59. Exum, *Song of Songs*, 219.

60. Robert Gordis, "The Root *dgl* in the Song of Songs," *JBL* 88 (1969): 203–4; see
also Zakovitch, *Das Hohelied*, 140.

61. Fox, *Song of Songs*, 108; Pope, *Song of Songs*, 375–78.

62. Gillis Gerleman, "Das Hohelied," in *Ruth: Das Hohelied*, 2nd ed., BKAT 18
(Neukirchen-Vluyn: Neukirchener Verlag, 1981), 117–18.

63. Daniel Lys, *Le plus beau chant de la création: Commentaire du Cantique des
cantiques*, LD 51 (Paris: Cerf, 1968), 219–20; Longman, *Song of Songs*, 170.

64. Leo G. Krinetzki, *Das Hohelied: Kommentar zu Gestalt und Kerygma eines alttestamentlichen Liebeslied* (Düsseldorf: Patmos, 1964), 189. More recently, a military interpretation of Song 5:10 has been supported by Frolov, "Comeback of Comebacks," 41–64.

65. Krinetzki, *Das Hohelied*, 189.

tingue," nullify any warlike nuance.[66] Finally, Jennifer Andruska's recent contribution is worth mentioning. The author rightly reads the root דגל occurring in 5:10 in light of all other occurrences in the Song and in the rest of the Hebrew Bible and argues in favor of its military interpretation. According to Andruska, "the man in 5:10 is not just preeminent among ten thousand. He is an astonishing sight, as fearsome to behold as a bannered host or an awe-inspiring warrior approaching."[67] Andruska's reading of 5:10 is very close to my own.[68]

Several arguments suggest that (1) the root דגל always has a military sense in the Bible, and therefore there is no need for speculating on the occurrence of *dgl* II in biblical texts; (2) דֶּגֶל is to be read as "army" and cognate translations; and (3) the meaning of "banner" is a frame metonymy. First, outside the Song, דגל always occurs in military scenarios, suggesting that the root belongs to the conceptual domain of WAR. In Num 1; 2; and 10 it refers to the military units of Israel's tribes, and in Ps 20:6 to Israel's deployed military troops.[69] Second, as George Gray has shown, the military meaning of דגל is supported by the Septuagint, as well as by the Peshitta.[70] Third, the root דגל occurs in a number of extrabiblical sources that, despite their different geographical origins, provide evidence of a widespread martial comprehension and use of the root in question during the fifth to first centuries BCE—the period when the Song was probably written. For instance, it occurs twenty times in a number of Aramaic papyri with reference to military detachments, as in the following from the eleven documents of the Mibtahiah archive (471–410 BCE):

---

66. Joüon, *Le cantique des cantiques*, 246; Luzarraga, *Cantar de los Cantares*, 439.

67. Jennifer L. Andruska, "The Strange Use of דגל in Song of Songs 5:10," *VT* 68 (2018): 7.

68. Verde, "War-Games," 185–97.

69. Stanislaw Bazyliński, *I salmi 20–21: Nel contesto delle preghiere regali* (Roma: Miscellanea Francescana, 1999), 110–13.

70. In the LXX, while in Ps 20:6 נדגל is rendered as μεγαλυνθησόμεθα (μεγαλύνω) ("to exalt, to magnify")—probably reading נגדל instead of נדגל—in Num 1:52; 2:17, דגל is translated as ἡγεμονία ("leadership, chief command"). On other occurrences, the LXX uses τάγμα ("military group, troop, division, camp") (Num 2:2, 3, 10, 18, 25, 31, 34; 10:14, 18, 22, 25). In the context of the Song, דגול (5:10) is translated as ἐκλελοχισμένος (ἐκλοχίζω) ("picked out of a troop"); נדגלות (6:4, 10) is translated as τεταγμέναι (τάσσω) ("deployed troops"); and דגלו (2:4) is rendered by the imperative τάξατε (τάσσω) ("deploy"), which implies דגלו. See George B. Gray, "The Meaning of the Hebrew Word דֶּגֶל," *JQR* 11 (1899): 92–101.

אמר קוניה בן צדק ארמי מסון לדגל וריזת למחסיה בן ינדיה ארמי לדגל וריזת
לאמר...

Konaiah, son of Zadak, an Aramean of Syene, of the detachment of Varyazata, said to Mahseiah, son of Jenadiah, an Aramean of Syene, of the
detachment of Varyazata, saying ...[71]

In his renowned volume on the Elephantine archives, Bezalel Porten shows
that דגל indicated Jewish sociomilitary units that protected the interests of the Persian Empire at the southern border of Egypt.[72] As Arthur
Cowley had previously explained, "Several men are described in different
documents as belonging to two *degalin*, which may mean that they were
transferred from one detachment to another.... The *degalin* (composed of
Jews) formed the garrison (חילא), or an important part of it, in Elephan-
tine-Syene."[73] Likewise, at Qumran דגל refers to "both a conscription and
a combat unit."[74]

The meaning of "banner," however, cannot easily be dismissed, especially when we consider the occurrence of דגל in Ps 20:6. The expression
בשם־אלהינו נדגל could be rendered by "may we unfurl banners" as a sign
of military victory, in parallel with the previous colon, that is, ־נרננה בישו
עתך, "may we shout for joy in your victory." Consequently, דגל seems to
be a polysemous root belonging to the conceptual domain of WAR, and it
may refer to both the conceptual frame ARMY and its metonymic element
"banner." Metonymy is usually understood as referring to a qualitative
part-whole relationship (e.g., author for work) and is distinguished from
synecdoche, which would indicate a quantitative part-whole relationship
(e.g., genus for species). Cognitive linguistics, however, more generally
describes metonymy as any "use of some entity A to stand for another
entity B with which A is *correlated*."[75] More specifically, a frame metonymy
establishes a correlation between parts of the same frame, namely, a chunk

---

71. *TAD* B2.1:2–3. See also *TAD* B2.1:9; 2.7:10; C3.8IIIA:7.8.9; C3.8IIIB:35.36;
3.19:4; D22.7:1; 23.1.6B:1.

72. Bezalel Porten, *Archives from Elephantine: The Life of an Ancient Jewish Military Colony* (Berkeley: University of California Press, 1968), 28–35.

73. Arthur E. Cowley, *Aramaic Papyri of the Fifth Century B.C.* (Oxford: Clarendon, 1923), 12. See also *DNWSI* 240–41.

74. Yigael Yadin, *The Scroll of the War of the Sons of Light against the Sons of Darkness* (London: Oxford University Press, 1962), 49–51. See also the references to the
Dead Sea Scrolls in *DCH*.

75. Dancygier and Sweetser, *Figurative Language*, 101.

of knowledge structure, and the frame as a whole. Kövecses designates as "vehicle entity" the term that directs attention to another term, which is named "target entity." The author clarifies that the conceptual access to the target through the vehicle is possible because both terms/entities are tightly linked in experience and belong to the same conceptual domain.[76] Concerning דגל, since troops were made visible by their standards, and banners were planted as a sign of victory and conquest, both concepts probably overlapped in the same root.

The noun דֶּגֶל can be translated by "army" in 2:4, keeping in mind the idea of banner during the explanation of the metaphor. The verbal forms דגול in 5:10 and נדגלות in 6:4, 10 can be both translated by "deployed," despite the fact that דגול and נדגלות are morphologically different. Indeed, the former is a *qal* passive participle, and the latter is a *niphal* participle. It is well-known that the *qal* passive participle and the *niphal* participle are semantically very similar, although as Muraoka explains, "The Qal passive participle mostly denotes a completed action or a state, whereas the Niphal participle underscores an action in process."[77] In this view, in Song 5:10 the participle דגול mostly functions as an adjective qualifying the man and pictures a static image of him as a deployed soldier. As for 6:4–10, the participle נדגלות conveys a more dynamic image of an army *while its troops/banners are being deployed*. We must admit that due to its semantic density, the construction מן + דגול in 5:10 is very difficult to render in English through only one phrase that would simultaneously express the military meaning of the root דגל, the passive voice דגול, and the idea, conveyed by the preposition מן, that the beloved emerges *from* and therefore is special among myriads. The translation "deployed among myriads" has the advantage of underscoring the passive form and the military meaning of דגל, while other semantic aspects of the phrase דגול מרבבה can be left to the explanation of the metaphor.

SONG 2:4
He brought me to the house of wine,
and his *army* on me is love

SONG 5:10
My beloved is radiant and ruddy,
deployed among myriads

---

76. Kövecses, *Metaphor*, 171–94.
77. Joüon §121q.

SONG 6:4
You are beautiful, my love, like Tirzah,
longed for like Jerusalem,
frightening like an army with deployed banners

SONG 6:10
Who is this that looks forth like the dawn,
fair as the moon, bright as the sun,
frightening
as *an army with deployed banners*?

In sum, contrary to the reading of many scholars, the occurrence of the
Akkadian *dagālu* in the Song is an unnecessary and misleading specula-
tion. As Gordis recognizes at the very outset of his proposal, the suggestion
of the Akkadian *dagālu* aims at overcoming the problem of dealing with
a military root (דגל) that, in his view, is inappropriate to a love poem. In
other words, דגל presents a conceptual problem rather than a philological
one: "How can we put together *love* and *war*?" Looking for the easiest text,
the unfortunate result of the exegetical maneuver of Gordis and others is
the suppression of what Ricœur calls "l'impertinence ou l'incompatibilité
sémantique," which is the very core of metaphorical phenomena.[78] By
blending together different conceptual elements (i.e., BEAUTY, DESIRABIL-
ITY, FEAR) of distinct conceptual domains (i.e., CITY, WAR, WOMAN, MAN),
the Song contains such a semantic and conceptual "impertinence," which
needs to be explained rather than removed.

Going back to Song 6:4, it contains three similes, which present a
focused cross-mapping; namely, they specify the properties in which "A
is like B" (BEAUTIFUL, LONGED FOR, and FRIGHTENING). As shown in
figure 2.3 (see below), the generic space can be identified with the general aspects that the source domains (i.e., CITY and WAR) and the target
domain (i.e., WOMAN) have in common—the aspects that activate the process of comparison. Since 6:4 belongs to the strophe 6:4–10, in which the
man describes what the woman looks like, there must be something in her
stunning appearance that recalls to the man the domains CITY and WAR
(generic space). Once the comparison is triggered, Song 6:4 specifies the
properties in which the target domain WOMAN is like the source domains
CITY and WAR, that is, BEAUTIFUL, LONGED FOR, and FRIGHTENING. The

---

78. Paul Ricœur, *La métaphore vive*, OP (Paris: Seuil, 1975), 169.

conceptual properties of the source domains are attributed to the woman, who is thereby conceptualized as simultaneously attractive and intimidating. In order to express the blending of BEAUTIFUL, LONGED FOR, and FRIGHTENING, the concept of SUBLIME is particularly appropriate, a concept that over the centuries has been understood and expressed in many ways.[79] *Sublime* here means the experience of beauty that simultaneously attracts and overpowers, entailing the conceptual metaphor BEAUTY IS A FORCE. According to Kövecses, the conceptual metaphor BEAUTY IS A FORCE conveys two interrelated ideas, namely, that our reaction to beauty is essentially passive and that the self loses control.[80] Both ideas, "feeling compelled" and "losing control/power," emerge in Song 6:5: "Turn away your eyes from me, for they overwhelm me [הרהיבני]." Outside the Song, the verb רהב is often associated with the conceptual domain FORCE, suggesting the idea of exerting force on/against/in favor of somebody.[81] In 6:5, רהב seems to indicate that the woman's gaze is an overwhelming force that is irresistible to such an extent that the man cannot even hold her gaze, while at the same time he cannot but keep staring at her and longing for her beauty (6:6–10).

---

79. Robert Doran, *The Theory of the Sublime: From Longinus to Kant* (Cambridge: Cambridge University Press, 2015); Harold Bloom, ed., *The Sublime* (New York: Infobase, 2010); Philip Shaw, *The Sublime* (London: Routledge, 2006).

80. Zoltán Kövecses, *Metaphors of Anger, Pride, and Love: A Lexical Approach to the Structure of Concepts*, Pragmatics and Beyond 7.8 (Amsterdam: Benjamins, 1986), 69.

81. In Isa 3:5, רהב refers to the young who will rise up against/attack the old. In Ps 138:3, רהב might refer to God's empowering the psalmist. In Prov 6:3, it expresses the necessity of badgering the neighbor. The connection with the conceptual domain POWER/FORCE is also suggested by the substantive רַהַב, which is used in order to indicate a mythological monster under the power of God in Job 9:3; 26:12; Pss 51:9; 89:11. The useless/weak Egypt is called "Rahab who sits still" in Isa 30:7. Psalm 40:5 calls blessed those who takes refuge in YHWH, instead of turning to the powerful (NRSV: "proud"). Finally, according to Ps 90:10, the power (NRSV: "span") of the human life is just trouble and harm.

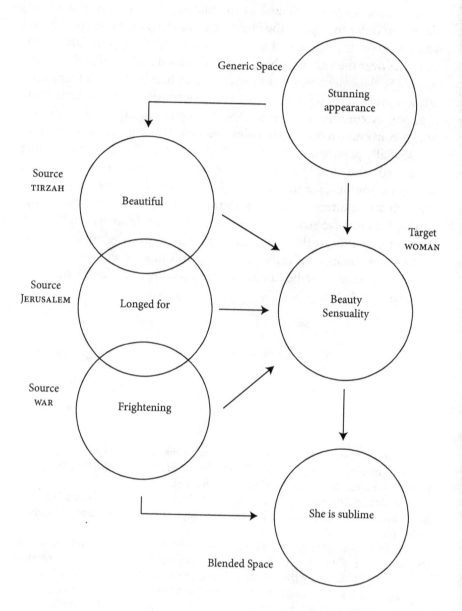

Fig. 2.3. Conceptual structure of Song 6:4

2.2.3. The Power of Beauty: The Subjugating Female

Within the seventh literary unit (6:4–7:11), 6:4 forms part of a group of strophes ending in 6:10. While in the strophe 6:4–7 the man praises his beloved and her beauty by describing her body, in the strophe 6:8–10 he refers to other women, namely, her mother, unspecified girls, queens, and concubines:

SONG 6:4–10

You are beautiful as Tirzah, my love,	יפה את רעיתי כתרצה
longed for as Jerusalem,	נאוה כירושלם
frightening as an army with deployed banners.	אימה כנדגלת
Turn away your eyes from me,	הסבי עיניך מנגדי
for they overwhelm me.	שהם הרהיבני
Your hair is like a flock of goats	שערך כעדר העזים
that gamboled down from the mountains.	שגלשו מן־הגלעד
Your teeth are like a flock of ewes	שניך כעדר הרחלים
that have come up from the washing,	שעלו מן־הרחצה
all of them bearing twins	שכלם מתאימות
and not one among them bereaved.	ושכלה אין בהם
Like a slice of pomegranate is your cheek	כפלח הרמון רקתך
behind your veil.	מבעד לצמתך
Sixty are the queens	ששים המה מלכות
and eighty the concubines	ושמנים פילגשים
and maidens without number;	ועלמות אין מספר
one alone is she, my dove, my perfect one,	אחת היא יונתי תמתי
she the only one to her mother;	אחת היא לאמה
she is splendid to the one who conceived her.	ברה היא ליולדתה
The girls saw her and called her blessed;	ראוה בנות ויאשרוה
the queens and the concubines praised her:	מלכות ופילגשים ויהללוה
"Who is this, who looks forth like the dawn,	מי־זאת הנשקפה כמו־שחר
beautiful as the moon,	יפה כלבנה
splendid as the sun,	ברה כחמה
frightening as an army with deployed banners."	אימה כנדגלות

The phrase אימה כנדגלות, occurring in both 6:4 and 6:10, constitutes the "enveloped figure" or *inclusion* that frames a section by means of repeated key words.[82] Song 6:4 introduces the dense concept of the sublime, which the following verses, so to speak, unravel. While 6:5–6 develops

---

82. Roland Meynet, *Trattato di retorica biblica*, RetBib 10 (Bologna: EDB, 2008),

the tumultuous aspect of the sublime by mentioning the woman's overwhelming eyes and by comparing her hair to goats gamboling down from the mountains, 6:7–8 develops the concepts of BEAUTIFUL/DESIRABLE through the mention of fertile ewes and slices of pomegranates. As far as 6:9 is concerned, it emphasizes that the woman is unique, as suggested by the repetition of the expression אחת היא in 6:9. She is unique to such an extent that not only her mother but even other girls, queens, and concubines recognize how special she is and praise her beauty. Finally, Song 6:10 explains what constitutes the woman's uniqueness, through the repetition of the key-phrase אימה כנדגלות: she is not just beautiful (many women are); rather, she is "beautiful as the moon, splendid as the sun, frightening as an army with deployed banners"; namely, she is sublime. Due to the repeated key-phrase אימה כנדגלות, therefore, Song 6:4–10 is enveloped by the same conceptualization of the woman as sublime; however, while in 6:4 the concept of SUBLIME is produced by the blending of the domains WAR and CITY, in 6:10 it is constructed by the overlap of the domains WAR and HEAVENLY BODIES. The vision of heavenly bodies and their order in the sky often suggested to the ancients the analogy with military troops and, thereby, feelings of intense astonishment.[83]

The overlap of the domains CITY and WAR in 6:4 compels the reader to go back to 4:4, in which the man has already described the woman as a fortified city and their game of seduction as a military conquest. The description of the woman's beauty as elusive that we have seen in 4:4 now acquires new conceptual elements: she is elusive *and* overwhelming, resistant *and* irresistible, evasive *and* invasive. Furthermore, the occurrence of the root דגל in 6:4, 10 recalls the description of the man in 2:4 and 5:10. As already mentioned and as will be further explained in the next chapter, in both 2:4 and 5:10 the root דגל is used to describe the man as a conquering warrior. Song 6:4, 10 turns 2:4 and 5:10 upside down: not only does the conqueror experience boundaries (4:4), but he now becomes the one who is conquered (6:4); the overwhelming man becomes the overwhelmed. The presentation of the woman as אימה כנדגלות, therefore, might be considered another example of the aforementioned *estrangement effect*. By *disturbing* the soft characterization of the woman as beautiful and longed for and

82, 216; Wilfred G. E. Watson, *Classical Hebrew Poetry: A Guide to Its Techniques*, JSOTSup 26 (Sheffield: Sheffield Academic, 1985), 282–87.

83. Shelomo D. Goitein, "*Ayumma Kannidgalot* (Song of Songs VI. 10)," *JSS* 10 (1965): 220–21.

by turning the already established siege motif upside down, it challenges the reader to rethink both the woman and the interaction between the lovers in order to acquire a broader comprehension of the many complex dynamics of love.

The Song's representation of the woman as sublime certainly is embedded in the aesthetics of the Hebrew Bible and its cultural milieu, in which the conceptual metaphor BEAUTY IS A FORCE and the conceptual association BEAUTY ↔ POWER play a remarkable role.[84] The conceptual metaphor BEAUTY IS A FORCE emerges in several biblical texts, which often enlighten the dangerous aspect of beauty's power, the "the dark side of beauty."[85] Furthermore, several texts convey a very widespread conceptual pattern, in which BEAUTY appears to be conceptually connected to the ideas of ROYAL POWER and DOMINION. This is the case, for instance, in Ps 45:3, according to which *the king* is the most beautiful man.[86] The concepts of BEAUTY and POWER are joined together in the vast majority of the occurrences of the lexeme תפארה ("beauty"). For instance, in Exod 28:2, 40, תפארה is used to describe the sacred vestments and the glorious adornment of Aaron and his family and to emphasize their power and prestige within ancient Israel's community.[87] The concepts of BEAUTY and POWER are often blended

---

84. On the concept of beauty in the Hebrew Bible, see F. W. Dobbs-Allsopp, "Beauty," *NIDB* 1:415–16; Dobbs-Allsopp, "Delight of Beauty"; Luke Ferretter, "The Power and the Glory: The Aesthetics of the Hebrew Bible," *LT* 18 (2004): 123–38; Francis Landy, *Beauty and the Enigma: And Other Essays on the Hebrew Bible*, JSOTSup 312 (Sheffield: Sheffield Academic, 2001).

85. James A. Loader, "The Dark Side of Beauty in the OT," *OTE* 25 (2012): 334–50; Loader, "The Pleasing and the Awesome," *OTE* 24 (2011): 652–67. The experience of erotic beauty seems to blind some biblical characters, forcing them to make foolish decisions and actions, such as Potiphar's wife, drawn to Joseph's beauty (Gen 39); David and Bathsheba (2 Sam 11); and Susanna (Dan 1). The book of Proverbs repeatedly warns the young against the trap of female beauty, which can be fatal (e.g., Prov 2:16–19; 5:1–23; 7:1–27; 11:22). All these texts make an aspect of the conceptualization BEAUTY IS A FORCE emerge, namely, the destructive potential of the power of beauty.

86. In Ps 48:3, Mount Zion is "beautiful in elevation … the city of the great king." In Ezek 16:13, Jerusalem "grew exceedingly beautiful, fit to be a queen." In Ezek 31:3, 7, 9 the power of Assyria is described through the image of a beautiful and impressive cedar of Lebanon.

87. In Isa 63:12, תפארה refers to Moses's powerful arm, while in Isa 60:7; 64:10; 1 Chr 22:5, it characterizes the temple and is a manifestation of God's dominion. In Isa 52:1, תפארה refers to Israel, set high above all nations that God has made, and

in the occurrences of the term כבוד ("glory"). It is well-known that כבוד
has to do with the basic concept of TO BE HEAVY, WEIGHTY, from which
the concept of a WEIGHTY, IMPRESSIVE, AND RESPECTABLE PERSON derives
(see Exod 20:12; 1 Kgs 11:21; Isa 29:13; 40:5; Mal 1:6; Pss 24:7–10; 66:2;
79:91; Prov 21:21; 22:4; 26:1; 1 Chr 29:28). The manifestation of the glory
of YHWH is perceived as simultaneously stunning and powerful, as in Ps
145:5: "On the glorious *splendour* of your *majesty*, and on your wondrous
works, I will meditate."[88]

The association of BEAUTY with POWER also occurs in Ugaritic literature, usually with reference to gods and goddesses,[89] and in Egyptian
love poems, the association of BEAUTY with POWER is often entailed in the
descriptions of the lovers. The beautiful man is described as a powerful
royal horse, "the choicest of a thousand among all the steeds, the foremost of the stables."[90] According to the beloved woman, there is no captain
who can overtake him, suggesting that his allure resides in his untamable
strength.[91] The woman's beauty is described as able to subdue the beloved
man.[92] Especially when she looks at him, the man feels captured, although
he seems to be more delighted than overwhelmed: "Indeed it is she who
captured my heart, when she looks at me, (I) am refreshed."[93]

The Song's conceptualization of the woman's beauty as a force able to
subjugate her beloved in Song 6:4 is, therefore, embedded in the aesthetics of the Hebrew Bible and its milieu, in which BEAUTY and POWER are

---

in several texts to YHWH, who rules over the world (Pss 71:8; 79:6; Jer 33:9; 1 Chr
29:11, 13).

88. Likewise, in Isa 4:2 "the branch of YHWH" is described as beautiful and glorious, and in Isa 60:1 the restoration of Israel is caused by the shining glory of YHWH.
Theophanies are often described by Ezekiel as sublime experiences of the overwhelming power of God's beauty (e.g., Ezek 1:27–28; 43:2). The creation often produces the
experience of the sublime, in which the contemplation of beauty goes hand in hand
with feelings of awe and even of fear (e.g., Pss 8:3; 19:4–5; 29; Job 9:10; 26:5–14; 36:27–
37:13).

89. In the myth The Gracious Gods, for instance, El and his two wives Athirat and
Rahmay are described as beautiful deities of high rank (*KTU* 1.23). The powerful Anat
is, on the one hand, the loveliest and the most gracious of Baal's sisters (*KTU* 1.10,15)
and a model of beauty (*KTU* 1.14), and, on the other hand, a ferocious, powerful warrior (*KTU* 1.6 II 30–37).

90. P.Beatty 1.B.39 (Fox, *Song of Songs*, 66).

91. P.Beatty 1.B.39 (Fox, *Song of Songs*, 66).

92. P.Beatty 1.A.31 (Fox, *Song of Songs*, 52).

93. O.Gardiner 304 (Fox, *Song of Songs*, 81).

tightly intertwined. Nevertheless, Song 6:4 is the only biblical text that blends BEAUTY with POWER in order to positively characterize a woman as sublime. Thanks to 6:4, woman is held in the Hebrew Bible as one of the *loci* of the sublime, in which female beauty simultaneously displays its attractive and dominating force.[94]

2.3. The Mature Woman (Song 8:10)

SONG 8:10
I am a city wall,
and my breasts are like towers;
thus, I have seemed to him[95]

אני חומה
ושדי כמגדלות
אז הייתי בעיניו

---

94. One can certainly recall the heroines Esther and Judith, who thanks to their beauty were able to conquer the heart of Ahasuerus and Holofernes respectively. Yet, these stories do not aim to celebrate female beauty; they rather focus on the heroism of Esther and Judith, and the emphasis on their beauty only serves the plot. In contrast, Song 6:4 is all about the woman's bewildering beauty.

95. Many current translations render the reference to the eyes literally (e.g., NRSV: "I was in his eyes"; Murphy: "I have become in his eyes"; Luzárraga: "he sido a sus ojos"; Barbiero: "sono diventata ai suoi occhi"; Schwienhorst-Schönberger: "in seinem Augen bin ich geworden"), and several commentators argue that 8:10 refers to the man's loving gaze for his beloved. See, for instance, Barbiero, *Song of Songs*, 480; Longman, *Song of Songs*, 215–18. In my view, בעיניו is an example of grammaticalization of body-part terms. In several languages, terms for body parts are used as pre- and post-position, especially to express spatial concepts. For instance, the body parts *back, face, head, stomach, side,* and *foot* are very often used to indicate the concepts of BEHIND, IN FRONT, ABOVE, WITHIN, NEXT TO, and UNDER respectively. See Bernd Heine, "The Body in Language: Observations from Grammaticalization," in *The Body in Language: Comparative Studies of Linguistic Embodiment*, ed. Matthias Brenzinger and Iwona Kraska-Szlenk, BSLCC 8 (Leiden: Brill, 2014), 11–32; Iwona Kraska-Szlenk, "Semantic Extension of Body Part Terms: Common Pattern and Their Interpretation," *LS* 44 (2014): 15–39; Toni Suutari, "Body Part Names and Grammaticalization," in *Grammar from the Human Perspective: Case, Space, and Person in Finnish*, ed. Marja-Liisa Helasvuo and Lyle Campbell, CILT 177 (Amsterdam: Benjamins, 2006), 101–28. Such a cross-linguistic phenomenon also occurs in Biblical Hebrew, in which, for instance, פנים ("face") may acquire the spatial meaning of "in front" (e.g., 2 Sam 10:9; Ezek 2:10; Ps 3:1; 2 Chr 19:10; 20:16) as well as the temporal meaning of "formerly, beforehand" (e.g., Deut 2:12, 20; Josh 11:10; Isa 41:26). On several occasions, the construction ב + עין is used to express a point of view and an opinion (e.g., Gen 16:4, 5; 21:11, 12; 34:18; Exod 15:26; Judg 2:11; 2 Sam 10:3; Esth 1:16; 3:6). Note the phrases והייתי בעיניו כמתעתע (Gen 27:12) and ויהיו בעיניו כימים אחדים (Gen 29:20), with the meaning "being

like one who finds and provides peace.[96]   כמוצאת שלום

As Exum recognizes, the woman's words here are particularly enigmatic.[97] Scholars generally acknowledge that 8:10 employs military/architectural imagery, yet current interpretations of it diverge considerably. According to some exegetes, Song 8:10 is about the woman's chastity (e.g., Pope), while according to others she is claiming her autonomy (e.g., Zakovitch), and for still others she is presenting herself as ready for love (e.g., James).[98] While in Keel's view Song 8:10 suggests that the man does not take the woman's strength too seriously, Murphy argues that she speaks of "the man's loving acceptance of her."[99] In the following, I will argue that 8:10 conceptualizes the woman as an adult in full possession of her sexuality. This interpretation is certainly in line with some current readings of 8:10, while at the same time adds some new observations on the complexity of the syntactic construction of the verse, the phenomenon of enjambment, and the resulting, unconventional portrayal of the woman.

2.3.1. Syntax and Forward Movement

Song 8:10 presents three clauses: two verbless clauses connected by the conjunction ו (אני חומה and ושדי כמגדלות) and a verbal clause (אז הייתי בעיניו כמוצאת שלום) introduced by the adverb אז. While the first two verbless clauses do not display peculiar syntactic features, the final verbal clause requires special investigation, regarding (1) the function of the

---

seen/considered like *x*" or "to seem like *x* to someone." In 8:10, therefore, the expression הייתי בעיניו can legitimately be translated "I have seemed to him."

96. The verb (כמוצאת) can be either a *qal* of מצא ("to find") or a *hiphil* of יצא ("to bring out"). The former reading certainly has some advantages: (1) the dynamic of "searching and finding" is crucial in the poem; (2) the *qal* of מצא occurs in 3:1–4; 5:6–7, while the *hiphil* of יצא never occurs in the poem; (3) the expression evokes the common idiom "to find grace in someone's eyes"; and (4) the meaning of "finding" is supported by the LXX (εὑρίσκουσα). As a matter of fact, however, the participle מוצאת can be read either way, which suggests that the Song might deliberately intend both meanings. The expression כמוצאת שלום, therefore, is here translated "like one who finds and provides peace."

97. Exum, *Song of Songs*, 257.

98. Pope, *Song of Songs*, 683–86; Zakovitch, *Das Hohelied*, 278–79; James, *Landscapes of the Song of Songs*, 113.

99. Keel, *Song of Songs*, 279; Murphy, *Song of Songs*, 193.

adverb אז and (2) the "syntactic overflow"[100] from the first colon (אז הייתי בעיניו) to the second (כמוצאת שלום), that is, the so-called phenomenon of enjambment.

Scholars understand the meaning of the adverb אז in two different ways. While a group of commentators read the adverb as having an adversative value ("yet"), creating a contrast between 8:10ab (אני חומה ושדי כמגדלות) and 8:10c (אז הייתי בעיניו כמוצאת שלום), according to most scholars אז introduces a logical sequence ("then," "thus," "thereby").[101] Upon closer inspection, the first interpretation seems to be highly conjectural, since in the Hebrew Bible there is no evidence of an adversative value in אז. Nor do the supporters of the adversative value of אז justify their interpretation by quoting other examples from the Hebrew Bible. The adverb אז occurs 141 times in the Hebrew Bible—including the occurrences of מאז and מן־אז ("from that time") (see Gen 39:5; Prov 8:22; Isa 48:8; Jer 44:18)—to which one should add the three occurrences of the by-form אזי in Ps 124:3, 4, 5. BDB distinguishes two main meanings of אז, namely, a strictly temporal meaning ("then, at that time") and one expressing logical consequence ("then, thus, thereby").[102] Likewise, according to *A Biblical Hebrew Reference Grammar*, "אָז is primarily an adverb of time," and it often "functions as a *conjunctive adverb* to introduce the *logical outcome* of the accomplishment of an event."[103] When אז has a temporal meaning, "the stretch in time referred to is that of the duration of events in the immediately preceding context."[104] This is not the case in Song 8:10, in which nothing connects אז temporally to the "immediately preceding context." Consequently, the adverb needs to be read as introducing a consequence ("thus, I have seemed to him"). The remaining question is how

---

100. Clive Scott, "Rejet," in *New Princeton Encyclopedia of Poetry and Poetics*, 4th ed., ed. Roland Greene (Princeton: Princeton University Press, 2012), 1153.

101. Keel: "yet"; Barbiero: "ma"; Schwienhorst-Schönberger: "doch." Alter: "then"; Luzarraga: "así"; Exum: "so"; Pope: "thus."

102. When אז has a temporal value, it can refer to both the past (e.g., Gen 4:26; 12:6, 13:7; Exod 4:26; Josh 10:33; 14:11; Judg 8:3; 13:21; 2 Sam 23:14; Jer 22:15) and the future (e.g., Lev 26:41; 1 Sam 20:12; 2 Sam 5:24; Isa 35:5, 6; 60:5; Mic 3:4). When אז is used to express logical sequence, it introduces the apodosis of a condition, sometimes after אם (e.g., Isa 58:14; Prov 2:5), לו or לולא (e.g., 2 Sam 2:27), אחלי (e.g., 2 Kgs 5:3), and a suppressed protasis (e.g., 2 Kgs 13:19; Job 3:13).

103. *BHRG* §40.6, pp. 372–73.

104. *BHRG* §40.6, pp. 372–73.

to understand the logical transition from 8:10ab to 8:10cd, a question that first requires a correct understanding of the employed imagery (see *infra*).

As far as the enjambment is concerned, the occurrence of this phenomenon in 8:10cd has not received any attention. While the colon 8:10c ends in בעיניו, the syntax of 8:10c (אז הייתי בעיניו) runs over into 10d (כמוצאת שלום). As a result, 8:10d completes the clause both syntactically and semantically.[105] As Dobbs-Allsopp has shown, the enjambment has not only aesthetic value but also communicative effect.[106] In 8:10, the use of enjambment both creates a sense of cohesion between the colons (aesthetic dimension) and provides a sense of forward movement (pragmatic dimension). Since the syntax and the meaning of 10c are left open, the reader is compelled to read forward looking for resolution. In forcing the reader to do so, not only does the text control the pace of the verse, but it also directs and controls the reader's attention. In 8:10c, the adverb "thus" has already created a sense of forward movement, from 8:10ab ("I am a city wall and my breasts are like towers") to 8:10c ("*thus*, I have seemed to him"). In 8:10cd, the enjambment reinforces such a forward movement and crescendo, driving the reader's attention to the conclusion ("like one who finds and provides peace"). As a result, Song 8:10d should be considered the most important part of the entire utterance. The phrase כמוצאת שלום is both the most important and the most baffling part, not only due to the morphological and semantic ambiguity of the participle מוצאת,[107] but also because it modifies the idiomatic expression למצא־חן בעיניו, "to find favor in his eyes," raising the question of the semantic implications of such a modification (see *infra*).

---

105. The Song contains several cases of enjambment. The following types of enjambment can be found: (1) vocative enjambment, in which the *rejet*, namely, the term/s starting the second colon, is a vocative phrase (e.g., 1:5, 7, 8; 5:9; 6:1); (2) adjunct enjambment, in which the *rejet* consists of an adjunct phrase, such as a prepositional phrase (e.g., 3:7, 8; 4:1, 9; 5:5; 8:8, 14); (3) appositional enjambment, in which the *rejet* qualifies the referent of the previous colon (e.g., 2:1, 15; 4:4; 8:6); and (4) verb enjambment, in which the *rejet* is the main verb of the clause (e.g., 1:9; 2:17; 3:1). Song 8cd is a unique case of enjambment within the Song, in which the *rejet* (כמוצאת שלום) is the object of the *contre-rejet* (אז הייתי בעיניו).

106. F. W. Dobbs-Allsopp, "The Enjambing Line in Lamentations: A Taxonomy (Part 1)," *ZAW* 113 (2001): 219–39; Dobbs-Allsopp, "The Effects of Enjambment in Lamentations (Part 2)," *ZAW* 113 (2001): 270–85; Watson, *Classical Hebrew Poetry*, 332–36.

107. See n. 96.

2.3.2. Standing between the Family and the Beloved

The lexeme חומה forms part of a group of words indicating the notion of "wall." While other lexemes indicate generic and/or different kinds of walls, חומה usually refers to city walls.[108] Archaeological data indicates that, from the ninth century BCE onward, surrounding walls became the main architectural and military structure employed to defend ancient Israel's cities.[109] Several cities were encircled by a double defense line, as also suggested by Isa 26:1: "We have a strong city, he sets up inner walls [חומה] and outer walls [חל] to protect us." In these cases, חומה seems to refer to the inner wall, which was meant to be the most resistant part of fortifications and the last structure of defense to collapse in the event of military attack. In order to protect the walls, other installations were built, such as ramparts, moats, and towers.

Given the defensive function of city walls, the Hebrew Bible occasionally employs the lexeme חומה to metaphorically represent the concept

---

108. See, e.g., Lev 25:29–31; Deut 3:5; 28:52; Josh 2:16; 6:5, 20; 1 Sam 31:10, 12; 2 Sam 11:20, 21, 24; Isa 2:15; 25:12; Jer 1:15; 39:4; Pss 51:20; 55:11; Prov 25:28. The lexeme קיר has a wide range of meaning, such as city walls, residential structures, and structures of the temple, as well as the sides of the altar (e.g., Num 35:4; 1 Kgs 6:5; 2 Kgs 20:2; Ezek 41:22). The lexeme גדר indicates a generic wall made of field stones (Num 22:24; Ezek 13:15; 22:30; 42:10; Ps 62:4; Qoh 10:8; Ezra 9:9). The lexeme טירה indicates a row of stones or a camp protected by a wall of stones (Gen 25:16; Num 31:10; Ezek 25:4; 46:23; Ps 69:26; Song 8:9; 1 Chr 6:39). The lexeme נד indicates a dam of water or a heap (Exod 15:8; Josh 3:13, 16; Isa 17:11; Pss 33:7; 78:13). The lexeme שור and its by-form שורה indicate a generic wall, maybe a terrace wall on a hill (Gen 49:22; 2 Sam 22:30; Job 24:11; Ps 18:30). The lexeme חיץ indicates a generic wall (Ezek 13:10). The lexeme כתל seems to indicate the wall of a house (Song 2:9).

109. As Mazar explains: "From the mid-ninth century onwards, the Israelites and their neighbours constructed massive fortification systems that were similar to those attested also in contemporary northern Syria. They include massive city walls with protruding towers, often with a second wall on the slope of the mound. Moats and earth or stone glacis were added in certain cases. City gates were massive and contained four or six guard chambers. An outer defence prevented direct approach to the gate structure. Such fortifications were intended to withstand the battering rams and other siege devices used by the Assyrian army." See Amihai Mazar, "The Divided Monarchy: Comments on Some Archaeological Issues," in *The Quest for the Historical Israel: Debating Archaeology and the History of Early Israel; Invited Lectures Delivered at the Sixth Biennial Colloquium of the International Institute for Secular Humanistic Judaism, Detroit, October 2005*, ed. Israel Finkelstein, Amihai Mazar, and Brian B. Schmidt, ABS 17 (Atlanta: SBL Press, 2007), 170.

of PROTECTION. In 1 Sam 25:16, for instance, Nabal's servants compare David's men to protective walls ("they were a wall to us"). According to Prov 18:10–11, while the righteous finds refuge in YHWH, who is compared to a strong tower ("The name of YHWH is a strong tower"), the rich find safety in their own wealth, which is compared to a high wall ("like a high wall in his own imagination"). In Zech 2:9, Jerusalem will eventually have no need of walls, since YHWH himself will be a wall of fire around her ("I—declares YHWH—will be a wall of fire around her, and I will be the glory in her midst"). In addition, the lexeme חומה is connected to the concepts of STRENGTH and RESILIENCE. For instance, in Jer 1:18 YHWH makes the prophet as a fortified city, as an iron pillar, and as bronze walls, able to resist forthcoming attacks. The same idea is repeated in Jer 15:20, where Jeremiah is transformed into inaccessible walls of bronze, against which his enemies will fight without prevailing. Conversely, in Isa 30:13 the idea of weakness generated by iniquity is represented through the image of a break in a high wall ("this iniquity shall become for you like a break in a high wall, bulging out, and about to collapse").

In the Song, the lexeme חומה occurs three times. In 5:7, it refers to the city walls guarded by sentinels. In 8:9–10, it is used metaphorically twice, both times in reference to the woman. In order to better understand the meaning of חומה in 8:9–10, we must read the two verses together with 8:8:

SONG 8:8–10

We have a little sister,	אחות לנו קטנה
and she has no breasts.	ושדים אין לה
What shall we do for our sister	מה־נעשה לאחתנו
on the day she is spoken for?	ביום שידבר־בה
If she is a wall,	אם־חומה היא
we will build on her a silver turret,	נבנה עליה טירת כסף
but if she is a door,	ואם־דלת היא
we will barricade her with cedar boards.	נצור עליה לוח ארז
I am a city wall,	אני חומה
and my breasts are like towers;	ושדי כמגדלות
thus, I have seemed to him	אז הייתי בעיניו
like one who provides peace.	כמוצאת שלום

The image of wall evokes the concept of SELF-PROTECTION in both 8:9 and 8:10, although it acquires different meanings in the two verses. Song 8:8–9, spoken by the woman's brothers, expresses the involvement of the woman's family in her personal life.[110] The brothers, wondering how to arrange their little sister's life (מה־נעשה לאחתנו), make conditional plans that depend on her conduct. Hypothesizing about the woman's behavior, they use two metaphors, that is, "if she is a wall" and "if she is a door." The meaning of these two images is clarified by what the brothers say about their consequent reactions. If she is a wall, they will react positively by enhancing her beauty and value (נבנה עליה טירת כסף). On the contrary, if she is a door, they will try to protect and reinforce her (נצור עליה לוח ארז). It seems, therefore, that while the image of the door bespeaks the woman's bad behavior, the image of the wall refers to her good, acceptable behavior. Within the context of an erotic poem, the brothers' concern for her behavior cannot but refer to her sexual life. The wall image used by the woman's brothers, therefore, seems to indicate her ability to protect her chastity by warding off possible lovers, in opposition to the door image, which seems to indicate a more permissive attitude to possible lovers, letting them in and out. Both reactions by the woman's brothers, however, are presented as very negative and as an actual siege. The lexeme טירת can be understood as both a row of stones and an encampment (see Gen 25:16; Num 31:10; Ezek 25:4; 46:23; Ps 69:26). The phrase בנה על often indicates siege actions (see Deut 20:20; 2 Kgs 25:1; Jer 52:4; Ezek 4:2; Lam 3:5), and in 8:9 it might refer to the action of building encampments against the city, either beside or outside the city walls. Likewise, in the expression נצור עליה לוח ארז, the phrase צור על evokes siege language, bespeaking military attacks against the city (see Deut 20:12; 2 Sam 11:1; 20:15; 1 Kgs 15:27; 16:17; 20:1; 2 Kgs 6:24–25; 16:5; 17:5; 18:9; 24:11; Isa 29:3; Jer 21:9; 32:2; 37:5; 39:1). In other words, the text presents the brothers not only as wanting to protect

---

110. Although some scholars (James, Exum, and Landy) question whether Song 8:8 is spoken by the woman's brothers, several arguments suggest that this is indeed the case. First, the expression אחות לנו קטנה easily leads to the identification of the speakers with the woman's brothers. Second, her brothers are mentioned in 8:1–2, and third, their presence at the end of the poem perfectly corresponds to their presence at the beginning (1:6). Attributing 8:8–9 to either the woman (Exum) or the daughters of Jerusalem (Landy), who would be talking about a different "little sister," is unnecessary. James's recent reading, according to which 8:8–9 is spoken by suitors, describing their interest in the Song's woman, is a conjecture that does not have enough ground in the text. The Song never mentions these characters elsewhere, and their introduction at the very end of the poem seems to occur out of the blue. See Exum, *Song of Songs*, 256; Landy, *Paradoxes of Paradise*, 153 n. 24; James, *Landscapes of the Song of Songs*, 109.

their "little sister"; it also portrays them as conquerors trying to dominate her.[111] While in the brothers' mouths חומה refers metaphorically to her chastity, in 8:10 the wall image transmits a completely different meaning. By affirming that she is a city wall, the woman cannot be saying that she is chaste because the rest of the poem disproves such a possibility. She must be saying therefore that she is strong enough to protect herself. At the same time, however, she is showing her strength and resilience in front of and against her brothers' paternalistic attitude, subtly portrayed as a siege. Not only is she able to autonomously look after her sexuality, but she is also able to ward off the attacks of her brothers, namely, their intrusive, patronizing attitude.

As for the lexeme שלום, its core meaning is notoriously disputed.[112] It is often established in light of the root שלם, the basic meaning of which is, however, equally disputed. While according to Gillis Gerleman the main ideas conveyed by the root are expressed by the *piel* form of the verb, "to pay, to reward," other scholars argue that the basic meaning of שלם is expressed by the *qal* form, "to be completed, ended."[113] In the former case, the main meaning of the noun שלום is "satisfaction, sufficiency," while in the latter the noun conveys the ideas of "completeness, wholeness, totality." Franz Stendebach tries to combine these two ideas, arguing that "'wholeness' and 'sufficiency' mark points on a continuum between which the meaning of *šālôm* flickers; it cannot be fixed at one point or the other.... *Šālôm* is a comprehensive expression denoting all that the people of ancient Near East wish for as the substance of blessing." The author argues that "*šālôm* denotes a supremely positive quality of being, which can be instantiated in the most various ways in various contexts."[114] Nev-

---

111. The siege language of Song 8:8–9 has already been noticed by James, although with a different reading. See Elaine T. James, "A City Who Surrenders: Song 8:8–10," *VT* 67 (2017): 448–57.

112. Franz J. Stendebach, "שָׁלוֹם," *ThWAT* 8:12–46; Philip J. Nel, "שלם," *NIDOTTE* 4:130–35.

113. Gillis Gerleman, "שלם *šlm* to Have Enough," *TLOT* 3:1337–48; Gerleman, "Die Wurzel שלם *šlm*," *ZAW* 85 (1973): 1–14; Walter Eisenbeis, *Die Wurzel שלם im Alten Testament*, BZAW 113 (Berlin: de Gruyter, 1969); Gerhard von Rad, "שָׁלוֹם in the Old Testament," *TDNT* 2:402–6. Furthermore, Torczyner suggests that שלום is actually to be connected with the root שלה ("to be calm, at ease"). See Harry Torczyner, *Die Entstehung des semitischen Sprachtypus: Ein Beitrag zum Problem der Entstehung der Sprache* (Wien: Löwit, 1916), 243.

114. Stendebach, "שָׁלוֹם," 19–20.

ertheless, if put in this way, it is difficult to explain (1) why the supposed basic meanings of either "satisfaction" or "wholeness" do not always occur and (2) how the different meanings that שלום acquires in different contexts are connected to each other within the conceptual system of the lexeme.[115]

In this regard, the notions of *meaning potential* and *prototype* might be very helpful. While the conceptual system of the lexeme שלום presents a very broad meaning potential, its specific meanings in different contexts are connected to each other through the same prototypical meaning, namely, "welfare." The prototypical meaning of "welfare" is the fundamental and essential idea underlying all occurrences of the lexeme. In different contexts, the basic concept of WELFARE acquires other attributes and thereby develops into more complex concepts such as (1) HEALTH (e.g., Gen 29:6; 37:14; 43:28; Exod 18:7; 1 Sam 17:18, 22; Esth 2:11), which is also implicit in greeting formulas (e.g., Gen 37:4, 21; Judg 18:5; 19:20; 1 Sam 10:4; 18:28; 25:6; 30:21); (2) SAFETY (e.g., Gen 28:21; Judg 8:9; 11:31; 1 Sam 20:7, 13, 21; 25:35; Isa 32:18), in contexts of hostilities and troubles; (3) FRIENDLINESS (e.g., Josh 9:1; Isa 27:5; Jer 9:7; Pss 28:3; 35:20), in contexts of relationship; (4) PEACE (e.g., Deut 20:11; Judg 4:17; 1 Sam 7:14; Zech 9:10), in contexts of war, often indicating peace agreements and terms of peace; and (5) PROSPERITY (e.g., Lev 26:6; Isa 60:17; Jer 29:7, 11; Zech 8:12), in contexts that refer to natural resources, agricultural scenarios, and fertility. Furthermore, especially in the prophetic texts (but not only in prophetic texts), שלום presents a more comprehensive idea that is difficult to render by a single lexeme, since it blends together all the aforementioned profiles. In these cases, שלום seems to be close to the concepts of WHOLENESS, FULFILLMENT, and FULLNESS OF GOODS (e.g., Num 6:26; Isa 9:5–6; 26:3, 12; 32:17; Jer 29:11; 33:6; Ezek 34:25; 37:26; Hag 2:9; Zech 6:13; 8:12; Lam 3:17). "Wholeness," therefore, is by no means the core meaning of שלום, but it is one of its many profiles.

It should also be noted that, when שלום occurs in military contexts, it is usually something offered by the stronger to the weaker (e.g., Deut 20:10–11; Judg 21:13; Isa 27:5)—something expressing, on the one hand, the dominance of the victorious over the defeated and, on the other hand, the servitude and submission offered by the defeated to the victorious. As Shemaryahu Talmon puts it, in military contexts שלום is an "imposed

---

115. For a more recent investigation of the root שלם in light of cognitive linguistics, see Chin Hei Leong, "Completeness—Balance: Revisiting the Biblical Hebrew Verb שלם from the perspective of Cognitive Semantics" (PhD diss., KU Leuven, 2019).

peace," and, as Chin Hei Leong argues, "If there is any notion of peace at all, it would more accurately be the *conqueror's peace*."[116]

As far as Song 8:10 is concerned, despite the fact that the term שלום has a broad meaning potential and does not always have military connotation, here the term acquires the meaning of "peace," in the sense of the "end of a war," due to the context's architectural and warlike imagery. In other words, in 8:10 the conceptual domain WAR is activated not by means solely of military terms (שלום as such is not necessarily a military term), but rather by the architectural imagery of the context (8:8–10) and by the siege motif that has been subtly introduced in 8:8–9. That elsewhere in the poem the domain CITY explicitly overlaps with the domain WAR (4:4; 6:4) also supports a military reading of 8:10. Within the general context of the Song, which is all about the expression of desire and the longing for satisfaction, and in light of the Song's representation of eros in terms of military conquest, שלום cannot express a generic notion of welfare, but rather the denser and richer concept of FULFILLMENT.

Finally, the expression אז הייתי בעיניו כמוצאת שלום evokes the common expression מצא חן בעיני (e.g., Gen 6:8; Exod 33:12; 1 Sam 20:29) although in 8:10 בעיניו is syntactically subordinated to הייתי rather than to מוצאת. On some occasions, the expression "to find favor in someone's eyes" is used within the context of the relationship between men and women (e.g., Gen 6:8; Exod 33:12; 1 Sam 20:29). Song 8:10 might have deliberately used the expression כמוצאת שלום instead of כמוצאת חן both (1) in order to develop and conclude the siege motif and (2) in order to emphasize the equal status of man and woman in matters of love. The expression "to find favor" (חן) always entails a hierarchical relationship between the one who finds favor and the one who shows favor. In 8:10, the woman says something completely different, namely, that the man has recognized her (הייתי בעיניו) as a woman able to both find and provide peace (כמוצאת שלום), to both receive and give fulfilment. Granted, the overall picture seems to portray the woman as a city surrendered to the conqueror and love seems to be represented in the most stereotypical way: the victorious man conquers the capitulated, defeated woman. Nevertheless, due to the ambiguity of מוצאת and to the modification of the most common phrase

---

116. Shemaryahu Talmon, "The Signification of שָׁלוֹם and Its Semantic Field in the Hebrew Bible," in *The Quest for Context and Meaning: Studies in Biblical Intertextuality in Honor of James A. Sanders*, ed. Craig A. Evans and Shemaryahu Talmon, BibInt 28 (Leiden: Brill, 1997), 100; Leong, "Completeness—Balance," 217, emphasis original.

כמוצאת חן in כמוצאת שלום, Song 8:10 seems to ironically suggest that, at least in matters of love and at least in the Song, it is not very clear who the stronger is, who offers שלום to whom, since man and woman are in a mutually fulfilling relationship.

In light of cognitive metaphor theory, Song 8:10 can be represented as in figure 2.4 below.[117] The conceptual domains involved are FORTI-FIED CITY and WAR as sources and WOMAN as target. The source domain FORTIFIED CITY is activated by the lexemes חומה and מגדל, which trigger the military meaning of the lexeme שלום and, thereby, the source domain WAR. The source domain WAR is also activated by the previously intro-duced siege motif (4:4; 6:4; 8:8–9). The target domain WOMAN is activated by the pronoun אני and the mention of her breasts (שדים); context sug-gests that the conceptual element at stake is her sexual maturity (8:8–9). The generic space can be identified with the fact that both fortified cities and the woman face external attacks (conquerors/brothers). The concepts of SELF-PROTECTION, STRENGTH, GRANDEUR, POWER, and PEACE of the source domains are projected into the target domain WOMAN. The con-cepts of PROTECTION and STRENGTH are conveyed by the lexeme חומה. The concept of GRANDEUR is conveyed by the lexeme מגדל. In §2.1.3, I argued that the Song's metaphorical use of מגדל blends the concepts of SELF-DEFENSE, INACCESSIBILITY, POWER, GRANDEUR, and BEAUTY (Song 4:4; 7:5). In 8:10, however, only the concepts of GRANDEUR and POWER seem to be highlighted, since the woman's words respond to her brothers' words in 8:8, which present the woman as a little girl, sexually imma-ture. Finally, the concept of PEACE/FULFILLMENT is conveyed by the term שלום. The resulting conceptualization of the woman blends the activated conceptual elements, representing the woman as mature. She is not a "little girl" needing protection, as her brothers think; on the contrary,

---

117. Song 8:10 presents one metaphor (8:10a) and two similes (8:10b, 8:10cd). The metaphor אני חומה presents the structure "A *is* B," and the two similes, i.e., שדי כמגד-לות and [אני] כמוצאת שלום, present the formula "A is *like* B." Since, however, the two similes do not provide the properties in which "A is *like* B" and, thereby present *open mapping*, here they will be considered "metaphor like." For the notion of *open map-ping*, as opposed to the notion of *focused cross-mapping*, see Croft and Cruse, *Cognitive Linguistics*, 211–21; Carol Moder, "Two Puzzle Pieces: Fitting Discourse Context and Constructions into Cognitive Metaphor Theory," *ETC* 3 (2008): 294–320; Moder, "It Is Like Making a Soup: Metaphors and Similes in Spoken News Discourse," in *Language in the Context of Use: Discourse and Cognitive Approaches to Language*, ed. Andrea Tyler, Yiyoung Kim, and Mari Takada, CLR 37 (Berlin: de Gruyter, 2008), 301–20.

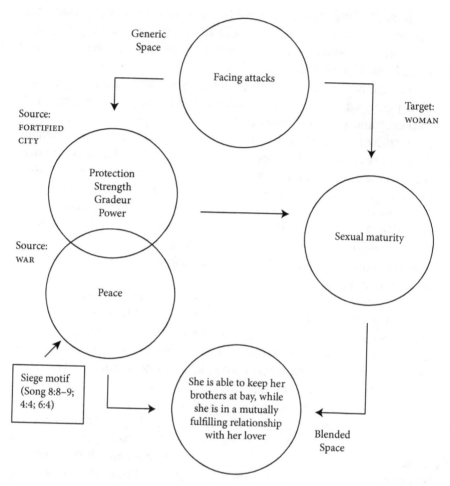

Fig. 2.4. Conceptual structure of Song 8:10

like a fortified city surrounded by walls, she has her own resources, with which to protect her sexuality from whomever wants to approach her and from her family's paternalistic attitude. She is not a little girl whose sexuality still needs to develop, as her brothers think; on the contrary, her sexuality is visibly developed, like the towers of a city. Regardless of what her brothers think about her, her sexual maturity has been recognized by the man. She is able, therefore, to establish with him a mutually fulfilling relationship, like a city that at the end of a war stipulates a peace treaty, beneficial to both the city and its conqueror. Contrary to what some exegetes think,[118] the fulfillment is made possible not *despite the fact* but *due to the fact* (as the adverb אז suggests) that she is like a fortified city, namely, thanks to the fact she is a woman in full possession and fully aware of her sexuality.

Song 8:10, therefore, represents the woman as mature, a complex concept blending several aspects: she is able to emancipate herself from her family, she is aware of the power of her sexuality, and she is able to stay in an equal relationship with her beloved, a relationship in which she both gives and receives. The woman's maturity presented by 8:10 is, therefore, double-sided. It concerns, on the one hand, the relationship with her family and, on the other hand, the relationship with her lover.

2.3.3. A Challenging Peripheral Voice

Song 8:10 forms part of the poem's last literary unit (8:5–14). After the formula of mutual union in 7:11, which concludes the section 6:4–7:11 ("I am my beloved's, and his desire is upon me"), the Song presents two new sections (7:12–8:4 and 8:5–14), which are enveloped by a double invitation. In 7:12, the woman invites the man to go with her and receive her love ("Come, my lover, let us go out into the fields; let us spend the night in the villages"). In 8:14, she urges him to run away ("Flee, my lover, and be like a deer or like a gazelle on the spice mountains").[119] Within the section 7:12–8:14, we can distinguish four parts that, however fragmented, are sewn together by the theme *love is strife*.

(1) Love against social censure (7:12–8:4): After inviting the beloved to join her (7:12–14), the woman expresses her wish that her beloved might be one of her brothers ("O that you were a brother to me, suckling my mother's breasts!"). Had they been siblings, they could have been together since the very beginning of life and experience the most profound intimacy. If he were her brother, she could now express her love without enduring the obstruction of social restrictions and judgments ("I would find you in the street, would kiss you, and no one would even despise me"). If he were her brother, she could now bring him home, and

---

118. E.g., Keel, *Song of Songs*, 277–79; Barbiero, *Song of Songs*, 472–82.

119. As Alter has pointed out, the woman's final words seem to contain a "purposeful ambiguity." While she is saying that it is time for him to leave, she is actually inviting him to join her once again. The phrase הרי בשמים, indeed, might allude to her breasts (see Song 2:8, 17; 4:1, 6, 8). Alter, *Writings*, 617.

they could be close to each other ("I would lead you, I would bring you to my mother's house").

(2) Love against all opposing forces (8:5–7): A voice-over, recalling 3:6, introduces the second unit ("Who is this coming up from the desert?"). After the enigmatic association of the man's sexual arousal with his own conception ("Under the apple tree I roused you, there your mother conceived you"), the woman emphasizes the unstoppable power and tenacity of love. Love cannot be stemmed, just as the arrival of death cannot be hindered ("For strong as death is love, fierce as Sheol is passion"), and a raging fire cannot be quenched even by a torrential deluge. Rather than being fought against, therefore, love should be accepted and valued as the most precious treasure ("If one offered for love all the wealth of one's house, it would be utterly scorned").

(3) Love against family (8:8–10): The third unit, as I have argued, is about the conflictual relationship between the woman and her brothers.

(4) Love against wealth (8:11–14): Finally, the last unit returns to representing love as priceless (8:7) and presents the woman as more valuable than King Solomon's wealth ("My vineyard is my own. You can have the thousand, Solomon, and two hundred for the keepers of its fruits").[120]

The opposition "woman versus brothers" in 8:8–10 recalls the very beginning of the poem, in which the woman's brothers were introduced through the circumlocution בני אמי ("my mother's sons"):

SONG 1:6

My mother's sons were incensed with me;	בני אמי נחרו־בי
they made me a keeper of the vineyards.	שמני נטרה את־הכרמים
My vineyard, which is mine, I have not kept.	כרמי שלי לא נטרתי

Both 1:6 and 8:10, on the one hand, present the brothers as trying to control the woman's sexuality and, on the other hand, present the woman as teasing her brothers. As in 8:10, in 1:6 the woman not only cheekily affirms that she has taken her sexual freedom—regardless of her brothers' punitive measures and restrictions—but also that she is in sole and independent control of her sexual life. Nevertheless, although 1:6 and 8:10 present the

---

120. The identification of the speakers in Song 8:11–14 is debated. I prefer to read Song 8:11–14 as spoken by the woman, since there is no clear indication of a shift of speakers. Furthermore, the phrase כרמי שלי (Song 8:12) occurs in 1:6, which is undeniably spoken by the woman.

same theme, the resulting representations of the woman are very different, due to the use of different source domains. In 1:6, the woman uses the metaphor of the vineyard, which always has strong erotic connotations in the Song.[121] The image of the woman as vineyard in 1:6 and, thereby, of the woman's vivacious sexuality gives way to the much more imposing image of the fortified city in 8:10. Song 8:10 makes it clear that her claim for sexual freedom is not the tantrum of a frivolous girl but the demand of a mature woman, fully aware and in control of her sexuality. In 8:10, sexual freedom is not something that she has to surreptitiously steal from her brothers as in 1:6, but rather something that she imposes as her right. The teasing and playful woman of 1:6 appears to be resolute and steadfast in 8:10.

As for the other side of the image, that is, her relationship with the man, 8:10 is the only line of the poem in which the woman applies to herself the metaphor of the fortified city that has been used by the man in 4:4 and 6:4. In other words, in 8:10 the woman proposes an image of herself and of her relationship with her beloved, drawing on the man's views, metaphors, and words. At the same time, however, she profoundly modifies the metaphor. The man had compared her neck (4:4; 7:5) and her nose (7:5) to towers to describe her as parrying his advances, whereas she applies such an image to her breasts in 8:10 to affirm her sexual maturity in front of her brothers. The man had portrayed her as a fortified city to emphasize her elusive attitude (4:4) and her sublime beauty (6:4); she uses the same image in 8:10 to respond to her family. In 4:4 and 6:4 the man had used the image of the fortified city to describe the dynamic of courtship; in 8:10 the woman emphasizes the result of the lovers' war-games. More importantly, the portrayal of herself as "pacified and pacifying city" that she attributes to the experience of the man ("I have seemed to him") is entirely made up. As I have shown, the man's representation of the woman as a fortified city in both 4:4 and 6:4 is far from peaceful; on the contrary, it features the man's discomfort because of her elusiveness and his interior upheaval when faced with her beauty. Furthermore, the man has never represented

---

121. On some occasions, the vineyard bespeaks the woman's body (1:14; 8:12), whereas on some other occasions it constitutes the scenario of the lovers' sexual experience (2:15; 7:13). Related to the vineyard is the image of the wine, which seems to indicate the joyful and intoxicating aspect of the lovers' sexual experience (1:2, 4; 2:4; 4:10; 5:1; 7:3, 10; 8:2). By representing herself as a vineyard, therefore, in 1:6 the woman emphasizes the exuberance and even the euphoria of her sexual life.

his experience of love in terms of peace elsewhere in the poem. He has certainly experienced love, joy, and an assault on the senses, but also turmoil, resistance, and emotional disruption. In 8:10, the woman shrewdly reelaborates the man's metaphor for her own purposes, namely, to support her claim for freedom in front of her brothers: she is able to find and even provide the שלום that her beloved man has experienced (except that, in actuality, he never said that!). Song 8:10, therefore, certainly coheres with the poem's representation of the woman, of her relationship with her family and with her beloved; at the same time, it underscores the firmness and the shrewdness through which the woman tries to wriggle out of her brothers' control.

Besides being unique on the figurative level—as previously mentioned, the representation of a woman as fortified city cannot be found either in the rest of the Hebrew Bible or in the ancient Near East—Song 8:10 is also very unconventional with respect to its content. In the Hebrew Bible, there is no woman who dares to decide about her romantic life independently from and in opposition to her family. This is mainly due to the fact that in ancient Israel the sexuality of an unmarried woman was considered as belonging to the father, and marriages were agreements arranged by and between families.[122] This does not necessarily imply that the bride was always forced to do something contrary to her will. For instance, when Abraham tries to arrange his son's marriage, his servant makes it clear that women could reject his offer (Gen 24:5). Rebekah is asked explicitly whether she wants to marry Isaac (Gen 24:57–58). Furthermore, the fact that the marriage between Michal and David takes place after she steps forward (1 Sam 18:20) suggests that women were not always and totally

---

122. For instance, the decision that Isaac had to marry a woman from his country and among his relatives was made by his father, Abraham, and was arranged in agreement with Rebekah's family (Gen 24). Jacob and Rachel could get married only after Laban's approval (Gen 28–31). When Shechem wanted to marry Dinah, he had to ask his father Hamor: "Get me this young girl to be my wife" (Gen 34:4). Moses is said to have received Zipporah from Reuel, her father (Exod 2:21). Hagar chose a wife for Ishmael from Egypt (Gen 21:21), and Bathsheba fostered the marriage between Adonijah and Abishag (1 Kgs 2:17–18). The brothers' bride must have had authority in these matters too, as suggested by the narrative of Rebekah's marriage and the role that her brother Laban played in it (Gen 24). See Jennie R. Ebeling, *Women's Lives in Biblical Times* (London: T&T Clark, 2010), 83–85; Hennie J. Marsman, *Women in Ugarit and Israel: Their Social and Religious Position in the Context of the Ancient Near East*, OTS 49 (Leiden: Brill, 2003), 49–73.

at the mercy of their families' arrangements, but they could also be active and take the initiative. However, except for the Song, there is no record in the Hebrew Bible of women opposing their family's will with respect to issues such as love, sexuality, and marriage.

Likewise, the idea of a woman providing and receiving fulfillment cannot be found elsewhere in the Hebrew Bible. As Susan Ackerman writes, "The Hebrew Bible is a book that was primarily written by men, for men, and about men," in which women's experience of love is either out of focus or presented through a male perspective.[123] Such a widespread male perspective on love emerges even more when we consider that in the Hebrew Bible only one woman is said to love a man, namely, Michal (1 Sam 18:20, 28), while many men are said to love their women.[124] Not only does female experience of love have almost no place in the Hebrew Bible, but women are usually considered dangerous when it comes to issues such as love and sexuality (see, for instance, Potiphar's wife, Delilah and Bathsheba, and the strange/foreign/adulterous woman in the book of Proverbs). Even when in Prov 5:18–19 the woman's sexuality is characterized positively, it is still considered something for the man's joy and satisfaction:

PROVERBS 5:18–19

Let your fountain be blessed	יהי־מקורך ברוך
and rejoice in the wife of your youth,	ושמח מאשת נעורך
a lovely deer, a graceful doe.	אילת אהבים ויעלת־חן
May her breasts satisfy you at all times;	דדיה ירוך בכל־עת
may you be intoxicated always by her love.	באהבתה תשגה תמיד

In Song 8:10, on the contrary, the woman is portrayed as both satisfying and satisfied, fulfilling and fulfilled, pacifying and pacified, by using a very strong term, that is, שלום, which in the Hebrew Bible often indicates ancient Israel's most desired condition.

The highly exceptional character of 8:10 raises the question of how such a concept of womanhood could have taken shape within ancient Israel's patriarchal society. One should bear in mind that the category of

---

123. Susan Ackerman, "Women in Ancient Israel and in the Bible," Oxford Research Encyclopedia of Religion, April 2016, https://tinyurl.com/SBL2645a"

124. E.g., Isaac loves Rebekah (Gen 24:67), Jacob loves Rachel (Gen 29:18, 20, 30), Elkanah loves Hannah (1 Sam 1:5), Ahasuerus loves Esther (Esth 2:17), and Rehoboam loves Maacah (2 Chr 11:21).

patriarchy is a Western construction that describes the social reality of ancient Israel and the role of women within it only in part. As Meyers has convincingly shown, even though ancient Israel certainly was an andro-centric society with no gender equality, Israelite women were preeminent actors within the household, rather than submissive chattels in a tyrannical male society.[125] Simply stated, the conceptualization of women as com-pletely subdued by hegemonic male power and reduced to silence does not belong to the experience of ancient Israel. The Hebrew Bible itself testi-fies to this, presenting women who often dare to challenge the status quo. In other words, ancient Israel's society, however androcentric, was able to produce many literary constructions of audacious female characters, with whom the Song's woman is perfectly in line (e.g., Tamar, Ruth, Esther, and Judith). Furthermore, sociological studies have shown that even the most conservative and rigidly structured societies present an inner dynamic between their *center* or *core*, that is, the dominant view and the establish-ment, and their *periphery*, that is, the minor voices that do not belong to the structures of power.[126] While the center guarantees steadiness and organization for society at large, as well as power to the establishment, minor voices provide society with flexibility and perspectives of emancipa-tion. In the Hebrew Bible, women often occupy the periphery, crossing the boundary lines of what was established as socially acceptable and making challenging and unexpected demands. Thinking of the Song's woman as one of ancient Israel's peripheral voices does not imply that the Song has political intentions, such as "subverting Ancient Israel's androcentrism."[127] The Song is a love poem, and the woman's demand for sexual indepen-

---

125. Carol L. Meyers, "Was Ancient Israel a Patriarchal Society?," *JBL* 133 (2014): 8–27; Meyers, *Rediscovering Eve: Ancient Israelite Women in Context* (New York: Oxford University Press, 2013); Meyers, "Material Remains and Social Relations: Women's Culture in Agrarian Households of the Iron Age," in *Symbiosis, Symbol-ism, and the Power of the Past: Canaan, Ancient Israel, and Their Neighbors from the Late Bronze Age through Roman Palaestina*, ed. William G. Dever and Seymour Gitin (Winona Lake, IN: Eisenbrauns, 2003), 425–44.

126. Martin Kilduff and Wenpin Tsai, *Social Networks and Organizations* (London: Sage, 2003).

127. Ricœur points out that such a "subversive hermeneutics," which has effected much feminist exegesis of the Song, seems to be led more by the ideology of the wom-en's liberation movement of the 1970s than by textual evidence. See Paul Ricœur, "La métaphore nuptiale," in *Penser la Bible*, ed. André LaCocque and Paul Ricœur, CI (Paris: Seuil, 1998), 446.

dence in 8:10 is not a political statement but the claim of a young woman who wants to be free to love whomever she wants and at any cost. Conceptualizing the Song's woman as one of ancient Israel's peripheral voices instead allows us to understand the Song's woman as simultaneously unconventional, given ancient Israel's society, and grounded in the biblical tradition of presenting female, challenging voices.

The siege motif seems to be a peculiarity of the Song's discourse on love, a motif that can barely be found either in Egyptian or Ugaritic literature. There are, however, two texts that are worth considering, namely, fragment DM 1079 of an Egyptian love poem, and the Ugaritic legend of King Keret. The first text, contained in a fragmentary ostracon from Deir el-Medineh (DM 1079), is not entirely clear, unfortunately, as the two following translations show:

Fox
> Bear is sweet,
> when I am at his side
> [and my] hands have not been far way.
> The wind blows
> as I say in my heart,
> " … with sweet wine.
> I am given to you
> By the powers of [love(?)]."
> …
> My voice is hoarse from saying,
> "(King) Mehi! Life, prosperity, health!"
> He is in his fortress.

Bresciani
> [Bel giorno di] dolce ebbrezza,
> durante il quale io sono accanto a lui
> e non lo abbandono nella tempesta di vento.
> Dico al mio cuore:
> "[Perché] i cuori lo amano?"
> Io, io sono consegnata a te dalla forza [del mio amore]
> La mia forza è spezzata a forza di dire: "[Salute a te]
> Mehi, vita, salute, forza!
> Egli si trova nella sua cittadella …"

While Fox thinks that the fragment is about a man talking to King Mehi, to whom the man is consecrated, Edda Bresciani's translation suggests that the poem is spoken by a woman, who presents herself as a city sur-rendering to her conqueror, namely, her beloved Mehi. The identification and the role of Mehi are contested too. In Fox's view, Mehi is neither a historical figure nor a lover, but rather a "cupid-figure who embodies the power of love. He wanders about the earth and holds young people in the bonds of love. Whoever turns himself over to love becomes one of Mehi's followers."[128] According to Paul Smither, Mehi represents a kind of Don Juan figure.[129] Other scholars, however, propose the identification of Mehi with Amenhotep II or an officer of Sethi I.[130] Furthermore, William Murnane argues that Mehi represents a warrior figure and a hero, whose military record was fresh in Egyptian memory.[131] As for the possible link with Mehi in the aforementioned love poetry, Murnane considers such a link difficult to dismiss, however unprovable. The ostracon is probably too fragmentary for scholars to draw definitive conclusions from it. If Bres-ciani and others are correct, however, we have a text with imagery bearing some resemblance to the Song's warlike imagery, especially Song 8:10, fea-turing the woman as a fortress, the man as a conqueror, and their union as the woman's surrender. The woman's words in the Egyptian ostracon ("Mehi! Life, prosperity, health!") recall 8:10, in which the end of the siege is described as a condition of שלום. The Song's siege motif, however, seems to be conceptually more complex.

As for the Ugaritic poem known as the Legend of Keret, it tells the story of King Keret and his siege of the land of Udumu, which would enable him to conquer the country and marry Ḥurrayu, the daughter of King Pabilu (*KTU* 1.14–16). In the face of the threat of Keret's siege, Ḥurrayu is given to him as wife, and, eventually, she bears the king two sons and six daughters. The differences between the Song and the legend of Keret are manifold and concern not only the literary genre but also the contents. First, the main issue in the Ugaritic poem is not Keret's love for Ḥurrayu but rather the king's offspring. Second, the plot of the Legend of Keret is clearly developed by the prominent presence of gods, who play no role in

---

128. Fox, *Song of Songs*, 66.

129. Paul Smither, "Prince Mehy of the Love Songs," *JEA* 34 (1948): 116.

130. See Mathieu, *La poésie amoureuse*, 155 nn. 521 and 522.

131. William Murnane, *The Road to Kadesh: A Historical Interpretation of the Battle Reliefs of King Sety I at Karnak*, SAOC 42 (Chicago: University of Chicago Press, 1985), appendix 5, "The Mysterious Mehy," 163–75.

the Song. Finally, the woman's role in Keret's epic is very marginal, since everything depends on the gods' plan, Keret's will, and his father's politics.

The Egyptian poem and the legend of Keret suggest that the siege motif in matters of love or marriage was part of the imagery present in the Song's broad literary context. While in these literary works the motif is clearly a very minor theme, it becomes prominent in the Song, demonstrating that the Song both draws on and develops ancient Near Eastern imagery.

***

Song 4:4; 6:4; and 8:10 are connected to one another thanks to the representation of the woman as fortified city. On the clause level, all these warlike metaphors and similes present their own peculiarities, which direct the reader's attention to such apparently odd imagery. On the conceptual level, Song 4:4; 6:4; and 8:10 present different conceptualizations of the woman. Song 4:4 features the woman as an elusive lover, who plays hard to get. Song 6:4 represents the woman as sublime, dominating her beloved through the power of her beauty. Song 8:10 presents a double-sided concept of maturity that, on the one hand, refers to the woman's attempt to wriggle out of her brothers' control and, on the other hand, emphasizes that she is able to establish an equal relationship with her beloved. Song 4:4; 6:4; and 8:10 are unique both on the figurative and the conceptual level. Thanks to the estrangement effect, the text is able to introduce original metaphors and similes to the conceptual universe of the Song's milieu.

3

Man Is Conqueror

> Over this fallen soldier fight your war, then make him burn still more as
> you withdraw.
>
> —Yehuda Halevi, *Love's War* (trans. Halkin)

This chapter shows that the surface military images in Song 2:4; 5:10; and
6:12 are conceptually linked via the metaphor MAN IS WARRIOR. Song
2:4 and 5:10 do not present peculiar characteristics on the clause level,
whereas 6:12 contains a very problematic text. Both 2:4 and 6:12 conceptualize the man in the throes of passion, and 5:10 presents him as beautiful
and terrible. The metaphor MAN IS WARRIOR contributes to the portrayal
of erotic experience as a dominating force (2:4) and, simultaneously,
makes the poem's discourse more romantic and intimate (5:10), moving
the reader's attention from what the man sees to what the man feels (6:12).
The poem's metaphor MAN IS WARRIOR clearly represents a case of conventional metaphor, embedded in the most stereotypical ideal of masculinity
in the ancient Near East. However, due to the interplay with the poem's
other military images, the Song's metaphor MAN IS WARRIOR and its concept of masculinity undergo a process of reconceptualization that subverts
that ideal.[1]

The following is reworked and extended version of Danilo Verde, "When the War-
rior Falls in Love: The Shaping and Reshaping of Masculinity in the Song of Songs," in
The Song of Songs Afresh: Perspectives on a Biblical Love Poem, ed. Stefan Fischer and
Gavin Fernandes, HBM (Sheffield: Sheffield Phoenix, 2019), 188–212.

1. This chapter is slightly different from and shorter than both the previous chapter and those following. Since I have already discussed current scholarship on 2:4 and
5:10, I will not repeat the state of the investigation. As for 6:12, I will discuss different
readings during the analysis. Likewise, I have already established the military meaning
of both 2:4 and 5:10. I will thus not repeat the semantic analysis of the root דגל. Fur-

3.1. The Virile and Passionate Man (Song 2:4)[2]

SONG 2:4
He has brought me to the house of wine,   הביאני אל־בית היין
and his army on me is love.[3]   ודגלו עלי אהבה

3.1.1. The Intoxicating Male Dominance

Two very different images, belonging to two distant conceptual domains,
make up the figurative language in 2:4, that is, the image of the wine
(DRINKS) and the image of the army (WAR).

Song 2:4a (הביאני אל־בית היין) closely recalls 1:4 and 8:2. In 1:4, after
describing the beloved man as a king who has brought his lover into his
chambers (הביאני המלך חדריו), the woman refers to the same image of
wine (נזכירה דדיך מיין). In 8:2, the woman wishes she could bring her lover
to her mother's house (אביאך אל־בית אמי) and fantasizes about giving him
wine to drink (אשקך מיין הרקח). In the poem, wine imagery always has
strong erotic connotations, referring to the consummation of eros as a
joyful and intoxicating experience (see Song 1:2, 4; 2:4; 4:10; 5:1; 7:10; 8:2).
The use of the image of the wine throughout the poem and the similarities between 2:4a; 1:4; and 8:2 suggest that the phrase הביאני אל־בית היין
should be considered a metaphorical expression indicating lovemaking,
rather than referring to a specific place (the house of the wine) that needs
to be identified.[4] The lovemaking is here initiated by the man (הביאני) and
is described from the woman's point of view.

---

thermore, I will treat the relationship between the Song's metaphor MAN IS WARRIOR,
the Hebrew Bible, and cognate literature together at the end.

2. The following is a reworked and extended version of Danilo Verde, "War-
Games in the Song of Songs: A Reading of Song 2,4 in Light of Cognitive Linguistics,"
SJOT 30 (2016): 185–97.

3. On the clause level, Song 2:4 does not display peculiar characteristics. It
includes a verbal clause (הביאני אל־בית היין) and a nominal clause (ודגלו עלי אהבה).
Neither clause displays peculiar syntactic features: the former presents a predicate
(הביאני) followed by a prepositional phrase (אל־בית היין), and the latter presents the
default word order subject (ודגלו) + modifier (עלי) + predicate (אהבה). In the second
clause, אהבה functions as the focus of the utterance, i.e., the constituent that conveys
the salient information about the topic (דגלו).

4. Among the many proposals: "tavern, wine shop" (Lys), "cellar" (Robert and
Tournay), "a licentious funeral banquet" (Pope).

As far as 2:4b is concerned, I have already argued that the root דגל belongs to the conceptual domain WAR and that it might simultaneously refer to both "army" and "banner." While in 2:4a the woman describes the lovemaking as a joyful, inebriating encounter, 2:4b suddenly changes imagery to emphasize a different aspect of the same experience. Song 2:4b uses hyperbole (army) to portray lovemaking as a military occupation, in which the beloved man is atop the woman (עלי) like a conquering warrior planting his banner (which might be a not-so-subtle phallic allusion). When we read 2:4 as a whole, the man emerges as intoxicating her (the image of the wine) through his dominant virility (the image of the army/banner).

This apparently violent image might certainly disturb the modern reader, especially due to current gender concerns, leading some exegetes to sugarcoat the metaphor. For instance, commenting on the woman's description of her erotic experience as "love" (דגלו עלי אהבה), Barbiero remarks, "The woman ... has been conquered not by *force* but by *love*."[5] To my mind, however, removing the conceptual element FORCE from the military description of lovemaking contradicts the metaphor. War is an experience of force, and love becomes a force if it is conceptualized in military terms. One of the main points of the Song's military imagery seems to be that force and love are by no means mutually exclusive. The woman's final remark, "his army is love," is rather to be considered her personal experience of the man's force: it is during this experience of being taken by her lover that she has felt loved. In other words, she has experienced the force of love also thanks to and together with her powerful, passionate lover. Some other exegetes suggest that 2:4 conceptualizes the man as a refuge for the woman.[6] Many different readings are certainly possible, due to the density of the Song's metaphors. However, it is difficult to argue convincingly that the image of the man as a warrior who is equipped with a banner is a reassuring metaphor. It seems more plausible that 2:4 portrays the woman as conquered and overwhelmed by her lover's passion. The

---

5. Barbiero, *Song of Songs*, 90, emphasis added.

6. Hunt, for instance, comments: "It [i.e., דגל] could be intended here to simply represent his protection over her as a primary idea, but also alluding to the fact that through his love she would become part of his family and thus under his family banner through marriage." See Hunt, *Poetry in the Song of Songs*, 250. See also Exum, *Song of Songs*, 115.

woman's words that follow immediately after support this interpretation; she describes herself as fainting and exhausted rather than reassured:

SONG 2:5
Sustain me with raisins,   סמכוני באשישות
refresh me with apples,   רפדוני בתפוחים
because I am lovesick   כי־חולת אהבה אני

Furthermore, the already discussed image of 6:4, in which the same root דגל occurs, confirms that the Song's military imagery is anything but reassuring.

The conceptualization of the man in 2:4, therefore, might be represented as in figure 3.1 below. The woman's beloved man and warriors probably share the fact that they both are outstanding males in the woman's eyes. The image of the wine in 2:4a and the woman's characterization of her experience of the warrior as "love" in 2:4b (דגלו עלי אהבה) highlight the experience positively and hide the most violent aspects of the domain WARRIOR (e.g., *violence, killing, hatred*). The conceptual elements of the source domain WARRIOR are projected onto the target domain MAN and are cross-mapped with the conceptual elements BEAUTY and SENSUALITY, suggested by the context (2:3–4a). The blended space contains the image of the man as a virile and passionate lover, two aspects that as such do not belong to the source domain WARRIOR. By definition, a warrior is not a passionate lover but rather a person who is engaged or experienced in warfare. Nor is the concept of virile, passionate lover intrinsic to the target domain MAN. Men are not necessarily passionate lovers. The concept of virile, passionate lover, rather, is the result of the metaphorical process.

3.1.2. The Medium of the Vigor of Love

Song 2:4 forms part of the first literary unit of the Song (1:2–2:7), containing many of the themes that will be developed throughout the poem.[7] More precisely, 2:4 belongs to a strophe (2:1–7) that first describes the lovers (2:1–3ab), then presents their intimate union (2:3cd–6), and finally ends with an invitation to the daughters of Jerusalem (2:7). When we consider the imagery of 2:1–7, the military metaphor of 2:4b might sound very odd:

---

7. Elliott, *Literary Unity of the Canticle*, 43.

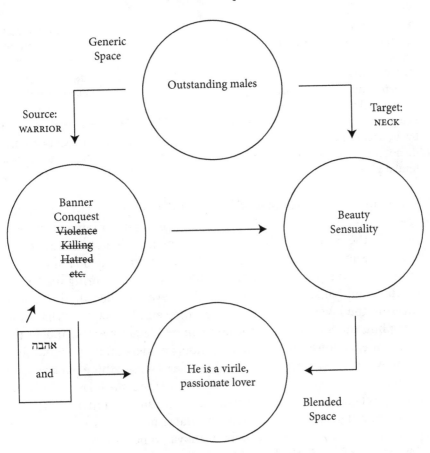

Fig. 3.1. Conceptual structure of Song 2:4

SONG 2:1–7
I am the *lily* of Sharon,
a lotus *flower* of the *valley*.[8]
Like a *lotus flower* among the *thorns*
so is my friend among the young women.
Like an *apple tree* among the *trees* of the *forest*
so is my lover among the young men.
In its shade, I luxuriated and I sat,
and its *fruit* was sweet to my taste.
He has brought me to the house of wine,

אני חבצלת השרון
שושנת העמקים
כשושנה בין החוחים
כן רעיתי בין הבנות
כתפוח בעצי היער
כן דודי בין הבנים
בצלו חמדתי וישבתי
ופריו מתוק לחכי
הביאני אל-בית היין

8. It is well-known that the identification of the flowers here called חבצלת and שושן is very problematic. I am following Keel, *Song of Songs*, 78–80.

and his army on me is love.   וְדִגְלוֹ עָלַי אַהֲבָה
Sustain me with *raisin cakes*;   סַמְּכוּנִי בָּאֲשִׁישׁוֹת
support me with *apples*,   רַפְּדוּנִי בַּתַּפּוּחִים
for I am lovesick.   כִּי־חוֹלַת אַהֲבָה אָנִי
His left hand is beneath my head,   שְׂמֹאלוֹ תַּחַת לְרֹאשִׁי
and his right hand embraces me.   וִימִינוֹ תְּחַבְּקֵנִי
I charge you, O daughters of Jerusalem,   הִשְׁבַּעְתִּי אֶתְכֶם בְּנוֹת יְרוּשָׁלַ͏ִם
by the *deer* or the *gazelles* of the *field*,   בִּצְבָאוֹת אוֹ בְּאַיְלוֹת הַשָּׂדֶה
do not rouse and do not stir love   אִם־תָּעִירוּ וְאִם־תְּעוֹרְרוּ אֶת־הָאַהֲבָה
until it pleases.   עַד שֶׁתֶּחְפָּץ

The main conceptual domain shaping 2:1–7 is NATURAL ENVIRONMENT. She is a flower; he is a tree in 2:1–3. Their intimate union is portrayed through the very erotic image of the woman sitting at the feet of an apple tree and savoring its fruit in 2:3. This is probably one of the best examples of the poem's use of metaphor to effectively bring the lovers' longing and satisfaction to the reader's eyes, while simultaneously covering the lovers' intimacy through the veil of metaphor. Thanks to metaphor, the Song's words for love can be blatantly erotic and, at the same time, endowed with striking candor: readers know, or think they know, what 2:3 is about, without being able to see anything but a woman eating from an apple tree. Song 2:5 continues the same imagery by mentioning raisin cakes and fruits, while 2:7 introduces animals. As for 2:6, it presents the lovers' voluptuous embrace, maybe while they hold a position as in *Eros and Psyche* by Canova. When we read 2:6 within the context of 2:1–7, the lovers' passionate embrace seems to take place against the luxuriant background of trees, flowers, fruits, and wine. The abrupt passage from the image of the wine in 2:4a to the image of the warrior in 2:4b underscores the clash between the domains NATURAL ENVIRONMENT and WAR. Yet, there is no reason to remove the friction within 2:4 and between 2:4b and 2:1–7, since cascades of metaphors, in which different source domains interweave and blend, characterize the Song's poetics. Something similar, for instance, occurs in 4:1–5, in which images of animals and fruits surround the unequivocal military metaphor of 4:4.

SONG 4:1–5
O you are so beautiful, my friend;   הִנָּךְ יָפָה רַעְיָתִי
O you are so beautiful.   הִנָּךְ יָפָה
Your eyes are *doves*   עֵינַיִךְ יוֹנִים

behind your veil.
Your hair is like a flock of *goats*
that gamboled down from *Mount* Gilead.
Your teeth are like *a flock of ewes*
that came up from the *washing*.
All of them are mothers of twins,
and none has lost its young.
Like a scarlet thread are your lips,
and your speech is desire.
Like a slice of *pomegranate* is your cheek
behind your veil.
Like the tower of David is your neck
built in courses.
Thousands of shields are hung on it,
all quivers of warriors.
Your two breasts are like two *fawns*,
twins of a *gazelle*
grazing among the *lotus flower*.

מבעד לצמתך
שערך כעדר העזים
שגלשו מהר גלעד
שניך כעדר הקצובות
שעלו מן-הרחצה
שכלם מתאימות
ושכלה אין בהם
כחוט השני שפתתיך
ומדבריך נאוה
כפלח הרמון רקתך
מבעד לצמתך
כמגדל דויד צוארך
בנוי לתלפיות
אלף המגן תלוי עליו
כל שלטי הגבורים
שני שדיך כשני עפרים
תאומי צביה
הרועים בשושנים

The apparent conflict between different domains and images might be read as surrealism *ante litteram*, in which disparate elements of human experience flow and merge into the same portrayal, which creates a strange, disturbing image.

The communicative function of 2:4 within the Song seems to be to present eros not only as a pleasant, pacifying, idyllic experience, but also as a conqueror and dominating force that has nothing negative, since it is not violence but passion. More precisely, 2:4 presents the man as the medium of the vigor and ardor of love, which completely subjugates the beloved. At the end of the Song, the woman will return to the vehemence of love (8:6–7). In 2:4, she makes it clear that being at the mercy of the power of love is not an abstract idea. Rather, it is a concrete experience, taking place during and through the passionate encounter with her belligerent lover.

3.2. The Sublime Man (Song 5:10)

SONG 5:10
My beloved is dazzling and ruddy,
deployed among myriads [of soldiers].[9]

דודי צח ואדום
דגול מרבבה

---

9. Like 2:4, the clause of 5:10 does not present remarkable constructions. It con-

3.2.1. The Interplay between the Colons

On the semantic/conceptual level, Song 5:10 presents the image of an awe-inspiring, aristocratic warrior. The description of the man recalls Lam 4:7, which employs the verb צחח ("to be dazzling"), together with the lexeme אדום:

LAMENTATIONS 4:7
Her princes were more radiant than snow,
whiter than milk;
their bodies were ruddier than coral,
their hair like sapphire.

זכו נזיריה משלג
צחו מחלב
אדמו עצם מפנינים
ספיר גזרתם

In the Hebrew Bible, the rare lexeme צח conveys the ideas of "warm/hot" (Isa 18:4; Jer 4:11), "bright/white" (Lam 4:7), and "arid/dry" (Isa 58:11).[10] As for אדם, it encompasses colors from brown to red.[11] The adjective אדם often occurs in connection with power/strength. According to Num 19:1–9, for instance, anyone who had contact with a corpse needed to be purified by using the ashes of a brown/reddish heifer. As John Hartley argues, "Although the symbolic force of the cow's color is neither stated nor obvious, the stress on the heifer's reddish brown color indicates that its color contributed to the cleansing potency of the ashes. Possibly, that significance lies in the association of the heifer's 'reddish brown' hide with blood."[12] In Isa 64:3, אדם describes a victorious warrior, and in Zech 1:8 and 6:2–7, it is used to describe apocalyptic horses, which represent God's ruling power over the earth. The cognate lexeme אדמוני is used three times. In Gen 25:25 it refers to Esau's hair or complexion, probably to indicate his roughness as opposed to the quiet temperament of Jacob (Gen 25:27). In

---

tains a standard nominal clause (דודי צח ואדום) in the first colon, extended by an apposition (דגול מרבבה) in the second colon. Song 5:10b might be considered a case of "adjunct enjambment," i.e., one of the mildest forms of enjambment, in which the adjunct of the second colon makes the description of the first colon progress, adding new information. See Dobbs-Allsopp, "Enjambing Line in Lamentations," 226.

10. Shlomo Talmon, "צח," ThWAT 6:983–84; Roland Gradwohl, Die Farben im AT, BZAW 83 (Berlin: de Gruyter, 1963), 7.

11. John E. Hartley, The Semantics of Ancient Hebrew Colour Lexemes, ANESSup 33 (Leuven: Peeters, 2010), 119; Athalya Brenner, Colour Terms in the Old Testament, JSOTSup 21 (Sheffield: Sheffield University Department of Biblical Studies, 1982), 80.

12. Hartley, Semantics of Ancient Hebrew Colour Lexemes, 118.

1 Sam 16:12 and 17:42, it refers to David, to which I will return. The different shades of red often convey the ideas of wealth and luxury. In Jer 22:14
and Ezek 23:13–14, for instance, the lexeme ששר ("vermillion") seems to
indicate a paint that was used to decorate the opulent houses of nobility.
In Exod 25–28 and 35–39, the color ארגמן ("purple, red-purple") is used in
the description of the splendor of the sanctuary. The same lexeme occurs
in Esth 1:6 and 8:15, in which it underlines the pomp of the royal palace.
Likewise, in Song 3:10 ארגמן describes the interior of the royal litter, and in
7:6 it describes the woman's hair. Due to the widespread conceptual association RED ↔ POWER/WEALTH/LUXURY in the Hebrew Bible, we should
not take the description of the Song's man as ruddy as a mere reference to
his complexion (contra Athalya Brenner) or to his youthful skin (contra
Hartley), but rather as an indication of his stunning appearance.[13] In Song
5:10 the combination of the lexemes אדום and צח presents the image of a
blinding fire and a dazzling splendor, the evocation of Lam 4:7 lends to the
man an aristocratic aspect,[14] and other biblical occurrences of the color
red and its different tonalities suggest that the beloved man is not simply
"ruddy"; he is magnificent.

In the second colon, scholars usually translate דגול by "distinguished"
(e.g., Barbiero, Longman) or "standing out/outstanding" (e.g., Alter, Exum,
Murphy).[15] Yet, since דגל belongs to the conceptual domain WAR, its military meaning needs to be present in the translation. The military scenario
of the line is also suggested by the lexeme רבבה, which usually occurs in
military contexts and bespeaks a conspicuous number of soldiers (see Lev
26:8; Deut 32:30; 1 Sam 18:7–8; Ps 3:7).[16] Since דגל refers to military troops
both in the Hebrew Bible and in a number of extrabiblical sources (see
§2.2.2), the passive participle דגול might be translated by "deployed" or
cognate expressions. Given the widespread military connotation of רבבה, I
propose to render the expression דגול מרבבה as "deployed among myriads

---

13. Brenner, *Colour Terms in the Old Testament*, 74; Hartley, *The Semantics of Ancient Hebrew Colour Lexemes*, 115.

14. Song 5:10–14 recalls the description of the princes of Jerusalem in Lam 4 also through the same use of three different lexemes for gold, i.e., זהב (Lam 4:1; Song 5:14), כתם (Lam 4:1; Song 5:11), and פז (Lam 4:2; Song 5:11, 15). Several authors have noted that the expression צח ואדום can be read as a hendiadys. See the discussion in Hartley, *Semantics of Ancient Hebrew Colour Lexemes*, 63.

15. Barbiero, *Song of Songs*, 249; Longman, *Song of Songs*, 163; Alter, *Writings*, 604; Exum, *Song of Songs*, 184; Murphy, *Song of Songs*, 164.

16. Frolov, "Comeback of Comebacks," 65–76.

[of soldiers]." After the dazzling image of the man in the previous colon, the image of the man deployed among a huge display of troops presents a bewildering portrayal of the woman's lover.

The final military image clarifies the initial chromatic description of the beloved man as צח ואדום. The lexeme אדום, indeed, often occurs in military contexts and is associated with the appearance of warriors. For instance, the color red is used to describe warriors in Nah 2:4–5:

NAHUM 2:4–5

The shields of his warriors are red;	מגן גבריהו מאדם
his soldiers are clothed in crimson.	אנשי־חיל מתלעים
The metal on the chariots flashes	באש־פלדות הרכב
on the day of its preparation;	ביום הכינו
the juniper arrows are poisoned.[17]	והברשים הרעלו
The chariots race madly through the streets,	חוצות יתהוללו הרכב
they rush to and fro through the squares;	ישתקשקון ברחבות
their appearance is like torches,	מראיהן כלפידם
they dart like lightning.	כברקים ירוצצו

As Duane Christensen argues, the text might imply both that shields and clothes are made red by blood in battle and that they are painted red prior to battle.[18] Marvin Sweeney suggests that the warriors' intention in reddening themselves was "to terrify and undermine the morale of the defending soldiers who will imagine their own blood splattered all over the attacking troops."[19] The image of a warrior clothed in red-stained garments also occurs in Isa 63:1–2:

ISAIAH 63:1–2

Who is this that comes from Edom,	מי־זה בא מאדום
from Bozrah in garments stained crimson?	חמוץ בגדים מבצרה
Who is this so splendidly robed,	זה הדור בלבושו
marching in his great might?...	צעה ברב כחו
Why are your robes red,	מדוע אדם ללבושך

---

17. For the translation of והברשים הרעלו, see Duane L. Christensen, *Nahum: A New Translation with Introduction and Commentary*, AB 24F (New Haven: Yale University Press, 2009), 274–76.

18. Christensen, *Nahum*, 270.

19. Marvin A. Sweeney, *Micah, Nahum, Habakkuk, Zephaniah, Haggai, Zechariah, Malachi*, vol. 2 of *The Twelve Prophets*, Berit Olam (Collegeville, MN: Liturgical Press, 2000), 438.

and your garments like someone treading the wine press?   ובגדיך כדרך בגת

Granted, חמוץ is *hapax*, and its meaning is therefore uncertain. Neverthe-less, the pun between אדום ("Edom") and אדם ("red") suggests the probable meaning of reddish or crimson (NRSV) or bright red (*HALOT*) for חמוץ. This reading of חמוץ is confirmed by the fact that the warrior's clothes turn out to be bloodstained in the following verses.[20] Mentions of red war-riors can also be found in Ezek 23:14, in which the color has both military and sexual connotations. Judah is here described as an unfaithful woman, whose lust is aroused by the sight of the Chaldean warriors portrayed in vermillion (חקקים בששר). Finally, David, one of the most famous war-riors in the Hebrew Bible, is said to be ruddy (הוא אדמוני) in 1 Sam 16:12. Despite the fact that such a characterization likely refers to his skin tone or hair, it is worth noting that the description of David as ruddy is imme-diately followed by military combat with Goliath (1 Sam 17:1–58). When the Philistine sees David, he disdains him, "because he was a boy, ruddy and handsome in appearance" (1 Sam 17:42). The description of David as ruddy could be more than a mere narrative frill, anticipating that David will be a valiant warrior and, therefore, that he is worthy of being king.[21]

A number of examples from ancient Near Eastern literature confirm the association of the color red with warriors.[22] The most compelling of these examples come from Ugaritic literature and more precisely from the story of Aqhatu (*KTU* 1.19, iv.28–61) and the story of Kirta (*KTU* 1.14, i.7–37). In the former, in order to avenge Aqhatu's death, his sister Pugatu decides to kill Yatpanu. The text explicitly mentions that Pugatu prepares herself by bathing and coloring her body in red (41–43), wearing military uniform and weapons (44–45). In the latter story, during his military cam-paign to conquer the city of Udmu and marry Hariya, Kirta washes and makes himself up to look red as a ritual preparation to the war. As Frank Ritchel Ames summarizes, "In and around ancient Israel, the bodies were at times stained red—a display of color that is both evocative and horrific."[23]

---

20. Blenkinsopp prefers the translation "glistening." See Joseph Blenkinsopp, *Isaiah 56–66: A New Translation with Introduction and Commentary*, AB 19B (New York: Doubleday, 2003), 245.

21. Hartley, *Semantics of Ancient Hebrew Colour Lexemes*, 122.

22. Frank Ritchel Ames, "The Red-Stained Warrior in Ancient Israel," in Kelle, Ames, and Wright, *Warfare, Ritual, and Symbol*, 83–110.

23. Ames, "Red-Stained Warrior," 83.

Before Ames's research, both Cyrus Gordon and Keel had already shown that in the ancient Mediterranean the color red was largely employed to refer to "heroic prowess."[24]

In light of the widespread association of the color red with warriors in the Song's *Umwelt*, I suggest that the military imagery of the second colon in Song 5:10 affects the reading of the first colon and explains why the beloved man is said to be ruddy: he is a warrior! Thanks to the interplay between the colons, Song 5:10 as a whole describes the man as an awe-inspiring, aristocratic warrior, deployed among an impressive number of soldiers.

The conceptualization of the man in 5:10, therefore, might be represented as in figure 3.2 below. As already said about 2:4, what instigates the metaphorical process is probably the fact that, in the woman's perspective, both warriors and the beloved man are outstanding males. Song 5:10 highlights some conceptual aspects of the source domain WARRIOR, such as SPLENDOR, POWER, ARISTOCRACY, DISTINCTIVENESS, and AWE. These elements are projected into the target domain MAN and cross-mapped with the conceptual element APPEARANCE, suggested by the context. The woman, indeed, is describing to the daughters of Jerusalem what the man looks like. These conceptual elements blend in the final representation of the man as SUBLIME, a concept that as such does not belong to either the definition of warriors or the definition of men. As already explained in the previous chapter, the concept of the sublime is particularly apt to describe the blending of the beautiful and the terrible. Song 5:10, therefore, mirrors the representation of the woman in 6:4, both on the lexical level—due to the occurrence of the root דגל—and on the conceptual level. The man is like an aristocratic warrior, who stands out among myriads of soldiers and blinds everybody with his stunning beauty, inspiring simultaneously attraction and awe.

3.2.2. Romance and the Military

Song 5:10 forms part of a group of songs (5:2–6:3) uttered by the woman. After the famous scene at the door that ends with the man's sudden departure, the woman goes around the city looking for her lover and implores

---

24. Cyrus H. Gordon, *The Common Background of Greek and Hebrew Civilizations* (New York: Norton Library, 1965), 230–31; Keel, *Song of Songs*, 198. Quoted in Hartley, *Semantics of Ancient Hebrew Colour Lexemes*, 121–22.

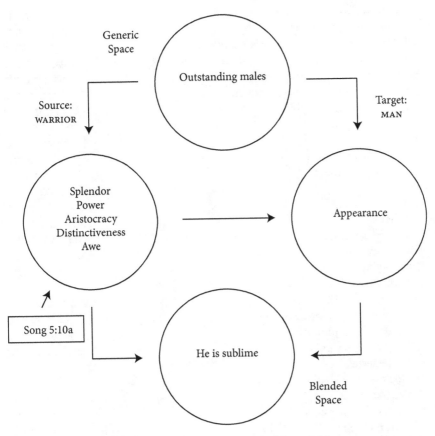

Fig. 3.2. Conceptual structure of Song 5:10

the daughters of Jerusalem to tell the beloved man about her love (5:2–8).
The daughters of Jerusalem ask the woman what makes her lover so different from any other man (5:9), and she starts singing her *waṣf* in 5:10.

The martial representation of the man in 5:10 brings up the question
of its function within the literary unit to which it belongs, that is, 5:8–16,
and within the poem as a whole.

Song 5:8–16
I charge you, daughters of Jerusalem,
should you find my beloved,
what will you tell him?
That I am lovesick.

השבעתי אתכם בנות ירושלם
אם־תמצאו את־דודי
מה־תגידו לו
שחולת אהבה אני

What makes your lover more than another,	מה־דודך מדוד
O fairest among women?	היפה בנשים
What makes your lover more than another,	מה־דודך מדוד
that you charge us so?	שככה השבעתנו
My beloved is radiant and ruddy,	דודי צח ואדום
deployed among myriads [of soldiers].	דגול מרבבה
His head is gold, pure gold;	ראשו כתם פז
his locks are spathes,[25]	קוצותיו תלתלים
black as a raven.	שחרות כעורב
His eyes are like doves	עיניו כיונים
by streams of water,	על־אפיקי מים
bathing in milk,	רחצות בחלב
sitting upon abundant waters.[26]	ישבות על־מלאת
His cheeks are like beds of spices,	לחיו כערוגת הבשם
exuding[27] aromatic scents.	מגדלות מרקחים
His lips are flowers of lotus,	שפתותיו שושנים
dripping liquid myrrh.	נטפות מור עבר
His arms are cylinders of gold,	ידיו גלילי זהב
inset with Tarshish stones.	ממלאים בתרשיש
His abdomen is a block[28] of ivory,	מעיו עשת שן
covered with sapphires.	מעלפת ספירים
His legs are ivory pillars,	שוקיו עמודי שש
set on pedestals of gold.	מיסדים על־אדני־פז
His look is like Lebanon,	מראהו כלבנון
choice like the cedars.	בחור כארזים
His mouth is sweetness,	חכו ממתקים
all of him is delight.	וכלו מחמדים
This is my lover and this is my friend,	זה דודי וזה רעי
O daughters of Jerusalem.	בנות ירושלם

---

25. The lexeme תלתלים is a disputed *hapax legomenon*. My translation is based on the LXX ἐλάται, which means either "silver fir" or "spathe of the date inflorescence" (*LSJ*).

26. The lexeme מלאת is a disputed *hapax legomenon*. My translation is based on the LXX πληρώματα ὑδάτων, "abundance of water."

27. For the translation of מגדלות מרקחים, see ch. 2, n. 26.

28. The term עשת is a disputed *hapax legomenon*. The LXX translates πυξίον, "a tablet of box-wood" (*LSJ*). According to Bloch and Bloch, the term is "used in Mishnaic Hebrew in reference to a work of artistic craftsmanship, specifically a polished block or bar" (*Song of Songs*, 187).

Enveloped by the woman's address to the daughters of Jerusalem (5:8, 16), Song 5:8–16 contains a description of the man that aims to answer the question as to what makes her lover so special (5:9). The woman starts with a general portrayal of the man (5:10) and then focuses on different parts of his body, that is, his upper part (5:11–13), his central part (5:14), and his lower part (5:15). At the end, the woman goes back to the man's mouth, which represents the object of her desire since the very beginning of the poem (1:2). The two conceptual domains on which the woman draws are PRECIOUS MATERIALS and NATURAL ENVIRONMENT. The former is employed to describe both the very top and the very bottom parts of the man, that is, the head, the feet, the arms, the abdomen, and the legs. The latter is used to describe the man's hair and face and his overall aspect (5:11, 15). Not only does the domain PRECIOUS MATERIALS lend to the man a statuary aspect, but it also represents him as a divine figure, recalling ancient Near Eastern statues of gods.[29] As far as the elements of the domain NATURAL ENVIRONMENT are concerned, they seem to evoke concepts such as LIFE (the streams of water), LOVE (the doves), and ABUNDANCE (the milk), as well as a MIXTURE OF LUXURIOUSNESS, SENSUALITY, and THE SACRED (the spices, the scents, the lotus flower, and the myrrh).[30]

At the same time, however, the beloved man also seems to have a dark, wild side. His locks are said to be black as a raven (שחרות כעורב). On the chromatic level, the image of the man's black hair creates a strong contrast with the mention of the gold. The mention of the raven also contrasts with the mention of the doves. Besides being of opposite color, the raven is an animal of the desert, whereas the doves are here connected to water and milk; the former is an unclean animal, whereas the second is a clean animal. The two birds occur together in the flood story (Gen 8:6–12), and, although the meaning of their presence within the narrative is far from clear,[31] Philo provides evidence that within Jewish tradition ravens and

---

29. Keel, *Song of Songs*, 198–207.

30. The lexeme מרקח is a *hapax*, but it is probably connected to the root רקח, "to prepare, mix spiced ointment" (*HALOT*). In the Hebrew Bible, water images evoke both chaos and death (e.g., Gen 1:2; 7:11) and life (e.g., Joel 4:18; Ps 42:2; Job 29:23). Dove images were used in the ancient Near East as messengers of love (see Keel, *Song of Songs*, 69–71). Milk is always used to indicate blessing and abundance (e.g., Exod 3:8, 17; 13:5; Deut 6:3; Jer 11:5; Ezek 20:6).

31. Robert W. L. Moberly, "Why Did Noah Send Out a Raven," *VT* 50 (2000): 345–56.

doves were respectively considered symbols of vice and virtue, evil and good (*QG* 2.35–39). These contrasts suggest that opposite features of the man are here at stake, features that might be expressed as "the beautiful and the terrible." The resulting portrayal of the man in 5:10–16 seems to blend attractive and awe-inspiring features: he is simultaneously like a god, like a source of life and abundance in a cloud of intense, arousing perfumes, but also with a touch of darkness, which makes his aspect more intriguing and perturbing. Should the daughters of Jerusalem meet the woman's lover, they would certainly recognize him. Within such an striking portrayal of the woman's lover, the function of 5:10 is to introduce the man's breathtaking beauty. The beautiful and the terrible, which are already blended in the image of the warrior (5:10), are developed through the following cascade of metaphors (5:11–16).

Song 5:10 needs to be read together with 2:4 and 6:4, 10. That these verses present the same root, דגל, can hardly be fortuitous. Song 2:4; 5:10; and 6:4, 10 certainly share the same emphasis on the bewildering experience of being in love. Yet, whereas 2:4 is more about the overwhelming experience of the lovers' sexual encounter, both 5:10 and 6:4, 10 are about the emotional tumult that the beauty of the lover's body produces in them. As has been said, Song 6:4, 10 expresses the man's feeling of being overwhelmed by the woman's beauty. Song 5:10, on the contrary, expresses the woman's feeling of being overwhelmed by the man's beauty. Both 6:4, 10 and 5:10, therefore, focus on a different aspect of being in love, less sexual and more emotional and aesthetic. Song 5:10 together with 2:4 and 6:4, 10 makes the poem's discourse romantic and intimate, rather than merely erotic. Romance is here created primarily through the conceptual domain WAR, which is as such the furthest thing from romance.

3.3. The Man in the Grip of His Longing (Song 6:12)

SONG 6:12
I am shocked; she turned me   לא ידעתי נפשי שמתני
into chariots of Amminadib   מרכבות עמי־נדיב

3.3.1. A Sensible Conjecture for a Difficult Clause

Song 6:12 presents a number of difficulties that make both its translation and interpretation highly conjectural.

First, who is the speaker? Although some scholars attribute 6:11–12
to the woman,[32] I find that the attribution of these two verses to the man
is much more compelling. In Song 6:11, the speaker says, "I went down
to the nut garden." In the poem, the metaphor of the garden always refers
to the woman (4:12, 16; 5:1; 6:2); hence, 6:11 is very likely spoken by the
man. As for 6:12, since the text does not provide any evidence that the
speaker changes, its attribution to the woman is unnecessary. Second, it is
not clear whether נפשי is the object of ידעתי or the subject of שמתני. Third,
the phrase שמתני מרכבות עמי-נדיב might either contain a case of double
accusative or imply the preposition "in/on" before מרכבות. Finally, עמי-
נדיב might be understood as either a proper name or "my noble people."
Song 6:12 was already difficult for ancient translations, as emerges when
we compare the MT, the LXX, and the Vulgate:

MT	LXX	Vulgate
לא ידעתי נפשי שמתני	οὐκ ἔγνω ἡ ψυχή μου ἔθετό με my soul did not know; it made me[33]	nescivi anima mea conturbavit mea I did not know; my soul disturbed me
מרכבות עמי-נדיב	ἅρματα Αμιναδαβ chariots of Aminadab	propter quadrigas Aminadab because of the chariots of Aminadab

Whereas the LXX understood נפשי as the subject of both ידעתי and שמתני,
the Vulgate considered it as the subject of שמתני. Furthermore, both versions differ as far as the meaning of the verb שים is concerned, although
they agree on the reading of עמי-נדיב as a proper name (reading עמינדב).

I understand נפשי as the object of לא ידעתי, since the phrase לא ידעתי
נפשי has a parallel in Job 9:21: תם-אני לא-אדע נפשי אמאס חיי, "I am blame-
less; I do not know myself; I loathe my life" (NRSV). Furthermore, as
Shalom Paul has shown, the expression "he does not know himself" occurs
in some Mesopotamian medical texts to describe a loss of consciousness

---

32. E.g., Exum, *Song of* Songs, 211.

33. The basic meaning of the verb τίθημι is "to put/to place." However, when it is
constructed with the double accusative it can also mean "to establish/to make someone something" (Acts 13:47; Rom 4:17).

and a mental disturbance.[34] The expressions לא ידעתי נפשי in Song 6:12 and לא־אדע נפשי in Job 9:21 might indicate a loss of mental balance and a state of profound confusion and shock, due to either an intense experience of joy (Song 6:12) or an intense experience of sorrow and pain (Job 9:21).

As for the phrase שמתני מרכבות עמי־נדיב, it seems close to the construction of שים + double accusative that we find in Gen 21:13, 18 and Isa 28:17, in which it indicates a change of status of something/somebody.[35] The question arises as to who is the subject of the verb שמתני in Song 6:12. The verb שמתני requires a feminine subject. Since, according to my reading, the feminine noun נפש is the object of לא ידעתי, thus the only possible subject of שמתני is the woman, about whom the beloved man has talked immediately before (6:4–11). I read עמי־נדיב as a proper name "Amminadib." Although no character bearing this name exists in the Hebrew Bible, עמי־נדיב closely recalls the name עמינדב ("Amminadab"). This is the name in the Hebrew Bible of the father of Naashon, that is, the leader of the tribe of Judah in the desert (see Exod 6:23; Num 1:7; 2:3; 7:12, 17; 10:14; Ruth 4:19, 20; 1 Chr 2:10), as well as one of the Levites in charge of carrying the ark (see 1 Chr 15:10, 11). Given the military scenario suggested by the mention of chariots, the more likely connection is with the former. In Num 2:3 and 10:14 the name of Amminadab (Naashon's father) occurs in the context of the description of Judah's army (דגל). Furthermore, the same Amminadab is one of Solomon's ancestors according to Ruth 4:19, 20. The fact that in Song 6:12 we find the name עמי־נדיב ("my people is noble"), rather than עמינדב might be explained as a pun mirroring the description of the woman as בת־נדיב ("noble daughter") that occurs immediately after (7:2). By changing the name from עמינדב to עמי־נדיב, the man acquires noble origins.[36] The incredible difficulty of 6:12, however,

---

34. Shalom M. Paul, "An Unrecognized Medical Idiom in Canticles 6,12 and Job 9,21," *Bib* 59 (1978): 545–47.

35. In Gen 21:13, YHWH promises to Abraham that he will change the status of Ishmael from being just the son of a slave (Hagar) to being the ancestor of a great nation, i.e., the Ishmaelites. The same promise is made to Hagar in Gen 21:18. In Isa 28:17, the prophet announces that "justice" and "righteousness" will become the instruments through which YHWH will judge his own people, and, thereby, YHWH will change from a salvific presence to a punisher. In these verses, however, the direct object is introduced by the preposition ל, which is missing in Song 6:12, probably because the text is corrupted.

36. Keel, *Song of Songs*, 228.

makes every reading extremely conjectural. As Longman says, "Whatever interpretation is adopted, it should be held very lightly."[37]

If this reading is correct, Song 6:12 contains two verbal clauses, which do not present particular syntactic constructions. The Masoretic accent on שָׂמַתְנִי, however, creates another example of enjambment since, regardless of how we read the syntax of לֹא ידעתי נפשי שמתני, the utterance expressed by the verb שמתני runs over into 6:12b (מרכבות עמי־נדיב). In so doing, Song 6:12b emerges as the most important part of the verse, clarifying both why the man is so confused and what the woman made of him.

3.3.2. The Male Unrestrainable Desire

Song 6:12 presents the man in military terms, since the lexeme מרכבות belongs to the conceptual domain WAR.

Despite the fact that different kinds of chariot existed in Israel and throughout the ancient Near East (e.g., for hunting, ceremonial occasions, transportation, etc.), in the Hebrew Bible both מרכבות and רכב mainly refer to military chariotry.[38] The term מרכבות occurs forty-four times in biblical texts,[39] with reference to the enemies' war chariots (see Exod 14:25; 15:4; Josh 11:6, 9; Judg 4:15; Jer 4:13; Nah 3:2), to Israel's war chariots (see 2 Sam 15:1; 1 Kgs 10:29; 12:18; 2 Chr 1:17; 9:25; 10:18), and to YHWH's war chariots (see Isa 66:15; Hab 2:8). "Horse and chariot" constitutes a hendiadys indicating "military cavalry" in the most important war stories in the Hebrew Bible (see Exod 14–15; Judg 4–5; 1 Kgs 22; 2 Kgs 6–7; 18–19).[40] The Hebrew Bible claims that Israel already possessed military chariots during the reign of Solomon, who is said to have "forty thousand stalls of horses for his chariots, and twelve thousand horsemen" (1 Kgs 5:6). Solomon's introduction of chariots in Israel's army formed part of

---

37. Longman, *Song of Songs*, 185.

38. Luis Jonker, "רכב," *NIDOTTE* 3:1109–14; W. Boyd Barrick and Helmer Ringgren, "רָכַב," *ThWAT* 7:508–15.

39. See Gen 41:43; 46:29; Exod 14:25; 15:4; Josh 11:6, 9; Judg 4:15; 5:28; 1 Sam 8:11; 2 Sam 15:1; 1 Kgs 7:33; 10:29; 12:18; 20:33; 22:35; 2 Kgs 5:21, 26; 9:27; 10:15; 23:11; 1 Chr 28:18; 2 Chr 1:17; 9:25; 10:18; 14:8; 18:34; 35:24; Isa 2:7; 22:18; 66:15; Jer 4:13; Joel 2:5; Mic 1:13; 5:9; Nah 3:2; Hab 3:8; Hag 2:22; Zech 6:1–3.

40. Aarnoud van der Deijl, *Protest or Propaganda: War in the Old Testament Book of Kings and in Contemporaneous Ancient Near Eastern Texts*, SSN 51 (Leiden: Brill, 2008), 129.

his attempt to reinforce the kingdom, by transforming "the Israelite army from a light infantry force into an army whose chariots were its arm of decision."[41] The presence of chariots in ancient Israel is supported by both Assyrian sources and archaeological excavations, which provide evidence of military chariots during the kingdoms of Ahab and Omri.[42] According to Yigael Yadin, the function of chariots was twofold: chariots "served as a movable platform within the battlefield, from which relatively limited fire-power can be rushed to and brought to bear on decisive spots in the midst of the fighting,"[43] and they also intimidated the enemy ranks. In other words, not only did chariots help win battles and wars; they also impressed and subdued enemies by the display of power, prestige, and wealth.

In biblical texts, the mention of chariots is often metonymically used to conceptually represent the idea of MILITARY POWER, in which ancient Israel put its trust instead of relying on God. Isaiah 2:7, for instance, portrays Israel's arrogant confidence in the power of its chariots and horses: "Judah is full of horses; there is no end to their chariots" (אין קצה למרכבתיו). In Isa 31:1, God peremptorily excludes the possibility that salvation might come from military power, symbolized by chariots and horsemen.[44] According to Elisha, the prophet Elijah is the real "chariots of Israel and its horseman" (2 Kgs 2:11), namely, Israel's only strength.[45]

Besides evoking the concept of POWER, in the imagery of both ancient Israel and the ancient Near East, chariots evoked ideas of pres-tige and wealth. As Jacob Wright has argued, building chariots was extremely expensive, and possessing and showing an impressive number of chariots contributed to building the monarch's self-image and his

---

41. Richard A. Gabriel, *The Military History of Ancient Israel* (London: Praeger, 2003), 35.

42. Brad E. Kelle, *Ancient Israel at War 853–586 BC*, EH 67 (Oxford: Osprey, 2007), 20–22.

43. Yadin, *Art of Warfare*, 4.

44. "Woe to those who go down to Egypt for help and rely on horses, who trust in chariots because they are many and in horsemen because they are very strong, but do not look to the Holy One of Israel or consult YHWH!"

45. As van der Deijl explains: "Since God is the sender, the destinateur of history, the important thing is to listen to his word. The strength of a human, a king, and a people lies in this word. God is stronger than horse and chariot. The word of God, the prophecy, is to Israel what 'horses and chariots' are to the peoples" (van der Deijl, *Protest or Propaganda*, 138).

royal propaganda.[46] This point clearly emerges in 2 Sam 15:1 and 1 Kgs 1:5, in which Absalom and Adonijah start their bids for the throne by acquiring chariots, together with horses and runners.[47] This emphasis on chariots as both military equipment and royal propaganda was widespread in the ancient Near East, as in the descriptions of Sennacherib's military actions.[48]

Song 6:12 might suggest that the woman, with her beauty (6:4–10) and her blossoming sexuality (6:11), has made the man feel as though he is an army of which the chariots are a metonymic element. Namely, she has made him feel in the grip of his impetuous and irresistible longing for her. The man is therefore described as profoundly overwhelmed by both the woman's magnificence (6:4, 5, 10) and his own yearning (6:12), causing his mental and emotional state of shock and confusion.

The metaphorical process in 6:12 might be described as in figure 3.3 (see below). The source domain WAR CHARIOTS is used to conceptualize the target domain MAN. The aspect that might have activated the metaphorical process could be the impetuous force that both military chariots and the beloved man have in common. Within the source domain WAR CHARIOTS, the highlighted conceptual elements seem to be POWER, WEALTH, and NOBILITY, which were commonly associated with military chariots in both the Hebrew Bible and the ancient Near East. The blending shapes the representation of the man as yearning with an unrestrainable desire, which conjures the furious and glorious chariots of ancient Israel.

3.3.3. The Man's Inner Experience

Song 6:12 belongs to a group of songs spoken by the beloved man (6:4–7:10a) and closed by the woman's final words (7:10b–11). Within this group of songs, it is possible to distinguish four strophes. As already said, the first strophe (6:4–10) is enveloped by military representations of the woman as אֲיֻמָּה כַּנִּדְגָּלוֹת ("frightening as an army with deployed banners"), underscoring the disconcerting power of her beauty. The second stro-

---

46. Jacob L. Wright, "Military Valor and Kingship: A Book-Oriented Approach to the Study of a Major War Theme," in Kelle and Ames, *Writing and Reading War*, 33–56.

47. Wright, "Military Valor and Kingship," 40.

48. Carly L. Crouch, *War and Ethics in the Ancient Near East: Military Violence in Light of Cosmology and History*, BZAW 407 (Berlin: de Gruyter, 2009), 128.

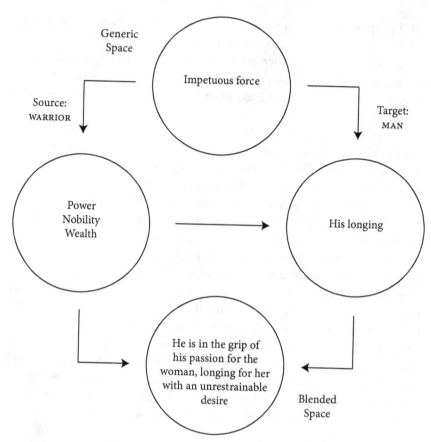

Fig. 3.3. Conceptual structure of Song 6:12

phe (6:11–7:1) resumes the military imagery introduced in 6:4, 10 twice, through the description of the man's impetuous desire (6:12) and through the mention of a military dance (7:1).[49] The third strophe (7:2–6) contains a *waṣf*, in which the man describes the woman's body. Finally, the fourth strophe (7:7–11) continues the previous description of the woman and expresses the man's longing for her (7:7–10a). At the very end, the woman responds to the man mid-sentence (7:10b–11) to summarize their mutual love: "I am my beloved, and his desire is on me" (7:11).

The main themes of 6:4–7:10a are, on the one hand, the woman's beauty and, on the other hand, what such beauty elicits in the man. Not

_____

49. For analysis of Song 7:1, see ch. 4.

only does the man repeatedly describe the woman; he also gives voice to his emotional reactions to her formidable allure. In 6:5, the man expresses his feeling of being overwhelmed by her: "Turn away your eyes from me, for they overwhelm me"; in 6:12, he expresses his feeling of being overwhelmed by the power of his own desire for her; and in 7:9, he finally makes the decision to let his desire loose: "I said to myself: I will climb up the palm, I will squeeze its clusters. May your breasts be like clusters of the vine, and the scent of your nose like apples, and your palate like good wine." Before the beauty of his beloved woman, therefore, the man, on the one hand, trembles, due to the power of her beauty (6:5) and, on the other hand, cannot but pursue her, due to the power of his desire (6:12). The function of 6:12 is therefore to give the reader access to the man's interior experience. More precisely, it pictures the strength of the man's passion, which allows him to pass from fearing the woman to enjoying her.[50] The woman is the one who confirms the man's emotions in 7:11: "I am my beloved's, and his desire is upon me."[51]

When we consider 6:11–12 together, the imagery appears to be similar to the imagery in 2:1–4 and 4:1–7, insofar as a military metaphor is abruptly introduced among images belonging to the source domain NATURAL ENVIRONMENT:

SONG 6:11–12
To the *walnut garden* I went down
to see the *buds* of the *brook*,
to see if the *wine* had *blossomed*,
if the *pomegranate trees* were in *flower*.
I am shocked; she made me
into the chariots of Amminadib

אל־גנת אגוז ירדתי
לראות באבי הנחל
לראות הפרחה הגפן
הנצו הרמנים
לא ידעתי נפשי שמתני
מרכבות עמי־נדיב

While the imagery of 6:11 describes the blossoming body and sexuality of the woman, the imagery of 6:12 portrays the impetuous rise of the man's desire. The introduction of an off-key image (i.e., the military one) conveys the idea of the emotional shock that the woman's body produces in

---

50. On another occasion in the poem the man gives voice to his interior experience, i.e., in Song 4:9: "You have ravished my heart, my sister" (לבבתני אחתי).

51. Despite the fact that many interpreters translate עלי by "for me" (e.g., Barbiero and Alter), I prefer "upon me," since it better renders the basic meaning of the preposition על and fits the representation of the man on top of the woman. Furthermore, it recalls Song 2:4: ודגלו עלי אהבה.

the man. The sudden interruption of the flowing of images belonging to the domain NATURE reflects the sudden and uncontrollable shift in the man from looking at the woman's body to yearning for it: when he looks at her, his own desire overpowers him.

Finally, Song 6:12 likens the lovers to one another by mirroring each other's feelings. Reading 6:12, the reader's mind goes straight to 1:9, the only other line in the poem in which the image of military chariots occurs:

SONG 1:9

To a mare that is among Pharaoh's chariots   לססתי ברכבי פרעה
I liken you, my friend   דמיתיך רעיתי

While I will comment extensively on 1:9 in the next chapter, here it suffices to say that the image of the mare among Pharaoh's chariots represents the woman's beauty as an uncontrollable, tumultuous, even chaotic power. Song 6:12 portrays the man in similar terms, through the already mentioned mirroring technique.[52] Throughout the poem, the two lovers seem to mirror each other, not only because they each in turn reciprocate what the other says, but also because what the lovers see in each other reflects what they experience inside. For instance, Song 2:4 and 5:10 respectively represent the woman's interior experience of being conquered (2:4) and the exterior perception of the man as a warrior (5:10). Likewise, Song 1:9 and 6:12 respectively represent the man's exterior perception of the woman as untamable (1:9) and his interior experience of his untamable desire (6:12). In so doing, Song 6:12 steers the reader from what the man sees to what the man feels.

3.4. The Song's Warrior and the Embodiment of Masculinity

Several cross-cultural studies on gender construction have argued that every society develops its own "hegemonic masculinity," namely, a dominant model of maleness to be imitated and propagated, even though in each society minor construal and performances of masculinity may certainly coexist.[53] As far as ancient Israel is concerned, we still know very

---

52. On the mirroring technique in the Song, see Elliott, *Literary Unity of the Canticle*, 246–51.

53. Raewyn W. Connell and James W. Messerschmidt, "Hegemonic Masculinity: Rethinking the Concept," *GS* 19 (2005): 829–59; Jeff Hearn, "From Hegemonic

little about this subject, and much research needs to be done.[54] Despite the fact that the Song has not received any attention from this perspective hitherto, it represents an invaluable source to understand ancient Israel's construal of both of the male and the female.[55] Granted, the Song's figurative language creates idealized portrayals of both man and woman, and therefore the poem cannot be considered a description of the actual relations between sexes in biblical times. At the same time, however, the Song's figurative language, and especially its more conventional metaphors, sheds light on the conceptual categories through which ancient Israel thought of the female and the male. The Song's military representations of the beloved man are such a case of conventional metaphor. The intertwining of the conceptual domains MAN, WAR, and SEXUALITY embodies an ideal of masculinity that was widespread in both ancient Israel and its *Umwelt*.

As Harry Hoffner has argued, "The masculinity of the ancient was measured by two criteria: (1) his prowess in battle, and (2) his ability to sire children."[56] In the ancient Near East, these two aspects occasionally merge

---

Masculinity to the Hegemony of Men," *FT* 5 (2004): 49–72; Pierre Bourdieu, *Masculine Domination* (Stanford, CA: Stanford University Press, 2001); Tim Carrigan, Bob Connell, and John Lee, "Toward a New Sociology of Masculinity," in *The Making of Masculinities: The New Men's Studies*, ed. Harry Brod (Boston: Allen & Unwin, 1987), 63–100.

54. See Marc Z. Brettler, "'Happy Is the Man Who Fills Quiver with Them' (Ps 127:5): Constructions of Masculinities in the Psalms," in *Being a Man: Negotiating Ancient Constructs of Masculinity*, ed. Ilona Zsolnay (London: Routledge, 2017), 198–220; Peter-Ben Smit, *Masculinity and the Bible: Survey, Models, and Perspectives*, BRP (Leiden: Brill, 2017); Stephen Wilson, *Making Men: The Male Coming-of-Age Theme in the Hebrew Bible* (Oxford: Oxford University Press, 2015); Ovidiu Creangă and Peter-Ben Smit, eds., *Biblical Masculinities Foregrounded*, HBM 62 (Sheffield: Sheffield Phoenix, 2014); Ovidiu Creangă, ed., *Men and Masculinities in the Hebrew Bible and Beyond*, BMW 33 (Sheffield: Sheffield Phoenix, 2010). For an overview of biblical masculinity studies, see Susan E. Haddox, "Masculinity Studies of the Hebrew Bible: The First Two Decades," *CurBR* 14 (2016): 176–206.

55. This is probably due to the fact that, both inside and outside feminist exegesis, scholars have often underscored the prominent role and the unconventional characterization of the Song's woman, to such an extent that the emphasis on the poem's representation of femininity has almost completely overshadowed the poem's representation of masculinity. For an overview of feminist exegesis, see Exum, *Song of Songs*, 80–81.

56. Harry H. Hoffner, "Symbols for Masculinity and Femininity: Their Use in Ancient Near Eastern Sympathetic Magic Rituals," *JBL* 85 (1966): 327.

and emerge on the lexical level, as in the case of the Hittite noun LÚ-*natar*, which means both "male genitalia" and "military exploit."[57] On different occasions, male virility is clearly associated with the military. Some Hittite rituals to cure sexual impotence involved giving bow and arrow to the impotent man. Hoffner quotes an interesting Hittite text containing a ritual in which the supplicant expresses his desire to deprive his enemies of their masculinity using the image of taking away their weapons.[58] The military emerges as a distinguished feature of maleness also in Ugaritic literature. In the tale of Aqhat (*KTU* 1.17–19), for instance, when Anat tries to buy Aqhat's bow and arrows, the young hero reminds her that the bow belongs to men, not to women. In the tale of Keret (*KTU* 1.14–16), the king resolves the problem of not having any offspring through a military campaign of conquest. In so doing, not only does Keret fulfil the tale's narrative program; he also realizes himself as both king and male. The warrior embodies the ideal of masculinity also in Egyptian love poems, in which Mehi is described as a soldier in his chariots and as a warrior conquering a fortress.[59] The beloved man is portrayed as a horseman with no respite until he reaches his lover's house and as an invincible warrior who cannot be overtaken by any of the captains of military troops.[60] Love itself is portrayed as the arrival of a soldier.[61]

Biblical texts also suggest that the warrior embodied the ideal of maleness. In Ps 127:4–5, for instance, male sexual potency is metaphorically represented through the image of a warrior, whose quiver is full of arrows—that is, a man who has generated many children. On the contrary, in 2 Sam 3:29 David's curse on the warrior Joab and on his male descendants involves sexual illness and a process of emasculation: David dooms Joab and his children to holding the spindle (מחזיק בפלך)—that is, to lose their virility and masculinity and be like women. The spindle, indeed, was a typical object for women, whereas weapons were considered "male objects."[62] Furthermore, the aforementioned biblical descriptions of military defeats in terms of emasculation and feminization conversely suggest that, since being a victorious warrior was commonly regarded as the quin-

---

57. Hoffner, "Symbols for Masculinity," 327 n. 4.
58. Hoffner, "Symbols for Masculinity," 327.
59. P.Beatty 1.A.33 (Fox, *Song of Songs*, 53); DM 1079 (Fox, *Song of Songs*, 80).
60. P.Beatty 1.B.38 (Fox, *Song of Songs*, 66); P.Beatty 1.B.39 (Fox, *Song of Songs*, 66).
61. P.Harr. 500.A.2 (Fox, *Song of Songs*, 9).
62. P.Harr. 500.A.2 (Fox, *Song of Songs*, 9).

tessence of masculinity, losing in battle equaled losing masculinity. David Clines has also provided several cases suggesting that being a warrior is a crucial characteristic of biblical construal of masculinity and even one of the main attributes of the male biblical God.[63] However disturbing the image of the warrior God might be to our modern sensitivity, in a society in which survival depended on (male) warriors and in which being a warrior was quintessential masculinity, the male/military representation of the divine must have sounded particularly appropriate for inspiring feelings of trust, awe, fear, and submission.

Not only does the Hebrew Bible provide evidence that in ancient Israel military might was at least one of the most important traits of maleness; it has also fostered such a construal of maleness through its stories and poems. The majority of biblical men were warriors, from Joshua to Samson, from Gideon to Saul and David, from Ahab to Omri, from Barak to the Maccabees. The rhetoric on the strength of Israelite military troops in the book of Joshua, as well as in the book of Chronicles (1 Chr 11:10–12:39), together with war narratives and war poems on the military feats of ancient Israel's (male) leaders and (male) heroes, suggest that ancient Israel was very proud of its (male) warriors.[64] Hence, the Prophets and the Psalms denounce trusting too much in warriors and too little in God (e.g., Hos 10:13; Ps 33:16–17). That wisdom literature had to remind Israel's men that being wise was much more important than being a warrior (Prov 16:32; 21:22; Qoh 9:16) suggests that being a warrior was commonly regarded as a male ideal to pursue.

---

63. David J. A. Clines, "Dancing and Shining at Sinai: Playing the Man in Exodus 32–34," in Creangă, *Men and Masculinities*, 54–63; Clines, "He-Prophets: Masculinity as a Problem for the Hebrew Prophets and Their Interpreters," in *Sense and Sensitivity: Essays on Reading the Bible in Memory of Robert Carroll*, ed. Alastair G. Hunter and Phillip R. Davies, JSOTSup 348 (Sheffield: Sheffield Academic, 2002), 311–28; Clines, "'Ecce Vir,' or, Gendering the Son of Man," in *Biblical Studies/Cultural Studies: The Third Sheffield Colloquium*, ed. Cheryl J. Exum and Stephen D. Moore, JSOTSup 266 (Sheffield: Sheffield Academic, 1998), 352–75; Clines, "David the Man: The Construction of Masculinity in the Hebrew Bible," in *Interested Parties: The Ideology of Writers and Readers of the Hebrew Bible*, ed. David J. A. Clines, JSOTSup 205 (Sheffield: Sheffield Academic, 1995), 212–43.

64. Mark S. Smith, *Poetic Heroes: Literary Commemorations of Warriors and Warrior Culture in the Early Biblical World* (Grand Rapids: Eerdmans, 2014); Smith, "Warfare Song as Warrior Ritual," in Kelle, Ames, and Wright, *Warfare, Ritual, and Symbol*, 165–86.

The Song's representation of the beloved man as warrior not only confirms the tight conceptual connection MALENESS ↔ WAR in the Hebrew
Bible and cognate literature; it also confirms that the warrior in ancient
Israel was considered the ultimate male or, at least, one of the ultimate
males. The military conceptualization of the man's virile strength in 2:4
and his overwhelming desire in 6:12 could make good sense and characterize the man positively only if the military represented a highly regarded
male value. In 5:10, the woman could effectively use the image of the warrior to convince the daughters of Jerusalem of the excellence of her lover
only if being a warrior was generally recognized as an important feature of
the Israelite alpha male. The Song's metaphor MAN IS WARRIOR, therefore,
is an example of stereotypical construal of masculinity embedded in the
conceptual universe of the poem's cultural milieu.

Despite the fact that the Song's metaphor MAN IS WARRIOR is conventional, the Song's image of the warrior and thereby the concept of
masculinity undergo a process of reconceptualization, due to the interplay between the metaphor MAN IS WARRIOR and the poem's other military
images. First, Song 4:4 scales down the representation of the man as a
powerful conqueror. The woman, who in 2:4 declares herself conquered
by her lover, in 4:4 becomes elusive and apparently unconquerable. In 6:4,
the man is completely subjugated by the woman's beauty, to such an extent
that in 6:5 he needs to ask her to turn away her eyes. In other words, not
only does the man experience boundaries (4:4); he is also the one who is
conquered: the yearning male becomes the yearned-for male. A warrior
is certainly meant to win his war, but in the battlefield of love he is not
alone: he has to deal with a belligerent woman (see next chapter). Thanks
to the mutual tension of the Song's military metaphors, the Song's overall construal of maleness becomes as unconventional as its construal of
femaleness, on which much of feminist exegesis has notoriously insisted.
The Song's overall construal of maleness certainly implies the concepts of
POWER, VALOR, and BEAUTY, but also the concepts of LIMITED POWER (4:4)
and LOSING CONTROL (6:4; 7:6). In the Song, "being man" implies both
being the subject (6:12) and being the object (6:4–5) of sexual desire, both
being active in the relationship with the woman and being passive and
even being fulfilled by her (8:10).

The Song's construal of maleness, therefore, both reflects and subverts
the poem's cultural milieu. Such a reversal ultimately depends on the fact
that the Song is a love poem between a man and a woman and that the
relational dynamics between the two shape the very idea of maleness (and

femaleness), as well as its metaphorical representations. This suggests that in the Hebrew Bible different constructions of masculinities may coexist that, in spite of their common cultural background, are ultimately forged by the peculiar perspectives of each biblical book.

***

Besides the Song's representation of the woman as fortified city, the poem contains the representation of the man as conqueror. The surface metaphor MAN IS CONQUEROR emerges through several figurative expressions, each of which underlines a specific aspect of the beloved man, for example, his dominant virility (2:4), his awe-inspiring beauty (5:10), and his overwhelming desire (6:12). The Song's conceptualization of the beloved man as conqueror is profoundly embedded in the ideal of masculinity that ancient Israel shared with its *Umwelt*. Nevertheless, the interplay with the Song's military metaphors reshapes that ideal.

4
Woman Is Conqueror

That you have shed my blood, I have two witnesses—your lips and cheeks.

—Yehuda Halevi (trans. Halkin)

The following section analyzes two military images in Song 1:9 and 7:1 representing the woman as conqueror. On the clause level, Song 1:9 contains a defamiliar word order, which I explain as the text's attempt to draw the reader's attention to the warlike imagery. On the semantic/conceptual level, the image of the mare conceptualizes the woman's beauty and sensuality as OVERWHELMING and IRRESISTIBLE. On the communicative level, Song 1:9 introduces a new metaphor and a new positive and challenging conceptualization of female eros. The motif of the woman-mare indeed was uncommon in the ancient Near East, whereas Greek authors very often (but not always) used it to blame and ridicule women. In 1:9, this image conveys the idea of the woman's sexuality as active and even dominant within the context of the lovers' games of seduction, without any hint of judgment. As for 7:1, it recalls biblical representations of military dances performed at the end of a war to celebrate the victorious return of the hero. By drawing on and reworking a repertoire of biblical and non-biblical motifs, Song 7:1 pictures the woman as the winner of the lovers' war-game.

4.1. The Irresistible Woman (Song 1:9)[1]

SONG 1:9

To a mare[2] that is among Pharaoh's chariots[3]   לססתי ברכבי פרעה
I liken you, my friend   דמיתיך רעיתי

Exaggerating somewhat, Black defines 1:9 as "almost incomprehensible,"
although it is true that scholars heatedly debate its meaning.[4]

On the one hand, some exegetes read a martial connotation in the
metaphor of the mare. According to Pope, Song 1:9 alludes to the practice of sending an estrous mare among enemy cavalry to create confusion
among horses, as happened during an Egyptian military campaign of
Thutmose III.[5] Pope suggests that in 1:9 the man is describing his beloved
as able to drive men crazy, arousing their sexual desire. However sug-
gestive this interpretation may appear, there is no evidence of such a
military expedient either in 1:9 or in other texts of the Hebrew Bible.
Granted, absence of evidence is not necessarily evidence of absence; yet,
it still makes scholarly argumentation extremely conjectural. Barbiero
rightly emphasizes that the mention of the woman's cheeks, neck, and
jewels in 1:10 suggests that the focus lies on her aesthetic appearance
and that 1:11 calls to mind the pompous decorations of Egyptian military

---

1. This section is a reworked and extended version of Danilo Verde and Pierre
Van Hecke, "The Belligerent Woman in Song 1,9," *Bib* 98 (2017): 208–26.

2. The final *ḥireq* in לססתי is here regarded as a *littera compaginis*, expressing the
construct state ברכבי פרעה, as happens in other poetic texts: e.g., מלאתי משפט, "she
that was full of justice" (Isa 1:21); שרתי במדינות, "she that was great among the nations"
(Lam 1:1). See *GKC* §90; Joüon §93 l–q; Robyn C. Vern, "Case: Vestiges of Case Inflections," *EHLL* 1:400–1j.

3. This is the only plural occurrence of the collective name רכב ("group of chariots") in the entire Hebrew Bible. Hence, scholars suggest it refers to stallions (see Pope,
Song of Songs, 337). Nevertheless, this is not necessary, since רכבי could be either a
simple plural (chariots) or a "plural of generalisation" (chariotry), which mainly
occurs in poetry: e.g., נקמות ("vengeance"; 2 Sam 4:8); במסתרים ("hidden place"; Jer
23:24); הררי ציון ("mountain of Zion"; Ps 133:3); הררי נמרים ("mountain of the leopards"; Song 4:8). For more examples, see Joüon §136.

4. Black, *Artifice of Love*, 170.

5. Marvin H. Pope, "A Mare in Pharaoh's Chariotry," *BASOR* 200 (1970): 56–61;
Pope, *Song of Songs*, 336–43. Pope is followed by a number of scholars, e.g., Keel, *Song
of Songs*, 56–58; Schwienhorst-Schönberger, *Das Hohelied*, 49–51; Zakovitch, *Das
Hohelied*, 127–28.

cavalry.[6] Unfortunately, Barbiero does not develop his interpretation by explaining exactly which aspects of the woman's beauty are foregrounded by the metaphor of the mare and what such a metaphor adds to the Song's description of its female character. Moreover, Barbiero's statement that the emphasis is aesthetic rather than erotic separates between two dimensions (i.e., aesthetic and erotic) that in the Song are closely interwoven.[7] Landy's comment on 1:9 makes the metaphorical complexity of 1:9 emerge. While he recognizes that the military image of the mare emphasizes the powerful attractiveness of the woman, at the same time he argues ironically that "it hints at her proper subservience, as a member of the king's entourage, as an adornment to his court."[8] Likewise, Yvonne Thöne recently suggested that the image evokes "a strong and precious being but one simultaneously under male command."[9] The Song's metaphors may certainly condense and combine many different meanings; to my mind, however, Song 1:9 does not seem to highlight the concept of SUBMISSION.

On the other hand, many other exegetes reject military readings of 1:9. Fox, for instance, argued that in the Hebrew Bible the lexemes "chariot" and "horse" do not always have military meaning, and, in his opinion, the line is rather to be considered as belonging to royal imagery.[10] Likewise, Garrett asserts that "the text says nothing about a military setting for this verse," and many scholars do not provide any martial interpretation.[11] I will suggest not only that 1:9 first and foremost requires a martial interpretation, but also that the opposition between military and royal imagery is deceptive, since the domains WAR and ROYALTY were tightly interlaced in the cultural experience and conceptual universe of the ancient Near East.

---

6. Barbiero, *Song of Songs*, 71.

7. Barbiero, *Song of Songs*, 77.

8. Landy, *Beauty and the Enigma*, 90.

9. Yvonne S. Thöne, "Female Humanimality: Animal Imagery in the Song of Songs and Ancient Near Eastern Iconography," *JSem* 25 (2016): 389.

10. Fox, *Song of Songs*, 105.

11. Garrett, *Song of Songs*, 144. See also Anselm C. Hagedorn, "What Kind of Love Is It: Egyptian, Hebrew, or Greek," *WO* 46 (2016): 90–106. See also Murphy, *Song of Songs*, 134; Luzarraga, *Cantar de los Cantares*, 193–97.

4.1.1. Another Case of Marked Word Order

Song 1:9 presents a case of marked word order that underscores the impor-tance of its military metaphor. In 1:9, the verb is preceded by a fronted constituent (לססתי), which is itself modified by an adnominal phrase (ברכבי פרעה). This nondefault order calls for an explanation.

Noun Phrase	Verbal Phrase	Prep. Phrase[2]	Prep. Phrase[1]
	Main Field		Preverbal Field
רעיתי	דמיתיך	ברכבי פרעה	לססתי
my friend	I liken you	that is among Pharaoh's chariots	To a mare
Extension	↔	Fronting	

Nicholas Lunn suggests that in 1:9 the fronted word order depends on the fact that the line introduces a new section containing the very first words of the male character.[12] Marking the start of a new section is indeed one of the common functions of marked word order.[13] Note also the *setumah* mark at the end of 1:8. Lunn's reading implies that 1:9 does not continue the discourse of the preceding 1:8. In his opinion, the latter is spoken by an unspecified voice, and 1:9 by the man. In this regard, Lunn is in line with many authors according to whom the appellative "most beautiful among women" (1:8) is used by the daughters of Jerusalem in the rest of the poem (5:9; 6:1), proving that this verse is pronounced by a chorus.[14] Many others, however, consider 1:8–9 together as belonging to the man's speech.[15] In this view, since 1:7 clearly addresses the man ("Tell me, O you whom my soul loves"), the reply in 1:8 might be attributed to him as well, with 1:9 continuing his discourse. Also in this case, the marked word order in 1:9 could indicate a new section, for example, within the man's speech: after his indications to the woman on where to find him (v. 8), he now

---

12. Nicholas P. Lunn, *Word-Order Variation in Biblical Hebrew Poetry: Differentiating Pragmatics and Poetics*, PBM (Milton Keynes, UK: Paternoster, 2006), 223–24.

13. Joüon §155nd.

14. E.g., Keel, *Song of Songs*, 53; Garrett, *Song of Songs*, 138; Exum, *Song of Songs*, 97; Barbiero, *Song of Songs*, 48.

15. E.g., Fox, *Song of Songs*, 100–05; Murphy, *Song of Songs*, 130; Longman, *Song of Songs*, 100–02; Zakovitch, *Das Hohelied*, 124–28.

turns to a description of her beauty (vv. 9–11). To my understanding, there are no conclusive arguments to settle the discussion.

A second, pragmatic explanation is that the word order explicitly marks the fronted constituent as what is technically called the clause's focus, highlighting the unexpected or remarkable nature of the comparison.[16] It indicates that the clause does not simply state that the man compares his beloved to a mare, but that of all things "it is to *a mare among Pharaoh's chariots*" that he compares her. Additionally, stylistic reasons are to be considered. As Michael Rosenbaum argues, the changes in word order might result from the author's decision to avoid common forms and trite expressions.[17] By building an unfamiliar word order, the text draws attention to the content of the clause.

4.1.2. Overwhelming Female Beauty

The image of the mare in 1:9 recalls the conceptual domain MILITARY CAVALRY, due to the lexemes סוס and רכב, their combination with the mention of pharaoh, and other military texts in which horse, chariot, and pharaoh occur together.

The lexeme סוס as such might certainly indicate different kinds of horses, not necessarily military. Nevertheless, it refers to generic, unspecified horses in only a few biblical texts, while it indicates military horses in the vast majority of its occurrences.[18] Likewise, while רכב can indicate different kinds of chariots (e.g., for hunting, ceremonial occasions, or transportation), it is mainly used in contexts of war.[19]

---

16. It has been argued that comparative adjuncts often take marked positions in the clause by virtue of their role in the clause's completive focus, which is larger than that of other adjuncts. In clauses with a comparative adjunct, comparing one of the clause constituents to something else is one of the clause's focal points, and this is often indicated by a marked order (see Van Hecke, *From Linguistics to Hermeneutics*, 189, 195–97).

17. Michael Rosenbaum, *Word-Order Variation in Isaiah 40–55: A Functional Perspective*, SSN 36 (Assen: Van Gorcum, 1997), 149–208. For a discussion of Rosenbaum's position on defamiliar word orders, see Van Hecke, *From Linguistics to Hermeneutics*, 68. Rosenbaum's idea is very close to the already mentioned concept of "defamiliarization" described by Russian formalism.

18. Franz J. Stendebach, "סוס," *ThWAT* 5:782–91; Robert B. Chisholm, "סוס," *NIDOTTE* 3:234–36.

19. Jonker, "רכב," 8206; Barrick and Ringgren, "רָכַב," 508–15.

Moreover, horse and chariot often occur together in the Hebrew Bible in war scenes, and, on some occasions, they constitute a hendiadys referring to military cavalry (e.g., Josh 11:4; Isa 43:17; Ps 76:7).[20] Such an abundant use of the two lexemes in literary warlike scenes is grounded in the experience of warfare in the ancient Near East. Indeed, chariots were first used to provide mobility during battles, and horses and chariots together were considered the most powerful and threatening weapons throughout the ancient Near East.[21] Since the meaning potential of סוס and רכב is broad, however, the question remains whether their frequent military meaning is also activated in 1:9. I suggest it is, taking into consideration the combination of the terms "horse" and "chariot" and their collocation with the following "Pharaoh," as well as the occurrences of the three lexemes together in other military texts (i.e., what Allwood calls "the memory of past activations").[22] Pharaoh's cavalry is mentioned in many texts of the Hebrew Bible, referring to Egypt's military power and to the strength of its cavalry (e.g., Deut 11:3–4; Isa 43:17; Ps 136:15). The three terms סוס, רכב, and פרעה occur together in one of the most emblematic war scenes in the Hebrew Bible: the story of the crossing of the Red Sea in Exod 14–15. Here we find references to "all Pharaoh's horses [and] chariots" (Exod 14:9), "all Pharaoh's horses [and] his chariot" (Exod 14:23), and "Pharaoh's horse with his chariot" (Exod 15:19).[23] The objection, mentioned above, that 1:9 refers to royal imagery seems to overlook the fact that the conceptual domains ROYALTY and MILITARY CAVALRY were by no means distant in the ancient Near Eastern milieu. While the two domains in question are not associated in the modern, Western world—the queen of England and the king of Belgium do not immediately evoke concepts such as army tanks or military weapons—in the ancient Near East kings were warriors and their

---

20. See Martinus Beek, "The Meaning of the Expression 'The Chariots and the Horsemen of Israel' (ii Kings ii 12)," *OtSt* 17 (1972): 1–10.

21. Fabrice de Backer, "Evolution of War Chariot Tactics in the Ancient Near East," *UF* 41 (2010): 29–46; de Backer, "Some Basic Tactics of Neo-Assyrian Warfare," *UF* 39 (2008): 69–116; Nigel Tallis, "Ancient Near Eastern Warfare," in *The Ancient World at War*, ed. Philip de Souza (New York: Thames & Hudson, 2008), 47–66; Stephanie Dalley, "Ancient Mesopotamian Military Organization," in *Civilizations of the Ancient Near East*, ed. Jack M. Sasson (New York: Scribner, 1995), 413–22.

22. Allwood, "Meaning Potential," 43.

23. This entails that the aforementioned texts chronologically precede the composition of the Song.

armies were expressions and tools of their royal dominion. As Deborah O'Daniel Cantrell shows, literary and visual representations of horses and chariots and their parades and lavish adornments were widespread in ancient Near Eastern rhetoric establishing and exhibiting royal/military power.[24] The conceptual domain MILITARY CAVALRY, therefore, is not to be considered either opposed or an alternative to the conceptual domain ROYALTY, but rather as part of it.

Given that in 1:9 the mare recalls the conceptual domain MILITARY CAVALRY, from the perspective of cognitive semantics it is important to investigate which specific aspect(s) of the domain in question is/are highlighted by the lexeme סוסה. Archaeological and literary research on warhorses and chariots in Israel provides evidence that mares were regularly used in battle throughout the ancient Near East.[25] Both stallions and mares were the most lethal weapons in battle, receiving special training to pull chariots (in the case of stallions), to carry warriors, to smite the opposing army, and even to kill fallen soldiers by trampling them.[26] Biblical texts often mention the furious, appalling force of horses, acknowledged as exceptionally frightening and brave (e.g., Isa 5:28; Ezek 26:10–11; Nah 3:2–3; Hab 1:8; Job 39:20–25). Due to their irrepressible strength, horses were considered, on the one hand, difficult to tame and, on the other, the most reliable arm in battle (e.g., Pss 20:7; 32:9; 33:17; 76:6; Prov 26:3). Egyptian horses especially were regarded as particularly strong and impressive (e.g., Deut 17:16; 1 Kgs 10:28; 2 Kgs 18:23–24; Isa 31:1). Cantrell convincingly shows that the mention of warhorses, both in literature and in visual arts, belonged to widespread propaganda in the ancient Near East that aimed at inspiring feelings of awe, admiration, reverence, threat, and submission.[27]

From a conceptual point of view, therefore, Song 1:9 should be read in light of widespread imagery, both in Israel and in its *Umwelt*, in which horses were primarily associated with literary scenes and experiences of war and with concepts such as OVERWHELMING, STAGGERING, IRRESIST-

---

24. Deborah O'Daniel Cantrell, "'Some Trust in Horses': Horses as Symbols of Power in Rhetoric and Reality," in Kelle, Ames, and Wright, *Warfare, Ritual, and Symbol*, 131–48.

25. Deborah O'Daniel Cantrell, *The Horsemen of Israel: Horses and Chariotry in Monarchic Israel (Ninth–Eighth Centuries B.C.E.)*, HACL 1 (Winona Lake, IN: Eisenbrauns, 2011).

26. Cantrell, *Horsemen of Israel*, 136.

27. Cantrell, "Some Trust in Horses," 131–48.

IBLE POWER. The next paragraph will illustrate how these concepts are activated in the metaphorization of the woman.

In light of the insights coming from both conceptual metaphor theory and blending theory and drawing from the previous semantic/conceptual analysis, the metaphorization of the woman as military mare in 1:9 could be represented as in figure 4.1 below. The generic space could be identified with the jewelry worn by the Song's woman and recalling the ornaments of ancient military horses, as several scholars suggest (see *supra*). The text, however, does not provide clear hints. Since military horses were considered the most powerful, invincible weapons in ancient Near Eastern warfare, the concept of UNSTOPPABLE STRENGTH seems to play a major role in the metaphoric process. Other concepts such as LETHAL WEAPON and KILLER POWER are hidden. As for the target domain, the immediate context highlights the woman's sensual body. The mention of the woman's cheeks, neck, and jewels in 1:10 suggests that the man is admiring her alluring body:

SONG 1:10
Your cheeks among the ornaments are desirable,
your neck among jewels[28]

נאוו לחייך בתרים
צוארך בחרוזים

The man is not staring at, so to speak, neutral body parts. Cheeks surround the mouth, which is an erogenous body part, and 5:13 clearly emphasizes their seductive facet.[29] Likewise, the neck arouses erotic thoughts, since it moves the gaze toward both the mouth and the breasts. Cheeks and necks might be considered synecdoches: parts indicating the entire sensuality of the woman's body. The conceptual elements UNSTOPPABLE STRENGTH of the source restructures the target, conveying the turbulent, boisterous

---

28. The meaning of תרים is uncertain. It might come from תור ("to turn"), indicating "something twisted in a decorative fashion" (Garrett, *Song of Songs*, 145). The connection to the woman's cheeks suggests that it refers to some kinds of earrings, like those that one can see in ancient Near Eastern depictions of goddesses and of Egyptian military horses. Since the exact meaning is unclear, I prefer the vague translation "ornaments." As far as the lexeme חרוזים is concerned, it is *hapax*, probably indicating "something formed by perforating and then stringing together, such as a necklace" (Murphy, *Song of Songs*, 131). Also in this case, I prefer a vague translation, namely "jewels."

29. "His cheeks are like beds of spices, yielding fragrance. His lips are lilies, distilling liquid myrrh" (NRSV).

effect of the woman's beauty on the beloved and the emotional crash that she produces in him. Her beauty and sensuality are overwhelming and irresistible, so that if their love were a battlefield, she would be the victor. Note that the man addresses his beloved with the vocative רעיתי ("my friend"), which creates a strong contrast with לססתי. The two terms, לססתי and רעיתי, respectively open and close the line, with a probably intentional assonance created by the final *hireq*. While, on the one hand, לססתי ברכבי פרעה recalls a military, enemy scenario, the vocative רעיתי cancels the conceptual aspect of HOSTILITY. In other words, the man does not feel threatened or scared by such a majestic woman. On the contrary, he is fascinated to such an extent that in 1:11 he even wants to emphasize the powerful sensuality of her beauty, by making her new jewelry:

SONG 1:11
We will make you ornaments of gold,
studded with silver[30]

תורי זהב נעשה־לך
עם נקדות הכסף

He seems, so to speak, to welcome and enjoy such a magnificent woman: she is irresistible, and he loves it.

4.1.3. Empowering Poetry

Song 1:9 belongs to the first literary unit (1:2–2:7), which goes from the woman's expression of her longing for the man (1:2–4) to the fulfillment of her desire (2:4–5), passing through the woman's words to the daughters of Jerusalem (1:5–6), her search for the man (1:7–8), and the lovers' first dialogue (1:9–2:3).

It is unclear whether the man is absent in 1:7–8. As said above, on the one hand, since the woman addresses the man in 1:7, Song 1:8 might contain the man's reply.[31] On the other hand, the appellative היפה בנשים in 1:8 might indicate that the verse is spoken by an external voice, since the daughters of Jerusalem always use this appellative (5:9; 6:1).[32] Note that the woman has

---

30. נקדות is *hapax*. Since the root נקד occurs in Gen 30:32, 33 to indicate spots in Laban's sheep, we might speculate that Song 1:11 refers to dots or spangles of silver.

31. Alter, *Writings*, 589; Longman, *Song of Songs*, 101–2; Murphy, *Song of Songs*, 134.

32. Barbiero, *Song of Songs*, 67–68; Gordis, *Song of Songs*, 135–39; Schwienhorst-Schönberger, *Das Hohelied*, 48. For the question concerning who says what in the

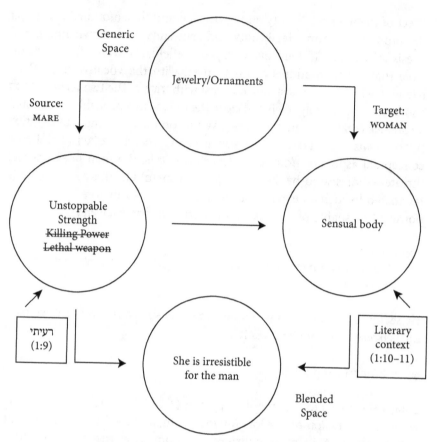

Fig. 4.1. Conceptual structure of Song 1:9

directly addressed the daughters of Jerusalem in 1:5–6; hence, they might be the speakers in 1:8. Furthermore, the expression "whom I love so" (שאהבה נפשי, trans. Alter) in 1:7 occurs again three times in 3:1–3, in a context in which the man is clearly absent. The woman's words in 1:7 might be read as an emotional exclamation while she is looking for him, and the answer in 1:8 might be an advice coming from an external voice, maybe the daughters of Jerusalem. Many readings are certainly possible, and looking for logical coherence from verse to verse in poetry is perhaps naïve. I here assume that the man starts talking in 1:9, since this is the first verse that unequivocally

Song, see Jean-Marie Auwers and Pieter Van Petegem, "Les interventions du choeur dans le Cantique des cantiques. Qui dit quoi dans le poème?," *ETL* 85 (2009): 439–48.

can be attributed to him. The vocative "my friend" (רעיתי), indeed, is one of
the typical ways through which the man addresses his lover (Song 1:15; 2:2,
10, 13; 4:1, 7; 5:2; 6:4). If my reading is correct, the warlike imagery in 1:9
acquires particular relevance, since this is the very first time that we hear
the man's voice: when he sees the woman and talks to her, he starts thinking
and talking in military terms. Her desire, which emerges at the very beginning of the poem, is so impetuous and her beauty is so bewildering that the
very first image that comes to the man's mind is the image of the Egyptian
military cavalry. Something similar happens to the woman: as we have seen,
when the daughters of Jerusalem ask her what is so special about her lover
(5:9), her very first description of the man is military (5:10).

The only reference to the woman as a mare is in 1:9, and this remark
credits a second peculiar aspect to the verse. The fauna of the Song (doves,
sheep, fawns, gazelles, etc.) seem to recall concepts such as GRACE, TEN-
DERNESS, MILDNESS, LIVELINESS, and VIVACITY. Likewise, the pastoral
imagery might here suggest a harmonious atmosphere of serenity and
innocence, and the numerous references to flowers and fruits appear to
be associated with ideas of delicacy, freshness, fruitfulness and readiness for love. Although an attentive interpretation of each single image
would certainly bring many more meanings to light, it could be said that
the Song, generally speaking, conveys a portrayal of an ideal, dreamlike,
conceptualization of the woman as SWEET, TENDER, FULL OF JOY, and LIFE.
Song 1:9, surprisingly, takes a different conceptual direction, emphasizing
the disconcerting power of the woman's beauty, building up a much more
complex character.

At the same time, however, the metaphor of the mare is conceptually
close to a cluster of images underlying the chaotic, tumultuous aspect of
the woman's beauty and sensuality. For instance, the image of goats gamboling down from the mountains (4:1) might serve to conceptualize the
woman as wild, and the mention of lions and leopards, presented as part of
her environment (4:8), suggests that she is also rather savage. Such a wild
aspect also emerges from the first metaphorical description of the woman,
which is found in 1:5:

SONG 1:5
I am black and/but beautiful,   שחורה אני ונאוה
O daughters of Jerusalem   בנות ירושלם
like the tents of Kedar,   כאהלי קדר
like the curtains of Solomon   כיריעות שלמה

While 1:5 seems to be an apology about her dark skin to the daughters of
Jerusalem, at the same time it presents the woman's beauty as wild (the
mention of Bedouins) and luxurious (the mention of Solomon's curtains).
Two conceptual domains, apparently distant and unrelated, here overlap:
WILD ENVIRONMENT (the Bedouins of the desert) and ROYAL ENVIRON-
MENT (the curtains of Solomon). This creates a short-circuiting paradox
in the final, astonishing portrayal: her beauty is both very rustic and very
sophisticated! These two elements, incompatible at first glance, are also
present in 1:9, where, as mentioned above, the woman is described as both
powerful/unstoppable and an elegant and regal military mare.

Furthermore, by drawing on the conceptual domain WAR, Song 1:9 is
in line with the poem's other clusters of military images. In this respect,
the already analyzed metaphor in 6:12 is particularly interesting, since it is
the only verse that mentions chariots; moreover, both verses are spoken by
the man. However, whereas 1:9 is about the woman's enormous seductive
power, Song 6:12 describes the man's impetuous longing for her. In both
cases, the man faces two powers that he can barely resist. Furthermore,
whereas the man evokes foreign military chariots (i.e., Pharaoh's chariots)
when he speaks to/about the woman (1:9), he evokes ancient Israel's glorious past (the chariots of Amminadib) when he speaks of himself (6:12).
In short, in 1:9 the woman is presented not only as a powerful military
mare, but also as having something exotic, which makes her beauty more
intriguing, unpredictable, and thrilling.

The uniqueness and novelty of 1:9 stand out when the line is read
within the broader literary context of the Hebrew Bible. Although none
of the many women of the Hebrew Bible are characterized in terms similar to 1:9, vaguely similar images are found in the prophets' description of
the relationship between YHWH and Israel. Jeremiah 2:23–24 describes
Israel chasing the Baals as a young camel and a wild ass in heat. The metaphors of wild animals in Jer 2:23–24 are particularly interesting because
they combine, on the one hand, the sexual and animal imageries and, on
the other hand, the metaphorization of Israel as YHWH's young fiancée,
introduced at the very beginning of the pericope (Jer 2:2). On another
occasion, Jeremiah represents Israel through the metaphor of sex-crazed
horses (Jer 5:8). At the same time, by referring to the sons of Israel (Jer
5:7) the prophet implicitly addresses his people as a wife who gave YHWH
rebellious children. Furthermore, the characterization of the stallions as
מיזנים משכים (Jer 5:8) introduces a warlike element. While the *qere* מוּזָנִים
is a *hophal* participle of זון ("to feed")—hence the translation "well-fed

horses" (NRSV)—the *ketib* מְיֻזָּנִים is a *pual* participle of יזן ("equipped, supplied"). The term משכים is usually understood as a *hiphil* participle of שכה ("to be mad, lustful"), yet it can also be read as a plural of מֶשְׁכִּי/ מֶשֶׁךְ, ("Meshech"), an Anatolian people who were very well-known as producers of warhorses.[33] The horses are therefore qualified as (military) equipped horses of Meshech (Jer 7:7), *each neighing for his neighbor's wife* (Jer 5:8). Once again, the sexual, animal, martial, and female domains overlap. Something similar happens in the book of Ezekiel, in which Oholah (representing the sanctuaries of the North?) and Oholibah (representing the Jerusalem temple?)[34] are portrayed as unfaithful women lusting after their lovers: Assyrian and Babylonian warriors and horsemen (Ezek 23:5–8). In Ezek 23:20 the prophet describes a sexual scene between Egyptians and Oholibah. The former are described as donkeys and stallions, and the latter is perhaps implicitly portrayed as a mare (Ezek 23:20).

This group of texts suggests that, in the conceptual system of the Hebrew Bible, domains such as WOMAN, WILD/INDOMITABLE ANIMALS, SEX, and WAR are occasionally tied together and blended, so that 1:9 is not to be regarded as made up in a conceptual vacuum. Nevertheless, the differences between 1:9 and the aforementioned prophetic texts by far exceed their similarities. The first, most evident difference concerns the target: while prophetic texts speak in female, animal, and belligerent terms about Israel, Song 1:9 targets a woman. More importantly, whereas the prophets employ the domains WOMAN, WILD/INDOMITABLE ANIMALS, SEX, and WAR to describe Israel's unfaithfulness, vilifying female sexual desire as LUSTFUL and UNRELIABLE, Song 1:9 enthusiastically lauds the woman's sensuality. Consequently, the metaphor of the military mare in 1:9 emerges as unique in the Hebrew Bible both linguistically and conceptually. By introducing a new metaphor and a new conceptualization of the woman, not only does it enrich the figurative language of the Hebrew Bible, but it also introduces positive and challenging ideas about the woman's beauty and eros.

Although the representation of a woman as mare never occurs either in the rest of the Song or in the Hebrew Bible, it is found in the poem's cog-

---

33. William L. Holladay, *Jeremiah 1: A Commentary on the Book of the Prophet Jeremiah, Chapters 1–25*, Hermeneia (Philadelphia: Fortress, 1986), 181.

34. On the controversial interpretation of Oholah and Oholibah, see Moshe Greenberg, *Ezekiel 21–37: A New Translation with Introduction and Commentary*, AB 22A (New York: Doubleday, 1997), 474–75.

nate literature. The portrayal of the woman in 1:9 might recall the image of some armed goddesses well attested in the ancient Near East.[35] For example, in Canaanite mythological texts from Ugarit, the goddess Anat is described as a tremendous, bloodthirsty female warrior. She is also present in Egyptian literary and iconographic representations.[36] Such a scary, cruel warrior, who in Johannes Cornelis de Moor's view was also the beautiful goddess of love and fertility, had incredible power, prestige, and independence within the Ugaritic pantheon.[37] Whereas one would expect Anat to be subservient to a male divinity in the androcentric mythology of the ancient Near East, in the Baal Cycle she is portrayed as a "virgin warrior" fighting against and defeating male gods such as Yam-Nahar (*KTU* 1.1–2), Mot (*KTU* 1.5–6), and even El (*KTU* 1.3–4). As David West and Izak Cornelius demonstrate, Anat and other armed goddesses were often portrayed on horseback, enhancing their belligerent, menacing depictions.[38] Furthermore, the Myth of Shapsh and the Mare presents a goddess-mare,[39] invoking all the deities to deal with her foal beaten by a snake (*KTU* 1.100). In ancient Near Eastern imagery, combining the domains LOVE (Anat was also the goddess of love and fertility),[40] WAR, HORSES, and WOMAN was not uncommon. Song 1:9 and its representation of the woman as a mili-

---

35. Izak Cornelius, *The Many Faces of the Goddess: The Iconography of the Syro-Palestinian Goddesses Anat, Astarte, Qedeshet, and Asherah c. 1500–1000 BCE*, OBO 204 (Fribourg: Academic Press, 2008), 1–4.

36. Arvid S. Kapelrud, *The Violent Goddess: Anat in the Ras Shamra Texts*, SUB (Oslo: Universitetsførlaget, 1969); Peggy L. Day, "Why Is Anat a Warrior and Hunter?," in *The Bible and the Politics of Exegesis: Essays in Honor of Norman K. Gottwald on His Sixty-Fifth Birthday*, ed. David Jobling (Cleveland: Pilgrim, 1991), 141–46; Day, "Anat: 'Ugarit's Mistress of Animals,'" *JNES* 51 (1992): 181–90; Neal H. Walls, *The Goddess Anat in Ugaritic Myth*, SBLDS 135 (Atlanta: Scholars Press, 1992).

37. Johannes Cornelis de Moor, *An Anthology of Religious Texts from Ugarit* (Leiden: Brill, 1987), 198; Walls, *Goddess Anat*, 77–112.

38. David R. West, *Some Cults of Greek Goddesses and Female Daemons of Oriental Origin: Especially in Relation to the Mythology of Goddesses and Daemons in the Semitic World*, AOAT 233 (Kevelaer: Butzon & Bercker, 1995), 116–23; Cornelius, *Many Faces of the Goddess*, 40–44.

39. Baruch A. Levine and Jean-Michel de Tarragon, "'Shapshu Cries Out in Heaven': Dealing with Snake-Bites at Ugarit (KTU 1.100, 1.107)," *RB* 95 (1988): 481–518. The identification of the mare with a goddess is, however, debated: Theodor H. Gaster, "Sharper than a Serpent's Tooth: A Canaanite Charm against Snakebite," *JANES* 7 (1975): 33–51.

40. De Moor, *Anthology of Religious Texts*, 198.

tary mare, therefore, fits into the broad conceptual universe of its *Umwelt*. Nevertheless, all these texts are myths about gods and goddesses, and they never employ the aforementioned domains to describe the desire between human men and women. Song 1:9 is therefore more different from than similar to this group of texts.

Egyptian love poems contain references to horses within the context of human love, describing the man's desire rather than the woman's. For example, the girl incites her beloved to reach her as soon as possible by using the metaphor of a military horse in battle: "Hasten to see your sister, like a horse (dashing) [onto a battle] field."[41] A similar image is found on another occasion:

> If only you would come to (your) sister swiftly ...
> All the (steeds of) the stables are harnessed for him,
> While he has horses (waiting) at the rest stations,
> A chariot is harnessed in its place—
> no respite for him on the way! ...
> If only you would come to your sister swiftly,
> Like a royal horse,
> The choicest of a thousand among all the steeds,
> the foremost of the stables.[42]

Finally, the fragment Deir el-Medineh 1078 is also worth mentioning, since it is the only case in which the domain HORSE is perhaps used with reference to a woman: "(I) will take/my horse/before the wind/in her love." It is actually unclear whether this line refers to the man's "hurry," as in the previous texts, or whether the expression "my horse" metaphorically refers to the man's beloved.[43] Even in the latter reading, the text would still provide a very different characterization of the woman from the one in 1:9. The Egyptian line describes the man's sexual desire in terms of a stallion that wants to take a mare and, therefore, represents the woman as a yearned-for and passive object of desire. Song 1:9 reverses the chase, since here it is the woman who seems about "to dash" toward her beloved.

Despite the fact that Greek literature falls outside the investigation of this book, it is worth mentioning here, since Greek literature makes ample use of

---

41. P.Harr. 500, A.2 (Fox, *Song of Songs*, 8).

42. P.Beatty 1.B.38–39 (Fox, *Song of Songs*, 66).

43. DM 1078, recto (Fox, *Song of Songs*, 79).

this motif. Sappho's famous line already makes it clear that the domains WAR and MILITARY CAVALRY considerably shaped the Greek concept of beauty:

Οἱ μὲν ἰππήων στρότον οἱ δὲ πέσδων
οἱ δὲ νάων φαῖσ' ἐπ[ὶ] γᾶν μέλαιναν
ἔ]μμεναι κάλλιστον ἔγω δὲ κῆν' ὅτ-
τω τὶς ἔπαται.
πά]γχυ δ' εὔμαρες σύνετον πόησαι
πά]ντι τ[ο]ῦτ', ἀ γὰρ πόλυ περσκόπεισα
κάλλος [ἀνθ]ρώπων Ἐλένα [τὸ]ν ἄνδρα
[τὸν [πανάρ]ιστον.

Some say a host of cavalry, others of infantry,
and others of ships, is the most beautiful thing on the black earth,
but I say it is whatsoever a person loves.
It is perfectly easy to make this understood by everyone:
for she who far surpassed mankind in beauty,
Helen, left her most noble husband. (*Frag.* 16 [Campbell])

Although this image of military cavalry does not describe Helen but justifies her decision to follow Paris, the poet refers rhetorically to a host of cavalry as a literary trope of one of the most beautiful sights. The match between "horse" and "woman" occurs especially in lyric poetry, from the seventh to fifth centuries BCE, but also in later authors.[44] Alcman used equestrian images in the longest and most famous of his fragments, the so-called *First Partheneion* or *Louvre-Partheneion* (*PMG* 1.40–60). The poem starts with a war, telling a myth about the local heroes and warriors called Hippokoöntidai. It continues by praising two women, Agido and Hagesichora, who run side by side like the best two horses, the Kolaxaian and the Ibenian. The equine metaphor emphasizes Agido's and Hagesichora's beauty, presented as outstanding and highly distinguished among women. By drawing on the domain HORSE RACE, the equine metaphor points out that nobody can be compared to Agido and Hagesichora.[45] While Alcman

---

44. Antonio Sestili, *Cavalli e cavalieri nell poesia greca dall'arcaismo al tardo antico*, vol. 2 of *L'equitazione nella Grecia antica* (Roma: Aracne, 2008), 21–22; Eva Stehle, "Greek Lyric and Gender," in *The Cambridge Companion to Greek Lyric*, ed. Felix Budelmann, CCL (Cambridge: Cambridge University Press, 2009), 58–71.

45. Diskin Clay, "Alcman's 'Partheneion,'" *QUCC* 39 (1991): 47–67; Emmet I. Robbins, "Alcman's Partheneion: Legend and Choral Ceremony," *ClQ* 44 (1994): 7–16.

celebrates women in comparing them to horses, the metaphor assumes negative connotations in Simonides's misogynistic satire (Semonides, *Frag.* 7). Here the poet composes a list of ten different categories of women, the eighth of which is the woman-horse,[46] a caricature of what the author considers "typical female flaws." While the horse-woman is attractive, she is also selfish, lazy, and, since she is only concerned with her beauty, abhorrent in her domestic duties. According to Phocylides, however, the horse-woman is the most beautiful, lively, and energetic one.[47] Beauty is also connected to equestrian imagery in one of Theognis's quatrains, in which a female voice praises herself as "beautiful and victorious," complaining about her rider—her husband whom she would like to unsaddle (*Eleg.* 257–60 [Gerber]). However, it is not very clear whether the image celebrates or ridicules both the woman and her husband.

In Anacreon's papyrus fragments, the metaphor of a woman as a horse appears twice. First, the poet addresses the beautiful Herotima, who "escaped to the fields of hyacinth, where Cyprian Aphrodite tied her horses freed from the yoke" (Anacreon, *Frag.* 346, P.Oxy. 2321 [Campbell]). The image seems to evoke the freedom of love but also the power of passion and apparently recalls Hector's military ardor portrayed by Homer as a stallion moving toward the pasture of horses (*Il.* 15).[48] Second, in a fragment referring to Anacreon's pain of love for an elusive woman, Heraclitus quotes Anacreon's words against his beloved for stubbornly fleeing from him like a Thracian filly. Ironically, the author asserts that he would surely be able to bridle and ride her.[49] The comparison of women to horses also occurs in the *Hippolytus* and in the *Bacchae* by Euripides (*Hipp.* 545; *Bacch.* 1056), in which unmarried women are presented as horses free from any harness. While for Euripides the equestrian image

---

46. Hugh Lloyd-Jones, ed., *Females of the Species: Simonides on Women* (London: Duckworth, 1975), 78–79; Ezio Pellizer and Gennaro Tedeschi, eds., *Semonide: Introduzione, testimonianze, testo critico, traduzione e commento*, LGE 9 (Roma: Ateneo, 1990), 135–36.

47. Pascale Derron, ed., *Pseudo-Phocylide: Sentences*, CUFSG (Paris: Belles Lettres), vv. 201–4; Martin Litchfield West, "Phocylides," *JHS* 98 (1978): 164–67.

48. Gregorio Serrao, "L'ode di Erotima: Da timida fanciulla a donna pubblica (Anacr. fr. 346, 1 P. = 60 Gent.)," *QUCC* 6 (1968): 36–51.

49. "Moreover Anacreon of Teos, abusing the meretricious spirit and arrogance of a haughty woman, used the 'allegory' of a horse to describe her frisky disposition: Thracian filly, why do you look at me from the corner of your eye and flee stubbornly from me, supposing that I have no skill?" (Heraclitus, *Alleg. Hom.* 417 [Campbell]).

seems to suggest the positive concepts of FREEDOM and RELEASE, for Eubulus it evokes concepts such as WANTONNESS and SEXUAL FRIVOLITY, and it mainly becomes an appellative for hetaerae (*Frag.* 84.2). Interesting enough, in the *Alphabetical Collection of All Words* by Hesychius, the word πῶλος ("filly") is labeled "prostitute."[50] Finally, Theocritus describes Helen's beauty as a Thracian horse (*Id.* 18.26–31). At first glance, the likening of Helen to a horse has the function of underlying the woman's attractiveness. The poet, however, might be subtly referring to the aforementioned subversive tradition of using equestrian imagery to represent a dangerous, unreliable woman. Nicholas Lane suggests that Theocritus's equine metaphor might express a subtle judgment on the woman: (1) in Theocritus's time, the representation of women as horses had become very popular as a way of indicating lecherous women; (2) Helen was condemned by many poets and writers because of her adultery; and (3) Helen's beauty was the cause of Menelaus's problems.[51] The interpretation of Theocritus's intention in *Id.* 18 is, however, debated. According to Ilaria Dagnini, for instance, the Greek author recalls Sappho, who celebrated Helen as a divinity.[52] The general positive tone in Theocritus's *Idyll* seems to support Dagnini's interpretation.

In sum, whereas describing a woman as a mare/horse is uncommon in the ancient Near East, Greek literature makes ample use of this motif. In one group of texts this motif praises female beauty, elegance, and freedom (Alcman, Phocylides, Euripides, Theocritus), but in another group of texts it conveys negative and sarcastic judgments on women's unreliable, stubborn behavior and lascivious sexuality (Simonides, Theognis, Anacreon, Eubulus, Hesychius). In Song 1:9, the image conveys the idea of a woman's sexuality as active and even dominant within the context of the lovers' games of seduction, without any hint of judgment. Song 1:9 is a significant metaphor that should be regarded as both in keeping with the Song's milieu and the creative result of the text's poetic genius. Despite some undeniable connections with the conceptual universe of the poem's *Umwelt* and cognate literature, Song 1:9 presents novel aesthetic and con-

---

50. Peter Allan Hansen and Kurt Latte, eds., *Hesychii Alexandrini Lexicon*, vol. 3, Π–Σ, SGLG 11/3 (Berlin: de Gruyter, 2005).

51. Nicholas Lane, "Some Illusive Puns in Theocritus, Idyll 18 Gow," *QUCC* 83 (2006): 23–26.

52. Ilaria Dagnini, "Elementi saffici e motivi tradizionali in Teocrito, Idillio XVIII," *QUCC* 24 (1986): 39–46.

ceptual aspects, enriching not only the figurative language but also the concept of woman in Israel's milieu.

4.2. The Extolled Heroine (Song 7:1)

SONG 7:1[53]

Come back, come back,[54] O Shulammite,	שובי שובי השולמית
Come back, come back, that we may admire[55] you!	שובי שובי ונחזה־בך
Why[56] do you want to admire the Shulammite	מה־תחזו בשולמית
like the dance of the two camps!	כמחלת המחנים

---

53. The identification of the speakers in 7:1 is difficult, for the text provides little information. The question in 7:1ab and the reply in 7:1cd only suggest a dialogue between two (groups of) speakers. The use of the first-person plural in 7:1a (נחזה) suggests that 7:1ab is spoken by a group of persons. All we can say is that the second masculine person of the verb חזה (תחזו) in 7:1c suggests that 7:1ab is spoken by either a group of men (one of whom could be the woman's lover) or a group in which there are men. As for the speakers in 7:1cd, it might be spoken either by the man or the woman, or a female chorus, or a male chorus. Since the text does not provide clear indications, and there are no conclusive arguments to settle the question, I consider the entire verse as an antiphonal exchange between a first group that includes men (7:1ab), and a second, nonspecified group (7:1cd).

54. שובי שובי. Many modern translations understand these imperatives as invitations to turn around, facing the speakers, rather than invitations to turn back (e.g., Barbiero, *Song of Songs*, 362–67). The objection to the translation "turn back" relies on the fact that nothing in the context suggests that the woman has gone somewhere. Nevertheless, I prefer the translation "turn back"—which also implies the invitation to turn around—because this is the most common meaning of the *qal* form of the verb שוב in biblical texts. See Alfred Jepsen, "חָזָה," *ThWAT* 2:822–35. The lack of narrative coherence is not a real issue, the Song is not a story. As Assis puts it, "In poetry it is not the event that is at the centre of interest, but the feeling it inspires" (*Flashes of Fire*, 206).

55. It is well known that the verb חזה does not simply indicate "to see," but rather "to observe," "to look upon," "to gaze," "to have visions." I translate it as "to admire," due to the subsequent preposition ב (בשולמית/בך). In the vast majority of its occurrences, the verb חזה is followed by the direct object without a preposition. Outside the Song, חזה is followed by the preposition ב only on four occasions, describing the action of beholding the creation (Job 36:25), or the beauty of YHWH in the temple (Ps 27:4), or the stars of the sky (Isa 47:13), or the destruction of Jerusalem, which gives pleasure to the nations assembled against Israel (Mic 4:11). The construction חזה + ב implies the experience of contemplating and finding inner gratification in what is seen. Hence, my translation is "to admire," which belongs to the conceptual domain of eyesight (Latin *admirare*) and conveys the idea of enjoying and marveling at the object.

56. The interrogative pronoun מה occurs in the Song with different meanings,

Even though scholars usually agree on the presence of a military scenario in 7:1, both the details and the overall meaning of this verse remain obscure.

As Murphy argues, the meaning of the simile מחלת המחנים ("dance of the two camps") is unclear: the expression might refer to something popular to the poem's audience but unknown to the modern reader.[57] The obscurity of the simile, however, is not the only problem in 7:1. There is a widespread uncertainty about who speaks this verse. In addition, both prepositions מה (מה-תחזו בשולמית) and כ (כמחלת המחנים) can be understood and translated in different ways, profoundly affecting the interpretation of the entire verse. Further, the elusive meaning of the appellative שולמית compounds the difficulties of interpreting 7:1.

There are three major trends among the many interpretations of this verse. One group of scholars argues that the simile compares looking on the woman to looking on a military dance (e.g., Murphy) or to looking on two armies battling with each other (e.g., Longman).[58] A second group, however, suggests that the simile implies a rebuke. For instance, Fox contends that 7:1 rebukes those who look at the woman "disdainfully as if she were a common dancer who roams the camps of the soldier."[59] Finally, according to other exegetes, the speaker portrays the woman performing a dance in front of her onlookers.[60]

As I will better explain below, I suggest reading the simile כמחלת המחנים not as an *Objektvergleich*, but rather as a *Subjektvergleich*. In other words, the target of the simile is neither the act of admiring nor the Shulammite (the chorus admires *the Shulammite* the way it admires *a military dance*) but the chorus itself (the *chorus* admires the Shulammite the way *dancers* admire the hero in a military dance). In my view, Song 7:1 recalls some well-known biblical scenes in which military dances extol the victorious hero returning home from war. In so doing, Song 7:1 represents the Shulammite not as a dancer but as the victorious heroine of the lovers' war games.

---

such as "what?" (5:8, 9; 8:8), "how ... !" (4:10; 7:2, 7), and "why?" (8:4). The translation mainly depends on the overall understanding of the verse.

57. Murphy, *Song of Songs*, 181.

58. E.g., Murphy, *Song of Songs*, 185; Longman, *Song of Songs*, 191–93.

59. Fox, *Song of Songs*, 158. Likewise, Munro argues that, out of jealousy, the beloved man urges a group of men not to look at his lover the way they look at female dancers at public celebrations of military victory (*Spikenard and Saffron*, 31). Keel also supports the idea "these lines indignantly reject the request to make Shulammite the object of voyeurism" (*Song of Songs*, 229).

60. E.g., Barbiero, *Song of Songs*, 363–67.

4.2.1. The Syntax of the Simile כמחלת המחנים: A New Proposal

On the clause level, the main peculiarity of 7:1 consists in the relationship between the predicate תחזו and the prepositional phrase כמחלת המחנים. Much of the interpretation of the entire verse depends on how we understand this construction.

That כמחלת המחנים + תחזו is particularly problematic emerges from the reading of both ancient and modern witnesses and translations. Besides the fact that several manuscripts read ב instead of כ (see *BHQ* and *BHS*), the LXX rendered the phrase as "going like choral dances of camps" (ἡ ἐρχομένη ὡς χοροὶ τῶν παρεμβολῶν), suggesting that the woman is performing a sort of dance. Among current interpretations, a group of scholars suggest that the preposition כ has an asseverative function, introducing a second, independent clause. Gordis, for instance, translates: "[What will you see in the maid of Shulem?] *Indeed*, the counter-dance!"[61] More recently, Barbiero has translated as follows: "[What do you want to admire in the Shulamite?] *What a question*: the dance of the two camps."[62] A second group of scholars renders the preposition כ as "in/during," either relying on the aforementioned textual variant ב (e.g., Bloch and Bloch) or attributing a temporal value to the preposition כ (e.g., Pope).[63] Alter, for instance, translates: "[Why should you behold the Shulammite] *in* the dance of the double rows?"[64] The author comments, "The choreography is beyond retrieval, but one may imagine two rows of dancers with the Shulamite as the star performer moving between them. The two rows may even be two choruses."[65] More widespread, however, is the solution adopted by a third group of modern translators and commentators, who read the preposition כ according to its most common meaning, that is, "like/as."[66] The NRSV, for instance, translates: "[Why should you look upon the Shulammite,] *as* upon a dance before two armies?" In this latter

---

61. Gordis, *Song of Songs*, 68, emphasis added.

62. Barbiero, *Song of Songs*, 319, emphasis added.

63. Bloch and Bloch, *Song of Songs*, 199–200; Pope, *Song of Songs*, 601.

64. Alter, *Writings*, 609, emphasis added.

65. Alter, *Writings*, 609. A similar interpretation can be found in Athalya Brenner, "'Come Back, Come Back the Shulammite' (Song of Songs 7:1–10): A Parody of the *waṣf* Genre," in *On Humour and the Comic in the Hebrew Bible*, ed. Yehuda T. Radday and Athalya Brenner, JSOTSup 92 (Sheffield: Almond, 1990), 251–75.

66. E.g., Longman, *Song of Songs*, 189; Exum, *Song of Songs*, 211.

view, the general meaning of the sentence is that looking on the woman is compared to looking on the enigmatic "dance before two armies" or "dance of the two camps."

All these interpretations are certainly legitimate attempts to understand an objectively difficult verse. Nevertheless, they all contain some drawbacks. First, despite the fact that in Biblical Hebrew the preposition כ might also have an asseverative function, in the Song it always introduces similes (Song 1:5, 7; 2:2; 3:4, 6; 4:1, 11; 5:11, 15; 6:4, 10; 7:1, 4, 9; 8:1, 6, 10).[67] Second, reading ב instead of כ relies on the *lectio facilior* provided by only a few manuscripts. The comparative interpretation of the phrase, therefore, is to be preferred, since it is more strongly grounded in both the Song's use of the preposition כ and the textual tradition. Nevertheless, scholars' interpretation and translation of the clause as "Why should you look upon the Shulammite like *upon* the dance of the two camps" is not the only possible solution, and perhaps it is not the best option either.

Translating "like *upon* the dance of the two camps" implies the ellipsis of the preposition ב in כמחלת and the phenomenon of the so-called double-duty preposition: in other words, according to this interpretation, the preposition ב in 7:1c (מה־תחזו בשולמית) is to be understood in the parallel 7:1d (כ[ב]מחלת המחנים). This phenomenon certainly occurs in the Hebrew Bible.[68] Nevertheless, Cynthia Miller's recent research has convincingly shown that the ellipsis of the bare preposition is not very widespread in Biblical Hebrew poetry.[69] When the ellipsis of the bare preposition does occur, it requires three specific syntactic configurations:

---

67. The exception is כמעט ("like a little") in 3:4, which is probably to be read as an adverb ("hardly, barely").

68. Mitchell Dahood, *Ugaritic-Hebrew Philology: Marginal Notes on Recent Publications*, BibOr 17 (Rome: Pontifical Biblical Institute, 1967), §13.44a.

69. Cynthia L. Miller, "A Reconsideration of 'Double-Duty' Prepositions in Biblical Poetry," *JANES* 31 (2008): 99–110; Miller, "A Linguistic Approach to Ellipsis in Biblical Poetry; Or, What to Do When Exegesis of What Is There Depends upon What Isn't," *BBR* 13 (2003): 251–70; Miller, "Ellipsis Involving Negation in Biblical Poetry," in *Seeking Out the Wisdom of the Ancients: Essays Offered to Honor Michael V. Fox on the Occasion of His Sixty-Fifth Birthday*, ed. Ronald L. Troxel, Kelvin G. Friebel, and Dennis R. Magary (Winona Lake, IN: Eisenbrauns, 2005), 37–52; Miller, "Constraints on Ellipsis in Biblical Hebrew," in *Studies in Comparative Semitic and Afroasiatic Linguistics Presented to Gene B. Gragg*, ed. Cynthia L. Miller, SAOC 60 (Chicago: University of Chicago Press, 2007), 165–80.

(1) "In the first configuration, a preposition that is the head of a preposition predicate elides forwards from the initial periphery of the clause."[70] An example:

ISAIAH 15:8
As far as Eglaim (is) her cry
and [as far as] Beer Elim (is) her cry

עד־אגלים יללתה
ובאר אילים יללתה

(2) "In the second syntactic configuration, the verb היה or a nominal predicate is deleted from the initial periphery of the clause. The preposition that immediately follows is also deleted."[71] For example:

ISAIAH 42:22
They have become plunder and no one rescues;
[they have become] spoil and no one says, "Restore!"

היו לבז ואין מציל
משסה ואין־אמר השב

(3) "In the third configuration, the preposition that is deleted is not immediately adjacent to the deleted verb."[72] An example:

ISAIAH 28:5–6
In that day, the LORD of hosts will be
(ל) a crown of beauty and (ל) a diadem of glory (ל)
for the remnant of his people
and [the LORD of hosts will be] (ל) a spirit of justice
(ל) for the one who sits in judgment,
and [the LORD of hosts will be] (ל) strength
[for] those who turn back battle at the gate.

ביום ההוא יהיה יהוה צבאות
לעטרת צבי ולצפירת תפארה
לשאר עמו
ולרוח משפט
ליושב על־המשפט
ולגבורה
משיבי מלחמה שערה

Song 7:1 does not present any of these three syntactic contexts. In addition, there is no actual need for a hypothetical ellipsis in כמחלת המחנים. If we read the text as it is, Song 7:1 is not saying, "Why do you want *to admire/look upon* the Shulammite like you *admire/look upon* the dance of the two camps" (*Objektvergleich*) but rather, "Why do you want *to admire/look upon* the Shulammite like the dance of the two camps *does* (*Subjektvergleich*)."

---

70. All following examples are provided by Miller, "Reconsideration of 'Double-Duty' Prepositions," 107.

71. Miller, "Reconsideration of 'Double-Duty' Prepositions," 107–8.

72. Miller, "Reconsideration of 'Double-Duty' Prepositions," 108–9.

4.2.2. The Conceptual Density of a Poetic Metaphor

In order to better understand the meaning of 7:1, a semantic/conceptual analysis of both the appellative השולמית and the phrase מחלת המחנים is required.

The appellative שולמית seems to many a variant of שונמית ("Shunammite"), indicating a woman from the town of Shunem and used to designate Abishag, the beautiful woman chosen to warm up David's bed at the end of his life (1 Kgs 1:3, 15; 2:17, 21, 22).[73] According to Carl Budde, Abishag became legendary for her beauty to such an extent that the appellative "the Shunammite" became a synonym of "the beautiful woman par excellence."[74] More recently, André LaCocque argued that "The Shulammite [of Song 7:1] is the anti-Shunammite! While the latter [i.e., Abishag] was a passive and reified woman, the former [the Song's woman] is quicksilver, an active subject whose first person pronoun dominates the poem from start to finish."[75] Harold Rowley, however, points out that, besides the fact that there is no record that Abishag ever became the emblem of female beauty in ancient Israel, the connection between the Song's woman and David's lover seems too tenuous.[76] Likewise, Longman wonders "why Abishag should play a role in the Song where … the main players are poetic types and not historical personages."[77]

In my view, the assonance between שולמית and שונמית is too strong to be considered fortuitous. In poetry in general and in oral cultures in particular, sound is not just an accident but often has semantic connotations.[78] The hypothesis that the Song intends to create a pun between שולמית and שונמית, and thereby between the two women, should not be dismissed. This does not necessarily imply either that in ancient Israel Abishag was the emblem of female beauty—which we cannot prove—or that the figure of the Shulammite is constructed ad hoc to subvert the

---

73. An anonymous wealthy woman (אשה גדולה), who gave hospitality to the prophet Elisha, is also called "Shunammite" in 2 Kgs 4:12, 25, 36.

74. Carl F. R. Budde, "Das Hohelied," in *Die fünf Megillot*, ed. Carl F. R. Budde, Alfred Bertholet, and Gerrit Wildeboer, KHC 17 (Freiburg: Mohr Siebeck, 1898), 36.

75. LaCocque, *Romance, She Wrote*, 145–46.

76. Harold H. Rowley, "The Shulammite," *AJSL* 56 (1939): 84–91.

77. Longman, *Song of Songs*, 192.

78. Jonathan G. Kline, *Allusive Soundplay in the Hebrew Bible*, AIL 28 (Atlanta: SBL Press, 2016); Luis Alonso Schökel, *A Manual of Hebrew Poetics*, SubBi 11 (Rome: Pontifical Biblical Institute, 1988), 20–33.

figure of the Shunammite—also difficult to determine—or that Abishag herself plays a role in the Song. More simply, by the word שולמית the Song might simply intend to conjure its audience's literary memory of the שונמית, a woman admired by men for her exceptional beauty. A second possibility is that שולמית (7:1) is the feminine form of שלמה. As Keel puts it: "Understood in this way, the name characterizes the woman as the female counterpart to the legendary Solomon of the Song (cf. 3:7; 8:11)."[79] Here again, the consonance between שולמית and שלמה is too strong to be accidental. Since Solomon is mainly presented as a royal figure in the Song, the epithet "Shulammite" may present her as a queen. Furthermore, both שולמית and שלמה recall שלום and ירושלם, that is, two terms that, besides occurring in the Song, play a crucial role in ancient Israel's imagery and worldview. She is the one who brings and finds peace in 8:10, and the one who is desirable like Jerusalem in 6:4. A third possibility is that the epithet שולמית recalls the Assyrian *šulmānītu*, that is, one of the epithets of Ishtar (the legendary goddess of war and love), who on several occasions is associated with the dance (see *infra*).[80] Ishtar was probably the most famous goddess in ancient Mesopotamia, though whether and on which occasions the Bible mentions Ishtar is doubtful. Ishtar, however, was certainly well-known in ancient Israel.[81] Furthermore, that Ishtar was the goddess of love and war, and that she is often connected with military dances, makes this proposal cohere with both 7:1 and the Song's warlike imagery. Contrary to Longman,[82] the persuasiveness of the connection between שולמית and *šulmānītu* does not depend on whether we have a cultic approach to the book, but rather on whether we want to recognize that in Biblical Hebrew poetry sound is semantically relevant. Instead of choosing among these possibilities, it seems more appropriate to consider that multiple meanings are conveyed by the lexeme שולמית. The sound of the lexeme שולמית blends and condenses

79. Keel, *Song of Songs*, 228. See also Edgar J. Goodspeed, "The Shulammite," *AJSL* 50 (1934): 102–4.

80. William F. Albright, *Yahweh and the Gods of Canaan: A Historical Analysis of Two Contrasting Faiths*, JLCR 7 (London: Athlone, 1968), 150; Albright, "The Syro-Mesopotamian God Šulmân-Ešmûn and Related Figures," *AfO* 7 (1931–1932): 164–69; Lys, *Le plus beau chant de la création*, 251.

81. Susan Ackerman, *Under Every Green Tree: Popular Religion in Sixth-Century Judah*, HSM 46 (Atlanta: Scholars Press, 1992), 32–34; 79–93; William J. Fulco, "Ishtar," *ABD* 3:521–22.

82. Longman, *Song of Songs*, 192.

more concepts simultaneously, such as BEAUTY (by evoking Abishag), DESIRABILITY (by evoking Jerusalem, used as a simile in 6:4), WAR and LOVE (by evoking Ishtar), ROYALTY (by evoking Solomon), and PEACE and WHOLENESS (by evoking שלום). Since the Song's woman embodies all these qualities at the same time, she can only be the center of everybody's attention and admiration.

The phrase מחלת המחנים is equally problematic. The Hebrew Bible contains several references to the practice of dance, but the syntagma מחלת המחנים only occurs in the Song, making the meaning of this expression particularly obscure and the entire utterance difficult to understand. The meaning of both מחלת המחנים and 7:1 as a whole, however, becomes much clearer when we consider the other occurrences of the lexeme מחלה, the basic meaning of the lexeme מחנים, and the biblical references to military dances. The Hebrew Bible contains a cluster of different verbs and dance-derived expressions referring to the act of dancing: that is, דלג, רקד, סבב, חגג (in the *piel* form), כרר (in the *piel* form), פזז (in the *piel* form), פסח (in the *piel* form), and שחק (in the *piel* form).[83] The lexeme מחלה, and its masculine form מחול, however, are the most used terms for "dance" (Exod 15:20; 32:19; Judg 11:34; 21:21; 1 Sam 18:6; 21:12; 29:5; Jer 31:4, 13; Pss 30:12; 149:3; 150:4; Lam 5:15). Whereas the different dance-derived expressions in the Hebrew Bible refer to either cultic dances or generic expressions of joy, the lexemes מחלה and מחול mostly occur in military contexts. In Exodus, for instance, when the Israelites see that YHWH has brought back the waters of the sea on the Pharaoh's horses and chariots, a chorus of women start playing musical instruments and dancing (Exod 15:20). In the book of Judges, after Jephthah defeats the Ammonites and conquers their cities, he is welcomed by his daughter's dance in Mizpah (Judg 11:34). In the book of Samuel, a chorus of women acclaims Saul and David after a famous military feat (1 Sam 18:6; 21:12; 29:5). The mention of the dance also relates to war in Ps 149:3–4. When we read Ps 149:5–9, it becomes clear that the military supremacy of Israel is the reason for praising YHWH. Likewise, the dance mentioned in Jer

---

83. Mayer I. Gruber, "Ten Dance-Derived Expressions in the Hebrew Bible," *Bib* 62 (1981): 328–46. See also Dvora Lapson, "Dance," *EncJud* 5:1262–74; William O. E. Oesterley, *The Sacred Dance: A Study in Comparative Folklore* (Cambridge: University Press, 1923); Julian Morgan, "The Etymological History of the Three Hebrew Synonyms for 'To Dance,' HGG, HLL and KRR, and Their Cultural Significance," *JAOS* 36 (1916): 321–32.

31:4, 13 is not a generic expression of joy but a dance following YHWH's military victory, which finally defeats the enemies and brings back the lost wealth. In Lam 5:15 the reference to Israel's dance that has been turned to mourning follows the description of the city devastated by the enemies' military invasion (Lam 5:11–14). Since the lexemes מחלה and מחול usually occur in contexts of war—with only a few exceptions (Exod 32:19; Judg 21:21; Pss 30:12; 150:4)—the chances that a military scenario is also evoked in Song 7:1 are very high. This interpretation becomes more than just a possibility when we consider the following lexeme, מחנים. Whereas it is true that the word מחנה sometimes indicates a temporary residence (e.g., Gen 32:22), it refers to a war camp in the vast majority of its occurrences.[84] The dual form in the Hebrew Bible only refers to a city in Gad (Gen 32:3; Josh 13:26; 21:38; 2 Sam 2:8–9; 17:24), which plays no role in the Song. Hence, the suggested translation "the dance of Mahnaim" makes no sense—and also the use of the determinate article before the name of a city in 7:1 (המחנים) makes a reference to the supposed city of Mahnaim highly improbable.[85] More likely, in 7:1 the syntagma מחלת המחנים refers to a military dance performed in two rows or circles of dancers.

Many scholars argue that 7:1 portrays the woman dancing, but Exum is correct when she states, "Nothing in the following description of the woman indicates that she is dancing or that a group of people is watching her dance."[86] The Shulammite might be dancing, but this does not seem to be the main point in 7:1. What the text does emphasize is that there are two rows of dancers admiring and extoling the Shulammite through a military dance. These two rows of dancers might be moving in circle (as the root חול would suggest) and might even be encircling the woman. The question then arises as to what such a scene represents.

Here, the category of cognitive scenarios might be very helpful. A cognitive scenario is a conceptual schema with which the mind represents human experience. The exposure to recurrent experiences creates a conceptual frame in the human mind, which allows the individual to recognize, interpret, and interact with new, similar experiences. For instance, the recurrent experience of having dinner in a restaurant creates the conceptual schema "restaurant" that heuristically functions as a script. We

---

84. Tremper Longman, "מַחֲנֶה," *NIDOTTE* 2:918–19.
85. *Pace* Luzarraga, *Cantar de los Cantares*, 490–95.
86. Exum, *Song of Songs*, 225.

know what a restaurant is and what it is not. We know how to behave and what our expectations should be. We can interpret and understand what happens around us and how to react.[87] Cognitive poetics argues that literary texts are also made of literary cognitive scenarios, conceptual patterns or scripts, shared by the text and the reader, that make the understanding of a text possible.[88] The conceptual pattern "love story," for instance, has peculiar characteristics that allow the reader to understand the text as being about romantic love and thus to have specific expectations about the story.[89] It goes without saying that different literary traditions may have different cognitive scenarios. The way a text uses a cognitive script may either confirm readers' schemas by presenting a faithful version of the script, or challenge readers' schemas by presenting a different version of the script, with changes such as new content, new language, or new style. In the latter case, the text forces readers to reorganize their script. In order to cause a reassessment of the cognitive scenario, the text must provide readers with two crucial elements. First, the text needs to provide a scenario that is sufficiently similar to the script; otherwise, readers would not be able even to recognize the script. Second, the text needs to be clearly different from the script; otherwise, readers would not be able to understand the challenge and refresh their script.

Song 7:1 recalls a well-established cognitive script in the biblical tradition, which might be labeled "dance after a war" (1 Sam 18:6–7; 2 Sam 1:20; 6:20; see also Exod 15:20–21; Judg 9:34). Sonnet considers the dance after a war one of the many "type scenes" of biblical literature.[90] Cognitive

---

87. Croft and Cruse, *Cognitive Linguistics*, 7.

88. Peter Stockwell, *Cognitive Poetics: An Introduction* (London: Routledge, 2002), 75–90. Note that the expressions "cognitive scenarios," "conceptual patterns," and "scripts" are quite interchangeable in cognitive poetics.

89. Gerard J. Steen, "Love Stories: Cognitive Scenarios in Love Poetry," in *Cognitive Poetics in Practice*, ed. Joanna Gavins and Gerard Steen (London: Routledge, 2003), 67–82.

90. Jean-Pierre Sonnet, "L'analyse narrative des récits bibliques," in *Manuel d'exégèse de l'Ancien Testament*, ed. Michaela Bauks and Christophe Nihan, MdB 61 (Labor et Fides: Genève 2008), 86–87. See also Laura Invernizzi, "La mano, il tamburello, la danza delle donne: La 'scena-tipo' del canto di vittoria," in *Extra ironiam nulla salus: Studi in onore di Roberto Vignolo in occasione del suo LXX compleanno*, ed. Matteo Crimella, Giovanni C. Pagazzi, and Stefano Romanello, Biblica 8 (Glossa: Milano 2016), 73–99; Josselin Roux, "La danse de la fille de Jephté (Jg 11, 29–40) ou l'enfantement de la vengeance," *SemCl* 5 (2012): 29–42; Roux, "La danse de la prophé-

script and type scenes, however, are not exactly the same thing. Whereas a type scene is a literary construction, a cognitive script is something more, insofar as a cognitive script is not only a literary property of the text, but also a conceptual scheme that both the text and the reader share and that is embedded in the reader's experience. The biblical cognitive script "dance after a war" contains the following basic elements: (1) a war, (2) a victorious warrior, (3) a chorus of women welcoming and admiring the victorious warrior, and (4) a dance performed by the chorus. Another element often present is that the dance is performed at the warrior's arrival, whether he returns to his place or enters the place he has conquered (Judg 11:34; 1 Sam 18:6; Jdt 3:7; 15:12–13). All these elements are present in 7:1, in which we find (1) a war scenario, suggested by the military connotation of the dance (מחלת המחנים) as well as by the previous warlike image in 6:12; (2) an admiring chorus, as the antiphonal exchange makes clear; and (3) a dance (מחלת המחנים). Furthermore, the insistent request "Return! Return!" might be explained as the text's attempt to follow the script: the victorious hero needs to return to be admired. But who is the hero? Since in 7:1 the center of admiration is the Shulammite, she is obviously the one who plays the role of the victorious hero. Therefore, the scene in 7:1 differs crucially from the recalled script: whereas in the script "dance after a war" a group of women admire a man (the hero), in 7:1 a group of men or, at the very least, including men, admire a woman (the heroine). In so doing, the Song attentively observes and profoundly rewrites the reader's script.

That a woman is the extolled heroine is not unique to the Song, since we find the same reversal in the deuterocanonical book of Judith. While in Jdt 3:7 Holophernes is welcomed "with garlands and dances and tambourines," in 15:12 the celebrated hero is Judith, who replaces the defeated Holophernes: "All the women of Israel gathered to see her, and bless her, and some of them performed a dance in her honour." Both the Shulammite and Judith, therefore, break the script, insofar as they occupy a role that, according to the script, belongs to male heroes.

---

tesse Miryam (Exode 15,20–21)," in *Présence de la danse dans l'antiquité, présence de l'antiquité dans la danse: Actes du colloque tenu à Clermont-Ferrand (11–13 Décembre 2008)*, ed. Rémy Poignault, Caesarodunum 42–43 (Paris: Centre de Recherches A. Piganiol, 2013), 15–33.

4.2.3. Who (This Time) Conquers Whom

As part of the seventh literary unit of the poem, Song 7:1 interrupts the man's discourse (6:4–10, 11–12), which continues immediately after (7:2–10a) and ends with the woman's final words (7:10b–11). The warlike imagery in 7:1 perfectly fits into the seventh literary unit since, on the one hand, it continues and develops the military imagery of the previous verses, and, on the other hand, it is coherently developed by what follows.

The man has described the woman as "frightening like an army with deployed banners" in 6:4, 10 and has made it clear that the woman has a perturbing effect on him in 6:5 ("Turn away your eyes from me, for they overwhelm me"). Furthermore, the man has described himself as transformed "into the chariots of Amminadib" in 6:12. In other words, not only has the woman's astonishing beauty an overwhelming power over the man, but it also elicits the man's desire to conquer her. Hence, the question arises as to who will, eventually, conquer whom. The chorus speaking in 7:1 seems to carry on the tension created by the previous warlike images and establish the Shulammite as the winner of the lovers' erotic battle. Instead of picturing the man as the male hero acclaimed by a chorus of women—as the biblical script would require—7:1 pictures the woman as the winner of the lovers' war-games: she is the beautiful one, the powerful one, the majestic one, the pacified and the pacifying one. In a word, she is the Shulammite. Not only does 7:1 continue, develop, and conclude the previous warlike imagery but, through a hint of irony, it also nuances the man's perception of his own unstoppable lust. Whereas in 6:12 the man has portrayed himself as a conqueror in the throes of his passion, 7:1 ironically seems to suggest that, no matter how impetuous his longing, the Shulammite is the victor.

The following verses confirm the Shulammite as the winner of the lovers' war-game. Through a cascade of metaphors, 7:2–10a describes the heroine's body from foot to head: she is noble and a masterpiece of beauty, who intoxicates her lover and fills him with abundance of life.[91] Particularly remarkable is the end of the *waṣf*:

SONG 7:5–6
Your neck is like an ivory tower.   צוארך כמגדל השן

---

91. For a detailed explanation of the imagery in 7:2–6, see Barbiero, *Song of Songs*, 367–90.

Your eyes are pools in Hesbon
by the gate of Bath-rabbim.
Your nose is like a tower of Lebanon,
overlooking Damascus.
Your head upon you is like Mount Carmel,
and the locks of your head are purple.
A king is caught in the tresses.[92]

עיניך ברכות בחשבון
על־שער בת־רבים
אפך כמגדל הלבנון
צופה פני דמשק
ראשך עליך ככרמל
ודלת ראשך כארגמן
מלך אסור ברהטים

By recalling the conceptual domain CITY of 6:4 (as well as 4:4 and 8:10), 7:5 emphasizes her magnificence, her unreachability, her being towering and in absolute control of whatever happens around her. Finally, 7:6 confirms and reinforces 7:1 and the idea that she dominates her lover by taking him prisoner. Interestingly, the seventh unit ends with a coda, in which the man is presented as everything but discouraged. Far from withdrawing, he is profoundly delighted by the woman (v. 7), attracted by her magnificence (v. 8), ready to climb on her (v. 9), and ready to be intoxicated by her kisses (v. 10). The way in which the woman takes the words right out of the man's mouth (v. 10b) confirms, on the one hand, that she is the very center of the entire unit and, on the other hand, that there is a profound complicity between the lovers. Finally, the ending formula (v. 11) subtlety makes it clear that the woman is the winner of the lovers' war-game, at least at this stage:

SONG 7:11
I am my beloved's
and on me is his desire

אני לדודי
ועלי תשוקתו

Outside the Song, the lexeme תשוקה only occurs in Gen 3:16 and 4:7:

GENESIS 3:16
To the woman he said, "I will greatly increase your pangs in childbearing; in pain you shall bring forth children, yet your desire shall be for your husband, and he shall rule over you."
אל־האשה אמר הרבה ארבה עצבונך והרנך בעצב תלדי בנים ואל־אישך תשוקתך
והוא ימשל־בך

---

92. The lexeme רהט is notoriously difficult. Outside the Song, it only occurs in Gen 30:38, 41 and Exod 2:16 with the meaning of "troughs," which in Song 7:6 makes no sense. The LXX translates by παραδρομαῖς, "a running beside or over, traversing" (*LSJ*), which suggests that the translator probably understood רהט as deriving from the Aramaic "to flow" (BDB). If this is the case, רהטים might refer to the woman's tresses, evoking the image of running water. The interpretation, however, is dubious.

GENESIS 4:7

If you do well, will you not be accepted? And if you do not do well, sin is lurking at the door; its desire is for you, but you must master it.

הלוא אם־תיטיב שאת ואם לא תיטיב לפתח חטאת רבץ ואליך תשוקתו ואתה תמשל־בו

Note that both in Gen 3:16 and 4:7 the lexeme תשוקה is followed by the verb משל, "to rule/to master." As Barbiero rightly points out, "The rarity and importance of these occurrences renders accidental correspondence improbable."[93] The question, however, arises of how to interpret this intertext. Scholars usually interpret the Song's reference to Genesis as emphasizing the reciprocity of sexual desire in positive terms, in opposition to the woman's submissive condition in Gen 3:16 (e.g., Exum, Barbiero). Several authors have even suggested that Song 7:11 portrays a sort of way back to the lost paradise and a restoration of a more balanced relationship between man and woman.[94] If 7:11 is read in light of the previous warlike imagery, the reference to Genesis might be read as ironic. In light of the previous warlike imagery, Song 7:11 not only represents reciprocity and equality between the lovers, but it might ironically subvert Gen 3:16 by portraying the man's longing (not the woman's) for his lover, while she is actually the one who has conquered him (6:4–5; 7:1; 7:6). Whatever the case might be, Song 7:11 also seems to suggest that the lovers' war-game is about to restart. The celebration of the victorious heroine did not end the lovers' mutual longing. The man is still there, longing for her, over and over again. Who knows who the winner will be next time?

When we consider 7:1 within the rest of poem, the scene of a military dance extolling the victorious heroine coheres with both the other war-like metaphors and similes and the overall characterization of the woman. Both lovers actively play the war-game. The conqueror woman (1:9; 7:1) corresponds to the conqueror man (2:4; 5:10; 6:12). She is not merely the recipient of the man's attentions and the elusive woman who attracts her lover by parrying his advances (4:4). Nor is she only the fulfilling and ful-filled lover (8:10). She is also the winner of the lovers' war-games, namely,

---

93. Barbiero, *Song of Songs*, 403.

94. See, for instance, Paul Beauchamp, *Accomplir les Écritures*, vol. 2 of *L'un et l'autre Testament*, PD 28 (Paris: Seuil, 1990), 186; Phyllis Trible, "Love's Lyric Redeemed," in Brenner, *Feminist Companion to the Song of Songs*, 100–120; Landy, "Song of Songs," 513–28.

the one who seduces, conquers, and takes possession of the man she longs for. The communicative function of 7:1 within the poem's warlike imagery therefore shows a different side of the lovers' war-game, namely, the woman's power to conquer the man.

Furthermore, Song 7:1 recalls a well-established Israelite literary tradition of biblical texts extolling war heroes. Smith has recently argued that literary texts about war, warriors, and war-heroes play an important role in the Hebrew Bible.[95] According to Smith, "The speech acts surrounding warriors and warfare that we see in the Bible … occur over three phases surrounding a battle: pre-battle preparations; post-battle practices; and later commemoration."[96] The role of women in biblical heroic literature is, first and foremost, to praise the male hero and the military victory (Exod 15:20–21; 1 Sam 18:6–7; 2 Sam 1:20; 6:20). Women may even have played a crucial role in the oral production of heroic songs and poems.[97] Furthermore, biblical literature recalls a few women actively involved in military battles, such as Deborah, Jael, the woman of Thebez (Judg 4–8), and Judith in her eponymous deuterocanonical book.[98]

Outside the heroic literature of the Hebrew Bible, the conceptual domain WAR is only used to extol a woman in Prov 31:10–31.[99] Al Wolters

---

95. Smith, *Poetic Heroes*; Smith, "Warfare Song as Warrior Ritual."

96. Smith, "Warfare Song as Warrior Ritual," 168.

97. The text of Ps 68:12, for instance, might allude to the women's role of spreading the good news of military victory (המבשרות צבא רב, "great is the company of the army's messengers [f.]"). So might the text of Isa 40:9, which asks female messengers (מבשרת ירושלם) to announce YHWH's military victory through a series of feminine participles (עלי־לך, "go"; הרימי בכח קולך, "lift up your voice with strength"; הרימי אל־, תיראי אמרי, "lift [it] up, do not fear, say"). See Susan Ackerman, "Otherworldly Music and the Other Sex," in *The "Other" in Second Temple Judaism: Essays in Honor of John J. Collins*, ed. Daniel C. Harlow, Karina Martin Hogan, Matthew Goff, and Joel S. Kaminsky (Grand Rapids: Eerdmans, 2011), 86–100; Carol L. Meyers, "Mother to Muse: An Archaeomusicological Study of Women's Performance in Israel," in *Recycling Biblical Figures: Papers Read at a NOSTER Colloquium in Amsterdam, 12–13 May 1997*, ed. Athalya Brenner and J. Willem van Henten, STR 1 (Leiden: Deo, 1999), 50–77.

98. Susan Ackerman, *Warrior, Dancer, Seductress, Queen: Women in Judges and Biblical Israel*, ABRL (New York: Doubleday, 1998), 28–51; Gale A. Yee, "By the Hand of a Woman," *Semeia* 61 (1993): 99–132.

99. Zakovitch has recently argued that Prov 31:10–31 is a polemic against the Song. He argues, "The poet who composed 'A Woman of Valor' sought to replace the paragon of femininity in Song of Songs with a different female ideal: instead of the clever, active, and bold woman who is not confined by conventions, the physically

points out that this so-called song of the valiant woman contains several military expressions describing the אשת־חיל ("woman of strength"; Prov 31:10).[100] Despite the fact that Wolters's classification of Prov 31:10–31 as "heroic hymn" finds little grounding in the text, and Prov 31:10–31 contains fewer military terms than the author assumes, the employed imagery does contain some martial innuendos. For instance, the expression אשת־חיל (Prov 31:10) is the female counterpart of גבור חיל, "mighty man of valor" or "mighty warrior." The syntagma חיל + עשה (Prov 31:29) often occurs in military contexts with the meaning of "doing valiantly" (e.g., Num 24:18; Deut 11:4; 1 Sam 14:18; Ps 60:14). The lexeme שלל (Prov 31:11) is often translated by "gain" (NRSV), but it usually means "prey, spoil, plunder, booty." Likewise, the lexeme טרף (Prov 31:15) is usually translated by "food" (NRSV), but it more often means "prey," with or without military connotations (e.g., Gen 49:9; Num 23:24; Isa 5:29; 31:4; Amos 3:4; Nah 2:13, 14; 3:1; Job 4:11; 38:39; Ps 104:21).

The peculiarity of Song 7:1 with respect to biblical tradition consists in the use of the literary motif of the victorious heroine to extol female beauty and positively underscore the power that female sensuality exercises over the man. It is true that Judith "was very beautiful, charming to see" (Jdt 8:7). When she was in front of Holophernes and his adjutant, "the beauty of her face astonished them all" (Jdt 10:23). Before enchanting the brutal general with her speech, she had already conquered him with her face: "There is no woman like her from one end of the earth to the other, so lovely of face and so wise of speech!" (Jdt 11:21). In the book of Judith, however, female beauty and sensuality mainly serve the plot. In the Song, on the contrary, female beauty and sensuality are the very core of the discourse. Judith is first and foremost acclaimed for her shrewdness, not for being a beautiful woman. In other words, whereas Judith is a *war heroine*, the Shulammite is an *eros heroine*. As for Prov 31:10–31, the conceptual domain WAR is not used to extol the woman's femininity but her

---

beautiful woman who is not afraid to wander outside her home and to arouse her lover's desire, the author of 'A Woman of Valor' put forward a smart, active woman of a different sort: a woman who remains inside her home and supervises the household." See Yair Zakovitch, "'A Woman of Valor (אשת חיל)' Prov 31:10–31: A Conservative's Response to Song of Songs," in *The Song of Songs: Riddle of Riddles*, LHBOTS 673 (London: Bloomsbury T&T Clark, 2019), 98.

100. Al Wolters, "Proverbs XXXI 10–31 as Heroic Hymn: A Form-Critical Analysis," *VT* 38 (1988): 446–57.

wisdom. Proverbs 31:30 boldly affirms: "Charm is deceitful, and beauty is vain, but a woman who fears YHWH is to be praised." In sum, whereas Song 7:1 is grounded in biblical literature and imagery, it is unique and unconventional enough that it might be considered a conscious attempt to defamiliarize not only well-known literary motifs but also established ways of conceiving female beauty in ancient Israel.

As for the ancient Near East, neither Egyptian love poems nor Ugaritic texts contain scenes even remotely similar to what we find in 7:1. Mesopotamian sources, however, often present a connection between Ishtar and the dance. As mentioned above, William Albright has argued that 7:1 presents a "transparent borrowing from a Northwest Semitic mythological theme."[101] Not only do several sources use the epithet *šulmānītu* to refer to Ishtar, but on several occasions the war goddess is called "she whose dance is battle," as well as the patroness of warriors "who dance into the onslaught of weapons."[102] More recently, Uri Gabbay has also shown that Mesopotamian sources provide evidence of ritual dances in honor of Ishtar, the goddess of love and war.[103] In the Agushaya Poem, for instance, the war goddess herself is presented as dancing "in her manliness," and liturgical celebrations in her honor are described as "the melee, staging the dance of battle."[104] In the same poem, the god Ea is said to establish "a whirling dance" (*gūštu*), which, according to Benjamin Foster, seems to refer to mock combat performed by people in honor of Ishtar.[105] That the domains LOVE, WAR, and DANCE overlap in the description of both the Shulammite and Ishtar does not necessarily imply that the Song has a mythological background, as the so-called cultic school has argued. It only suggests that vaguely similar images also occur in the poem's *Umwelt* and that the Song probably adopted motifs that were well-known among its recipients. In so doing, the Song made possible both communication with its audience and recognition of the extraordinary character of the Shulammite.

---

101. William F. Albright, "Archaic Survivals in the Text of the Canticles," in *Hebrew and Semitic Studies Presented to Godfrey Rolles Driver: In Celebration of His Seventieth Birthday, 20 August 1962*, ed. Winton Thomas and William D. MacHardy (Oxford: Clarendon, 1963), 1–7.

102. Pope, *Song of Songs*, 599–605.

103. Uri Gabbay, "Dance in Textual Sources from Ancient Mesopotamia," *NEA* 66 (2003): 103–4.

104. Benjamin R. Foster, *Before the Muses: An Anthology of Akkadian Literature*, 3rd ed. (Bethesda: CDL, 2005), 97–98.

105. Foster, *Before the Muses*, 105 n. I.

By borrowing a motif from its *Umwelt* and by elaborating it, the Song once more proves that it is both grounded in the literary and conceptual universe of its contexts and produced by the poetic genius of its author(s)/redactor(s).

***

Song 1:9 and 7:1 share the same positive conceptualization of the woman as a powerful lover, whom the beloved man cannot resist. She is unstoppable as a military mare. She is victorious in her conquest of love. The conquering man has to deal not only with a woman who delays the fulfillment of his desire (4:4), who knocks him out through her overwhelming beauty (6:4), who proudly asserts her maturity (8:10). He has also to deal with a woman whose sensuality is disruptive, out of his control (1:9), and even dominating (7:1). In this regard, the surface metaphors WOMAN IS CONQUEROR and MAN IS CONQUEROR mirror each other. However, the symmetry in not perfect, as I will explain in the conclusion.

5

Love Is Strife

JULIET: If they do see thee, they will murder thee.
ROMEO: Alack, there lies more peril in thine eye
Than twenty of their swords. Look thou but sweet,
And I am proof against their enmity.
—William Shakespeare, *Romeo and Juliet*

In this final chapter, I will analyze the last surface military metaphor, LOVE IS STRIFE, which occurs in Song 3:6–8 and 8:6–7. Both these texts are very elaborate, and the military imagery is not limited to the boundaries of the clause. Conceptually, both present the lovers struggling with external opposition. Song 3:6–8 develops the theme *love is strife* by reworking the cognitive script "wedding" in light of the biblical Solomonic tradition. Song 3:6–8, however, omits many elements of this script and only foregrounds the procession of the nuptial litter and its military escort. Song 8:6–7 presents Love/Passion as a powerful warlike deity by drawing on several mythological motifs, particularly the biblical representation of YHWH as a warrior. Against such a warlike deity, the lovers' hostile social environment can only capitulate. The communicative function of both 3:6–8 and 8:6–7 within the Song is to present love as a war *ad extra*: love is not just a game of seduction between the lovers, as it was in the previous warlike metaphors, but a force enabling the lovers to face and overcome whatever obstructions they might encounter.

5.1. The Powerful and Invincible Love (Song 3:6–8)

SONG 3:6–8
Who is this[1] going up from the desert

מי זאת עלה מן־המדבר

---

1. The pronouns מי and זאת might refer to the litter (NRSV). Note that the ques-

like columns of smoke,	כתימרות עשן
perfumed with myrrh and frankincense,	מקטרת מור ולבונה
from all kinds of the merchant's powders?	מכל אבקת רוכל
Look! Solomon's litter!	הנה מטתו שלשלמה
Sixty warriors are around it,	ששים גברים סביב לה
of the warriors of Israel.	מגברי ישראל
All of them are equipped with a sword,[2]	כלם אחזי חרב
experts in war.	מלמדי מלחמה
Each with his sword on his thigh	איש חרבו על־ירכו
because of terrifying nocturnal dangers.[3]	מפחד בלילות

The main problem that has concerned exegetes dealing with this text is the identification of the occupant of the litter. Current interpretations of the military language depend on how this question is solved. For instance, Exum, who attributes 3:6–11 to the woman, thinks that the litter is occupied by King Solomon. She reads these verses as an expression of both the woman's admiration for her beloved man and "the sense of security that she feels in his presence."[4] Zakovitch, however, supposes that 3:6–8 is a satirical portrayal of King Solomon, who seems to be represented as terrified on his bed/litter. According to Zakovitch, 3:6–8 creates a strong contrast between the scared Solomon and the fearless woman, who was ready to leave her bed in the middle of the night to look for her beloved (3:1–5).[5] Murphy remains guarded about the identification of who is on the litter. Whoever is on the litter, in his view these verses are meant to extol the man.[6] In contrast, Barbiero contends that the woman is the one sitting on the litter and that the warriors are protecting her against the nocturnal

---

tion "what is that?" seems to receive an answer in 3:7 (NRSV: "Look, it is the litter of Solomon!"). Nevertheless, the translation "who is this?" is also possible, since (1) the pronoun מי usually enquires about a person; (2) the interrogative מי זאת occurs in 6:10 and 8:5, where it unequivocally refers to the beloved woman; and (3) Song 8:5 presents the same interrogative clause as 3:6.

2. אחזי חרב. Passive participles often indicate the result of the action expressed by the verb (Joüon §121o; GKC §50f): e.g., ידוע חלי ("acquainted with infirmity"; Isa 53:3), זכור כי־עפר אנחנו ("he is mindful of the fact that we are dust"; Ps 103:14). I therefore prefer the translation "equipped with a sword."

3. The preposition מן can mean "by reason of," "due to." See Deut 28:34; Isa 65:14; Ps 12:6.

4. Exum, *Song of Songs*, 148.

5. Zakovitch, *Das Hohelied*, 173–80.

6. Murphy, *Song of Song*, 151.

demons evoked by the expression פחד בלילות (3:8). Furthermore, Barbiero argues that the procession described by 3:6–8 recalls the exodus journey, centered on the ark of the covenant.[7] Finally, Luzarraga and Keel agree that the litter is occupied by the woman, although the former author reads the presence of the military escort as a symbol of Solomon's protection, while the latter interprets the military escort as a symbol of the woman's enchanting allure and awesome magnificence.[8]

In my view, 3:6–8 presents the metonymy litter-woman, and therefore the scene describes the litter carrying the bride,[9] in line with ancient Near Eastern cognitive script "wedding." At the same time, 3:6–8 reworks that script, conceptualizing love as POWERFUL and INVINCIBLE, able to brave all kinds of obstacles.

5.1.1. A Very Long and Elaborate Military Scene

Song 3:6–8 presents a very long and syntactically elaborate scene, starting with an interrogative clause (v. 6), continuing with an exclamation (v. 7a), and ending with a sequence of verbless clauses (vv. 7b–8).

The interrogative clause is governed by the preposition מי, introducing a rhetorical question: a question that is asked not to gain information but rather to point something out.[10] Rhetorical questions in Biblical Hebrew may have several different functions.[11] In 3:6, מי זאת seems to be first and foremost an expression of admiration, aiming at involving the reader in the speaker's wonder and driving the reader's attention on the ongoing event: the woman/litter is going up from the desert (עלה מן־המדבר).

The interrogative clause is followed by two phrases that modify the pronoun זאת: the former compares the woman's/litter's ascent to columns

---

7. Barbiero, *Song of Songs*, 148.

8. Luzarraga, *Cantar de los Cantares*, 324–25; Keel, *Song of Songs*, 128.

9. See n. 1.

10. Cornelia Ilie, *What Else Can I Tell You? A Pragmatic Study of English Rhetorical Questions as Discursive and Argumentative Acts* (Stockholm: Almqvist & Wiksell, 1994), 38, 45.

11. Adina Moshavi, "Between Dialectic and Rhetoric: Rhetorical Questions Expressing Premises in Biblical Prose Argumentation," *VT* 65 (2015): 136–51; Moshavi, "What Can I Say? Implications and Communicative Functions of Rhetorical 'WH' Questions in Classical Biblical Hebrew Prose," *VT* 64 (2014): 93–108; Moshavi, "Two Types of Argumentation Involving Rhetorical Questions in Biblical Hebrew Dialogue," *Bib* 90 (2009): 32–46.

of smoke (כתימרות עשן), while the latter describes her/the litter as shrouded in a cloud of myrrh and frankincense (מקטרת מור ולבונה). Finally, the last phrase (מכל אבקת רוכל) is a pleonastic adjunct to the previous one, specifying that the woman/litter is perfumed with all sorts of perfumes. Note the asyndetic coordination, which speeds up the reading pace and gives life to the description.

The first interrogative clause is followed by an exclamation introduced by הנה, a particle that zooms in and directs the reader's attention to what follows (הנה מטתו שלשלמה). The syntactic construction of מטתו שלשלמה is neither awkward (Garrett) nor particularly emphatic (Murphy) but is rather a syntactic construction expressing possession, which is typical of postbiblical Hebrew: *nomen regens* (מטה) + proleptic suffix (מטתו) + של + personal name (שלמה).[12] Furthermore, the clause as such does not necessarily suggest that Solomon is in the litter, but it may imply that Solomon owns it.

A series of verbless clauses follows that, in the absence of actions, carries on the process of zooming in introduced by the particle הנה and focuses on the military escort around the litter. The subject of the first verbless clause (ששים גברים) is modified by (1) an adverbial phrase (סביב לה) that specifies the position of the warriors, (2) a prepositional phrase that specifies their nationality (מגברי ישראל), and (3) two more clauses underscoring how well-trained these warriors are in sword-fighting (כלם אחזי חרב) and warfare more generally (מלמדי מלחמה). The end of verse 8 continues the description of the escort through a verbless clause zooming in on the warriors' swords (איש חרבו על-ירכו), also enjambing in a final prepositional phrase, which gives the reason for this military deployment (מפחד בלילות).

5.1.2. The Song's Warriors and the Ancient Script "Wedding"

The warriors are here described with respect to their number, position, nationality, expertise, and readiness for battle.

The warriors are said to be sixty, maybe alluding to the thirty warriors accompanying David and emphasizing that the soldiers around Solomon's litter are twice the number of David's bodyguards (2 Sam 23:18–19, 23).

---

12. Miguel Pérez Fernández, *An Introductory Grammar of Rabbinic Hebrew* (Leiden: Brill, 1997), 32.

Whether 3:6 alludes to David's bodyguards or not, in the Hebrew Bible ששים often indicates a remarkable quantity. For instance, the rams, the male goats, and the male lambs for the sacrifice of well-being need to be sixty (Num 7:88). The Israelites conquered sixty cities belonging to King Og of Bashan (1 Kgs 4:13). The temple built by Solomon is said to be sixty cubits long (1 Kgs 6:2; 2 Chr 3:3) and so are the pillars of the future temple (Ezek 40:14). The descendants of Adonikam were sixty males (Ezra 8:13), and Rehoboam is said to have sixty concubines and sixty daughters (2 Chr 11:21). In the Song, the number sixty is also used in 6:8, with reference to the innumerable women of Solomon's harem. In 3:6, therefore, the mention of sixty warriors is a stock phrase emphasizing the number of soldiers around the woman/litter and, thereby, the importance of both the litter and its occupant.

Not only are these warriors numerous, but they also are Israel's best. Besides the fact that the nationalist remark (מגברי ישראל) may indicate ancient Israel's pride in its military forces, the central idea seems to be that the litter's escort is composed of the most valiant warriors chosen from ancient Israel's soldiers, as the partitive מן indicates. The warriors are said to be around the woman/litter (סביב לה). This remark is not a futile detail; it envisions an inaccessible woman/litter, well defended all around. Further, the text specifies that all warriors are armed (כלם אחזי חרב). The lexeme חרב is usually translated by "sword," although it can also refer to a dagger (Josh 5:2), to a knife (Judg 3:16, 21), and even to a chisel (Exod 20:25).[13] Whatever the case might be in 3:8, חרב certainly indicates a short-range weapon, which makes the reader glimpse the possibility of hand-to-hand combat and a high-powered battle scene around Solomon's litter. That the warriors are all armed (כלם) conveys both danger and safety: on the one hand, the litter is in good hands; on the other, the litter is clearly in danger, to such an extent that *all warriors* need to be equipped with a sword. Reinforcing this double idea, the text points out that the warriors are all experts in war (מלמדי מלחמה). In the Hebrew Bible, the *pual* participle of למד only occurs five times. In Isa 29:13, the feminine singular form (מלמדה) qualifies God's commandment, which has become a commandment of men learned by rote (מצות אנשים מלמדה), and, in Hos 10:11, it qualifies Ephraim as "a trained heifer" (עגלה מלמדה). The construct state of the plural masculine form (מלמדי) only occurs in 1 Chr 25:7 and Ps 119:99,

---

13. Peter Enns, "חֶרֶב," *NIDOTTE* 2:259–62; Otto Kaiser, "חֶרֶב," *ThWAT* 3:164–76.

to indicate professional figures. In the former text, it refers to the temple's singers (מלמדי־שיר), and, in the latter, it refers to teachers of wisdom (מכל־מלמדי השכלתי). The syntagma מלמדי מלחמה in Song 3:8 might therefore indicate not only that these warriors are "trained" (all warriors are, at least, to some extent), but rather that they are *experts* in warfare, professional figures, the best of the best.

Furthermore, 3:8c returns to the theme of the sword (איש חרבו על־ירכו), focusing on the soldiers' weapons. Note the passage from "all of them" (כלם) to "each" (איש), which directs the reader's attention to the weapon that every single warrior is carrying.[14] The double mention of the sword is not redundant. Rather, it heightens the drama of possible, imminent battle, for which the warriors are ready.

Finally, 3:8d reveals the reason for the presence of military troops around the litter: the presence of warriors is due to terrifying nocturnal dangers (מפחד בלילות). In the Hebrew Bible, the lexeme פחד indicates a profound emotion of dread, as well as what causes the dread; hence, it sometimes translates as "terrifying danger" (e.g., Pss 53:6; 91:5; Job 3:25; 39:22; Prov 1:26–27, 33; 3:25).[15] Given that Biblical Hebrew contains many lexemes belonging to the conceptual domain FEAR,[16] the question arises as to what semantic content is peculiar to the lexeme פחד. Bruna Costacurta and Joüon argued that the root פחד conveys the idea of shivering.[17] This is certainly true especially when פחד is combined with verbs indicating the experience of trembling (e.g., רגז, רעד, and חרד; see, e.g., Deut 2:25; Job 4:14; Isa 19:16; Mic 7:17). Nevertheless, "shivering" cannot be considered a constant of the experience of פחד but one of its many somatic expressions. By looking at the occurrences of the substantive פחד, the idea more constantly connected with the use of this lexeme

---

14. Outside the Song, the image of the sword at one's thigh occurs four times in the Hebrew Bible: in contexts of imminent battles (Exod 32:27; Judg 3:16), in the middle of a battle (Judg 3:21), or describing the king as a majestic warrior riding on victoriously for the cause of truth and defending the right (Ps 45:4).

15. See Hans-Peter Müller, "פָּחַד," *ThWAT* 6:551–62.

16. E.g., אים ("terrible, dreadful"), אימה ("terror, dread"), בהל ("to be disquieted"), בעת ("to fall upon, to startle, to terrify"), גור III ("to be afraid, dread"), דאג ("to be anxious, concerned"), זכל II ("to fear"), חרד ("to tremble"), חתת ("to be shattered"), יגר ("to be afraid, to fear"), ירא ("to fear"), ערץ ("to tremble/to cause to tremble"), קוץ ("to feel a loathing/abhorrence/sickening dread").

17. Costacurta, *La vita minacciata*, 48–51; Paul Joüon, "Crainte et peur en hébreu biblique: Etude de lexicographie et de stylistique," *Bib* 6 (1925): 175.

seems to be a profound feeling of terror inspired by a higher power—a powerful and invincible reality. The clearest examples of the connection of פחד with the experience of being at the mercy of something/someone more powerful and invincible are the frequent expressions פחד־יהוה ("the terror of YHWH"; e.g., 1 Sam 11:7; Isa 2:10, 19, 21; 2 Chr 14:13; 17:10; 19:7), פחד אלהים ("the terror of God"; e.g., Ps 37:2; 2 Chr 20:29), and פחד יצחק ("the terror of Isaac"; e.g., Gen 31:42, 53), which all refer to God as the most powerful, invincible, and therefore fear-inspiring reality. In Job 13:11 the experience of terror is linked with the majesty of God: "Will not his majesty terrify you, and the dread [פחד] of him fall upon you?" Likewise, in Job 25:2 the experience of terror is connected with the experience of God's dominion: "Dominion and fear [פחד] are with God; he makes peace in his high heaven." God's majesty, however, is not the only reality producing פחד. Isaiah 24:17 refers to dangers that are on the inhabitants of the earth ("Terror [פחד], and the pit, and the snare are upon you, O inhabitant of the earth!"; see also Jer 48:43, 44; Job 22:10), and Isa 51:13 refers to the destructive, unstoppable fury of the enemy ("You fear [ותפחד] continually all day long because of the fury of the oppressor, who is bent on destruction"). In Jer 49:5, terror is produced by the experience of not having a way out: "I am going to bring terror [פחד] upon you, says YHWH the lord of hosts, from all your neighbors." In Ps 14:5 the enemies' terror is triggered when they realize that God is with the righteous and, therefore, that their defeat is imminent: "There they shall be in great terror [פחד], for God is with the company of the righteous." The experience of פחד reduces one to silence (Exod 15:16) and generates confusion (Deut 2:25) and a profound sense of precariousness (Deut 11:25; 28:66), anxiety (Deut 28:66), restlessness (Job 3:25), or panic (Jer 30:5). One's skin may even bristle (Ps 119:120). The lexeme פחד quite often indicates the experience of terror in military contexts. When it is the subject of נפל + על, or היה + על, or simply paired with על, it clearly suggests overwhelming terror as part of war.[18]

As for Song 3:8, many attempts have been made to clarify the meaning of the expression פחד בלילות. Some scholars suggest that it evokes a folktale in which nocturnal demons threaten lovers at night.[19] This is

---

18. על + נפל: e.g., Exod 15:16; 1 Sam 11:7. על + היה: e.g., 2 Chr 14:13; 17:10; 19:7; 20:29. Simply paired with על: e.g., Deut 2:25; 11:25; Isa 24:17; Jer 48:43.

19. E.g., Barbiero, *Song of Songs*, 151–52; Keel, *Song of Songs*, 128–29; Pope, *Song of Songs*, 434–37.

certainly a possibility, since the book of Tobit suggests that such a folktale did exist in Israel. Furthermore, wedding ceremonies often contain apotropaic rites, and, in several societies, weapons are used during weddings to chase away evil spirits.[20] There is no clear evidence, however, that this is what 3:8 refers to. As a matter of fact, outside the Song a similar expression to פחד בלילות can only be found in Ps 91:5 ("You will not fear for the terror of the night [מפחד לילה], or for the arrow that flies by day"). In this text, the lexeme פחד seems to refer to a feeling of terror that might be experienced either by night or by day, due to unexpected and unpredictable plagues and diseases. Note the mention of דבר, "pestilence," and קטב, "destruction," in verse 6. Nor can we better identify the precise cause of the experience of terror underlying the use of פחד by looking at the other occurrences of the lexeme in the Hebrew Bible, since פחד might be produced by God, by Israel, by enemies, or, more generally, by the experience of suffering.[21] Given that 3:6–8 describes a procession through the desert, פחד בלילות might refer to attacks by animals and/or by highwaymen. What is significant, however, is that further information is left out, and this increases the drama and heightens the suspense around Solomon's litter. What are these nocturnal terrifying dangers, then? Nobody knows. What we do know is that the threat is strong, the tension is high, and the warriors are ready to fight.

All in all, Song 3:6–11 seems to refer to an essential part of ancient wedding ceremonies and to a key part of the cognitive script/scenario "wedding" in antiquity: the nuptial procession accompanying the bride to the bridegroom. Even though the Hebrew Bible provides little information about the ceremonial aspects of marriage in ancient Israel, we have a general idea of what marriage looked like in biblical times thanks to those few biblical references to wedding ceremonies and to ancient Near Eastern sources.[22] Scholars agree that ancient Israel's weddings

---

20.. Edward Westermarck, *The History of Human Marriage* (New York: Allerton Book Company, 1922), 501.

21. פחד produced by God: e.g., Gen 31:42, 53; Isa 2:10, 19, 21; 19:16; 33:14; Jer 48:43; Job 13:11; 23:15; 25:2; 31:23; Pss 36:2; 119:120, 161; by Israel: e.g., Deut 2:25; 11:25; Isa 19:17; Jer 36:16; Ps 105:38; Esth 8:17; 9:2; by enemies: e.g., Exod 15:16; Deut 28:66, 67; Isa 51:13; Jer 30:15; Ps 64:2; Lam 3:47; by suffering: e.g., Isa 12:2; Job 3:25; 4:14; 21:9; 22:10; Prov 1:26, 27, 33; 3:24, 25.

22. For scholarly research on marriage in ancient Israel, see Bernard S. Jackson, "The 'Institutions' of Marriage and Divorce in the Hebrew Bible," *JSS* 56 (2011): 221–51; Angelo Tosato, *Il matrimonio israelitico: Una teoria generale*, AnBib 100 (Rome:

consisted of two main phases: the marriage contract and the wedding festivities. Whereas the former was mainly a juridical phase, in which the bridal couple's families entered into a contract, the second was a ritual phase aimed at performing that contract. Several rites formed part of the wedding festivities but, according to Roland de Vaux, the main part was the introduction of the bride into the bridegroom's house.[23] This crucial moment was marked by a procession accompanying the bride to the bridegroom's house. Psalm 45 refers to such a procession when it speaks of the bride led to the king by her companions (vv. 15–16).[24] Likewise, 1 Macc 9:36–41 makes it clear that wedding processions escorting the bride with a large retinue were common in ancient Israel, at least during the Hellenistic period.

Several ancient Near Eastern texts suggest that the procession also was the occasion in which the bride's dowry was transferred to the bride's new house, showing off her wealth. The nuptial procession during royal weddings was particularly ostentatious, as in the case of Taduhepa, daughter of Tushratta, king of Mitanni. Taduhepa is said to have traveled to Egypt to marry Amenophis III in a magnificent procession.[25] Likewise, on the occasion of the marriage between Ramesses II and a Hittite

---

Biblical Institute Press, 1982); Roland de Vaux, *Le nomadisme et ses survivances, institutions familiales, institutions civiles*, vol. 1 of *Les Institutions de l'Ancien Testament* (Paris: Cerf, 1958), 24–38; Gordon J. Wenham, "Weddings," in *The Oxford Companion to the Bible*, ed. Bruce M. Metzger and Michael D. Coogan (New York: Oxford University Press, 1993), 794–95; David R. Mace, *Hebrew Marriage: A Sociological Study* (London: Epworth, 1953); Millar Burrows, *The Basis of Israelite Marriage*, AOS 15 (New Haven: American Oriental Society, 1938). For scholarly research on marriage in the ancient Near East, see Karel van der Toorn, *Family Religion in Babylonia, Syria and Israel: Continuity and Change in the Forms of Religious Life*, SHCANE 7 (Leiden: Brill, 1996); Herbert Sauren, "Le mariage selon le Code d'Eshnunna," *RIDA* 33 (1986): 45–86; Joseph Klíma, "Le règlement du mariage dans les lois babyloniennes anciennes," in *Im Bannkreis des Alten Orients: Studien zur Sprach- und Kulturgeschichte des Alten Orients und seines Ausstrahlungsraumes*, ed. Wolfgang Meid and Helga Trenkwalder (Innsbruck: Amoe, 1986), 109–21; Samuel Greengus, "The Old Babylonian Marriage Contract," *JAOS* 89 (1969): 505–32; Greengus, "Old Babylonian Marriage Ceremonies and Rites," *JAOS* 20 (1966): 55–72.

23. De Vaux, *Le nomadisme et ses survivances*, 59.

24. Christoph Schroeder, "'A Love Song': Ps 45 in the Light of Ancient Near-ern Marriage Texts," *CBQ* 58 (1996): 417–32.

25. William L. Moran, ed., *The Amarna Letters* (Baltimore: Johns Hopkins University Press, 1992), 51–61, 72–84.

princess, the bridegroom traveled to Egypt accompanied by a long procession and an impressive dowry.[26] As Hennie Marsman and Adrianus
Van Selms have shown, the custom of the bride leaving the father's house
and traveling to the bridegroom's house/palace accompanied by her
dowry was also known at Ugarit. The dowry list of the queen Ahatmilku
suggests that the transfer of her dowry during her nuptial procession
must have been quite impressive.[27]

Several literary and archaeological sources suggest that the procession
accompanying the bride to her new home was the core and most public
event of both Greek and Roman weddings.[28] In Greece, the procession was
accompanied by torches and songs, which apparently were both decorative and apotropaic.[29] The bride's or the bridal couple's safety was a major
concern. For instance, Sappho's description of the wedding procession of
Hector and Andromache mentions Hector's friends with horses, chariots,
and charioteers. This procession, besides making the parade more flamboyant, also made the couple safe during the journey (*Frag.* 16). The protective
role of the escort clearly emerges in Hyperides's speech in defense of
Lycophron. Lycophron was accused of trying to approach a bride during
her nuptial procession to dissuade her from getting married. Hyperides
rejected this charge, pointing out that the bride was inaccessible due to her
escort of strong men and renowned wrestlers (*Par.* 496). Plutarch describes
a nuptial procession in which the groom's friends killed the drunk Hip-
poclus for trying to jump into the bride's cart (*Mor.* 244). According to
John Oakley and Rebecca Sinos, the cart was the usual vehicle for the
wedding procession. Nevertheless, they note that black-figure vases of the
wedding often represent the bridal couple riding a chariot. Since chariots
were first and foremost associated with warriors, the portrayal of bridal
couples riding chariots had the symbolic function of imparting "a heroic

26. *KRI* 2:149; Pinhas Artzi, "The Influence of Political Marriages on the International Relations of the Amarna-Age," in *La femme dans le Proche-Orient antique*, ed.
Jean-Marie Durand (Paris: Recherche sur les civilisations, 1987), 23–26.

27. Marsman, *Women in Ugarit and Israel*, 704–5; Adrianus Van Selms, *Marriage
and Family Life in Ugaritic Literature*, POS 1 (London: Luzac, 1954).

28. Karen K. Hersch, *The Roman Wedding: Ritual and Meaning in Antiquity* (New
York: Cambridge University Press, 2010); John H. Oakley and Rebecca H. Sinos, *The
Wedding in Ancient Athens* (Madison: University of Wisconsin Press, 2002).

29. As a character in *Phaon* by Plato Comicus says, λύχνων γὰρ ὀσμὰς οὐ φιλοῦσι
δαίμονες ("the gods [alias the demons] do not like the smell of lamps"). See *Test. and
Frag.* 188.15 (Storey).

flavor to the scene."[30] As far as Roman weddings are concerned, Karen Hersch argues that "the majority of all types of written evidence focuses on the procession of a bride before the eyes of her community."[31] The so-called *domum deductio*, the "the leading home" of the bride, was extremely important since it sanctioned the social status of the bridal couple in the community's eyes.[32]

Rabbinic literature also provides evidence not only that nuptial processions were part of Israel's culture, but also that brides were carried on a litter. In b. Sotah 9:14, the rabbis allow a bride to go around the city on the litter, even though this custom had been forbidden in time of war for safety reasons. In y. Sotah 1:17–20, a governor is allowed to take part in the procession of the litter during the nuptial procession of his daughter. Both texts use the term אפריון for litter, probably taken from Song 3:9. All these texts also support the idea that the litter, to which the Song refers, carries the bride and not Solomon.

The procession accompanying the bride to the bridegroom's house, therefore, was a crucial element of nuptial ceremonies in the Song's *Umwelt* and, possibly, the ancient cognitive script "wedding."[33] Song 3:6–11 bears signs of this ancient script. The text portrays the progressive arrival of the woman, carried by the litter in verse 6. It describes both the outside (the procession of warriors) and the inside (material and fabric) of the litter in verses 8–10. It clarifies that the wedding is Solomon's and that the point of arrival of the procession is Jerusalem in verse 11: "Go out, O daughters of Zion, and behold King Solomon, the crown with which his mother has crowned him on the day of his wedding, the day of the joy of his heart."[34] Song 3:6–11, however, does not merely use the cognitive script "wedding"; it reworks it by employing biblical traditions on Solomon. The pompous arrival of a woman in Jerusalem from the desert and the mention of exotic perfumes and spices (Song 3:6) recall the arrival in Jerusalem of the queen of Sheba, accompanied by "a very large retinue, with camels laden with spices and an immense quantity of gold and precious stones" (1 Kgs 10:2; see also 2 Chr 9:1). The mention of warriors (Song 3:7–8) is not extraneous to the figure of Solomon. Despite the fact that Solomon is usually con-

---

30. Oakley and Sinos, *Wedding in Ancient Athens*, 30.

31. Hersch, *Roman Wedding*, 58.

32. Hersch, *Roman Wedding*, 141.

33. See also the reference to a wedding procession in Matt 25:1–13.

34. I understand the preposition ב before both מלך and עטרה as a *signum accusativi*.

nected to the building of the temple and to wisdom rather than to warfare, in the biblical narrative he did play a crucial role in the reform of ancient Israel's military forces, transforming the old militia into a modern army.[35] The mention of wood from Lebanon (Song 3:9), from which Solomon made the litter, recalls Solomon's choice of the same material to build both the temple and the royal palace (1 Kgs 5:7, 24; 6:18, 20; 7:7, 11). The mention of the love of the daughters of Jerusalem (Song 3:10) evokes one of Solomon's main traits, his being a famous lover. Finally, Solomon's mother (Song 3:11) is an important figure in Solomon's narratives (1 Kgs 1:11–40).

Song 3:6–11 seems to rework the cognitive script "wedding" not only by alluding to the biblical tradition about Solomon, but also by omitting many of the elements that were typical of nuptial processions, such as baths, anointings, the transfer of the dowry, dancers, songs, and torches. In doing so, the text only foregrounds two elements of the nuptial procession: the litter and its military escort. Given the aforementioned metonymic relationship between the litter and the woman, the description of the litter also functions to characterize the bride. The sumptuousness of the litter, made of wood of Lebanon, silver, gold, purple, and precious embroideries, underscores the bride's splendor and majesty. As for the military escort, its presence is not surprising. Such a magnificent litter/woman cannot face a journey through the desert without protection. Since the litter is said to be Solomon's in 3:7, the text probably implies that the king sent his litter and his soldiers to make sure that the bride could have a safe travel, especially given the "terrifying nocturnal dangers" (3:8). A parallel scene appears in the description of the wedding of Ramesses II, who sent his army and his princes to escort his bride, already escorted by her Hittite troops.[36] More importantly, by omitting all other elements of the nuptial procession and by foregrounding the warriors around the litter/bride, the text emphasizes that something might hinder the wedding and that the union between Solomon and his bride might face a plethora of sinister threats. At the same time, the text empowers the bridal couple: given how well equipped and defended the litter/bride is, the wedding *will* take place, and the bridal couple's love *will* be fulfilled—no matter what.

---

35. Gabriel, *Military History of Ancient Israel*, 283.

36. *KRI* 2:150; James H. Breasted, ed., *The Nineteenth Dynasty*, vol. 3 of *Ancient Records of Egypt: Historical Documents from the Earliest Times to the Persian Conquest* (New York: Russell & Russell, 1906), 185–86.

An atmosphere of war, therefore, surrounds Solomon's wedding and bride. *The beautiful and the terrible* again emerge as two crucial aspects of the Song's aesthetics of love. The question then arises as to what the communicative function of this scene is.

5.1.3. When Love Is in Danger

Song 3:6–8 forms part of the fourth literary unit (3:6–11), ending with the invitation to the daughters of Zion to go out and attend Solomon's joyful wedding. As mentioned above, these verses occupy a central role within the unit and underscore, on the one hand, that great dangers might impede the lovers' union and, on the other hand, that the lovers are powerful and well-equipped to fight hostile opposition. By using military language, Song 3:6–8 picks up the Song's conceptual metaphor LOVE IS WAR but adds a different aspect: that love may imply a combat against external struggles. Whereas all other martial metaphors, similes, and scenes conceptualize love as a combat *ad intra*, namely, as a game of seduction through which the lovers try to conquer each other, Song 3:6–8 conceives of love as a combat *ad extra*, in which the lovers' powerful mutual attachment and longing struggles with surrounding foes. In doing so, Song 3:6–8 perfectly fits in the poem's representation of the relationship between the lovers and their environment.

In the Song, the interaction between the lovers and their environment is double-sided. On the one hand, the environment fully participates in the lovers' experience. A chorus of friends, who share the lovers' joy, surrounds both the woman and the man. In 1:3–4 other women are joined in the woman's love and euphoria for the man ("girls love you"; "rightly do they love you"). In 2:5 the daughters of Jerusalem constitute a support on which the woman can rely: "Sustain me with raisins, refresh me with apples; because I am lovesick." Likewise, in 5:8 ("I charge you, daughters of Jerusalem, should you find my beloved, what will you tell him? That I am lovesick") and in 6:1 ("Where has your beloved gone, O fairest among women? Which way has your beloved turned, that we may seek him with you?"), the daughters of Jerusalem provide help for the woman. In 6:9 girls, queens, and concubines rhapsodize about her ("The maidens saw her and called her happy; the queens and concubines also, and they praised her"), and in the already-analyzed 7:1, she is surrounded by a chorus of admirers. As for the man, in 5:1 he is in the company of a merry band of friends ("Eat, friends, drink, and be drunk with love"), and in 8:13 the man's companions long with him for the woman's voice ("friends are listening for your voice"). The natural environment is also profoundly supportive of the Song's couple insofar as it provides the lovers not only with much of the setting for their love experience, but also with words and thoughts through which the lovers can think of each other and can talk to each other.

On the other hand, however, the environment is also perceived as hostile. The words with which the woman addresses the daughters of Jerusalem in 1:5 sound quite confrontational and might allude to critical remarks on the color of her skin ("Black I am but beautiful, O daughters of Jerusalem"). In 1:6, the woman's brothers are clearly presented as trying to stop her sexual desires: "My mother's sons turned their anger on me, they made me look after the vineyards." In 5:7, the guards abuse her: "They beat me, they wounded me, they took my cloak away from me." In 8:1, the woman seems to refer to a possible social stigma that might weigh on the couple ("Ah, why are you not my brother, nursed at my mother's breast! Then if I met you outdoors, I could kiss you without people despising me"), and in 8:9 her family's paternalistic attitude emerges ("We have a little sister, she has no breasts"). Song 2:15, containing the woman's enigmatic invitation to catch the foxes that ruin the vineyards, seems to imply that something tries to hamper love. As Alter explains, "There are in the world pesky agents of interference that seek to obstruct love's fulfilment, as foxes despoil a vineyard, but our own special vineyard remains flourishing and intact, our love unimpeded."[37] Likewise, the idea that love is invincible in 8:7 implies that love experiences some kind of opposition ("flood cannot quench love, nor can torrents drown it").

The communicative function of 3:6–8 within the poem, therefore, is to underscore what the poem suggests on many occasions, namely, that love is not all sunshine and rainbows. It also brings with it conflicts and tensions. The martial imagery elevates the tension between the lovers and their social and natural environment, emphasizing the degree of conflict. At the same time, 3:6–8 points out that the stronger the opposition to love, the stronger love's resistance. In doing so, the poet conveys one of the most typical feelings connected with the human experience of romantic love: the feeling that love is powerful and invincible, able to overcome the most menacing threats. Modern psychology speaks of a so-called Romeo and Juliet effect, which occurs when external opposition to a couple's love

---

37. Alter, *Writings*, 594.

empowers their mutual attachment.[38] This effect is a widespread trope in world literature—often with tragic finales, as in *Romeo and Juliet*.

Within biblical literature as a whole, the Song's concept of love as a powerful experience able to overcome external oppositions appears unique. Biblical literature does present several couples struggling with all kinds of difficulties. Adam and Eve struggle with the interpretation of God's commands. Abraham and Sarah, Jacob and Rachel, Elkanah and Hannah face infertility. Isaac and Rebekah must tackle the conflict between their sons Jacob and Esau. Ruth and Boaz have to find a way to wed in spite of the levirate law. Hosea and Gomer grapple with her infidelity. Job and his wife are faced with the problem of illness. In all these cases, however, what is at stake is not the experience of love as such, which by no means constitutes the major concern and the real topic of these narratives.

In biblical tradition, only two couples experience direct obstruction to their love: Jacob and Rachel, and Tobit and Sarah. According to Gen 29, Rachel was shapely and beautiful (Gen 29:17), and Jacob fell in love with her (Gen 29:18). Jacob himself proposed to Laban to work for him for seven years, probably to pay the bride price. According to Gen 29:20, these seven years "seemed to him like a few days because he loved her so much." The story suggests that while the marriage contract had been made, Jacob was forced to wait seven years before he could celebrate the wedding and consummate the marriage. Indeed, according to Gen 29:21, after seven years Jacob said to Laban, "Give me my wife for my time is up and I want to go to her," which implies that Jacob and Rachel were already legally married. However, Laban famously deceived Jacob; he introduced Leah into the nuptial chamber, and Jacob, without his knowledge, consummated his marriage (Gen 29:23). Laban then forced Jacob to complete the week of festivities before Jacob could finally celebrate his marriage and consummate his love for Rachel (Gen 29:25–30). In addition, Laban imposed on Jacob seven more years of work to have Rachel. Genesis 29, therefore, tells a story of an obstructed, delayed wedding that Jacob was able to endure thanks to his love for Rachel. As for the deuterocanonical story of Tobit

---

38. H. Colleen Sinclair, Diane Felmlee, Susan Sprecher, and Brittany L. Wright, "Don't Tell Me Who I Can't Love: A Multimethod Investigation of Social Network and Reactance Effects on Romantic Relationships," *SPQ* 78 (2015): 77–99; H. Colleen Sinclair, "In Search of Romeo and Juliet," *SocPsy* 45 (2014): 312–14; Richard Driscoll, Keith E. Davis, and Milton E. Lipetz, "Parental Interference and Romantic Love: Romeo and Juliet Effect," *JPSP* 24 (1972): 1–18.

and Sarah, the problem that this couple has to face is the evil presence of the demon Asmodeus, who had already killed all Sarah's previous husbands during their wedding night (Tob 3:7). According to Tob 6:19, Tobit "fell so deeply in love with her and his heart profoundly attached to her." During their wedding night, Tobit was able to send Asmodeus away by burning a fish's liver and heart, as indicated by the angel Raphael (Tob 8:2), and by imploring God (8:4).

The idea that a couple has the necessary resources to overcome external oppositions to their union, therefore, is not extraneous to biblical literature. Nevertheless, the picture of love in 3:6–8 is remarkably different from these stories. First, in the stories of both Jacob and Rachel and Tobit and Sarah, love is exclusively presented as a male affair: only the male characters are said to be in love, and only the male characters engage with their struggles. Both Rachel and Sarah stay in the background. By contrast, in the scene of the litter surrounded by warriors in 3:6–8, the woman is foregrounded because of the metonymic relationship litter/ woman. Whether the warriors belong to the woman or are sent by Solomon to escort her, the image of the litter coming up from the desert with sixty armed warriors ready to fight makes the woman appear powerful and even intimidating for whoever/whatever wants to threaten her. Furthermore, even though both Jacob and Tobit are said to love their wives, love is not the real topic of these narratives. These love stories are subordinate to the narratives' developing characterizations of Jacob and Tobit. The dispute between Jacob and Laban is one of many struggles that Jacob has to face and perhaps ironically presents Jacob as "the trickster who is himself tricked" by his uncle. As for Tobit, love does not really seem to be what leads him against Asmodeus. During the dialogue between Tobit and Raphael in chapter 6, Tobit is very concerned about marrying Sarah because he does not want to die. According to Tob 6:16, Raphael convinces Tobit by reminding him of the obedience due to his father ("Have you forgotten your father's orders, when he commanded you to take a wife from your father's house?"). According to Tob 6:19, it is precisely Tobit's filial obedience and devotion—which are among the main leitmotifs of the book—that make him fall in love with Sarah and give him courage against Asmodeus ("When Tobit heard the words of Raphael and knew that Sarah was his relative, of the family line of his father, he loved her"). In other words, neither the story of Jacob nor the story of Tobit seems to be particularly concerned with the power of love. Such a focus on love as powerful and invincible is unique to the Song.

The depiction of love as powerful and invincible can be found in Egyptian love poems, though expressed through different figurative language. In the Cairo Love Songs, the beloved man says:

(A)   (My) sister's love
                is over there, on the other side.
        The river is about my body.
                The flood waters are powerful in (their) season
                        and a crocodile waits on the sandbank.
(B)   (Yet) I have gone down to the water
                that I may wade across the flood waters
                        my heart brave in the channel.
(C)   I found the crocodile (to be) like a mouse,
                and the face of the waters like dry land to my feet.
        It is her love
                that makes me strong.
                        She will cast a water spell for me!
(D)   I see my heart's beloved
                standing right before my face![39]

This scene describes the lovers as separated by a river; their union is impeded by the disquieting presence of a crocodile waiting to devour the beloved man. We do not know what both waters and the crocodile stand for. The text, however, seems to portray quite dramatically a strong opposition to the lovers' union. The mention of flood and crocodile evokes the primeval chaos, which makes the scene even more terrifying. Despite this menacing scenario, the man finds the courage to face the crocodile and the flood. Ironically, the man feels so powerful that the former suddenly seems like a mouse, and the latter like dry land. Philippe Derchain has observed that the second lexeme for crocodile (hnty) suggests a less threatening animal than the first one (dpy),[40] emphasizing that the danger becomes smaller and smaller as the man braves it. Although this poem at first seems to emphasize the man's courage, at the end it reveals that the woman's love empowered him through magic. In other words, the man and the woman are joined in overcoming the obstacles to their love, and they need each other to succeed in this endeavor.

---

39. Cairo Love Songs, A.20D (Fox, Song of Songs, 32).
40. Philippe Derchain, "Le lotus, la mandragore et la perséa," CdE 50 (1975): 68.

A different poem presents the lovers struggling for their "obstructed love":

(A)   My brother roils my heart with his voice,
           making me take ill.
      Though he is among the neighbors of my mother's house,
           I cannot go to him.
(B)   Mother is good in commanding me thus:
           "Avoid seeing him!"
      Yet, my heart is vexed when he comes to mind,
           for love of him has captured me.
(C)   He is senseless of heart
           and I am just like him!
      He does not know my desires to embrace him,
           or he would send (word) to my mother.
(D)   O brother, I am decreed for you
           by the Golden One.
      Come to me that I may see your beauty!
           May father and mother be glad!
(E)   May all people rejoice in you together,
           rejoice in you, my brother![41]

The lovers are here presented as separated by social conventions, personified by the neighbors. It is unclear whether the woman's mother is part of the group who obstructs the lovers' encounter or whether she stands on the woman's side and only suggests her prudence. Whatever the case might be, the woman's desire is too intense to follow social conventions: her heart is roiled by love; she is lovesick; she feels vexed when she thinks of her lover; she feels captured by him, confused and foolish, and even compelled to love her man. Consequently, she cannot resist and calls him instead of obeying her mother. The poem continues by describing the lovers as separated and longing for each other. The sixth stanza (group A, no. 36) is particularly interesting since it describes the lovers trying to steal glances at each other while kept apart by the man's family. It also describes the woman expressing her desire to kiss the man without being ashamed "because of anyone" (see Song 8:1). No military language, however, is used in any of the Egyptian love poems to represent the lovers' struggles.

---

41. P.Beatty 1.A.32 (Fox, *Song of Songs*, 52).

In sum, thanks to its military language, Song 3:6–8 conceptualizes love as powerful and invincible, able to brave all possible opposition. In doing so, Song 3:6–8 develops a different aspect of the conceptual metaphor LOVE IS WAR, namely, that love is also a combat *ad extra*. This idea of love is new when it comes to biblical tradition, but it can be found in Egyptian love poems, although represented through different images.

5.2. The Subjugating Love (Song 8:6–7)

SONG 8:6–7

Set me as a seal on your heart,	שימני כחותם על־לבך
as a seal on your arm,	כותם על־זרועך
for strong as death is love,	כי־עזה כמות אהבה
vehement as Sheol is passion.[42]	קשה כשאול קנאה
Its flashes are flashes of fire,	רשפיה רשפי אש
a raging flame of Yah.[43]	שלהבתיה
Many waters cannot quench love	מים רבים לא יוכלו לכבות את־האהבה
nor rivers drown it away.	ונהרות לא ישטפוה
Should one offer all the wealth of	אם־יתן איש את־כל־הון
his house for love,	ביתו באהבה
he would be utterly scorned	בוז יבוזו לו

---

42. Exegetes often render קנאה by "jealousy" (e.g., Fox, Landy). Nevertheless, קנא also conveys the idea of passion/ardor/zeal and even anger (e.g., Pss 69:10; 119:139). See Hendrik G. L. Peels, "קנא," *NIDOTTE* 3:938. Both "jealousy" and "passion/ardor" fit in Song 8:6, since they both are appropriate to a discourse about love. In line with other scholars (e.g., Murphy, *Song of Songs*, 190 ["ardor"]), I translate it "passion" mainly because jealousy does not emerge as a topic throughout the poem, and "passion" has a broader semantic range, which can also include jealousy.

43. The form שלהבתיה is morphologically close to מאפליה in Jer 2:31 and to מרחביה in Ps 118:5. In both cases, the ending seems to be an abbreviation of יהוה and seems to function as an intensifier of the noun. Hence the suggested translations "thick darkness" for מאפליה, "broad place" for מרחביה, and "raging flame" for שלהבתיה (e.g., NRSV). The ending in Song 8:6 can also be an explicit reference to יהוה (e.g., Barbiero, *Song of Songs*, 436; Zakovitch, *Das Hohelied*, 270 ["Gottesflamme"]). Even though the name YHWH never occurs in the poem, the idea that 8:6 may allude to YHWH is not unreasonable, since the Song constantly adopts biblical motifs that elsewhere always refer to YHWH/Israel. Furthermore, as explained below, 8:6–7 contain several innuendos to YHWH as warrior. In my view, Song 8:6 employs the suffix יה- to portray not a mere flame but a raging flame and, more precisely, the raging flame of the belligerent YHWH.

Song 8:6–7 is generally considered the climax of the Song and is certainly among the most commented-on verses of the entire poem. Since a comprehensive summary of the secondary literature on this verse goes far beyond my scope, I focus only on the main streams of current interpretations of its imagery.

I see two main tendencies in current scholarship. On the one hand, several exegetes argue that 8:6–7 represents love as victorious over chaos and death.[44] On the other hand, other scholars contend that the text does not pit love against death and chaos but rather compares love to death and chaos.[45] Only a few scholars focus on the verses' military imagery. Fox, for instance, suggests the presence of a warlike image in his translation of רשפי אש as "darts of fire," without, however, providing any interpretation.[46] Barbiero, on the contrary, does explain the employed military language, arguing that 8:6–7 describes the strenuous battle between love and death.[47] More recently, Aren Wilson-Wright argues that 8:6–7 identifies love with the divine warrior YHWH.[48]

I suggest that the conceptual metaphor LOVE IS WAR lies in the background of 8:6–7 and represents the conflict between the lovers and their social context rather than the conflict between love and death. The woman first urges the man to become one with her through the image of the seal (8:6ab), and she then explains and provides the motive for her request (8:6c–7): they need to become one because only in this way they can fight against the opposition their love receives.

44. See, for instance, Wilfred G. E. Watson, "Love and Death Once More (Song of Songs 8:6)," *VT* (1997): 384–87; Nicolas J. Tromp, "Wisdom and the Canticle. Ct., 8,6c–7b: Text, Character, Message and Import," in *La Sagesse de l'Ancien Testament*, ed. Maurice Gilbert, BETL 51 (Gembloux: Duculot, 1979), 88–95.

45. See for instance, Garrett, *Song of Songs*, 255; Roland E. Murphy, "Dance and Death in the Song of Songs," in *Love and Death in the Ancient Near East: Essays in Honor of Marvin H. Pope*, ed. John H. Marks and Robert M. Good (Guilford: Four Quarters, 1987), 117–19.

46. Fox, *Song of Songs*, 169.

47. Barbiero, *Song of Songs*, 460.

48. Aren M. Wilson-Wright, "Love Conquers All: Song of Songs 8:6b–7a as a Reflex of the Northwest Semitic Combat Myth," *JBL* 134 (2015): 333–45.

5.2.1. A Glance at the Syntax

Song 8:6ab contains a main verbal clause (שימני כחותם על־לבך) followed by a prepositional phrase (כחותם על־זרועך). The latter can be understood as a parallel clause with the ellipsis of the verb ([שימני] כחותם על־זרועך). The repetition of the simile כחותם and its first position in 8:6a gives the image of the seal special importance. Two parallel verbless clauses follow, in which the fronting position of the predicates marks the qualities (עזה and קשה) of the entities at stake (אהבה and קנאה) as the focus of the two utterances:

Subject	Prepositional Phrase (simile)	Predicate
אהבה	כמות	עזה
קנאה	כשאול	קשה

These two parallel clauses are introduced by the preposition כי, which is sometimes understood as having an asseverative function and which we could even leave untranslated.[49] In the Song, however, the preposition כי is always employed to give the reason for a previous request (1:2; 2:5, 10–11, 14). In 8:6a a request (שימני) precedes כי, suggesting that the preposition introduces here two causal subordinates. Being syntactically connected, 8:6ab and 8:6cd are to be read together.

The discourse about love/passion continues in 7a–b through a verbless clause (רשפיה רשפי אש) enjambing in an appositional phrase (שלהבתיה). Subject (רשפיה), predicate (אש רשפי), and apposition (שלהבתיה) are connected not only syntactically but also phonetically, semantically, and conceptually, thanks to the repetition of phonemes (שְׁ/שִׁ/אֲשׁ/שַׁ) and lexemes (רשפיה רשפי), as well as thanks to the repetition of the image of fire (שלהבת/אש/רשף). Furthermore, subject, predicate, and apposition present a *crescendo*: the concept of fire, evoked by the subject רשפיה, is taken up and made explicit by the predicate רשפי אש and further characterized by the apposition שלהבתיה, creating a powerful, cumulative effect.

As for the rest of verse 7, verse 7c–d contain two successive verbal clauses (ונהרות לא ישטפוה and מים רבים לא יוכלו לכבות את־האהבה). The fronting position of the subjects marks the entities מים רבים and נהרות as the focus of the utterances, as though the text said, "*Even* many waters cannot quench love, *even* rivers cannot drown it away." Finally, verse 7e–f

---

49. E.g., Zakovitch, *Das Hohelied*, 272.

presents a standard conditional proposition, with its protasis (אם־יתן איש
אֶת־כָּל־הוֹן בֵּיתוֹ בָּאַהֲבָה) and apodosis (בּוֹז יָבוּזוּ לוֹ).

5.2.2. Love, the Military, and the Divine

At first glance, Song 8:6–7 does not present any military scenario. Upon
closer inspection, however, some hints suggest that the conceptual metaphor LOVE IS WAR is also present in this verse, representing love in military
and divine terms. I will only focus on 8:6c–7b, since it is here that the conceptual metaphor LOVE IS WAR occurs.

    Some expressions and images in 8:6c–7b evoke a mythological sce-
nario of combat involving some ancient Near Eastern warlike gods, such
as Baal, Resheph, and YHWH.[50] For instance, the mention of death (מות)
in 8:6c and of Sheol (שאול) in 8:6d closely recall the Baal Cycle, in which
Baal is said to be strong as Mot/Death and ventures into the netherworld
to fight and defeat Mot/Death (*KTU* 1.6 vi.17, 19, 20). Wilson-Wright
has recently argued that the expression עזה כמות in 8:6c is a formula of
a Northwest Semitic combat myth.[51] A mythological/military scenario is
also evoked by the expression רשפיה רשפי אש. Resheph was a bellicose
Canaanite god, well known in the Mediterranean as a deity connected with
pestilence and death, often represented by fire and spear; he was simultaneously a "salvific god" and a god of disasters.[52] The lexemes קנא and אש
used in 8:6 only occur together in Deut 4:24 with reference to YHWH.
The final expression שלהבתיה, here translated as "a raging flame of Yah,"
is reminiscent of the biblical representation of YHWH as a warrior. Biblical texts often portray YHWH fighting with fire, thunder, and lightning
(e.g., Exod 9:23–24, 28; 1 Sam 7:10; 2 Sam 22:14, 15; Pss 18:9–15; 21:10;
29:7; 46:10; 97:4; 144:6).[53] As suggested by Wilson-Wright, two texts are

---

    50. Albright, "Archaic Survivals," 1–7.

    51. Wilson-Wright, "Love Conquers All," 338.

    52. Edouard Lipiński, *Resheph: A Syro-Canaanite Deity* 19, OLA 181 (Leuven:
Peeters, 2009).

    53. For the military representations of YHWH, see Charlie Trimm, *"YHWH
Fights for Them!": The Divine Warrior in the Exodus Narrative*, GDBS 58 (Piscataway,
NJ: Gorgias, 2014); Martin Klingbeil, *Yahweh Fighting from Heaven: God as Warrior
and as God of Heaven in the Hebrew Psalter and Ancient Near Eastern Iconography*,
OBO 169 (Fribourg: University Press, 1999); Tremper Longman and Daniel G. Reid,
God Is a Warrior, SOTBT (Carlisle, UK: Paternoster, 1995); Marc Z. Brettler, "Images
of YHWH the Warrior in Psalms," *Semeia* 61 (1993): 135–65; Patrick D. Miller, *The*

particularly important: Isa 30:30 and Ps 29:7. Both texts describe YHWH with flames of fire by using the expressions להבות אש ("flames of fire") and להב אש אוכלה ("flame of a devouring fire"), respectively. The employed lexeme להב contains the same root of שלהבתיה, that is, להב. The initial שֶׁ in שלהבתיה can be the š-prefix of the Semitic causative stem.[54] Song 8:6f, therefore, resorts to one of the most stereotypical representations of Israel's God, namely, the belligerent YHWH, to portray love in divine and military terms. The military and mythological/theological imagery continues in 8:7 through the mention of מים רבים and נהרות. In the Hebrew Bible, the expression מים רבים might simply refer to abundant waters (e.g., Isa 23:3; Jer 41:12; 51:13; Ezek 17:5, 8; 32:13; 2 Chr 33:4). On several occasions, however, מים רבים evokes mythological enemies against which the belligerent YHWH fights.[55] This is the case, for instance, in 2 Sam 22:17 and Ps 18:15–16, in which YHWH is depicted as a warrior drawing David/the psalmist out from many waters. Here we find the same metaphoric pattern fire-arrows/flashes-water of Song 8:7: first YHWH is depicted as being on fire (2 Sam 22:9, 13; Ps 18:9, 13) and sending out arrows and lightning (2 Sam 22:15; Ps 18:15); then he triumphs over the many waters and saves the supplicant (2 Sam 22:17; Ps 18:16). The idea that the mention of מים רבים in 8:7a has a mythological meaning is supported by its combination with the lexeme נהרות in 8:7b. Such combination only occurs in contexts of war between YHWH and aqueous enemies (e.g., Ezek 31:15; Hab 3:2–15; Ps 93:3–4). In sum, Song 8:6–7 uses and blends several mythological motifs belonging to ancient Near Eastern literature (e.g., Baal, Mot, Sheol, Resheph) and the Bible (i.e., the belligerent YHWH) to present love as a godlike warrior, or a warlike god.

The representation of love as a godlike warrior in 8:6–7 focuses on specific characteristics. The first is "strength," expressed by the adjective עז, meaning "strong, mighty, fierce" (BDB, *HALOT*). When we consider all occurrences of עז in the Hebrew Bible, the conceptual element HOSTILITY often emerges. As Siegfried Wagner convincingly shows, עז often means

---

Divine Warrior in Early Israel, HSM 5 (Cambridge: Harvard University Press, 1975); Henning Fredriksson, *Jahwe als Krieger: Studien zum alttestamentlichen Gottesbild* (Lund: Gleerup, 1945).

54. Edouard Lipiński, *Semitic Languages: Outline of a Comparative Grammar*, OLA 80 (Leuven: Peeters, 1997), 387.

55. Herbert G. May, "Some Cosmic Connotations of Mayim Rabbim, 'Many Waters,'" *JBL* 74 (1955): 9–21.

"strong/powerful" in a menacing sense.[56] By characterizing love as "strong like death," Song 8:6 introduces a scenario of strife and conceptualizes love as a FIERCE AND ROUGH FORCE AGAINST similar to death. The simile כמות amplifies enormously the power of love. Not only is love a "force against," but it also has the power proper to death: the ultimate power to subjugate everything and everybody.

The second characteristic of love is expressed by the adjective קשה, which occurs in the Hebrew Bible with a wide range of meanings, from difficult to rough, from severe to cruel, from obdurate to obstinate.[57] In 8:6, the nuance of vehemence/violence is suggested by both the parallelism with עז and the simile כשאול. Outside the Song, the combination of the root קשה with עז only occurs in the aforementioned Gen 49:7 and Isa 19:4, which describe a cruel and violent attitude. In Gen 49:7, Jacob curses his sons Simeon and Levi, whose swords are described as "implements of violence" (כלי חמס) in 49:5. This refers to the famous episode in which Simeon and Levi avenged their sister Dinah's rape by killing all the male inhabitants of the city of Shechem, taking their flocks, wealth, women, and children as spoils of war (Gen 34). In Isa 19:4, God punishes the Egyptians by leaving them in the hands of a tyrant. The simile כשאול is only used twice outside the Song, in Prov 1:12 and Hab 2:5, in both cases to portray ferocious and merciless behavior. The sage of Proverbs uses the simile to characterize the violence and ruthlessness of the sinners, and Habbakuk to describe the insatiable avidity of the oppressor. Note that Hab 2:5 is the only biblical text—besides Song 8:6—that uses

---

56. Siegfried Wagner, "עז," *ThWAT* 6:1–14. For instance, in Gen 49:7, עז is used to describe the violent anger (אף) of the brothers Simeon and Levi. According to Isa 19:4, one day Egypt will be given to the hands of a cruel lord (אדנים קשה) and a fierce king (מלך עז). In Num 13:28, powerful (עז) people occupied the promised land with large fortified cities. The explorers sent by Moses were terror-stricken by these people (Num 13:31), which suggests that they were perceived as not only powerful but also threatening. Samson describes the lion that attacked him as עז (Judg 14:14). In Isa 25:3, עז describes ruthless nations, and in Ps 18:18 describes the enemies. Proverbs 18:23 opposes the supplicant speech of the poor to the rough (עז) answers of the rich, and Prov 21:14 employs the adjective עז to qualify המה ("anger, wrath"). The condition of being without strength (עז) seems to be a synonym of being humble in Prov 30:25. Elsewhere, עז describes violent natural elements (Exod 14:21; Isa 43:16; Neh 9:11). The adjective עז, therefore, seems to convey not merely "strength," but rather "strength against."

57. Moshe A. Zipor, "קָשָׁה," *TDOT* 13:190.

the simile כשאול in parallel with כמות. The biblical use of the pairs עז/קשה and כשאול/כמות suggests that Song 8:6 characterizes passion as a violent power that nobody can resist.

The characterization of love continues through the expression רשפיה רשפי אש. Although the etymology of רשף is uncertain, it seems to contain the idea of fire.[58] In Deut 32:24 and Hab 3:5, the lexeme רשף seems to refer to a burning plague, in Ps 78:48 the meteorological imagery of the previous verse suggests the meaning "thunderbolts,"[59] and in Ps 76:4 the syntagma רשפי־קשת suggests the meaning of "(fiery) dart." In Job 5:7, בני־רשף is unclear. The NRSV translates it "sparks of fire," whereas several scholars understand it as a mythological reference to the sons of Resheph.[60] As mentioned above, the mythological background of Song 8:6 suggests that the poem's expression רשפיה רשפי אש might also evoke the Canaanite god Resheph. Even if this is not the case, the fire metaphor portrays love and passion/jealousy as an overpowering and destructive reality. Indeed, the Hebrew Bible usually employs fire metaphors to describe destructive realities. Some of these fire metaphors refer to human realities, such as the tongue of worthless men (Prov 16:27), sexual lust and adultery (Hos 7:6–7; Prov 6:27–29), and the human experience of suffering and persecution (Isa 43:2). However, most fire metaphors refer to God,[61] and fire is a significant element of YHWH's theophanies (e.g., Gen 15:17; Exod 3:2; 19:18; Isa 6; Ezek 1:4; Dan 7:9; Pss 18:14; 144:5–6). The lexeme שלהבתיה ("raging flame of Yah") intensi-

---

58. Martin J. Mulder, "רֶשֶׁף," ThWAT 7:683–90.

59. The parallelism with בְּרָד—which is often considered a scribal error for דֶּבֶר ("pestilence")—might also suggest the meaning of plague.

60. Marvin H. Pope, Job: Introduction, Translation and Notes, 3rd ed., AB 15 (New Haven: Yale University Press, 2008), 42–43; David J. A. Clines, Job 1–20, WBC 17 (Dallas: Word Books, 1989), 142.

61. To his devouring word (Jer 5:14; 23:29), to his purification (Jer 6:29), to his wrath (e.g., Isa 66:15; Jer 15:14; Hos 8:5; Nah 1:6; Job 41:19–21), and to his jealousy (Deut 4:24). As Lewis says, "The numinous quality of fire is one of the most (the most?) enduring of images used by the authors of the Hebrew Bible to depict divine presence. It appears in every literary (i.e., Pentateuchal) strand, in most literary genres, and throughout every period." See Theodore Lewis, "Divine Fire in Deuteronomy 33:2," JBL 132 (2013): 796. As Grant argues, "Theophany in fire highlights the sustaining but also dangerous nature of the deity.... To get too close to Yahweh is not only prohibited, but potentially lethal." See Deena E. Grant, "Fire and the Body of Yahweh," JSOT 40 (2015): 161.

fies the reference to the fire of YHWH, and love is conceptualized as the most fatal, overpowering force.

The exceptional force of love/passion is emphasized in Song 8:7 through the portrayal of love/passion as a fire impossible to extinguish even by many waters (מים רבים) and rivers (נהרות). Besides being images of abundance (e.g., Jer 51:13; Ezek 17:5, 8; 19:10; 31:27), water metaphors are more often employed to portray menacing scenarios, such as times of distress (Ps 32:6), chaos (Ps 93:4), enemies (Isa 17:12–13), and war and death (Ezek 32:13; Hab 3:15). In the conceptual universe of the Hebrew Bible, water is a synonym for overwhelming power, which only YHWH can dominate (e.g., Ps 29:3; Ezek 1:24; 43:2). Being the creator of water, and having established the water's boundaries (Gen 1), the God of Israel can use the water's power to destroy his creation (Gen 9), extinguish it (Ps 107:33; Isa 41:18; 50:2), and decide where it should flow to irrigate the land (Isa 41:18) at his own will. In short, in biblical literature, water symbolizes one of the most threatening powers, and there is only one who is stronger than water—YHWH. What biblical literature attributes to YHWH, Song 8:7 attributes to love/passion, which thereby acquires divine properties.

As shown in figure 5.1 below, Song 8:6 presents two similes. Love (אהבה) and passion (קנאה) can be considered a hendiadys and therefore constitute one target domain. The explicitly mentioned source domains are four: DEATH, SHEOL, FLASHES OF FIRE, and FLAME OF YAH. Moreover, a fifth source domain, WARLIKE GODS, stands in the background of the employed imagery. The generic space can be identified with the element "force," which both love/passion and DEATH/SHEOL/FIRE/FLAME OF YAH display. In light of the previous semantic/conceptual analysis, the conceptual elements of the source domains, which play a role in the conceptualization of love/passion, are the following:

(1) STRENGTH AGAINST (of the source domain DEATH) and VEHEMENCE (of the source domain SHEOL), which are explicitly mentioned (קשה/עזה).

(2) DESTRUCTION (of the source domain FIRE), which is the conceptual element more often associated with fire imagery in the Hebrew Bible and which fits in the context of strife of 8:6–7.

(3) RAGE (of the source domain FLAME OF YAH). The ending of the lexeme שלהבתיה suggests the image of a raging flame and evokes the terrifying image of YHWH as warrior. Furthermore, the strong contrast with the water images in 8:7 amplifies the violent and powerful aspect of the flame.

(4) MILITARY and DIVINE POWER (of the source domain WARLIKE GODS), which emerges due to mythological reminiscences of ancient Near Eastern warlike gods, such as Baal, Resheph, and YHWH. The conceptual elements of the source domains are projected into and restructure the target domain love/passion. The resulting conceptual blending can be phrased as follows: Love/Passion is as powerful as warlike deities. Nothing can oppose it, just as nothing can oppose death. It can subjugate all like Sheol, consume like fire, and is undefeatable like the raging flame of Yah.

The next paragraph will clarify that the aspects of the domain love/passion that constitute the target of the discourse are its social dimension, namely, the relationship between the lovers and their social environment. This will only emerge by closely looking at the context of Song 8:6–7.

5.2.3. Facing (and Overcoming) External Oppositions

Song 8:6–7 belongs to the ninth literary unit (8:5–14), which opens with the woman leaning on her beloved during their travel through the desert (8:5) and with her discourse on love (8:6–7). The unit develops with the words of the woman's brothers followed by her reply (8:8–10). It continues with the woman's words to Solomon (8:11–12) and finally ends with a concluding formula (8:13–14). As already said during the analysis of 8:10, even though this unit seems very fragmented, it is held together by the theme of love as strife. Song 8:6–7 presents a combat scenario, in 8:8–10 the woman argues with her brothers, and in 8:11–12 the woman contends that neither her brothers nor Solomon can decide about her body and sexuality. The theme *love is strife* was already evoked in the previous literary unit (7:12–8:4), in which the woman implies that the two lovers suffered from social obstruction and scorn (8:1). Furthermore, the *love is strife* theme emerges from the very beginning of the poem (1:6) and also occurs in other parts of the Song (3:7–8; 5:7). Note that the ninth literary unit is connected to the fourth literary unit through the catchphrase מי זאת עלה מן־המדבר (3:6; 8:5). I have discussed the military imagery and the theme of combat in 3:6–8 above. Before interpreting the communicative function of 8:6–7 in light of the *love is strife* theme of the Song's ninth literary unit, I will first explain the relationship between the imagery of strife in 8:6c–7 and the initial image of the seal in 8:6a–b.

Song 8:6–7 starts with the woman's request (8:6a–b), then supplies the reason for this request (8:6c–7b):

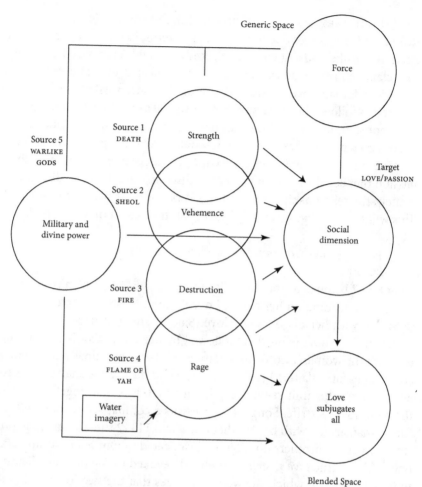

Fig. 5.1. Conceptual Structure of Song 8:6–7. Note that the target domain is left empty.

Song 8:6
Set me as a seal on your heart,
as a seal on your arm

שימני כחותם על־לבך
כחותם על־זרועך

The meaning of 8:6a–b has been elucidated by the use of seals in the ancient Near East.[62] Seals apparently had two main functions: (1) to secure

---

62. William W. Hallo, "For Love Is Strong as Death," *JANES* 22 (1993): 45–50; Hallo, "'As the Seal upon Thy Hearth': Glyptic Roles in the Biblical World," *BRev* 1

the closure of containers and, thereby, to protect and identify the owner; and (2) to authenticate administrative and legal documents.[63] Archaeological and literary sources provide evidence that when a person died, his seal was buried with him. This suggests that seals were considered special personal belongings that could not be passed down to others. Furthermore, seals also functioned as amulets against death. The mention of death in 8:6c leads some scholars to suggest that the woman's request to be a seal on her beloved's arm and heart expresses her desire that their love might survive death.[64] Barbiero, who adopts this perspective, explains: "In the embrace, the woman finds herself literally on the heart and on the arm of her beloved. She now seeks, therefore, that this union (the two are still embracing according to v. 5) will never be dissolved, that it will last forever."[65] Nevertheless, according to my reading, 8:6–7 is not about strife against death, since death is here used as a simile to characterize the strength of love.

A better comprehension of the simile of the seal may come from observing the figurative use of the lexeme חותם ("seal") in the Hebrew Bible. The biblical figurative use of the seal expresses ideas of closeness and attachment everywhere except Job 38:12.[66] In Hag 2:23, for example, the simile כחותם expresses the *close relationship* between YHWH and

---

(1985): 20–27; Hallo, "As the Seal upon thine Arm': Glyptic Metaphors in the Biblical World," in *Ancient Seals and the Bible*, ed. Leonard Gorelick and Elizabeth Williams-Forte (Malibu, CA: Undena 1983), 7–17; Oswald Loretz, "Siegel als Amulette und Grabbeigaben in Mesopotamien und HL 8,6–7," *UF* 25 (1993): 237–46.

63. Bonnie S. Magness-Gardiner, "Seals, Mesopotamian," *ABD* 5:1062–64.

64. Keel, *Song of Songs*, 272–75; Pope, *Song of Songs*, 666–67.

65. Barbiero, *Song of Songs*, 455. This interpretation of the seal has been strongly criticized by Loretz, according to whom "it is impossible that it would occur to an Israelite that he could confront death on equal terms with his love or even that he could hold on to his state of loving in the grave" (Loretz, "Siegel als Amulette," 228). Heinevetter, however, argues that the theme of love's victory over death stands at the very core of the Song—thus the mention of the seal in 8:6 may signify the woman's desire to overpower death, the enemy par excellence (Heinevetter, *Komm nun*, 190–98).

66. Job 38:12 contains a beautiful comparison of the dark earth to a piece of clay, and of the light of the morning to a seal. As Clines explains: "Just as a seal stamps on a flat and featureless piece of clay a design in relief, so the light of the morning changes the featureless dark earth." See David J. A. Clines, *Job 38–42*, WBC 18B (Nashville: Nelson, 2011), 1105.

Zerubbabel.[67] By contrast, in Jer 21:24, the action of tearing the seal off and giving it to somebody else expresses rejection of a *relationship*.[68] In Job 41:7, the metaphor of the seal is used to describe the Leviathan's scales as *closely attached* to his back.[69]

In Song 8:6ab the woman quite likely uses the image of the seal in the same way, to ask for a close relationship of mutual belonging, as though she says: "Let us be profoundly attached to each other; let us become one; let me be completely yours; and you be mine." A similar use of the image of the seal occurs in a parallel Egyptian text from the Cairo Love Songs:

> If only I were her little seal-ring,
> > the keeper of her finger!
> I would see her love
> > each and everyday ...
> [while it would be I] who stole her heart.[70]

The beloved man here clearly employs the image of the seal to express his desire to always be with his woman. The Song's expression שימני כחותם, therefore, seems to be a poetic variation of the Song's refrain דודי לי ואני לו, which is expressed not as a statement but as a wish in 8:6a–b, "May I be yours, and may you be mine." She probably wants to be sure, as does every person in love, that she is in a unique relationship with her lover, that she is his chosen one and even part of his identity, as Assis suggests.[71] She wants to be a seal on both his heart and his arm, to always be united with his thoughts, emotions, and inner world (the heart), as well as with his actions (the hand), that is, with the entire person of her beloved.

In my view, the causal preposition כי explains the connection between the image of the seal in 8:6ab with what follows in 8:6c–7 and with the *love is strife* theme of the ninth literary unit. After expressing to the beloved man her desire to become one through the image of the seal, she explains why they should be forever bonded with each other: since love is a battle-

---

67. "When that day comes—YHWH Sabaoth declares—I shall take you, Zerub-babel son of Shealtiel my servant—YHWH Sabaoth declares—and make you like a signet ring. For I have chosen—YHWH Sabaoth declares" (Hag 2:23).

68. "As I live—YHWH declares—even if Coniah son of Jehoiakim, king of Judah, were the signet ring on my right hand, I would still wrench you off!" (Jer 21:24).

69. "His back is like rows of shields sealed closely as with a seal" (Job 41:7).

70. Cairo Love Songs, B.21C (Fox, *Song of Songs*, 38).

71. Assis, *Flashes of Fire*, 238.

field and undergoes strenuous opposition (8:6c–7), she urges him to join her as one invincible force (8:6ab). The conceptual metaphor LOVE IS WAR, therefore, is used in 8:6c–7 to explain the crucial importance of becoming one (the image of the seal), that is, to overpower opponents (the images in 8:6c–7). In the Egyptian love poetry the image of the seal is used a second time in a text in which the beloved man first describes himself as "her little seal-ring" and then dreams of kissing her publicly in a quite confrontational spirit.

> Her little seal-ring is [on her finger],
> her lotus in her hand.
> I kiss [her] before everyone,
> that they may see my love[72]

The woman's final words in Song 8:6–7 reveal that her concern is about the lovers' concrete opponents rather than about death. In 8:7c–d, she comments critically against their surrounding society, which thinks of love as something that can be commercialized ("Should one offer all the wealth of his house for love, he would be utterly scorned"). It can be said that 8:6–7 is enveloped by the woman's desire for mutual belonging (at the beginning of her speech to the man, in 8:6a–b) and society's lack of understanding of what true love is (at the end, in 8:7c–d). In the middle, she figuratively represents the extent of the friction between love and society. Note that the verb בוז ("to despise, disdain, hold in contempt") used in 8:7 is the same verb that the woman used to indicate the scorn that she felt in 8:1. In 8:7, she turns the scorn back on her social environment.

Song 8:6–7 is therefore in line with 3:6–8: both texts portray a strife between the lovers and their social surroundings. However, 8:6–7 and 3:6–8 develop the common theme of strife in different ways. First, whereas 3:6–8 is spoken by the poet, the woman speaks in 8:6–7. Throughout the entire ninth unit, the woman is, so to speak, on the front line of the polemic against her social environment. In 8:6–7, she even becomes her lover's instructor, and teaches him a lesson about love and the necessity of uniting against external adversities. She does so by employing dramatic similes and metaphors to portray the opposition between love and society in hyperbolic terms, as a kind of cosmic battle in which the lovers have the power of warlike gods.

---

72. O.Gardiner 304 recto (*HO I, 38*); Ramses III (Fox, *Song of Songs*, 81).

This representation of love as a warlike god makes 8:6–7 unique, not only with respect to the rest of the poem but also with respect to the Hebrew Bible. As I have said, what the Bible says of YHWH, the Song says of love. This makes 8:6–7 not only the most unconventional and audacious conceptualization of human love in biblical literature but also a very provocative declaration: love is YHWH-like, so any opposition to love is not only useless—love is more powerful! But it would even seem nonsensical to a society that puts all its faith in YHWH.

Egyptian love songs also conceptualize love as POWERFUL AND INVINCIBLE, struggling against the lovers' society. However, the struggle between lovers and their social environment is never presented as forcefully as in Song 8:6–7. Water metaphors are used to represent the lovers' struggles, but not with the same dramatic tone that is used in the Song.[73] Furthermore, neither fire metaphors nor references to deities are employed to conceptualize the theme that love involves strife. Though Egyptian demotic literature is not my focus, it is worth mentioning that the topic of lovers fighting against society for their love appears commonly in this literary corpus.[74] For instance, Carlsbad 422.36 contains a discussion between a young man and his father about the possibility of him marrying a certain girl that he loved. The son's combative tone suggests that for some reason this love encountered some opposition. Indeed, he says to his father: "These things which I am saying, if they do not happen, death is the one who is with me as a friend and life is the one who is with me as an enemy."[75] In another papyrus, Carlsbad 159 1, 9–14, we find the following story:

> It happened one day that Hareus son of Pahat was strolling in the dromos of Atum, [lord of Heliopolis. He saw ...] the daughter of the prophet of Atum, as her head was stretched out of the windows of her [house ...]. His eyes which had been seeing, and his ears which

---

73. Water metaphors can be found in the following Egyptian texts: P.Harr. 500. A.2, 6, 8; Cairo Love Songs, A.20C.D.E, 20D; P.Beatty 1.A.33, 45. See Renata Landgráfová, "Water in Ancient Egyptian Love Songs," in L'acqua nell'antico Egitto, ed. Alessia Amenta, Maria Michela Luiselli, and Maria Novella Sordi, EA (Roma: L'Erma di Bretschneider, 2005), 69–80; Shih-Wei Hsu, "The Images of Love: The Use of Figurative Expressions in Ancient Egyptian Love Songs," Or 83 (2014): 407–16.

74. Joachim Friedrich Quack, "Where Once Was Love, Love Is No More? What Happens to Expressions of Love in Late Period Egypt?," WO 46 (2016): 62–89.

75. Quack, "Where Once Was Love," 68.

had been hearing, were taken. His spittle ceased (?). [...] He [went] away into his house and wrapped (?) himself in his garments, [without accepting food or drink. It was reported (?) to] his father. He came to the place where he was. He placed his hands upon him and said: "My son! Will [you] not [reveal to me what is the matter] with you? That which you will not reveal to me, to whom, then, will you reveal it?" He said: "Cease [from me! ..., the daughter of the] prophet of Atum—I have fallen in love with her very much. If I were not to sleep with her, I would die." [His father said to him: "...] ... in it. I will let her be given to you as wife."[76]

In sum, the Song's representation of the lovers struggling with their families is a literary topos, certainly found in the poem's cognate literature, but one that the Song develops and constructs in its own way through its remarkable dramatic imagery.

∗∗∗

The conceptual metaphor LOVE IS WAR emerges on the surface level of the Song's text not only to conceptualize and describe the relationship between the two lovers, but also to conceptualize and describe the tension between the lovers and the world. In both 3:6–8 and 8:6–7, the lovers seem to face external opposition, against which their passion appears to be powerful, invincible, and able to subjugate whoever or whatever dares to place obstacles in their way.

---

76. Quack, "Where Once Was Love," 68.

6

Conclusions

Here let me war; in these arms let me lie;
Here let me parley, batter, bleed, and die.
Thine arms imprison me, and my arms thee;
Thy heart thy ransom is; take mine for me.
Other men war, that they their rest may gain,
But we will rest that we may fight again.

—John Donne, *Love's War*

The conceptual metaphor LOVE IS WAR can be found throughout the Song's eight chapters and even constitutes one of the main *Leitmotifs* of the poem. LOVE IS WAR is an undercurrent conceptual metaphor, emerging through different military metaphors, similes, and scenarios. Several conclusive observations can be drawn, on both the thematic and the methodological level.

6.1. The Dialectic of the Song's Warlike Metaphors

Not only are warlike images spread out throughout the poem, but they are also conceptually interconnected. As shown in figure 6.1 below, in the Song it is possible to distinguish two groups of military metaphors.

The first group employs the domain WAR to describe a dynamic *ad intra*: the lovers' game of seduction and their mutual longing. The second group draws on the domain WAR to describe a dynamic *ad extra*: the strife between the lovers and the environment. In the first group, the surface metaphors WOMAN IS FORTIFIED CITY and MAN IS CONQUEROR appear to be conceptually intertwined. They create a metaphorical diptych: the man wants to conquer the woman, and the woman is like a city to be conquered. These two halves of the diptych need to be read together to properly understand the Song's discourse. The metaphor WOMAN IS FORTIFIED CITY

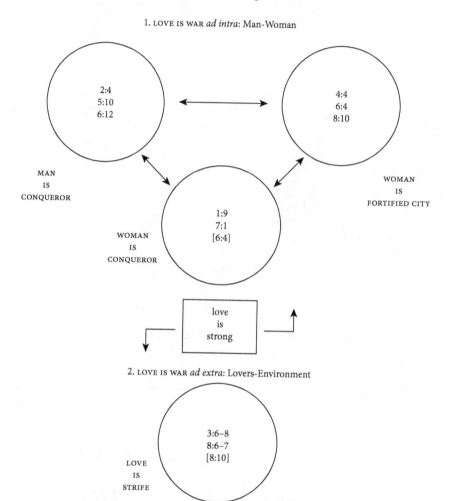

1. LOVE IS WAR *ad intra*: Man-Woman

Fig. 6.1. The mutual tension of the Song's warlike metaphors

empowers the woman in a unique way, picturing her as not immediately available (4:4), sublime (6:4), independent and able to both fulfill her lover and be fulfilled by him (8:10). However, when the metaphor WOMAN IS FORTIFIED CITY is read together with the metaphor MAN IS CONQUEROR, she suddenly appears to be completely in the man's grip (2:4), profoundly overwhelmed by such a stunning lover (5:10), and even responsible for his unstoppable passion (6:12). Likewise, the surface metaphor MAN IS CONQUEROR foregrounds the irrepressible and powerful passion of the beloved man, depicting him in a very conventionally masculine way. However, the interplay between MAN IS CONQUEROR and WOMAN IS FORTIFIED CITY shifts the Song's concept of masculinity: the beloved man is a stunning warrior, but his conquest also depends on the extent to which the woman makes herself available (4:4). While he conquers her, he feels conquered by her (6:4), and the result of the war is an experience of mutual fulfillment (8:10) that does not depend only on his agency.

In other words, in the mutual tension between MAN IS CONQUEROR and WOMAN IS FORTIFIED CITY, these two surface metaphors constantly modify each other, and consequently the poem's concepts of masculinity and femininity are constantly updated. The metaphor WOMAN IS FORTI-FIED CITY, in which the woman is portrayed as the *object* of the man's desire, is conceptually reversed by the metaphor WOMAN IS CONQUEROR. In this metaphor, the woman is not the object but the *subject* of an impetuous passion (1:9), even the victor of the lovers' war-games (7:1). The Song, however, does not present a metaphorical diptych perfectly mirroring WOMAN IS FORTIFIED CITY and MAN IS CONQUEROR. The metaphor MAN IS FORTIFIED CITY is indeed missing. One may certainly wonder whether this is because the Song is ultimately written from a stereotypical male perspective, in which the man is supposed to be the one who leads the conquest of love. If this were the case, however, the presence of the metaphor WOMAN IS CONQUEROR in the Song would be difficult to explain. The lack of the metaphor MAN IS FORTIFIED CITY is explained by the fact that the conceptual association CITY ↔ WOMAN, rather than CITY ↔ MAN, was widespread in both ancient Israel and the broader ancient Near East. However unconventional some of its metaphors are, the Song does not completely depart from the conceptual universe of its *Umwelt*.

The three surface metaphors of the first group share with the only surface metaphor of the second group the common idea that love is strong. Love manifests its strength through both the lovers' mutual longing and the way they face external opposition. The two groups of metaphors, therefore, are two sides of the same coin. Whereas the statement "love is strong" in 8:6 as such seems to refer to the conflictual relationship between the lovers and the environment, when read together with all other warlike metaphors, it becomes the key to the entire discourse. Certainly, it is not simply a case that 8:6 is one of the most memorable verses of the entire poem.

As for the individual metaphorical expressions, Song 6:4 stands out since it might be legitimately located within both the surface metaphor WOMAN IS FORTIFIED CITY and the surface metaphor WOMAN IS CON-QUEROR. On the one hand, the mention of Tirzah and Jerusalem presents the woman as a city to be conquered. On the other hand, the adjective "frightening," the reference to "an army with deployed banners," and the man's reaction in 6:5 ("Turn away your eyes from me, for they overwhelm me") suggest that the conqueror man is actually conquered by the city. Song 6:4 is therefore a polysemous image that condenses the entire dynamic of the first group of metaphors: the conqueror is conquered, and the conquered is conqueror. Likewise, Song 8:10 might be located within both the first group ("LOVE IS WAR *ad intra*: man-woman") and the second group of metaphors ("LOVE IS WAR *ad extra*: lovers-environment"), insofar as the conceptualization of the woman as mature is double-sided. It simultaneously refers to the shrewdness by which the woman tries to emancipate herself from her brothers' control and to the woman's relationship with her beloved man.

Conceptually, therefore, we can conclude that the poem's warlike metaphors display a high degree of *global coherence*, due to the root metaphor LOVE IS WAR. This metaphor makes the reader perceive the Song's discourse as *conceptually* unified, regardless of the different ways LOVE IS WAR emerges on the surface of the text. Thanks to the widespread use of the domain WAR, the reader creates a coherent overall concept of love as a circular dynamic, in which both lovers are conquered conquerors who both strongly desire each other, both passionately pursue each other, both knock each other out, and both surrender to each other. While *ad intra* the lovers are both invincible (they are irresistible to each other) and vincible (they can only capitulate in front of each other), *ad extra* they form one undefeatable force.

6.2. Global Coherence and the Reading Process

The global coherence of the Song's metaphor LOVE IS WAR builds gradually during the process of reading *one metaphor after another* throughout the poem. Through *hooks* to previous warlike metaphors, additions, adjustments, and shifts of focus, the various military metaphors eventually accumulate in the reader's mind to shape a multifaceted, coherent vision of love.

The text starts with the woman's longing for the man (1:2–4) and develops with her attempt to reach him (1:7–8). The very first time the lovers appear in front of each other, the man starts thinking of and talking to the woman in military terms (1:9). Here, the text introduces the man's first perception of the woman employing the first warlike surface metaphor (WOMAN IS CONQUEROR). Through the man's eyes, the reader starts seeing that LOVE IS WAR. The Song continues through a cascade of images of trees, flowers, exotic perfumes, spices, and fruits, creating a very sensual scene, which again turns into a battlefield in 2:4. A second warlike surface metaphor (MAN IS CONQUEROR) is here introduced, conceptually mirroring and matching the previous one. Through the woman's words, the reader starts creating a coherent vision of both the Song and love: in the Song and in love, both lovers are powerful conquerors. The poem seems to start *da capo* in 2:8–9 and continues first with the man's song (2:10–15) and then with the woman's search for the man (3:1–5). No military metaphor occurs until 3:6–8, when a third warlike surface metaphor (LOVE IS STRIFE) is introduced, allowing the reader to add a conceptual element to the network of warlike thoughts/concepts: the antagonistic relationship between the lovers and their environment. Chapter 4 begins with the man's song (4:1–15) and continues with the lovers' short dialogue (4:16–5:1). Right in the middle of the man's *waṣf*, a fourth warlike surface metaphor emerges (WOMAN IS FORTIFIED CITY), which perfectly fits in the previous military conceptualization of love. On the one hand, it is specular to the metaphor MAN IS CONQUEROR (2:4), and, on the other hand, it clarifies that metaphor: the man is a conqueror in the sense that he tries to conquer the woman like a warrior conquers a city. However, contrary to 2:4, in 4:4 the woman is not conquered yet. This *supposed* contradiction does not create incoherence but conceptual complexity, expressed as follows: the conquest of love is not something the man achieves once and for all; the woman is not always immediately available; the woman plays hard to get; and the love-war conquests never cease.

At this point, the pillars of the Song's literary motif *in love as in war* is established. The rest of the poem's warlike metaphors will consolidate, expand, and enrich what has taken shape during the reading of 1:9–4:4. The warrior man is described as sublime by the woman in 5:10, and the belligerent woman is described as sublime by the man in 6:4. Note that 6:4; 5:10; and 2:4 are lexically tied up through the root דגל and that 6:4 recalls both 4:4 (through the image of the city) and 1:9 (through the conceptualization of the woman's beauty as overwhelming). This allows readers to nestle 5:10 and 6:4 in the previous discourse and the metaphor LOVE IS WAR to grow in readers' minds. Likewise, 6:12 is drawn into the previous network of military images by the semantic linkage with 1:9 (מרכבות/רכב) and by the textual proximity to 6:4 (and 6:10), adding focus on the man's inner experience of being overwhelmed by his own passion. If LOVE

IS WAR, who is the hero? Who conquers whom? In 2:4, it is the man who conquers the woman, whereas in 7:1 it is the other way around. Once more, this contradiction does not make the Song less coherent, but more complex, dynamic, even dramatic—and, I would add, closer to the human experience of love, in which both lovers often find themselves in the grip of the other. Finally, not only do the last two metaphors take up the theme of the battle *ad intra* and *ad extra* (8:6–7 and 8:10), they also recapitulate and seal the literary motif and the reader's mental representation of love as war. Song 8:6 does so with its impressive imagery, and 8:10 by both blending most of the previous concepts and ending with the word שלום, which is exactly what we would expect at the end of a war (and toward the end of the Song). If the Song were a story, we would say that the narrative program started in 1:9 is fulfilled in 8:10. The Song, however, is not a story but a poem, in which the concatenation of metaphors throughout the chapters eventually culminates in a coherent narrative representation in the reader's mind: the war game that started in 1:9 is finally over in 8:10, with several developments in the middle.

Such global coherence of the Song's military imagery is therefore a mental representation that takes shape during and at the end of the reading process, a coherence fostered by the text itself, especially by its lexical linkages. The individual metaphorical expressions are connected to one another on the lexical level. This is the case of (1) Song 2:4; 5:10; and 6:4, due to the occurrence of the root דגל; (2) Song 6:12 and 1:9, due to the cognate lexemes מרכבות and רכב; and (3) Song 8:10 and 7:1, due to the presence of the root שלם in both verses. The presence of the root שלם in 3:6–8 also creates a connection between 8:10; 7:1; and the second group of military metaphors. Song 4:4 does not present lexical links with other metaphors belonging to the first group. Yet, it does have connections with the second group of metaphors, due to the lexeme גבור, which also occurs in 3:7, and the couple שלט/מגן that, together with the double mention of חרב occurring in 3:8, form part of the same conceptual domain WEAPONS.

6.3. The *Vexata Quaestio* of the Song's Literary Unity

The question then arises as to what extent the coherence of the Song's warlike metaphors can shed light on the long-standing problem of the unity of the Song.

The question of both the coherence and the unitary character of the Song greatly depends on how the exegete defines *coherence* and *unitary character*, as well as on whether these two are considered mutually inclusive. As stated in the introduction, coherence and unity are different categories that do not necessarily imply each other. Whereas the former is a mental representation, "an achievement of the reader, even as it is highly dependent on a text's cohesive ties," as Jeffrey Stackert puts it,[1] the latter is a compositional and authorial category. The root metaphor LOVE IS WAR in the Song per se is not an argument in favor of the unity of the poem, if by unity we mean a poem written by one author. What has been received as the Song might have been written by one or more authors and redacted by one or more redactors, who shared the same way of looking at LOVE in light of WAR. Nor does the widespread use of the conceptual metaphor LOVE IS WAR per se imply that the Song is one poem rather than a collection of poems. The Song might be an anthology of poems, sharing the same conceptual metaphor LOVE IS WAR. What the Song's widespread use of the conceptual metaphor LOVE IS WAR might rather suggest is the attempt of making the Song's discourse on love cohere. Whether such an attempt is authorial or editorial is difficult to determine, although the different degrees of cohesion of the Song's warlike metaphors make the latter possibility more likely. On the lexical level, only a few warlike metaphors present very strong interconnections (i.e., 2:4; 5:10; 6:4). As for grammar and style, my analysis has shown that the Song's warlike images present very different clause constructions. For instance, whereas some metaphors (i.e., 1:9; 4:4; 8:7) present cases of fronting phenomena, others do not. Whereas some metaphors (i.e., 5:10; 6:12; 8:7, 10) contain enjambing lines, this is not always the case. I have also noted that the warlike images are not perfectly symmetrical (e.g., the image of the man as a fortified city is missing). Furthermore, concerning the second group of military images, Song 3:6–8 and 8:6–7 have nothing in common on the lexical level, and 8:6–7 is not lexically connected to the first group. If the Song were written by one author and/or as one poem, it would probably present a much stronger linguistic cohesion.

It would be a worthwhile project to inquire into other extended metaphors, holding a clear distinction between coherence and cohesion, as well as between conceptual unity and literary unity. Doing so, one could see, on

---

1. Stackert, "Pentateuchal Coherence," 254.

the one hand, to what extent the Song is conceptually coherent both *thanks to and in spite of* its different surface metaphors and, on the other hand, whether the use of extended metaphors may be editorial tools with which the Song's redactors tried to satisfy the human mind's need for coherence.

6.4. Reading the Song *Da Capo* in Light of Its Military Imagery

Once we become aware of the Song's military imagery, we might want to read the Song *da capo* to see whether the poem's theme *in love as in war* can shed light on the interpretation of other verses.

The first of these verses is 1:5:

SONG 1:5
I am black and/but beautiful,   שחורה אני ונאוה
O daughters of Jerusalem   בנות ירושלם
like the tents of Kedar,   כאהלי קדר
like the curtains of Solomon   כיריעות שלמה

The MT vocalizes שלמה as שְׁלֹמֹה, a vocalization that Julius Wellhausen (*inter alios*) considered suspicious, since in the Hebrew Bible curtains are never directly connected to Solomon.[2] More importantly, "tents" and "curtains" occur in parallel lines in Hab 3:7, where they are both followed by the mention of tribes:

HABAKKUK 3:7
Under affliction, I saw the *tents of Cushan,*   תחת און ראיתי אהלי כושן
the *curtains of the land of Midian* trembled.   ירגזון יריעות ארץ מדין

Additionally, outside the Song, the syntagma אהלי קדר only occurs in Ps 120:5, in parallel with the mention of another tribe:

PSALM 120:5
How wretched I am, living in *Meshech,*   אויה־לי כי־גרתי משך שכנתי
dwelling in the *tents of Kedar!*   עם־אהלי קדר

---

2. Julius Wellhausen, *Prolegomena zur Geschichte Israels*, 6th ed. (Berlin: de Gruyter, 2001), 213.

Wellhausen, therefore, suggests vocalizing שלמה as שַׁלְמָה ("Shalma"), an ancient Arabian tribe, in order to restore the parallelism. Several scholars, throughout the twentieth century, accepted this emendation; nowadays, on the contrary, it is usually rejected,[3] mainly because the vocalization שְׁלֹמֹה is in line with the poem's other references to Solomon. The שְׁלֹמֹה reading has been adopted by ancient versions (see *BHQ*), and there is no textual evidence supporting the vocalization שַׁלְמָה. Nevertheless, if we consider the Song's warlike imagery, "Shalma" makes sense in the poem. The tribes of Ishmael were very well known during the Hellenistic period for their power and military strength.[4] Besides referring to the dark color of her skin, the woman's comparison to the tends of Kedar and the curtains of Shalma might also create an awe-inspiring image. Song 1:5 might picture the woman as though she is, so to speak, on the warpath trying to intimidate the daughters of the city of Jerusalem, who look down on her because of her complexion. In this view, Song 1:5 fits very well in the metaphor of love as a war *ad extra*.

The mentions of guards in 3:3 and 5:7 seem to be connected to the same metaphor cluster. Song 3:3 speaks of "guards who make their rounds through the city" (השמרים הסבבים בעיר), an expression also occurring in 5:7, which adds the characterization "guards/sentinels of the walls" (שמרי החמות) at the end. It is not entirely clear what kind of guards these are and whether this is a military image. They could be the sentries keeping guard on the city walls, or the Hellenistic institution of the *peripoloi* introduced in cities occupied by military troops, or simply an urban gang patrolling the streets of the city.[5] Whatever the case, the presence of these guards and their violent behavior against the woman in 5:7 makes sense when we consider the Song's metaphor of love as a war *ad extra*, the Song's idea that society opposes love. In this regard, the Song anticipates what will become one of the major leitmotifs in romantic literature.

---

3. Dominique Barthélemy, *Job, Proverbes, Qohélet et Cantique des cantiques*, vol. 5 of *Critique textuelle de l'Ancien Testament*, OBO 50.5 (Fribourg: Academic Press, 2016), 883–84. Pope provides a list of authors who adopted Wellhausen's proposal (*Song of Songs*, 320).

4. Ernst A. Knauf, "Kedar," *ABD* 4:9; Knauf, "Shalma," *ABD* 5:1154; Knauf, *Ismael: Untersuchungen zur Geschichte Palästinas und Nordarabiens im 1. Jahrtausend v. Chr*, ADPV (Wiesbaden: Harrassowitz, 1985).

5. Heinrich H. Graetz, *Schir Ha-Schirim oder das salomonische Hohelied* (Wien: Braumüller, 1871), 63.

In Song 4:13, the expression שְׁלָחַיִךְ is disputed. It is usually translated something either like "your channels" (e.g., NRSV) or like "your shoots" (e.g., Barbiero).[6] The root שלח occurs in Ezek 31:4–5 referring to irrigation canals, and in Isa 16:8 with the likely meaning of "branches," but it is difficult to pinpoint which of these two meanings is used in Song 4:13.[7] Given that the man is using this expression while describing the woman as a pomegranate orchard, both "your water-channels" and "your shoots" make sense. However, in the Hebrew Bible the lexeme שֶׁלַח often occurs also with the meaning of "weapon, dart" (e.g., Joel 2:8; Job 36:12; Neh 4:11, 17; 2 Chr 23:10; 32:5). In light of the poem's use of military imagery, it is not implausible that the poet plays with the lexeme שֶׁלַח, blending different metaphors in one word. Something similar happens in the title of the book by Frank Lalou and Albert Woda, *Tes seins sont des grenades*, where the French word for "grenade" means both "pomegranate" and "grenade."[8]

Song 7:5 uses urban/architectural imagery:

Song 7:5
Your neck is like an ivory tower.   צוארך כמגדל השן
Your eyes are pools in Hesbon   עיניך ברכות בחשבון
by the gate of Bath-rabbim.   על־שער בת־רבים
Your nose is like a tower of Lebanon,   אפך כמגדל הלבנון
overlooking Damascus   צופה פני דמשק

At first glance, nothing in this verse sounds military. Nevertheless, Song 7:5 follows several military images (1:9; 2:4; 3:7–8; 4:4; 5:10; 6:4; 7:1) that guide the reader to interpret this verse in the light of the poem's military-metaphorical diptych WOMAN IS FORTIFIED CITY—MAN IS CONQUEROR. The last expression, "overlooking Damascus," might especially evoke the image of watchmen on the tower, who are ready to spot the approaching enemy, to alert the city about a possible siege, and to fight back. In other words, Song 7:5 reiterates and expands the image of courtship as a siege.

---

6. See, for instance, NRSV and Barbiero, *Song of Songs*, 169.

7. For the meaning of this lexeme in postbiblical Hebrew, see Assis, *Flashes of Fire*, 137; Fishbane, *Song of Songs*, 125.

8. Frank Lalou and Albert Woda, *Tes seins sont des grenades: Pour en finir avec le Cantique des cantiques* (Paris: Alternatives, 2003).

The verse immediately before 7:5 is worth mentioning. Whereas the MT of 7:4 reads שני שדיך כשני עפרים ("Your two breasts are two fawns"), according to Torleif Elgvin's recent findings 4QSong of Songs[a] (4Q106 2 VII) contains the following variant: שני שדיך כמעז, "your two breast are like a fortification."[9] Elgvin argues that 4QSong of Songs[a] and 4QSong of Songs[b] represent recensions of the Song earlier than the MT.

Finally, Song 7:6 contains a very difficult expression that could be interpreted in light of the Song's military imagery: מלך אסור ברהטים ("A king is caught in the tresses"). Not only the meaning of the lexeme רהטים but also the employed imagery is dubious.[10] There are no elements that explicitly and unequivocally trigger the conceptual domain WAR, and the king may be described here as a "trapped animal." Yet, given the warlike imagery in the close context (6:4, 6:12, 7:1, and maybe 7:4 and 7:5), very likely this verse portrays the man as a prisoner of the woman's love: the conqueror is conquered, and the conquered is conqueror.

6.5. A Multilevel Approach to Metaphor

Since literary metaphors are very complex phenomena, the analysis of the Song's warlike imagery has been conducted on three different levels: the clausal level, the semantic or conceptual level, and the communicative level.

The clause analysis reveals that the Song's warlike metaphors, similes, and scenarios are usually very elaborate. There are three main characteristics of the clauses containing military images: inverted word order (1:9; 4:4; 6:4), enjambing lines (5:10; 6:12; 8:10), and long syntactic constructions (3:6–8; 4:4; 7:1; 8:6–7, 10). Moreover, some military metaphors (6:12; 7:1) present very tricky clauses, to which I have attempted to provide some possible solutions. The way the Song constructs its military metaphors reflects the authors' deliberately marking its warlike imagery. Using Alter's image of the Song as "the garden of metaphor,"[11] I suggest that in the Song's garden not all flowers and plants are particularly striking. Some metaphors stand out more than others also thanks to the way they are displayed—the way they are grammatically, syntactically, and stylistically constructed. The

---

9. Torleif Elgvin, *The Literary Growth of the Song of Songs during the Hasmonean and Early-Herodian Periods*, CBET 89 (Leuven: Peeters, 2018), 26–27.

10. See chapter 4, n. 91.

11. Alter, *Art of Biblical Poetry*, 231–54.

way the Song displays its military imagery foregrounds the poem's warlike
metaphors, similes, and scenarios as particularly prominent. Not all warlike metaphors, however, have the same prominence. For instance, 2:4 and
5:10 do not present peculiar clausal characteristics.[12] This is likely because
both 2:4 and 5:10 picture the man in stereotypically gendered terms, while
more unconventional metaphors (e.g., 4:4) require special constructions.
Or, perhaps, this is because 2:4 and 5:10 are marked differently on the lexical level through the root דגל. In any case, the way the Song constructs its
warlike metaphors has the pragmatic function of capturing and focusing
the reader's attention on its imagery. Much of the communicative power
of the Song's warlike metaphors depends not only on the use of military
vocabulary but also on how these words are connected to each other. The
analysis of the inner workings of metaphors, therefore, is not an end in
itself but a crucial step that allows the interpreter to better understand
what the text says by carefully observing *how* it is said. An attentive clause
analysis can even offer new insights on the meaning of particularly difficult metaphors, as in 6:12 and 7:1.

As for the semantic/conceptual analysis, cognitive linguistics is particularly beneficial to this research. Thanks to its theoretical framework,
especially the notion of *meaning potential*, the military meaning of some
disputed verses has been established (e.g., 1:9; 8:10). The semantic analysis has been strongly characterized not by the so-called dictionary view
of meaning—that is, what words mean—but first and foremost by the
encyclopedic view of meaning. According to the latter model, linguistic
expressions do not refer merely to isolated entities in an external objective
world but rather to vast repositories of knowledge and culture-specific
conceptual associations. For instance, *The Oxford English Dictionary*
alone would never explain why an abnormally large black cat named
Behemoth is present in Mikhail Bulgakov's *The Master and Margarita*.
The dictionary would tell us that the word *black* indicates "the darkest
color possible" and that the word *cat* indicates "a well-known carnivo-
rous quadruped (*Felis domesticus*) which has long been domesticated,
being kept to destroy mice, and as a house pet." What is crucial, however,
to know is that in Bulgakov's culture—as in many other cultures—*black
cat* was conceptually associated with *bad luck and evil*. Neither would

---

12. Song 5:10 does contain a case of "adjunct enjambment," yet this is one of the
mildest forms of enjambment.

the fact that in Russian *Begemot* means "hippopotamus" provide enough information to understand the role of that cat in the novel. It certainly would suggest Bulgakov's irony in portraying a cat as huge as a hippopotamus. Yet in order to fully understand the significance of the name of Bulgakov's cat, we also need to consider conceptual associations such as BEHEMOTH ↔ BIBLICAL MONSTER, DEMON ↔ ROUGHNESS, and AGGRESSIVENESS ↔ TROUBLE. Likewise, in my analysis of the Song's metaphors, while on some occasions it was pivotal to establish the dictionary meaning of some words (e.g., דגל), the mere definition of the Hebrew lexemes usually played a very marginal role. Nor was it important to linger on descriptions of what towers, walls, warriors, or weapons looked like in ancient Israel; an enormous amount of secondary literature already exists on these subjects. It was more important to understand which conceptual connections these terms carry in the Song and how these associations restructure the concepts of love and lovers.

Furthermore, in line with cognitive metaphor theory and contrary to current exegesis of the Song's figurative language, my metaphor analysis did not focus on what source and target domain have in common—the so-called *tertium comparationis*—but rather on the result of the metaphorical process. When it comes to very elaborate literary metaphors, the identification of the *tertium comparationis*, what might have activated the metaphorical process, is often highly speculative. Perhaps in 4:4 the simile of the tower has been suggested to the poetic mind by the shape of the neck, and maybe in the poetic mind the comparison of the woman to Jerusalem and Tirzah in 6:4 was triggered by the stunning appearance of these cities, but what does a woman have in common with a mare (1:9)? In any case, the very core of metaphor, from the perspective of cognitive linguistics, is neither the metaphor's origins nor what its source and target have in common; rather, the core is *what metaphor creates through domains that have little or even nothing in common*. In literature especially, the more distant source and target are from one another, and the less they have in common, the more effective a metaphor usually is. The Song's warlike metaphors are particularly powerful not because LOVE and WAR have something in common in reality (the *tertium comparationis*), but thanks to the fact that LOVE and WAR are in theory mutually exclusive, and yet, the metaphor paradoxically makes the poet grasp aspects of love that otherwise might be overlooked.

Metaphor is not a mere question of cross-mapping elements of the source domain with elements of the target domain—at least not from the perspective of blending theory. In my opinion, in interpreting literary metaphors, the precise identification of the cross-mapped conceptual elements not only is sometimes impossible, but it is not very helpful either. The cross-mapping might explain the metaphorical mechanism, but not what the metaphor conveys. Certainly, the entire target domain is not activated, but since the Song is a love poem, it goes without saying that the activated conceptual elements always concern beauty, passion, and sensuality. In light of blending theory, it is the blended space that is crucial. I suggested that within the surface metaphor WOMAN IS FORTIFIED CITY, the woman is conceptualized as elusive (4:4), sublime (6:4), and mature (8:10). Within the surface metaphor MAN IS CONQUEROR, the man is conceptualized as passionate (2:4), sublime (5:10), and in the grip of his own unstoppable longing (6:12). Within the surface metaphor WOMAN IS CONQUEROR, the woman is conceptualized as irresistible (1:9). Finally, within the surface metaphor LOVE IS STRIFE, love is conceptualized as subjugating all (8:6–7).

As for the use of the category of *cognitive scenario* or *script*, it can help elucidate some particularly problematic texts such as 3:6–8 and 7:1. When we consider the script "wedding," the procession of the litter and the presence of the military escort in 3:6–8 make much more sense, and *the beautiful and the terrible* emerge as two crucial aspects of the Song's concept of love. When we consider the script "military dance at the end of a war," the simile of 7:1 becomes much more intelligible, and the woman emerges as a victorious heroine, the winner of the lovers' war-game.

Finally, on the communicative level, the military representations of lovers and love stand out as novel and unconventional—with respect to the rest of the poem, biblical literature, and cognate literature. These representations are novel and unconventional not only linguistically but also conceptually in how they reconceive gender stereotypes. The positive depiction of the desire of the Song's female character (1:9) as well as the power of her apparent elusiveness (4:4); the characterization of the woman as sublime (6:4), as a love-heroine (7:1); the way she claims her independence in matters of love in front of her brothers and proudly asserts that she is the one who finds and brings שלום (8:10); the way she even instructs her beloved on the power of love (8:6–7)—all this de facto creates a novel and nonstereotypical concept of femininity in ancient Israel and its *Umwelt*.

6.6. Powerful and Powerless Gender

Gender construction in biblical literature has been at the center of academic interest over the past several decades, in line with the developments of the archipelago of interdisciplinary studies known as *gender studies*.[13] Despite the fact that gender theorists hold varying understandings of the definition and construction of gender, a basic, shared notion is that "sex" and "gender" refer to different realities.[14] Using Judith Butler's words, whereas the former is a "biological facticity," the latter is "the cultural interpretation or signification of that facticity," a performance of acts that are associated with the male and the female and that "are renewed, revised, and consolidated through time."[15]

As a love poem between a man and a woman, the Song has provided exegetes with abundant material to inquire into the construal of gender in biblical literature and in ancient Israel.[16] Closer inspection of the secondary literature, however, reveals that exegetes have been almost exclusively concerned with the Song's female character and construction of femininity, whereas the Song's male character and construction of masculinity have been profoundly neglected. This can only lead to partial comprehension, since in the Song gender is constructed and performed within the

---

13. Julian M. O'Brien, ed., *The Oxford Encyclopedia of the Bible and Gender Studies* (Oxford: Oxford University Press, 2014). For an overview of the last developments in gender studies, see Kathy Davis, Mary Evans, and Judith Lorber, eds., *Handbook of Gender and Women's Studies* (London: Sage, 2006).

14. Amy Blackstone, "Sex versus Gender Categorization," in *Encyclopedia of Gender and Society*, ed. Jodi A. O'Brien (Thousand Oaks, CA: Sage, 2008), 786–88; Wendy Cealey Harrison, "The Shadow and the Substance: The Sex/Gender Debate," in Davis, Evans, and Lorber, *Handbook of Gender*, 35–52.

15. Judith Butler, "Performative Acts and Gender Constitution: An Essay in Phenomenology and Feminist Theory," *ThJ* 40 (1988): 519–31. See also Judith Butler, *Bodies That Matter: On the Discursive Limits of Sex* (London: Routledge, 1993); Butler, *Gender Trouble: Feminism and the Subversion of Identity*, TG (London: Routledge, 1990). For one of the many critical reactions to Butler's theory, see Nancy Fraser, "False Antitheses: A Response to Seyla Benhabib and Judith Butler," in *Feminist Contentions: A Philosophical Exchange*, ed. Seyla Benhabib et al. (London: Routledge, 1995), 59–74. For a more refined version of Butler's understanding of gender as a performance, see Judith Butler, *Undoing Gender* (London: Routledge, 2004).

16. See, for instance, Exum's outstanding pages on this topic, which also provide several bibliographical references to the previous research on the Song from the perspective of gender (*Song of Songs*, 13–15, 17–22, 25–28).

relationship between man and woman. The Song's lovers express their "being woman" and "being man" while they long for each other, stand in front of each other, stare at each other, talk to each other, and draw on each other's feelings, words, and thoughts. An adequate understanding of the construal and performance of femininity in the Song is impossible if we disregard the construal and performance of masculinity. A more relational reading is required. The entanglement of femininity and masculinity in the Song emerges particularly when we observe the lovers' use of the metaphor LOVE IS WAR.

The lovers' use of the metaphor LOVE IS WAR reveals that the Song's man and woman shape each other's performance of gender. The concept of femininity, entailing the attributes *powerful*, *elusive*, and even *sublime*, is shaped by the man within his relationship with the woman. It is the man who initiates the metaphor LOVE IS WAR in 1:9 to portray her irresistible beauty when he first meets her. It is the man who sees the woman as an unconquerable fortified city in 4:4, when she plays hard to get, and as an awe-inspiring city in 6:4, when she drives him crazy with her gaze. In other words, it is the man who, standing in front of the woman, creates a set of unconventional metaphors that shape a very unconventional ideal of femininity. He does so by drawing on his own "male world," namely, on the world of war, which in ancient Israel was typically a male-dominated area. As Brettler argues, "As far as we know, war was fought almost exclusively by men against men: woman were not considered suitable for war.... Cross-culturally, war is almost always associated with males, and there is nothing in the Bible, or in the basic structure of Ancient Israel, that would suggest that this was exceptional."[17]

The man's male language and male world is so performative that in the end (8:10) the woman's sees herself through his eyes and affirms her femininity by drawing on his metaphors—his language, experience, and conceptual world. Granted, she also goes beyond the man's language by picturing herself as the one who both finds and provides peace (an idea lacking in the man's military words). However, the woman's expression of her femininity is still profoundly embedded in the man's discourse. In other words, the woman performs the man's ideal of femininity.

Likewise, the Song's construction of masculinity, entailing the attributes *strong*, *virile*, *valorous*, and also *sublime*, is shaped by the woman

---

17. Brettler, "Constructions of Masculinities in the Psalms," 203.

within the relationship with the man. It is the woman who underscores the man's virile passion by representing him as a warrior in 2:4. It is the woman who depicts him as an outstanding, noble warrior, when the daughters of Jerusalem ask her, "What is so special about him?" (5:9–10). Although in 6:12 the martial representation of the man in the grip of unstoppable passion is made by the man himself, he says that *she* made him feel so (at least, in my reading). The man feels like a warrior in 6:12 only after the woman has pictured him so in 2:4 and 5:10. Finally, in 8:6–7 the woman even uses the male world of war to leverage him against external oppositions. In sum, the woman uses the male ideal of the warrior, and the man performs her ideal.

Not only do the poem's lovers shape each other's performance of gender, but every single conceptualization of femininity implies a certain conceptualization of masculinity and vice versa. For instance, the conceptual representation of the woman as unstoppable (1:9), elusive (4:4), sublime (6:4), dominant (7:1), and able to both fulfill and be fulfilled (8:10) implies that being manly is not only associated with being active, powerful, and dominant, but also with being passive, not in control, feeling lost, receiving and not only giving. Likewise, the representation of the man as virile, passionate, and sublime (2:4; 5:10; 6:12) certainly implies that in the Song, being a woman is associated with the concept of being passive and dominated—and also that she is strong enough to contain and even elicit the ardor of the man's desire with her great ability to satisfy him.

Whereas scholars often emphasize the Song's unconventional and challenging construction of femininity against the backdrop of ancient Israel's androcentric society,[18] this reading does not sufficiently take into account that the poem's *overall* construction of masculinity is no less unconventional and challenging. If we consider the metaphor MAN IS WARRIOR as

---

18. See, for instance, Phyllis Trible, *God and the Rhetoric of Sexuality*, OBT (Minneapolis: Fortress, 1978); Athalya Brenner and Fokkelien van Dijk-Hemmes, *On Gendering Texts: Female and Male Voices in the Hebrew Bible*, BibInt 1 (Leiden: Brill, 1993), 3–13, 71–83; Marcia Falk, *Love Lyrics from the Bible: A Translation and Literary Study of the Song of Songs*, BLS 4 (Sheffield: Almond, 1982). Some exegetes argued against this reading (e.g., Clines, Polaski, Pardes). For a critical view of these and other studies, see Cheryl J. Exum, "Ten Things Every Feminist Should Know about the Song of Songs," in Brenner and Fontaine, *Song of Songs*, 24–35. All these studies certainly provided several important observations on the Song's male character. It seems to me, however, that the focus is very much on the woman.

an "isolated event of discourse," as Ricœur would say,[19] the Song's military construction of masculinity can only be viewed as the most stereotypical way of idealizing a man. The warrior certainly represented an ideal of masculinity in the ancient Near East, embodying what a man was supposed to be in ancient societies: active and dominant.[20] The Song does draw on that ideal. Nevertheless, if we read the Song's metaphor MAN IS WARRIOR within its network of military metaphors, the poem's construction of masculinity becomes much more complex and does not appear to be all about domination.[21] The Song's male character is not a stereotypical example of the ancient cultural ideal of male performance, although it does bear the signs of that ideal. The Song, on the contrary, builds up a new idealized performance of masculinity, which also entails the traits of being passive, powerless, and dominated, and it does so by portraying the man not just as warrior, but rather as "warrior in love." As Martti Nissinen says, in order to understand the different constructions of masculinity in biblical texts "it makes a difference whether the man in question is a king, slave, priest, prophet, or eunuch,"[22] or, I would add, a lover. Biblical texts present different constructions of masculinity, and the Song's is unique insofar as the poem's male lover simultaneously embodies, contradicts, and reshapes the ancient ideal of masculinity.

In sum, through the metaphor LOVE IS WAR, the lovers construct each other's gender and perform each other's ideal of gender on equal terms: both "being a woman" and "being a man" are constructed and performed as being powerful and powerless in matters of love.

6.7. The Song's Troublesome Metaphors

Over the past few years, I have had the privilege of presenting and discussing the Song's warlike metaphors at the European Association of Biblical Studies and Society of Biblical Literature Annual Meetings. Not only did

---

19. Ricœur, "Biblical Hermeneutics," 94.

20. Martti Nissinen, "Relative Masculinities in the Hebrew Bible/Old Testament," in Zsolnay, *Being a Man*, 224.

21. For the importance of reading the mutual tension between metaphors in the Hebrew Bible in general and in biblical Hebrew poetry in particular, see Danilo Verde, "On the Interplay of Metaphors in the Hebrew Bible," in Verde and Labahn, *Networks of Metaphors in the Hebrew Bible*, 1–11.

22. Nissinen, "Relative Masculinities," 237.

the insightful feedback of both senior and junior scholars challenge and profoundly improve my understanding of the Song; they also made me realize how disturbing the Song's military language might sound nowadays. During my conference presentations, several exegetes reacted to the metaphor MAN IS WARRIOR quite negatively (using expressions such as "I don't like this metaphor!"), while they were clearly more enthusiastic about the metaphors WOMAN IS CONQUEROR and WOMAN IS FORTIFIED CITY ("Now yes!" some of them exclaimed). The question often arose as to what we modern Western readers should make of the Song's metaphor LOVE IS WAR, since we live in a cultural context in which women do not enjoy gender equality, where violence against women can be perpetrated with relative impunity, and in which war is not regarded as an activity to be pursued, at least in theory. One cannot escape noticing, for instance, that the Song's portrayal of the elusive woman, who attracts by rejecting, seems to foster the very dangerous, misogynistic idea according to which when women *apparently* reject male courtship, they *actually* intend to encourage them. This book has only been an attempt to analyze, understand, and explain the Song's metaphor LOVE IS WAR, without being concerned with the value and the ethical implications of such a metaphor for modern readers. There are some implications, however, that I would like to point out.

First, we would be very naïve if we thought of the Song's metaphor LOVE IS WAR as a mere relic of the past. Modern, Western people make ample use of such a disturbing conceptual metaphor, as cognitive linguistics shows and pop culture suggests.[23] Other fields of research have also pointed out the crucial role that the military plays in our way of thinking. In 1961, for instance, Emmanuel Lévinas commented on Heraclitus's adage "War is the father and king of all" in his work *Totalité et infini: Essai sur l'extériorité*. Lévinas argues, "L'être se révèle comme guerre, à la pensée philosophique."[24] More recently, in 2004, psychologist James Hillman commented on Heraclitus's fragment in his work *A Terrible Love of War*,

---

23. For cognitive linguistics' research on LOVE IS WAR, see ch. 1, n. 6. As for the presence of this conceptual metaphor in pop songs, see, for instance, the lyrics of "Pillowtalk," "Titanium," "Love and War," "War of Hearts," or the French song "Que je t'aime" by Johnny Hallyday: "Quand on a fait l'amour/Comme d'autres font la guerre/Quand c'est moi le soldat/Qui meurt et qui la perd."

24. Emmanuel Lévinas, *Totalité et infini: Essai sur l'extériorité*, LLPB Essais 4120 (Dordrecht: Kluwer Academic, 1990), 5.

in which the author speaks of the "martial state of soul."[25] According to Hillman, "War fathers the very structure of existence and our thinking about it."[26] In other words, war is very much in the human mind, whether we like it or not, and the fact that poets, writers, thinkers, and common people throughout time even describe *love* as a warlike reality tells how profoundly war shapes our way of thinking and talking.

Second, it seems to me that the metaphor LOVE IS WAR sounds particularly unsettling because we immediately associate war with violence, which clashes with the common idea of love. Additionally, it hits some very somber notes of our society—the relationship between men and women, gender roles and stereotypes, and most recently, painful discussions about rape culture and consent. Nevertheless, the use of the metaphor LOVE IS WAR in poetry and elsewhere does not necessarily imply violence. As I explained in the introduction, when a certain source domain (e.g., WAR) is used to conceptualize a certain target domain (e.g., LOVE), only part of the structure of the source (and of the target as well) is activated. Some aspects are highlighted; others are hidden. The context in which the metaphor is used and how it is used foreground some elements and suppress others. In my view, violence and other truculent aspects connected with the human experience of war do not play any role in the way the Song uses the metaphor LOVE IS WAR. While in the Song WAR is used to shed light on some aspects of LOVE, the metaphor in turn *disarms* WAR by removing its most hideous features. As Percy Bysshe Shelley wrote in an essay titled *Defence of Poetry* in 1821, "Poetry is a mirror which makes beautiful that which is distorted."[27] The Song's metaphor LOVE IS WAR has several implications for the poem's construction and performance of gender that challenge our culture. This challenge emerges not *in spite of* but *thanks to* the Song's troublesome metaphors, as well as to the unavoidable clash—that should never be removed, I believe— between the world of the text and the world of the reader. In the end, it is completely up to the reader whether and to what extent the Song's metaphor LOVE IS WAR is a metaphor *to love by*.

---

25. James Hillman, *A Terrible Love of War* (New York: Penguin, 2004), 1.
26. Hillman, *Terrible Love of War*, 2.
27. Donald E. Reiman and Sharon Powers, eds., *Shelley's Poetry and Prose* (New York: Norton, 1977), 485.

NANNETTA
    The lip is the bow
FENTON
    And the kiss is the dart.
    Careful! I shoot the fatal arrow, from my mouth to your tress
    (he kisses her tress)
NANNETTA
    (while he kisses her tress, she ties it around his neck)
    I caught you!
FENTON
    Spare my life!
NANNETTA
    I am wounded, but you are defeated.
FENTON
    Mercy! Let's make peace, and then …
NANNETTA
    And then…?
FENTON
    If you wish, we shall start again!

                    —Giuseppe Verdi, *Falstaff* (my trans.)

Bibliography

Ackerman, Susan. "Otherworldly Music and the Other Sex." Pages 86–100 in *The "Other" in Second Temple Judaism: Essays in Honor of John J. Collins*. Edited by Daniel C. Harlow, Karina Martin Hogan, Matthew Goff, and Joel S. Kaminsky. Grand Rapids: Eerdmans, 2011.

———. *Under Every Green Tree: Popular Religion in Sixth-Century Judah.* HSM 46. Atlanta: Scholars Press, 1992.

———. *Warrior, Dancer, Seductress, Queen: Women in Judges and Biblical Israel.* ABRL. New York: Doubleday, 1998.

———. "Women in Ancient Israel and in the Bible." Oxford Research Encyclopedia of Religion. April 2016. https://tinyurl.com/SBL2645a.

Albrecht, Jason E., and Edward J. O'Brien. "Updating a Mental Model: Maintaining Both Local and Global Coherence." *JEP* 19 (1993): 1061–70.

Albright, William F. "Archaic Survivals in the Text of the Canticles." Pages 1–7 in *Hebrew and Semitic Studies Presented to Godfrey Rolles Driver: In Celebration of His Seventieth Birthday, 20 August 1962.* Edited by Winton Thomas and William D. McHardy. Oxford: Clarendon, 1963.

———. "The Syro-Mesopotamian God Šulmân-Ešmûn and Related Figures." *AfO* 7 (1931–1932): 164–69.

———. *Yahweh and the Gods of Canaan: A Historical Analysis of Two Contrasting Faiths.* JLCR 7. London: Athlone, 1968.

Allwood, Jens. "Meaning Potential and Context: Some Consequences for the Analysis of Variation in Meaning." Pages 29–65 in *Cognitive Approaches to Lexical Semantics*. Edited by Hubert Cuyckens, René Dirven, and John R. Taylor. CLR 23. Berlin: de Gruyter, 2003.

Alonso Schökel, Luis. *Il Cantico dei Cantici: La dignità dell'amore.* Casale Monferrato: Piemme, 1990.

———. *A Manual of Hebrew Poetics.* SubBi 11. Rome: Pontifical Biblical Institute, 1988.

Alter, Robert. *The Art of Biblical Poetry.* Rev. ed. New York: Basic Books, 2011.

———. *The Writings.* Vol. 3 of *The Hebrew Bible.* New York: Norton, 2019.

Ames, Frank Ritchel. "The Red-Stained Warrior in Ancient Israel." Pages 83–110 in *Warfare, Ritual, and Symbol in Biblical and Modern Contexts.* Edited by Brad E. Kelle, Frank Ritchel Ames, and Jacob L. Wright. AIL 18. Atlanta: Society of Biblical Literature, 2014.

Anacreon. *Greek Lyric.* Vol. 2, *Anacreon, Anacreontea, Choral Lyric from Olympus to Alcman.* Edited and translated by David A. Campbell. LCL. Cambridge: Harvard University Press, 1988.

Andersen, Francis I. *Habakkuk.* AB 25. New York: Doubleday, 2001.

Andruska, Jennifer L. "The Strange Use of דגל in Song of Songs 5:10." *VT* 68 (2018): 1–7.

Archilochus, Semonides, and Hipponax. *Greek Iambic Poetry: From the Seventh to the Fifth Centuries BC.* Edited and translated by Douglas E. Gerber. LCL. Cambridge: Harvard University Press, 1999.

Artzi, Pinhas. "The Influence of Political Marriages on the International Relations of the Amarna-Age." Pages 23–26 in *La femme dans le Proche-Orient antique.* Edited by Jean-Marie Durand. Paris: Recherche sur les civilisations, 1987.

Assis, Elie. *Flashes of Fire: A Literary Analysis of the Song of Songs.* LHBOTS 503. New York: T&T Clark, 2009.

Ast, Georg A. F. *Grundlinien der Grammatik, Hermeneutik und Kritik.* Landshut: Thomann, 1807.

Auwers, Jean-Marie. "Introduction." Pages 31–186 in *Le Cantique des Cantiques.* Edited by Jean-Marie Auwers. BA 19. Paris: Cerf, 2019.

———. "Les septante, lecteurs du Cantique des Cantiques." *Graphe* 8 (1999): 33–47.

Auwers, Jean-Marie, and Pieter Van Petegem. "Les interventions du choeur dans le Cantique des cantiques. Qui dit quoi dans le poème?" *ETL* 85 (2009): 439–48.

Backer, Fabrice de. "Evolution of War Chariot Tactics in the Ancient Near East." *UF* 41 (2010): 29–46.

———. "Some Basic Tactics of Neo-Assyrian Warfare." *UF* 39 (2008): 69–116.

Balzac, Honoré de. *Droll Stories.* Translated by J. Lewis May. New York: Skyhorse, 2015.

Banning, Edward B. "Towers." *ABD* 6:622–24.

Barbiero, Gianni. "Die Wagen meines edlen Volkes (Hld 6,12): Eine strukturelle Analyse." *Bib* 78 (1997): 174–89.

———. *Song of Songs: A Close Reading*. Translated by Michael Tait. VTSup 144. Leiden: Brill, 2011.

Barcelona Sánchez, Antonio. "Metaphorical Models of Romantic Love in *Romeo and Juliet*." *JP* 24 (1995): 667–88.

Barrick, W. Boyd, and Helmer Ringgren. "רָכַב." *ThWAT* 7:508–15.

Barthélemy, Dominique. *Job, Proverbes, Qohélet et Cantique des cantiques*. Vol. 5 of *Critique textuelle de l'Ancien Testament*. OBO 50.5. Fribourg: Academic Press, 2016.

Barthes, Roland. *Le bruissement de la langue: Essais critiques IV*. Paris: Seuil, 1984.

Bazyliński, Stanisław. *I salmi 20–21: Nel contesto delle preghiere regali*. Roma: Miscellanea Francescana, 1999.

Beauchamp, Paul. *Accomplir les Écritures*. Vol. 2 of *L'un et l'autre Testament*. PD 28. Paris: Seuil, 1990.

Beek, Martinus. "The Meaning of the Expression 'The Chariots and the Horsemen of Israel' (ii Kings ii 12)." *OtSt* 17 (1972): 1–10.

Ben Zvi, Ehud. "Observations on the Marital Metaphor of YHWH and Israel in Its Ancient Israelite Context: General Considerations and Particular Images in Hosea 1.2." *JSOT* 28 (2004): 363–84.

Bergmann, Claudia B. "We Have Seen the Enemy, and He Is Only a 'She': The Portrayal of Warriors as Women." Pages 129–42 in *Writing and Reading War: Rhetoric, Gender, and Ethics in Biblical and Modern Contexts*. Edited by Brad E. Kelle and Frank R. Ames. SymS 42. Atlanta: Society of Biblical Literature, 2008.

Biddle, Mark E. "The Figure of Lady Jerusalem: Identification, Deification, and Personification of Cities in the Ancient Near East." Pages 173–94 in *The Biblical Canon in Comparative Perspectives*. Edited by K. Lawson Younger, William W. Hallo, and Bernard Frank Batto. ANETS 11. Lewiston, NY: Mellen, 1991.

Black, Fiona C. *The Artifice of Love: Grotesque Bodies in the Song of Songs*. LHBOTS 392. London: T&T Clark, 2009.

Blackstone, Amy. "Sex versus Gender Categorization." Pages 786–88 in *Encyclopedia of Gender and Society*. Edited by Jodi A. O'Brien. Thousand Oaks, CA: Sage, 2008.

Blenkinsopp, Joseph. *Isaiah 56–66: A New Translation with Introduction and Commentary*. AB 19B. New York: Doubleday, 2003.

Bloch, Ariel A., and Chana Bloch. *The Song of Songs*. London: University of California Press, 1998.

Bloom, Harold, ed. *The Sublime*. New York: Infobase, 2010.

Borger, Rykle. "Die Waffenträger des Königs Darius." *VT* 22 (1972): 385–98.

Bourdieu, Pierre. *Masculine Domination*. Stanford, CA: Stanford University Press, 2001.

Bourguet, Daniel. *Des métaphores de Jérémie*. EBib 9. Paris: Gabalda, 1987.

Breasted, James H., ed. *The Nineteenth Dynasty*. Vol. 3 of *Ancient Records of Egypt: Historical Documents from the Earliest Times to the Persian Conquest*. New York: Russell & Russell, 1906.

Brenner, Athalya. *Colour Terms in the Old Testament*. JSOTSup 21. Sheffield: Sheffield University Department of Biblical Studies, 1982.

———. "'Come Back, Come Back the Shulammite' (Song of Songs 7:1–10): A Parody of the *waṣf* Genre." Pages 251–75 in *On Humour and the Comic in the Hebrew Bible*. Edited by Yehuda T. Radday and Athalya Brenner. JSOTSup 92. Sheffield: Almond, 1990.

Brenner, Athalya, and Fokkelien van Dijk-Hemmes. *On Gendering Texts: Female and Male Voices in the Hebrew Bible*. BibInt 1. Leiden: Brill, 1993.

Bresciani, Edda. *Letteratura e poesia dell'Antico Egitto*. I Millenni. Torino: Einaudi, 1990.

Brettler, Marc Z. "The 'Coherence' of Ancient Texts." Pages 411–19 in *Gazing on the Deep: Ancient Near Eastern and Other Studies in Honor of Tzvi Abusch*. Edited by Jeffrey Stackert, Barbara Nevling Porter, and David P. Wright. Bethesda, MD: CDL, 2010.

———. "'Happy Is the Man Who Fills Quiver with Them' (Ps 127:5): Constructions of Masculinities in the Psalms." Pages 198–220 in *Being a Man: Negotiating Ancient Constructs of Masculinity*. Edited by Ilona Zsolnay. London: Routledge, 2017.

———. "Images of YHWH the Warrior in Psalms." *Semeia* 61 (1993): 135–65.

———. "Unresolved and Unresolvable Problems in Interpreting the Song." Pages 185–98 in *Scrolls of Love: Ruth and the Song of Songs*. Edited by Peter S. Hawkins and Lesleigh Cushing Stahlberg. New York: Fordham University Press, 2006.

Brinton, Laurel J. *The Structure of Modern English: A Linguistic Introduction*. Amsterdam: Benjamins, 2000.

Broek, Paul van den, Kirsten Risden, and Elizabeth Husebye-Hartmann. "The Role of Readers' Standards for Coherence in the Generation of Inferences during Reading." Pages 356–67 in *Sources of Coherence in Reading*. Edited by Robert F. Lorch and Edward J. O'Brien. Hillsdale, NJ: Lawrence Erlbaum, 1995.

Budde, Carl F. R., Alfred Bertholet, and Gerrit Wildeboer. *Die fünf Megillot*. KHC 17. Freiburg: Mohr Siebeck, 1898.

Burrows, Millar. *The Basis of Israelite Marriage*. AOS 15. New Haven: American Oriental Society, 1938.

Buth, Randall. "Word Order in Verbless Clause: A Generative-Functional Approach." Pages 102–3 in *The Verbless Clause in Biblical Hebrew: Linguistic Approaches*. Edited by Cynthia L. Miller. LSAWS. Winona Lake, IN: Eisenbrauns, 1999.

Butler, Judith. *Bodies That Matter: On the Discursive Limits of Sex*. London: Routledge, 1993.

———. *Gender Trouble: Feminism and the Subversion of Identity*. TG. London: Routledge, 1990.

———. "Performative Acts and Gender Constitution: An Essay in Phenomenology and Feminist Theory." *ThJ* 40 (1988): 519–31.

———. *Undoing Gender*. London: Routledge, 2004.

Carrigan, Tim, Bob Connell, and John Lee. "Toward a New Sociology of Masculinity." Pages 63–100 in *The Making of Masculinities: The New Men's Studies*. Edited by Harry Brod. Boston: Allen & Unwin, 1987.

Carroll, Robert P. "Whorusalamin: A Tale of Three Cities as Three Sisters." Pages 67–82 in *On Reading Prophetic Texts: Gender-Specific and Related Studies in Memory of Fokkelien van Dijk-Hemmes*. Edited by Bob Becking and Meindert Dijkstra. BibInt 18. Leiden: Brill, 1996.

Chapman, Cynthia R. *The Gendered Language of Warfare in the Israelite-Assyrian Encounter*. HSM 62. Winona Lake, IN: Eisenbrauns, 2004.

Chisholm, Robert B. "סוס." *NIDOTTE* 3:234–36.

Christensen, Duane L. *Nahum: A New Translation with Introduction and Commentary*. AB 24F. New Haven: Yale University Press, 2009.

Clay, Diskin. "Alcman's 'Partheneion.'" *QUCC* 39 (1991): 47–67.

Clines, David J. A. "Dancing and Shining at Sinai: Playing the Man in Exodus 32–34." Pages 54–63 in *Men and Masculinities in the Hebrew Bible and Beyond*. Edited by Ovidiu Creangă. BMW 33. Sheffield: Sheffield Phoenix, 2010.

———. "David the Man: The Construction of Masculinity in the Hebrew Bible." Pages 212–43 in *Interested Parties: The Ideology of Writers and*

Readers of the Hebrew Bible. JSOTSup 205. Sheffield: Sheffield Academic, 1995.

———. "'Ecce Vir,' or, Gendering the Son of Man." Pages 352–75 in *Biblical Studies/Cultural Studies: The Third Sheffield Colloquium.* Edited by Cheryl J. Exum and Stephen D. Moore. JSOTSup 266. Sheffield: Sheffield Academic, 1998.

———. "He-Prophets: Masculinity as a Problem for the Hebrew Prophets and Their Interpreters." Pages 311–28 in *Sense and Sensitivity: Essays on Reading the Bible in Memory of Robert Carroll.* Edited by Alastair G. Hunter and Phillip R. Davies. JSOTSup 348. Sheffield: Sheffield Academic, 2002.

———. *Job 1–20.* WBC 17. Dallas: Word Books, 1989.

———. *Job 38–42.* WBC 18B. Nashville: Nelson, 2011.

Connell, Raewyn W., and James W. Messerschmidt. "Hegemonic Masculinity: Rethinking the Concept." *GS* 19 (2005): 829–59.

Cornelius, Izak. *The Many Faces of the Goddess: The Iconography of the Syro-Palestinian Goddesses Anat, Astarte, Qedeshet, and Asherah c. 1500–1000 BCE.* OBO 204. Fribourg: Academic Press, 2008.

Costacurta, Bruna. *La vita minacciata: Il tema della paura nella Bibbia ebraica.* AnBib 119. Rome: Pontifical Biblical Institute, 1988.

Coulson, Seana, and Todd Oakley. "Blending Basics." *CL* 11 (2000): 175–96.

Cowley, Arthur E. *Aramaic Papyri of the Fifth Century B.C.* Oxford: Clarendon, 1923.

Crawford, Lawrence. "Viktor Shklovskij: Différance in Defamiliarization." *CL* 36 (1984): 209–19.

Creangă, Ovidiu, ed. *Men and Masculinities in the Hebrew Bible and Beyond.* BMW 33. Sheffield: Sheffield Phoenix, 2010.

Creangă, Ovidiu, and Peter-Ben Smit, eds. *Biblical Masculinities Foregrounded.* HBM 62. Sheffield: Sheffield Phoenix, 2014.

Crim, Keith R. "Your Neck Is Like the Tower of David (The Meaning of a Simile in Song of Solomon)." *VT* 22 (1971): 70–74.

Croft, William, and Alan D. Cruse. *Cognitive Linguistics.* CTL. Cambridge: Cambridge University Press, 2004.

Crouch, Carly L. *War and Ethics in the Ancient Near East: Military Violence in Light of Cosmology and History.* BZAW 407. Berlin: de Gruyter, 2009.

Dagnini, Ilaria. "Elementi saffici e motivi tradizionali in Teocrito, Idillio XVIII." *QUCC* 24 (1986): 39–46.

Dahood, Mitchell. *Ugaritic-Hebrew Philology: Marginal Notes on Recent Publications*. BibOr 17. Rome: Pontifical Biblical Institute, 1967.

Dalley, Stephanie. "Ancient Mesopotamian Military Organization." Pages 413–22 in *Civilizations of the Ancient Near East*. Edited by Jack M. Sasson. New York: Scribner, 1995.

Dancygier, Barbara, and Eve Sweetser. *Figurative Language*. CTL. Cambridge: Cambridge University Press, 2014.

Davis, Kathy, Mary Evans, and Judith Lorber, eds. *Handbook of Gender and Women's Studies*. London: Sage, 2006.

Day, Peggy L. "Anat: 'Ugarit's Mistress of Animals." *JNES* 51 (1992): 181–90.

———. "The Personification of Cities as Females in the Hebrew Bible: The Thesis of Aloysius Fitzgerald." Pages 283–302 in *Social Location and Biblical Interpretation in Global Perspective*. Vol. 2 of *Reading from This Place*. Edited by Fernando F. Segovia and Mary Ann Tolbert. Minneapolis: Fortress, 1995.

———. "Why Is Anat a Warrior and Hunter?" Pages 141–46 in *The Bible and the Politics of Exegesis: Essays in Honor of Norman K. Gottwald on His Sixty-Fifth Birthday*. Edited by David Jobling. Cleveland: Pilgrim, 1991.

Deijl, Aarnoud van der. *Protest or Propaganda: War in the Old Testament Book of Kings and in Contemporaneous Ancient Near Eastern Texts*. SSN 51. Leiden: Brill, 2008.

Delitzsch, Franz. *Hoheslied und Kohelet*. BKAT 4. Leipzig: Dörffling & Franke, 1875.

Dempsey, Carol J. "The 'Whore' of Ezekiel 16: The Impact and Ramifications of Gender-Specific Metaphors in Light of Biblical Law and Divine Judgment." Pages 57–78 in *Gender and Law in the Bible and the Ancient Near East*. Edited by Victor H. Matthews. JSOTSup 261. Sheffield: Sheffield Academic, 1998.

Derchain, Philippe. "Le lotus, la mandragore et la perséa." *CdE* 50 (1975): 65–86.

Derron, Pascale, ed. *Pseudo-Phocylide: Sentences*. CUFSG. Paris: Belles Lettres.

Dijk-Hemmes, Fokkelien van. "The Metaphorization of Woman in Prophetic Speech: An Analysis of Ezekiel XXIII." *VT* 43 (1993): 162–70.

Dik, Simon C. *The Structure of the Clause*. Part 1 of *The Theory of Functional Grammar*. FGS 20. Berlin: de Gruyter, 1997.

Dobbs-Allsopp, F. W. "Beauty." *NIDB* 1:415–16.

———. "The Delight of Beauty and Song of Songs 4:1–7." *Int* 59 (2005): 260–77.

———. "The Effects of Enjambment in Lamentations (Part 2)." *ZAW* 113 (2001): 270–85.

———. "The Enjambing Line in Lamentations: A Taxonomy (Part 1)." *ZAW* 113 (2001): 219–39.

———. "Late Linguistic Features in the Song of Songs." Pages 27–77 in *Perspectives on the Song of Songs/Perspektiven der Hoheliedauslegung*. Edited by Anselm C. Hagedorn. BZAW 346. Berlin: de Gruyter, 2005.

Doran, Robert. *The Theory of the Sublime: From Longinus to Kant*. Cambridge: Cambridge University Press, 2015.

Doyle, Brian. *The Apocalypse of Isaiah Metaphorically Speaking: A Study of the Use, Function and Significance of Metaphors in Isaiah 24–27*. BETL 151. Leuven: Peeters, 2000.

Driscoll, Richard, Keith E. Davis, and Milton E. Lipetz. "Parental Interference and Romantic Love: Romeo and Juliet Effect." *JPSP* 24 (1972): 1–18.

Eagleton, Terry. *How to Read a Poem*. Malden, MA: Blackwell, 2007.

———. *How to Read Literature*. New Haven: Yale University Press, 2014.

Ebeling, Jennie R. *Women's Lives in Biblical Times*. London: T&T Clark, 2010.

Eco, Umberto. *The Name of the Rose*. Translated by William Weaver. London: Book Club Associates, 1983.

Eichrodt, Walther. *Ezekiel: A Commentary*. OTL. Philadelphia: Westminster, 1970.

Eisenbeis, Walter. *Die Wurzel שלם im Alten Testament*. BZAW 113. Berlin: de Gruyter, 1969.

Elgvin, Torleif. *The Literary Growth of the Song of Songs during the Hasmonean and Early-Herodian Periods*. CBET 89. Leuven: Peeters, 2018.

Elliott, Mary Timothea. *The Literary Unity of the Canticle*. EUS 23: Theology 371. Frankfurt am Main: Lang, 1989.

Enns, Peter. "חָרֵב." *NIDOTTE* 2:259–62.

Exum, Cheryl J. *Song of Songs*. OTL. Louisville: Westminster John Knox, 2005.

———. "Ten Things Every Feminist Should Know about the Song of Songs." Pages 24–35 in *The Song of Songs: A Feminist Companion*. Edited by Athalya Brenner and Carol R. Fontaine. FCB 2/6. Sheffield: Sheffield Academic, 2000.

Falk, Marcia. *Love Lyrics from the Bible: A Translation and Literary Study of the Song of Songs.* BLS 4. Sheffield: Almond, 1982.

Fauconnier, Gill, and Mark Turner. "Rethinking Metaphors." Pages 53–66 in *The Cambridge Handbook of Metaphor and Thought.* Edited by Raymond W. Gibbs. Cambridge: Cambridge University Press, 2008.

———. *The Way We Think: Conceptual Blending and the Mind's Hidden Complexities.* New York: Basic Books, 2002.

Fernández, Miguel Pérez. *An Introductory Grammar of Rabbinic Hebrew.* Leiden: Brill, 1997.

Ferraris, Maurizio. *Storia dell'ermeneutica.* Milano: Bompiani, 2008.

Ferretter, Luke. "The Power and the Glory: The Aesthetics of the Hebrew Bible." *LT* 18 (2004): 123–38.

Fillmore, Charles J. "Frame Semantics." Pages 11–37 in *Linguistics in the Morning Calm.* Edited by the Linguistic Society of Korea. Seoul: Hanshim, 1982.

———. "Frames and the Semantics of Understanding." *Quaderni di semantica* 6 (1985): 222–54.

Fisch, Harold. "Song of Solomon: The Allegorical Imperative." Pages 80–103 in *Poetry with a Purpose: Biblical Poetics and Interpretation.* ISBL. Bloomington: Indiana University Press, 1990.

Fischer, Stefan. *Das Hohelied Salomos zwischen Poesie und Erzählung.* FAT 72. Tübingen: Mohr Siebeck, 2010.

Fishbane, Michael A. *Song of Songs: The Traditional Hebrew Text with the New JPS Translation.* Lincoln: University of Nebraska Press, 2015.

Foster, Benjamin R. *Before the Muses: An Anthology of Akkadian Literature.* 3rd ed. Bethesda, MD: CDL, 2005.

Fox, Michael V. *The Song of Songs and the Ancient Egyptian Love Song.* Madison: University of Wisconsin Press, 1985.

Fraser, Nancy. "False Antitheses: A Response to Seyla Benhabib and Judith Butler." Pages 59–74 in *Feminist Contentions: A Philosophical Exchange.* Edited by Seyla Benhabib, Judith Butler, Drucilla Cornell, and Nancy Fraser. London: Routledge, 1995.

Fredriksson, Henning. *Jahwe als Krieger: Studien zum alttestamentlichen Gottesbild.* Lund: Gleerup, 1945.

Freeman, Donald C. "Catch[ing] the Nearest Way: *Macbeth* and Cognitive Metaphor." *JP* 24 (1995): 689–708.

Frolov, Serge. "The Comeback of Comebacks." Pages 41–64 in *On Prophets, Warriors, and Kings: Former Prophets through the Eyes of Their*

Interpreters. Edited by George J. Brooke and Ariel Feldman. BZAW 470. Berlin: de Gruyter, 2016.

Fulco, William J. "Ishtar." *ABD* 3:521–22.

Gabbay, Uri. "Dance in Textual Sources from Ancient Mesopotamia." *NEA* 66 (2003): 103–4.

Gabriel, Richard A. *The Military History of Ancient Israel*. London: Praeger, 2003.

Gadamer, Hans G. *Wahrheit und Methode*. Tübingen: Mohr Siebeck, 1960.

Galambush, Julie. *Jerusalem in the Book of Ezekiel: The City as Yahweh's Wife*. SBLDS 130. Atlanta: Scholars Press, 1992.

Garbini, Giovanni. *Cantico dei Cantici*. Biblica: Testi e Studi 2. Brescia: Paideia, 1992.

Garrett, Duane A. "Song of Songs." Pages 3–265 in *Song of Songs, Lamentations*. WBC 23B. Nashville: Nelson, 2004.

Gaster, Theodor H. "Sharper than a Serpent's Tooth: A Canaanite Charm against Snakebite." *JANES* 7 (1975): 33–51.

Gault, Brian P. *Body as Landscape, Love as Intoxication: Conceptual Metaphors in the Song of Songs*. AIL 36. Atlanta: SBL Press, 2019.

Gavins, Joanna. "Metaphor Studies in Retrospect and Prospect: An Interview with Gerard Steen." *RCL* 12 (2014): 493–510.

Gerleman, Gillis. "Die Wurzel שלם *šlm*." *ZAW* 85 (1973): 1–14.

———. *Ruth; Das Hohelied*. 2nd ed. BKAT 18. Neukirchen-Vluyn: Neukirchener Verlag, 1981.

———. "שלם *šlm* to Have Enough." *TLOT* 3:1337–48.

Goitein, Shelomo D. "*Ayumma Kannidgalot* (Song of Songs VI. 10)." *JSS* 10 (1965): 220–21.

Goodspeed, Edgar J. "The Shulammite." *AJSL* 50 (1934): 102–4.

Goodwin, Charles W. "On Four Songs Contained in an Egyptian Papyrus in the British Museum." *TSBA* 3 (1874): 380–88.

Gordis, Robert. "The Root *dgl* in the Song of Songs." *JBL* 88 (1969): 203–4.

———. *The Song of Songs and Lamentations: A Study, Modern Translation, and Commentary*. New York: KTAV, 1974.

Gordon, Cyrus H. *The Common Background of Greek and Hebrew Civilizations*. New York: Norton Library, 1965.

Gordon, Pamela, and Harold C. Washington. "Rape as Military Metaphor in the Hebrew Bible." Pages 308–25 in *A Feminist Companion to the Latter Prophets*. Edited by Athalya Brenner. FCB 8. Sheffield: Sheffield Academic, 1995.

Gradwohl, Roland. *Die Farben im AT*. BZAW 83. Berlin: de Gruyter, 1963.

Grady, Joseph E., Todd Oakley, and Seana Coulson. "Blending and Meta-phor." Pages 101–24 in *Metaphor in Cognitive Linguistics.* Edited by Raymond W. Gibbs and Gerard J. Steen. Amsterdam: John Benjamins, 1999.

Graetz, Heinrich H. *Schir Ha-Schirim oder das salomonische Hohelied.* Wien: Braumüller, 1871.

Grant, Deena E. "Fire and the Body of Yahweh." *JSOT* 40 (2015): 139–61.

Gray, George B. "The Meaning of the Hebrew Word דֶּגֶל." *JQR* 11 (1899): 92–101.

Greenberg, Moshe. *Ezekiel 21–37: A New Translation with Introduction and Commentary.* AB 22A. New York: Doubleday, 1997.

Greengus, Samuel. "Old Babylonian Marriage Ceremonies and Rites." *JAOS* 20 (1966): 55–72.

———. "The Old Babylonian Marriage Contract." *JAOS* 89 (1969): 505–32.

Gruber, Mayer I. "Ten Dance-Derived Expressions in the Hebrew Bible." *Bib* 62 (1981): 328–46.

Gunkel, Hermann. "Ägyptische Parallelen zum Alten Testament." *ZDMG* 63 (1909): 531–39.

Haddox, Susan E. "Masculinity Studies of the Hebrew Bible: The First Two Decades." *CurBR* 14 (2016): 176–206.

Hagedorn, Anselm C. "What Kind of Love Is It: Egyptian, Hebrew, or Greek." *WO* 46 (2016): 90–106.

Halkin, Hillel. *The Selected Poems of Yehuda Halevi.* New York: Schocken, 2010.

Halliday, Michael A. K., and Ruqaiya Hasan. *Cohesion in English.* ELS 9. London: Longman, 1976.

Hallo, William W. "'As the Seal upon Thine Arm': Glyptic Metaphors in the Biblical World." Pages 7–17 in *Ancient Seals and the Bible.* Edited by Leonard Gorelick and Elizabeth Williams-Forte. Malibu, CA: Undena, 1983.

———. "'As the Seal upon Thy Hearth': Glyptic Roles in the Biblical World." *BRev* 1 (1985): 20–27.

———. "For Love Is Strong as Death." *JANES* 22 (1993): 45–50.

Hansen, Peter Allan, and Kurt Latte, eds. *Hesychii Alexandrini Lexicon.* Vol. 3, Π–Σ. SGLG 11/3. Berlin: de Gruyter, 2005.

Harland, Peter J. "Vertical or Horizontal: The Sin of Babel." *VT* 68 (1998): 515–33.

Harrison, Wendy Cealey. "The Shadow and the Substance: The Sex/Gender Debate." Pages 35–52 in *Handbook of Gender and Women's Studies.*

Edited by Kathy Davis, Mary Evans, and Judith Lorber. London: Sage, 2006.

Hartley, John E. *The Semantics of Ancient Hebrew Colour Lexemes.* ANES-Sup 33. Leuven: Peeters, 2010.

Hatfield, Elaine, and Richard L. Rapson. *Love and Sex: Cross-cultural Perspectives.* Lanham, MD: University Press of America, 2005.

Hearn, Jeff. "From Hegemonic Masculinity to the Hegemony of Men." *FT* 5 (2004): 49–72.

Heine, Bernd. "The Body in Language: Observations from Grammaticalization." Pages 11–32 in *The Body in Language: Comparative Studies of Linguistic Embodiment.* Edited by Matthias Brenzinger and Iwona Kraska-Szlenk. BSLCC 8. Leiden: Brill, 2014.

Heinevetter, Hans-Josef. *"Komm nun, mein Liebster, Dein Garten ruft Dich!": Das Hohelied als programmatische Komposition.* BBB 69. Frankfurt am Main: Athenäum, 1988.

Henderson, Greig. "A Rhetoric of Form: The Early Burke and Reader-Response Criticism." Pages 127–42 in *Unending Conversations: New Writings by and about Kenneth Burke.* Edited by Greig Henderson and David Cratis Williams. RPT. Carbondale: Southern Illinois University Press, 2001.

Hersch, Karen K. *The Roman Wedding: Ritual and Meaning in Antiquity.* New York: Cambridge University Press, 2010.

Hiebert, Theodore. "The Tower of Babel and the Origin of the World's Cultures." *JBL* 126 (2007): 29–58.

Hillman, James. *A Terrible Love of War.* New York: Penguin, 2004.

Hirsch, Eric Donald. *The Aims of Interpretation.* Chicago: University of Chicago Press, 1976.

———. *Validity in Interpretation.* New Haven: Yale University Press, 1967.

Hoffner, Harry H. "Symbols for Masculinity and Femininity: Their Use in Ancient Near Eastern Sympathetic Magic Rituals." *JBL* 85 (1966): 326–34.

Holladay, William L. *Jeremiah 1: A Commentary on the Book of the Prophet Jeremiah, Chapters 1–25.* Hermeneia. Philadelphia: Fortress, 1986.

Hopf, Matthias. *Liebesszenen: Eine literaturwissenschaftliche Studie zum Hohenlied als einem dramatisch-performativen Text.* ATANT 108. Zurich: Theologischer Verlag, 2016.

Horst, Friedrich. "Die Formen des althebräischen Liebesliedes." Pages 176–87 in *Gottes Recht: Studien zum Recht im Alten Testament.* Edited by Friedrich Horst and Hans W. Wolff. TB 12. München: Kaiser, 1961.

Hrushovski, Benjamin. *Explorations in Poetics*. Stanford, CA: Stanford University Press, 2007.

———. "Poetic Metaphor and Frames of Reference: With Examples from Eliot, Rilke, Mayakovsky, Mandelshtam, Pound, Creeley, Amichai, and the New York Times." *PT* 5 (1984): 5–43.

Hsu, Shih-Wei. "The Images of Love: The Use of Figurative Expressions in Ancient Egyptian Love Songs." *Or* 83 (2014): 407–16.

Hunt, Patrick. *Poetry in the Song of Songs: A Literary Analysis*. StBibLit 96. New York: Lang, 2008.

Ilie, Cornelia. *What Else Can I Tell You? A Pragmatic Study of English Rhetorical Questions as Discursive and Argumentative Acts*. Stockholm: Almqvist & Wiksell, 1994.

Invernizzi, Laura. "La mano, il tamburello, la danza delle donne: La 'scena-tipo' del canto di vittoria." Pages 73–99 in *Extra ironiam nulla salus: Studi in onore di Roberto Vignolo in occasione del suo LXX compleanno*. Edited by Matteo Crimella, Giovanni C. Pagazzi, and Stefano Romanello. Biblica 8. Glossa: Milano, 2016.

Iser, Wolfgang. *The Act of Reading: A Theory of Aesthetic Response*. London: Routledge, 1978.

Jackson, Bernard S. "The 'Institutions' of Marriage and Divorce in the Hebrew Bible." *JSS* 56 (2011): 221–51.

James, Elaine T. "A City Who Surrenders: Song 8:8–10." *VT* 67 (2017): 448–57.

———. *Landscapes of the Song of Songs: Poetry and Place*. New York: Oxford University Press, 2017.

Jankowiak, William R. *Intimacies: Love and Sex across Cultures*. New York: Columbia University Press, 2008.

Jepsen, Alfred. "חָזָה." *ThWAT* 2:822–35.

Jonker, Luis. "רכב." *NIDOTTE* 3:1109–14.

Joüon, Paul. "Crainte et peur en hébreu biblique: Etude de lexicographie et de stylistique." *Bib* 6 (1925): 174–79.

———. *Le cantique des cantiques: Commentaire philologique et exégétique*. Paris: Beauchesne, 1909.

Kaiser, Otto. "חֶרֶב." *ThWAT* 3:164–76.

Kapelrud, Arvid S. *The Violent Goddess: Anat in the Ras Shamra Texts*. SUB. Oslo: Universitetsforlaget, 1969.

Karandashev, Victor. *Romantic Love in Cultural Contexts*. Cham, Switzerland: Springer, 2017.

Keel, Othmar. *Das Hohelied*. BKAT 18. Zürich: Theologischer Verlag, 1986.

————. *Deine Blicke sind Tauben: Zur Metaphorik des Hohen Liedes.* SBS 114/115. Stuttgart: Katholisches Bibelwerk, 1984.

————. *The Song of Songs: A Continental Commentary.* Translated by Frederick J. Gaiser. CC. Minneapolis: Fortress, 1994.

————. *The Symbolism of the Biblical World: Ancient Near Eastern Iconography and the Book of Psalms.* Winona Lake, IN: Eisenbrauns, 1997.

Kelle, Brad E. *Ancient Israel at War 853–586 BC.* EH 67. Oxford: Osprey, 2007.

————. "Wartime Rhetoric: Prophetic Metaphorization of Cities as Female." Pages 95–111 in *Writing and Reading War: Rhetoric, Gender, and Ethics in Biblical and Modern Contexts.* Edited by Brad E. Kelle and Frank R. Ames. SymS 42. Atlanta: Society of Biblical Literature, 2008.

Kellerman, Diether. "מִגְדָּל." *ThWAT* 4:642–46.

Kilduff, Martin, and Wenpin Tsai. *Social Networks and Organizations.* London: Sage, 2003.

King, Philip J., and Lawrence E. Stager. *Life in Biblical Israel.* LAI. Louisville: Westminster John Knox, 2001.

Kingsmill, Edmée. *The Song of Songs and the Eros of God: A Study in Biblical Intertextuality.* Oxford Theological Monographs. Oxford: Oxford University Press, 2009.

Klíma, Joseph. "Le règlement du mariage dans les lois babyloniennes anciennes." Pages 109–21 in *Im Bannkreis des Alten Orients: Studien zur Sprach- und Kulturgeschichte des Alten Orients und seines Ausstrahlungsraumes.* Edited by Wolfgang Meid and Helga Trenkwalder. Innsbruck: Amoe, 1986.

Kline, Jonathan G. *Allusive Soundplay in the Hebrew Bible.* AIL 28. Atlanta: SBL Press, 2016.

Klingbeil, Martin. *Yahweh Fighting from Heaven: God as Warrior and as God of Heaven in the Hebrew Psalter and Ancient Near Eastern Iconography.* OBO 169. Fribourg: University Press, 1999.

Knauf, Ernst A. *Ismael: Untersuchungen zur Geschichte Palästinas und Nordarabiens im 1. Jahrtausend v. Chr.* ADPV. Wiesbaden: Harrassowitz, 1985.

————. "Kedar." *ABD* 4:9–10.

————. "Shalma." *ABD* 5:1154.

Kövecses, Zoltán. *Metaphor: A Practical Introduction.* Oxford: Oxford University Press, 2010.

——. *Metaphor in Culture: Universality and Variation.* Cambridge: Cambridge University Press, 2007.

——. *Metaphors of Anger, Pride, and Love: A Lexical Approach to the Structure of Concepts.* Pragmatics and Beyond 7.8. Amsterdam: Benjamins, 1986.

——. *Where Metaphors Come From: Reconsidering Context in Metaphor.* Oxford: Oxford University Press, 2015.

Kraska-Szlenk, Iwona. "Semantic Extension of Body Part Terms: Common Pattern and Their Interpretation." *LS* 44 (2014): 15–39.

Krinetzki, Leo G. *Das Hohelied: Kommentar zu Gestalt und Kerygma eines alttestamentlichen Liebesliedes.* Düsseldorf: Patmos, 1964.

Labahn, Antje, ed. *Conceptual Metaphors in Poetic Texts: Proceedings of the Metaphor Research Group of the European Association of Biblical Studies in Lincoln 2009.* PHSC 18. Piscataway, NJ: Gorgias, 2013.

LaCocque, André. *Romance, She Wrote: A Hermeneutical Essay on Song of Songs.* Harrisburg, PA: Trinity Press International, 1998.

Lakoff, George. "The Contemporary Theory of Metaphor." Pages 202–51 in *Metaphor and Thought.* Edited by Andrew Ortony. Cambridge: Cambridge University Press, 1993.

——. *Women, Fire, and Dangerous Things: What Categories Reveal about the Mind.* Chicago: University of Chicago Press, 1987.

Lakoff, George, and Mark Johnson. *Metaphors We Live By.* Chicago: University of Chicago Press, 1980.

Lakoff, George, and Mark Turner. *More than Cool Reason: A Field Guide to Poetic Metaphor.* Chicago: University of Chicago Press, 1989.

Lalou, Frank, and Albert Woda. *Tes seins sont des grenades: Pour en finir avec le Cantique des cantiques.* Paris: Alternatives, 2003.

Landgráfová, Renata. "Water in Ancient Egyptian Love Songs." Pages 69–80 in *L'acqua nell'Antico Egitto.* Edited by Alessia Amenta, Maria Michela Luiselli, and Maria Novella Sordi. EA. Roma: L'Erma di Bretschneider, 2005.

Landgráfová, Renata, and Hana Navrátilová. *Sex and the Golden Goddess I: Ancient Egyptian Love Songs in Context.* Prague: Czech Institute of Egyptology, 2009.

Landy, Francis. *Beauty and the Enigma: And Other Essays on the Hebrew Bible.* JSOTSup 312. Sheffield: Sheffield Academic, 2001.

——. *Paradoxes of Paradise: Identity and Difference in the Song of Songs.* BLS 7. Sheffield: Almond, 1987.

————. "The Song of Songs and the Garden of Eden." *JBL* 98 (1979): 513–28.

Lane, Nicholas. "Some Illusive Puns in Theocritus, Idyll 18 Gow." *QUCC* 83 (2006): 23–26.

Langacker, Ronald W. "The Contextual Basis of Cognitive Semantics." Pages 229–52 in *Language and Conceptualization*. Edited by Jan Nuyts and Eric Pederson. LCC 1. Cambridge: Cambridge University Press, 1997.

Lapson, Dvora. "Dance." *EncJud* 5:1262–74.

Leong, Chin Hei. "Completeness—Balance: Revisiting the Biblical Hebrew Verb שלם from the Perspective of Cognitive Semantics." PhD diss., KU Leuven, 2019.

Lévinas, Emmanuel. *Totalité et infini: Essai sur l'extériorité*. LLPB Essais 4120. Dordrecht: Kluwer Academic, 1990.

Levine, Baruch A., and Jean-Michel de Tarragon. "'Shapshu Cries Out in Heaven': Dealing with Snake-Bites at Ugarit (KTU 1.100, 1.107)." *RB* 95 (1988): 481–518.

Lewis, Theodore. "Divine Fire in Deuteronomy 33:2." *JBL* 132 (2013): 791–803.

Linafelt, Tod. Review of *Spikenard and Saffron: The Imagery of the Song of Songs*, by Jill M. Munro. *JBL* 118 (1999): 350–51.

Lipiński, Edouard. *Resheph: A Syro-Canaanite Deity*. StPho 19. OLA 181. Leuven: Peeters, 2009.

————. *Semitic Languages: Outline of a Comparative Grammar*. OLA 80. Leuven: Peeters, 1997.

Litchfield West, Martin. "Phocylides." *JHS* 98 (1978): 164–67.

Lloyd-Jones, Hugh, ed. *Females of the Species: Simonides on Women*. London: Duckworth, 1975.

Loader, James A. "The Dark Side of Beauty in the OT." *OTE* 25 (2012): 334–50.

————. "The Pleasing and the Awesome." *OTE* 24 (2011): 652–67.

Long, Gary A. "A Lover, Cities, and Heavenly Bodies: Co-Text and the Translation of Two Similes in Canticles (6:4c; 6:10d)." *JBL* 115 (1996): 703–9.

Longman, Tremper. "מַחֲנֶה." *NIDOTTE* 2:918–19.

————. *Song of Songs*. NICOT. Grand Rapids: Eerdmans, 2001.

Longman, Tremper, and Daniel G. Reid. *God Is a Warrior*. SOTBT. Carlisle, UK: Paternoster, 1995.

Loprieno, Antonio. "Searching for a Common Background: Egyptian Love Poetry and the Biblical Song of Songs." Pages 105–35 in *Perspectives on the Song of Songs/Perspektiven der Hoheliedauslegung.* Edited by Anselm C. Hagedorn. BZAW 346. Berlin: de Gruyter, 2005.

Loretz, Oswald. "Siegel als Amulette und Grabbeigaben in Mesopotamien und HL 8,6–7." *UF* 25 (1993): 237–46.

Lowin, Shari. *Arabic and Hebrew Love Poems of al-Andalus.* CCME 39. London: Routledge, 2013.

Lunn, Nicholas P. *Word-Order Variation in Biblical Hebrew Poetry: Differentiating Pragmatics and Poetics.* PBM. Milton Keynes, UK: Paternoster, 2006.

Luzarraga, Jesús. *Cantar de los Cantares: Sendas del amor.* NBE. Estella: Verbo Divino, 2005.

Lys, Daniel. *Le plus beau chant de la création: Commentaire du Cantique des cantiques.* LD 51. Paris: Cerf, 1968.

Mace, David R. *Hebrew Marriage: A Sociological Study.* London: Epworth, 1953.

Magness-Gardiner, Bonnie S. "Seals, Mesopotamian." *ABD* 5:1062–64.

Marcovich, Miroslav. *Heraclitus: Greek Text with a Short Commentary.* Merida: The Los Andes University Press, 1967.

Marsman, Hennie J. *Women in Ugarit and Israel: Their Social and Religious Position in the Context of the Ancient Near East.* OTS 49. Leiden: Brill, 2003.

Mathieu, Bernard. *La poésie amoureuse de l'Égypte Ancienne: Recherche sur un genre littéraire au Nouvel Empire.* BEIFAO 115. Cairo: Institut français d'archéologie orientale du Caire, 1996.

May, Herbert G. "Some Cosmic Connotations of Mayim Rabbim, 'Many Waters.'" *JBL* 74 (1955): 9–21.

Mazar, Amihai. "The Divided Monarchy: Comments on Some Archaeological Issues." Pages 159–79 in *The Quest for the Historical Israel: Debating Archaeology and the History of Early Israel; Invited Lectures Delivered at the Sixth Biennial Colloquium of the International Institute for Secular Humanistic Judaism, Detroit, October 2005.* Edited by Israel Finkelstein, Amihai Mazar, and Brian B. Schmidt. ABS 17. Atlanta: Society of Biblical Literature, 2007.

Mazor, Yair. "The Song of Songs or the Story of Stories." *SJOT* 4 (1990): 1–29.

Merwe, Christo van der. "Explaining Fronting in Biblical Hebrew." *JNSL* (1999): 173–86.

Meyers, Carol L. "Gender Imagery in the Song of Songs." Pages 197–212 in *A Feminist Companion to the Song of Songs*. Edited by Athalya Brenner. FCB 1. Sheffield: Sheffield Academic, 1993.

———. "Material Remains and Social Relations: Women's Culture in Agrarian Households of the Iron Age." Pages 425–44 in *Symbiosis, Symbolism, and the Power of the Past: Canaan, Ancient Israel, and Their Neighbors from the Late Bronze Age through Roman Palaestina*. Edited by William G. Dever and Seymour Gitin. Winona Lake, IN: Eisenbrauns, 2003.

———. "Mother to Muse: An Archaeomusicological Study of Women's Performance in Israel." Pages 50–77 in *Recycling Biblical Figures: Papers Read at a NOSTER Colloquium in Amsterdam, 12–13 May 1997*. Edited by Athalya Brenner and J. Willem van Henten. STR 1. Leiden: Deo, 1999.

———. *Rediscovering Eve: Ancient Israelite Women in Context*. New York: Oxford University Press, 2013.

———. "Was Ancient Israel a Patriarchal Society?" *JBL* 133 (2014): 8–27.

Meynet, Roland. *Trattato di retorica biblica*. RetBib 10. Bologna: EDB, 2008.

Miller, Cynthia L. "Constraints on Ellipsis in Biblical Hebrew." Pages 165–80 in *Studies in Comparative Semitic and Afroasiatic Linguistics Presented to Gene B. Gragg*. Edited by Cynthia L. Miller. SAOC 60. Chicago: University of Chicago Press, 2007.

———. "Ellipsis Involving Negation in Biblical Poetry." Pages 37–52 in *Seeking Out the Wisdom of the Ancients: Essays Offered to Honor Michael V. Fox on the Occasion of His Sixty-Fifth Birthday*. Edited by Ronald L. Troxel, Kelvin G. Friebel, and Dennis R. Magary. Winona Lake, IN: Eisenbrauns, 2005.

———. "A Linguistic Approach to Ellipsis in Biblical Poetry; Or, What to Do When Exegesis of What Is There Depends upon What Isn't." *BBR* 13 (2003): 251–70.

———. "A Reconsideration of 'Double-Duty' Prepositions in Biblical Poetry." *JANES* 31 (2008): 99–110.

Miller, Patrick D. *The Divine Warrior in Early Israel*. HSM 5. Cambridge: Harvard University Press, 1975.

Moberly, Robert W. L. "Why Did Noah Send Out a Raven." *VT* 50 (2000): 345–56.

Moder, Carol. "It Is Like Making a Soup: Metaphors and Similes in Spoken News Discourse." Pages 301–20 in *Language in the Context of Use: Dis-*

course and Cognitive Approaches to Language. Edited by Andrea Tyler, Yiyoung Kim, and Mari Takada. CLR 37. Berlin: de Gruyter, 2008.

———. "Two Puzzle Pieces: Fitting Discourse Context and Constructions into Cognitive Metaphor Theory." *ETC* 3 (2008): 294–320.

Moor, Johannes Cornelis de. *An Anthology of Religious Texts from Ugarit.* Leiden: Brill, 1987.

Moran, William L., ed. *The Amarna Letters.* Baltimore: Johns Hopkins University Press, 1992.

Morgan, Julian. "The Etymological History of the Three Hebrew Synonyms for 'To Dance,' HGG, HLL and KRR, and Their Cultural Significance." *JAOS* 36 (1916): 321–32.

Moshavi, Adina. "Between Dialectic and Rhetoric: Rhetorical Questions Expressing Premises in Biblical Prose Argumentation." *VT* 65 (2015): 136–51.

———. "Two Types of Argumentation Involving Rhetorical Questions in Biblical Hebrew Dialogue." *Bib* 90 (2009): 32–46.

———. "What Can I Say? Implications and Communicative Functions of Rhetorical 'WH' Questions in Classical Biblical Hebrew Prose." *VT* 64 (2014): 93–108.

Mulder, Martin J. "רֶשֶׁף." *ThWAT* 7:683–90.

Müller, Friedrich M. *Die Liebespoesie der Alten Ägypter.* 2nd ed. Leipzig: Hinrichs, 1932.

Müller, Hans-Peter. "פָּחַד." *ThWAT* 6:551–62.

———. *Vergleich und Metapher im Hohenlied.* OBO 56. Freiburg: Universitätsverlag, 1984.

Munro, Jill M. *Spikenard and Saffron: The Imagery of the Song of Songs.* JSOTSup 203. Sheffield: Sheffield Academic, 1995.

Murnane, William. *The Road to Kadesh: A Historical Interpretation of the Battle Reliefs of King Sety I at Karnak.* SAOC 42. Chicago: University of Chicago Press, 1985.

Murphy, Roland E. "Dance and Death in the Song of Songs." Pages 117–19 in *Love and Death in the Ancient Near East: Essays in Honor of Marvin H. Pope.* Edited by John H. Marks and Robert M. Good. Guilford: Four Quarters, 1987.

———. *The Song of Songs: A Commentary on the Book of Canticles or the Song of Songs.* Hermeneia. Minneapolis: Fortress, 1990.

Murray, John D. "Logical Connectives and Local Coherence." Pages 107–25 in *Sources of Coherence in Reading.* Edited by Robert F. Lorch and Edward J. O'Brien. Hillsdale, NJ: Lawrence Erlbaum, 1995.

Myers, David G. "Robert Penn Warren and the History of Criticism." *MQ* 34 (1993): 369–82.

Nel, Philip J. "שלם." *NIDOTTE* 4:130–35.

Newsom, Carol A. "A Maker of Metaphors: Ezekiel's Oracles against Tyre." *Int* 38 (1984): 151–64.

Niccacci, Alviero. "Cantico dei cantici e canti d'amore egiziani." *SBFLA* 31 (1991): 61–85.

Nissinen, Martti. "Relative Masculinities in the Hebrew Bible/Old Testament." Pages 221–47 in *Being a Man: Negotiating Ancient Constructs of Masculinity*. Edited by Ilona Zsolnay. London: Routledge, 2017.

Noegel, Scott B., and Gary Rendsburg. *Solomon's Vineyard: Literary and Linguistic Studies in the Song of Songs*. AIL 1. Atlanta: Society of Biblical Literature, 2009.

Oakley, John H., and Rebecca H. Sinos. *The Wedding in Ancient Athens*. Madison: University of Wisconsin Press, 2002.

O'Brien, Julian M., ed. *The Oxford Encyclopedia of the Bible and Gender Studies*. Oxford: Oxford University Press, 2014.

O'Daniel Cantrell, Deborah. *The Horsemen of Israel: Horses and Chariotry in Monarchic Israel (Ninth–Eighth Centuries B.C.E.)*. HACL 1. Winona Lake, IN: Eisenbrauns, 2011.

———. "'Some Trust in Horses': Horses as Symbols of Power in Rhetoric and Reality." Pages 131–48 in *Warfare, Ritual, and Symbol in Biblical and Modern Contexts*. Edited by Brad E. Kelle, Frank Ritchel Ames, and Jacob L. Wright. AIL 18. Atlanta: Society of Biblical Literature, 2014.

Oesterley, William O. E. *The Sacred Dance: A Study in Comparative Folklore*. Cambridge: Harvard University Press, 1923.

Olmo Lete, Gregorio del. *Mitos, legendas y rituales de los semitas occidentales*. Barcelona: Trotta, Edicions de la Universität de Barcelona, 1998.

Ovid. *Heroides; Amores*. Translated by Grant Showerman. Revised by George P. Goold. LCL. Cambridge: Harvard University Press, 1914.

Paul, Shalom M. "An Unrecognized Medical Idiom in Canticles 6,12 and Job 9,21." *Bib* 59 (1978): 545–47.

Peels, Hendrik G. L. "קנא." *NIDOTTE* 3:937–40.

Pellizer, Ezio, and Gennaro Tedeschi, eds. *Semonide: Introduzione, testimonianze, testo critico, traduzione e comment*. LGE 9. Roma: Ateneo, 1990.

Pope, Marvin H. *Job: Introduction, Translation and Notes*. 3rd ed. AB 15. New Haven: Yale University Press, 2008.

Sinclair, H. Colleen. "In Search of Romeo and Juliet." *SocPsy* 45 (2014): 312–14.

Sinclair, H. Colleen, Diane Felmlee, Susan Sprecher, and Brittany L. Wright. "Don't Tell Me Who I Can't Love: A Multimethod Investigation of Social Network and Reactance Effects on Romantic Relationships." *SPQ* 78 (2015): 77–99.

Smit, Peter-Ben. *Masculinity and the Bible: Survey, Models, and Perspectives.* BRP. Leiden: Brill, 2017.

Smith, Mark S. *Poetic Heroes: Literary Commemorations of Warriors and Warrior Culture in the Early Biblical World.* Grand Rapids: Eerdmans, 2014.

——. "Warfare Song as Warrior Ritual." Pages 165–86 in *Warfare, Ritual, and Symbol in Biblical and Modern Contexts.* Edited by Brad E. Kelle, Frank Ritchel Ames, and Jacob L. Wright. AIL 18. Atlanta: Society of Biblical Literature, 2014.

Smither, Paul. "Prince Mehy of the Love Songs." *JEA* 34 (1948): 116.

Sonnet, Jean-Pierre. "Du chant érotique au chant mystique: Le ressort poétique du Cantique des cantiques." Pages 79–105 in *Regards croisés sur le Cantique des cantiques.* Edited by Jean-Marie Auwers. LR 22. Bruxelles: Lessius, 2005.

——. "Figures (anciennes et nouvelles) du lecteur: Du Cantique des cantiques au Livre entier." *NRTh* 113 (1991): 75–86.

——. "L'analyse narrative des récits bibliques." Pages 47–94 in *Manuel d'exégèse de l'Ancien Testament.* Edited by Michaela Bauks and Christophe Nihan. MdB 61. Labor et Fides: Geneva, 2008.

——. "Le Cantique, entre érotique et mystique: Sanctuaire de la parole échangée." *NRTh* 119 (1997): 481–502.

——. "Le Cantique: La fabrique poétique." Pages 159–84 in *Les nouvelles voies de l'exégèse: En lisant le Cantique des cantiques.* Edited by Jacques Nieuviarts and Pierre Debergé. LD 190. Paris: Cerf, 2002.

Stackert, Jeffrey. "Pentateuchal Coherence and the Science of Reading." Pages 253–68 in *The Formation of the Pentateuch: Bridging the Academic Cultures of Europe, Israel, and North America.* Edited by Jan C. Gertz, Bernard M. Levinson, Dalit Rom-Shiloni, and Konrad Schmid. FAT 111. Tübingen: Mohr Siebeck, 2016.

Steen, Gerard J. "Analyzing Metaphor in Literature: With Examples from William Wordsworth's 'I Wandered Lonely as a Cloud.'" *PT* 20 (1999): 499–522.

———. "The Cognitive-Linguistic Revolution in Metaphor Studies." Pages 117–42 in *The Bloomsbury Companion to Cognitive Linguistics*. Edited by Jeannette Littlemore and John R. Taylor. BC. London: Bloomsbury, 2014.

———. "The Contemporary Theory of Metaphor—Now New and Improved!" *RCL* 9 (2011): 26–64.

———. "Love Stories: Cognitive Scenarios in Love Poetry." Pages 67–82 in *Cognitive Poetics in Practice*. Edited by Joanna Gavins and Gerard Steen. London: Routledge, 2003.

———. "Metaphor and Style." Pages 315–28 in *The Cambridge Handbook of Stylistics*. Edited by Peter Stockwell and Sara Whiteley. Cambridge: Cambridge University Press, 2014.

———. "Metaphor in Language and Thought: How Do We Map the Field." Pages 117–56 in *Cognitive Linguistics: Convergence and Expansion*. Edited by Mario Brdar, Stefan Thomas Gries, and Milena Žic Fuchs. HCP 32. Amsterdam: Benjamins, 2011.

———. "The Paradox of Metaphor: Why We Need a Three-Dimensional Model of Metaphor." *MS* 23 (2008): 213–41.

Steen, Gerard J., and Raymond W. Gibbs. "Questions about Metaphor in Literature." *EJES* 8 (2004): 337–54.

Stehle, Eva. "Greek Lyric and Gender." Pages 58–71 in *The Cambridge Companion to Greek Lyric*. Edited by Felix Budelmann. CCL. Cambridge: Cambridge University Press, 2009.

Stendebach, Franz J. "סוּס." *ThWAT* 5:782–91.

———. "שָׁלוֹם." *ThWAT* 8:12–46.

Stockwell, Peter. *Cognitive Poetics: An Introduction*. London: Routledge, 2002.

Stoop-Van Paridon, Petronella W. T. *The Song of Songs: A Philological Analysis of the Hebrew Book Shir Ha-Shirim*. Leuven: Peeters, 2005.

Storey, Ian C., ed. *Fragments of Old Comedy*. Vol. 3, *Philonicus to Xenophon; Adespota*. LCL. Cambridge: Harvard University Press, 2011.

Suutari, Toni. "Body Part Names and Grammaticalization." Pages 101–28 in *Grammar from the Human Perspective: Case, Space, and Person in Finnish*. Edited by Marja-Liisa Helasvuo and Lyle Campbell. CILT 177. Amsterdam: Benjamins, 2006.

Sweeney, Marvin A. *The Twelve Prophets*. Vol. 2, *Micah, Nahum, Habakkuk, Zephaniah, Haggai, Zechariah, Malachi*. Berit Olam. Collegeville, MN: Liturgical Press, 2000.

Tallis, Nigel. "Ancient Near Eastern Warfare." Pages 47–66 in *The Ancient World at War*. Edited by Philip de Souza. New York: Thames & Hudson, 2008.

Talmon, Shemaryahu. "The Signification of שָׁלוֹם and Its Semantic Field in the Hebrew Bible." Pages 75–115 in *The Quest for Context and Meaning: Studies in Biblical Intertextuality in Honor of James A. Sanders*. Edited by Craig A. Evans and Shemaryahu Talmon. BibInt 28. Leiden: Brill, 1997.

Talmon, Shlomo "צַח." *ThWAT* 6:983–84.

Talmy, Leonard. *Toward a Cognitive Semantics*. 2 vols. Cambridge: MIT Press, 2000.

Thöne, Yvonne S. "Female Humanimality: Animal Imagery in the Song of Songs and Ancient Near Eastern Iconography." *JSem* 25 (2016): 389–408.

Toorn, Karel van der. *Family Religion in Babylonia, Syria and Israel: Continuity and Change in the Forms of Religious Life*. SHCANE 7. Leiden: Brill, 1996.

———. "The Significance of the Veil in the Ancient Near East." Pages 327–33 in *Pomegranates and Golden Bells: Studies in Biblical, Jewish, and Near Eastern Ritual, Law, and Literature in Honor of Jacob Milgrom*. Edited by David Wright. Winona Lake, IN: Eisenbrauns, 1995.

Torczyner, Harry. *Die Entstehung des semitischen Sprachtypus: Ein Beitrag zum Problem der Entstehung der Sprache*. Wien: Löwit, 1916.

Tosato, Angelo. *Il matrimonio israelitico: Una teoria generale*. AnBib 100. Rome: Biblical Institute Press, 1982.

Tov, Emanuel. "Canticles." Pages 195–219 in *Qumran Cave 4.XI: Psalms to Chronicles*. Edited by Eugene Ulrich et al. DJD 16. Oxford: Clarendon, 2000.

———. "Three Manuscripts (Abbreviated Texts?) of Canticles from Qumran Cave 4." *JJS* 46 (1995): 88–11.

Trible, Phyllis. *God and the Rhetoric of Sexuality*. OBT. Minneapolis: Fortress, 1978.

———. "Love's Lyric Redeemed." Pages 100–120 in *A Feminist Companion to the Song of Songs*. Edited by Athalya Brenner. FCB 1. Sheffield: Sheffield Academic, 1993.

Trimm, Charlie. *"YHWH Fights for Them!": The Divine Warrior in the Exodus Narrative*. GDBS 58. Piscataway, NJ: Gorgias, 2014.

Tromp, Nicolas J. "Wisdom and the Canticle. Ct., 8,6c–7b: Text, Character, Message and Import." Pages 88–95 in *La Sagesse de l'Ancien Testament*. Edited by Maurice Gilbert. BETL 51. Gembloux: Duculot, 1979.

Van Hecke, Pierre, ed. "Conceptual Blending: A Recent Approach to Metaphor: Illustrated with the Pastoral Metaphor In Hos 4,16." Pages 215–31 in *Metaphor in the Hebrew Bible*. Edited by Pierre Van Hecke. BETL 187. Leuven: Peeters, 2005.

———. *From Linguistics to Hermeneutics: A Functional and Cognitive Approach to Job 12–14*. SSN 55. Leiden: Brill, 2011.

———. *Metaphor in the Hebrew Bible*. BETL 187. Leuven: Peeters, 2005.

Van Hecke, Pierre, and Antje Labahn, eds. *Metaphors in the Psalms*. BETL 231. Leuven: Peeters, 2010.

Van Selms, Adrianus. *Marriage and Family Life in Ugaritic Literature*. POS 1. London: Luzac, 1954.

Vaux, Roland de. *Le nomadisme et ses survivances, institutions familiales, institutions civiles*. Vol. 1 of *Les Institutions de l'Ancien Testament*. Paris: Cerf, 1958.

Verde, Danilo. "Love Is Thirst and Hunger: Extended Metaphors and the Coherence of the Song's Words for Love." Pages 359–75 in *The Song of Songs in Its Context: Words for Love, Love for Words*. Edited by Pierre Van Hecke. BETL 310. Leuven: Peeters, 2020.

———. "Metaphor as Knowledge: A Hermeneutical Framework for Biblical Exegesis with a Sample Reading from the Song of Songs (Song 8:10)." *BibAn* 6 (2016): 45–72.

———. "On the Interplay of Metaphors in the Hebrew Bible." Pages 1–11 in *Networks of Metaphors in the Hebrew Bible*. Edited by Danilo Verde and Antje Labahn. BETL 309. Leuven: Peeters, 2020.

———. "Playing Hard to Get: The Elusive Woman in Song 4:4." *ETL* 94 (2018): 1–25.

———. "War-Games in the Song of Songs: A Reading of Song 2,4 in Light of Cognitive Linguistics." *SJOT* 30 (2016): 185–97.

———. "When the Warrior Falls in Love: The Shaping and Reshaping of Masculinity in the Song of Songs." Pages 188–212 in *The Song of Songs Afresh: Perspectives on a Biblical Love Poem*. Edited by Stefan Fischer and Gavin Fernandes. HBM. Sheffield: Sheffield Phoenix, 2019.

Verde, Danilo, and Pierre Van Hecke. "The Belligerent Woman in Song 1,9." *Bib* 98 (2017): 208–26.

Verde, Danilo, and Antje Labahn, eds. *Networks of Metaphors in the Hebrew Bible*. BETL 309. Leuven: Peeters, 2020.

Vern, Robyn C. "Case: Vestiges of Case Inflections." *EHLL* 1:400–401.

Vernus, Pascal. "Le Cantique des Cantiques et l'Égypte pharaonique." Pages 150–62 in *Perspectives on the Song of Songs/Perspektiven der Hoheliedauslegung*. Edited by Anselm C. Hagedorn. BZAW 346. Berlin: de Gruyter, 2005.

Wagner, Siegfried. "עזז." *ThWAT* 6:1–14.

Walls, Neal H. *The Goddess Anat in Ugaritic Myth*. SBLDS 135. Atlanta: Scholars Press, 1992.

Watson, Wilfred G. E. *Classical Hebrew Poetry: A Guide to Its Techniques*. JSOTSup 26. Sheffield: Sheffield Academic, 1985.

———. "Love and Death Once More (Song of Songs 8:6)." *VT* (1997): 384–87.

Weems, Renita J. *Battered Love: Marriage, Sex, and Violence in the Hebrew Prophets*. Minneapolis: Fortress, 1995.

Wellhausen, Julius. *Prolegomena zur Geschichte Israels*. 6th ed. Berlin: de Gruyter, 2001.

Wenham, Gordon J. *Genesis 1–15*. WBC 1. Waco, TX: Word, 1987.

———. "Weddings." Pages 794–95 in *The Oxford Companion to the Bible*. Edited by Bruce M. Metzger and Michael D. Coogan. New York: Oxford University Press, 1993.

Werth, Paul. "Extended Metaphor: A Text-World Account." *LL* 3 (1994): 79–103.

West, David R. *Some Cults of Greek Goddesses and Female Daemons of Oriental Origin: Especially in Relation to the Mythology of Goddesses and Daemons in the Semitic World*. AOAT 233. Kevelaer: Butzon und Bercker, 1995.

Westermarck, Edward. *The History of Human Marriage*. New York: Allerton Book Company, 1922.

White, John B. *A Study of the Language of Love in the Song of Songs and Ancient Egyptian Poetry*. SBLDS 38. Missoula, MT: Scholars Press, 1978.

Wilson, Gerald H. "נוה." *NIDOTTE* 3:54–56.

Wilson, Ian D. "Tyre a Ship: The Metaphorical World of Ezekiel 27 in Ancient Judah." *ZAW* 125 (2013): 249–62.

Wilson, Stephen. *Making Men: The Male Coming-of-Age Theme in the Hebrew Bible*. Oxford: Oxford University Press, 2015.

Wilson-Wright, Aren M. "Love Conquers All: Song of Songs 8:6b–7a as a Reflex of the Northwest Semitic Combat Myth." *JBL* 134 (2015): 333–45.

Wimsatt, William K., and Monroe C. Beardsley. "The Intentional Fallacy." *SR* 54 (1946): 468–88.

Wolde, Ellen van. "The Creation of Coherence." *Semeia* 18 (1998): 159–74.

———. *Stories of the Beginning: Genesis 1–11 and Other Creation Stories.* London: SCM, 1996.

Wolf, Friedrich A. *Museum der Altertumswissenschaft.* Berlin: Realschulbuchhandlung, 1807–1810.

———. *Vorlesungen über die Enzyklopädie der Altertumswissenschaft.* Leipzig: Lehnhold, 1831.

Wolters, Al. "Proverbs XXXI 10–31 as Heroic Hymn: A Form-Critical Analysis." *VT* 38 (1988): 446–57.

Wright, Jacob L. "Military Valor and Kingship: A Book-Oriented Approach to the Study of a Major War Theme." Pages 33–56 in *Writing and Reading War: Rhetoric, Gender, and Ethics in Biblical and Modern Contexts.* Edited by Brad E. Kelle and Frank R. Ames. SymS 42. Atlanta: Society of Biblical Literature, 2008.

Wyatt, Nicolas. *Religious Texts from Ugarit: The Words of Ilimilku and His Colleagues.* BibSem 53. Sheffield: Sheffield Academic, 2002.

Yadin, Yigael. *The Art of Warfare in Biblical Lands in the Light of Archaeological Discovery.* London: Weidenfeld and Nicolson, 1963.

———. *The Scroll of the War of the Sons of Light against the Sons of Darkness.* London: Oxford University Press, 1962.

Yee, Gale A. "By the Hand of a Woman." *Semeia* 61 (1993): 99–132.

Zakovitch, Yair. *Das Hohelied.* HThKAT. Freiburg: Herder, 2004.

———. *The Song of Songs: Riddle of Riddles.* LHBOTS 673. London: Bloomsbury T&T Clark, 2019.

Zimmerli, Walther. *Ezekiel: A Commentary on the Book of the Prophet Ezekiel.* 2 vols. Hermeneia. Philadelphia: Fortress, 1979–1983.

Zipor, Moshe A. "קָשָׁה." *TDOT* 13:189–95.

Ancient Sources Index

Modern Authors Index